American Politics and the Environment

Glen Sussman
Old Dominion University

Byron W. Daynes
Brigham Young University

Jonathan P. West
University of Miami

Longman

New York   San Francisco   Boston
London   Toronto   Sydney   Tokyo   Singapore   Madrid
Mexico City   Munich   Paris   Cape Town   Hong Kong   Montreal

Vice President/Publisher: Priscilla McGeehon
Senior Acquisitions Editor: Eric Stano
Associate Editor: Anita Castro
Senior Marketing Manager: Megan Galvin-Fak
Supplements Editor: Kelly Villella
Text Design, Project Coordination and Electronic Page Makeup: Pre-Press Co., Inc.
Cover Designer/Manager: John Callahan
Production Manager: Charles Annis
Manufacturing Buyer: Al Dorsey
Printer and Binder: Courier/Stoughton
Cover Printer: Phoenix Color Corp.

Library of Congress Cataloging-in-Publication Data

Sussman, Glen.
    American politics and the environment / by Glen Sussman, Byron W. Daynes,
Jonathan P. West.
        p. cm.
    Includes bibliographical references and index.
    ISBN 0-205-29643-2 (alk. paper)
        1. Environmental policy—United States. 2. Environmental protection—Govern-
ment policy—United States. I. Daynes, Byron W. II. West, Jonathan P. (Jonathan
Page), 1941–   III. Title.

GE180 .S87 2001
363.7'056'0973—dc21   2001038008

Copyright © 2002 by Addison Wesley Longman, Inc.

Please visit our website at http://www.ablongman.com

ISBN 0-205-29643-2

10 9 8 7 6 5 4 3 2 1—CRS—04 03 02 01

To Elizabeth, *whose loving support is never taken for granted but is always appreciated; whose love for the environment, and creatures large and small, makes the world a better place.*
—GLEN—

To Kathy, *who has been able to successfully blend her academic prowess as historian with her outstanding accomplishments as wife and mother to our three children.*
—BILL—

To Colleen, *whose love, support, and constructive criticism have made this a better book and made me a better person.*
—JONATHAN—

BRIEF CONTENTS

DETAILED CONTENTS

Chapter 3
Public Opinion, the Media, and Environmental Issues   *55*

Chapter 6
The Environmental Presidency   *158*

Chapter 7

LIST OF TABLES AND FIGURES

Tables

Guest Essay Tables

Figures

PREFACE

Environmental policy is largely a composite of contributions and input from elected and appointed officials operating in political institutions at every level of government. Students of public policy know less about the politics involved in these institutional decisions that have shaped environmental policy than about the decisions themselves. At the same time, political parties, organized interests, the mass media, and public opinion have also played a significant role in the policy process. Without knowledge of the politics of decision making and political activism, the nature of environmental policy making will continue to be haphazard, defying reasonable focus and making change difficult.

The importance of the environment (and the need to protect it for future generations) has been recognized throughout the history of our country. In his book *Notes on the State of Virginia*, prior to discussing politics and government, education, trade and commerce, Thomas Jefferson gave attention first to the natural environment.[1] While thinking about the quality of life of future generations, Benjamin Franklin said long ago, "It has been my opinion, that he who receives an Estate from his ancestors is under some kind of obligation to transmit the same to their posterity."[2] Early in the twentieth century, the environment captured the attention of President Theodore Roosevelt, who convened a White House conference to address the issue. He argued that the "occasion for the meeting lies in the fact that the natural resources of our country are in danger of exhaustion if we permit the old wasteful methods of exploiting them longer to continue."[3] And during his last year in office, John Kennedy warned us that "The history of America has been the story of Americans seizing, using, squandering and belatedly protecting their natural heritage."[4] Today, "sustainable development" has become the integrative mechanism to bring the nations of the world together in an effort to work toward environmental preservation.

For those of us who teach courses on environmental politics and policy, we do best when choosing appropriate books for our courses. Many, if not all, books about the subject tend to stress the policy dimension of environmentalism or offer a philosophical or socioeconomic approach, with less attention given to the importance of the political actors in the environmental policy process. A review of recent books in the field shows that most of them provide an overview of the institutions involved in environmental politics but with primary emphasis on specific issues (e.g., air pollution, water pollution) in individual chapters.

This book takes an institutional and behavioral approach to the study of environmental politics and policy. In doing so, it examines the role of political institutions and investigates the connection between them and environmental policy making. We include a discussion of the evolution of American environmentalism at the national and subnational level, political activism, electoral politics, the mass media and public opinion, the role of national political institutions, and the global environment.

A *common framework* links each chapter, as the reader is first introduced to the role and functions of specific institutions prior to an analysis of the institution and environmentalism. In Chapter 1, a host of *questions* are raised for the reader to consider as he or she reads each of the forthcoming chapters. In order to provide the reader with additional analytical tools, three *box inserts* are included in Chapters 2–9 focusing on a person, case study, and issue. The issue in each of these box inserts involves air pollution, providing another *integrative mechanism* for the reader. In this case, the reader will see how air pollution as a policy issue has been addressed from a variety of institutional perspectives. The concluding chapter, Chapter 10, presents a series of *propositions*. These propositions serve as a summary of the chapters as well as a basis for future research. Finally, environmental *Web sites* are included at the end of each chapter. These Web sites should encourage the reader to seek out additional information on their own to learn more about environmental politics and policy.

An undertaking such as this project requires the assistance of many people in order to bring it to fruition. We would like to express our deep appreciation to Longman Publishers and in particular to Eric Stano, political science editor, and Anita Castro, associate political science editor. Eric was sensitive to personal concerns that arose during our work on this project, resulting in his generous extension of time. That helped in the completion of this book. We thank Anita Castro for her patience, encouragement, assistance, and gentle reminders in bringing this project to a conclusion. We want to acknowledge the valuable assistance provided by our research assistants—Leticia Adams, Jeff Haymore, Emilie Leibovitch, Joseph Spector, Ken Taninaka, and Jaya Tiwari. We also thank Elizabeth Marie Burt for her thorough copyediting and for compiling a comprehensive index for this book. And we extend our appreciation to the reviewers who volunteered their time to review the manuscript: Stephen Meinhold, University of North Carolina at Wilmington; Susan J. Buck, University of North Carolina at Greensboro; Ronald Keith Gaddis, University of Oklahoma; John Frendreis, Loyola University, Chicago; Matthew Cahn, California State University, Northridge; James L. McDowell, Indiana State University; W. Douglas Costain, University of Colorado, Richard Young, Seattle University and Robert J. Duffy, Rider University. Finally, but most importantly, we want to recognize the support given by our wives and families, and the sacrifice they made while we spent countless hours working on this book.

Endnotes

[1] See Thomas Jefferson, *Notes on the State of Virginia* (Harper & Row, Publishers, 1964).

[2] See **http://www.state.gov/www/global/oes/earth.html**. Retrieved June 10, 1999.

[3] Theodore Roosevelt quoted in "Publicizing Conservation at the White House," in Roderick Nash, ed. *The American Environment: Readings in the History of Conservation* (Reading, MA: Addison-Wesley Publishing Company, 1968), 47–48.

[4] John Kennedy quoted in "How Conservation Grew from a Whisper to a Roar," *National Wildlife* magazine 38 (December/January 2000), 23.

CHAPTER 1

Introduction:
The American Political
Setting and the Environment

Throughout the twentieth century, the United States, as well as other industrialized and developing countries, has engaged in activities that have increasingly threatened the health of the environment. In the case of the United States, as one observer recently commented, "The economic prosperity of the Industrial Revolution—indeed, the rise of America—came at a steep price: lost wilderness, contaminated waters, dirty skies, endangered animals and plants."[1] Environmentalism is one among many complex and increasingly technical public policy issues that has challenged political leaders nationally and globally.

To what extent, however, have public officials included environmental issues as a central feature of the public agenda? For some, the question of environmental protection concerns value conflicts between preservation and development, where trade-offs are demanded of contending forces. While some public officials have advocated that the federal government play a strong role in protection of the environment, some of their colleagues are reluctant to impose governmental authority over citizens, with respect to the environment. Still others argue that state and local government, rather than the federal government, should play the primary role in managing the environment. Moreover, acrimonious debate has occurred regarding environmental policy, as some have questioned whether the environment is at risk at all.

The history of the environmental policy process has been associated with state-level politics, where the tendency has been for policymakers, more often than not, to support economic development over environmental quality. Over the past several decades, however, the federal government has begun to assume increasing responsibility for environmental affairs. At the same time, public opinion informs us that American citizens generally have supported protecting the environment over economic development.[2] Moreover, Americans are more likely to prefer that the federal government take action to protect the environment rather than rely on business and industry to do so.[3]

The political struggle regarding the environment is framed within the American Constitution's system of government. Our primary consideration is what role federal and state governments should play in environmental management.

Political conflict regarding environmental issues involves the role of national political institutions and intergovernmental relations, political parties, and interest-group activities, in addition to the role played by the media and public opinion. It also includes the question of the integration of science and environmental policy making and the ongoing value debate now framed within an evolving postindustrial American society. Consequently, environmental management can be viewed as being subject to a variety of influences that have affected the decision-making process. Before addressing these important aspects of environmental politics and policy, we first present a brief overview of environmentalism in the United States.

Background on Environmental Politics and Policy

During the first half of the twentieth century, the United States experienced periods of growth and depression, both of which militated against substantive political efforts to address the quality of the environment. World War I, the Great Depression of the 1930s, World War II, and the Korean War turned the attention of political leaders to issues of economic and national security. The period of the Roaring Twenties as well as the postwar prosperity of the 1950s created a mindset of unchecked growth, development, and continued exploitation of natural resources to meet consumer demands, industrial development, and national defense. Consequently, although environmentalists argued for years in favor of public policy initiatives to address issues ranging from proper management of public lands and natural resources to resource depletion to air and water pollution, public officials tended to move incrementally rather than implementing comprehensive national environmental policy.

However, it is also important to note that during the late nineteenth and the early twentieth centuries, appropriate measures to manage the environment were promoted by several prominent individuals and environmental groups (e.g., John Muir, Gifford Pinchot, Sierra Club, National Wildlife Federation)—measures that were the outcome of the continuing debate between conservationists and preservationists. For example, as Glen Sussman and Mark Kelso note, the environmental measures that were advocated by the modern presidents beginning with Franklin D. Roosevelt were grounded in the conservation philosophy begun during the Theodore Roosevelt administration:

> As Theodore Roosevelt moved the nation forward through industrial development and the politics of the Progressive era, he also had the vision to protect a large part of the nation's natural heritage by reserving huge tracts of public land for national parks, national forest, and wildlife preserves, embodying a conservationist strategy set forth by Gifford Pinchot, who would lead what we now know as the U.S. Forest Service.[4]

The conservationist philosophy of Theodore Roosevelt and Gifford Pinchot had a profound impact on American national politics. Not only did Roosevelt set a model for his successors, but also the philosophy "was broadly accepted by

Congress as well as by the public, and to a large extent extraction industries that were ensured access to resources."[5] Moreover, despite the fact that John Muir, president of the Sierra Club, promoted preservationist principles, Gifford Pinchot was successful in promoting the idea of conservation over preservation. As Pinchot argued:

> The first great fact about conservation is that it stands for development. . . . Conservation does mean provision for the future, but it means also and first of all the recognition of the right of the present generation to the fullest necessary use of all the resources with which this country is so abundantly blessed. Conservation demands the welfare of this generation first, and afterward the welfare of the generations that follow [6]

Although the idea of conservation can be traced to the very foundation of American society and gained salience almost a century ago when Gifford Pinchot and President Theodore Roosevelt embraced the notion of conservation over John Muir's ideas about preservation, this study of American politics and the environment focuses on the period beginning with the presidency of Franklin D. Roosevelt through the Clinton administration. We begin our study with the 1930s because this period was characterized by both the expansion of the federal government generally and the increasing role of the federal government in environmental policy in particular.[7]

Environmentalism: 1930s–1990s

Prior to the 1930s, the role of the federal government in environmental policy tended to focus on land management and the conservation of natural resources. However, during the era of Franklin D. Roosevelt, new and influential environmental groups were established including the Wilderness Society (1935) and the National Wildlife Federation (1936). These groups began to exert pressure on political leaders, adding to the efforts already underway by groups including the Sierra Club and the Audubon Society.

Moreover, the federal government became increasingly involved in environmental issues, in such initiatives as Franklin D. Roosevelt's Civilian Conservation Corps (CCC), the Tennessee Valley Authority (TVA), and the Soil Conservation Service. For example, the CCC played a significant role socially and economically by putting to work millions of unemployed young men, and environmentally through planting of millions of new trees, fighting soil erosion, and protecting wildlife refuges. As a result of the Tennessee Valley Authority project, which provided much needed low-cost energy for American citizens, the environmental damage to the Tennessee Valley wrought by lack of planning was resolved and millions of trees were planted.[8] Also, the TVA has been cited as attracting the attention of more foreign government leaders than any other resource conservation project, due to its success.[9]

A.L. Owen described the conservation efforts of the 1930s in terms of the quality of planning: "The leadership necessary for the integration of any comprehensive plan was supplied here by Franklin D. Roosevelt. Throughout his presidential terms, he insisted upon the need for thoughtfully devised plans that would carry out an overall conservation policy."[10] As Franklin Roosevelt himself stated to the Congress as he began his first term in office in 1933, programs like the CCC were:

an established part of our national policy. It will conserve our precious natural resources. It will pay dividends to the present and future generations. It will make improvements in national and state domains which have been largely forgotten in the past few years of industrial development.[11]

At this time, Congress was instrumental in passing important environmental legislation signed into law by the president. These include the Taylor Grazing Act (1934), which addressed the problem of overgrazing on America's grasslands, and the Flood Control Act (1936), in which the U.S. Army Corps of Engineers assumed responsibility for implementing a policy to protect watersheds and improve flood control. The Roosevelt era also saw the United States engaged in several important international treaties that protected flora and fauna, including a treaty with Canada to protect salmon and halibut fisheries and a treaty with Mexico to protect migratory birds and animals.[12]

During the early postwar period of the late 1940s and the 1950s, presidents Harry S Truman and Dwight D. Eisenhower were most concerned about national security issues and the communist threat rather than with the environment. Although they issued several environmental executive orders that were confined to land use and/or national parks and national forests initiatives, during a fifteen-year period, Congress passed and Truman and Eisenhower signed only a few pieces of significant environmental legislation. Moreover, Eisenhower had asserted that pollution issues should be considered a state and local responsibility rather than falling within federal jurisdiction.[13] James Sundquist has argued that the Eisenhower years were a time when "the federal government undertook few major new departures to conserve or improve the outdoor environment."[14]

The decades of the 1960s and 1970s were characterized by increasing levels of environmental initiatives in terms of both governmental authorities and the public, which involved interest-group activism, presidential action, congressional legislation, court decisions, state-level programs, among others. The Clean Air Act (1963) and Clean Water Act (1972), for instance, were passed by Congress and signed into law by the president. Subsequent clean air amendments were added in 1970 and again in 1977. Amendments were added to the Clean Water Act in 1977. The Endangered Species Act, which was passed in 1966, was amended and expanded in scope in 1969 and again in 1973. Although many other important pieces of environmental legislation were passed by Congress and signed into law by the president, what was most significant was the increasing role the federal government began to assume in environmental policy making. This was highlighted when both the government and the public embraced Earth Day in April 1970. Moreover, during that same year, the Environmental Protection Agency was created—a major development despite the failed effort to create a cabinet level Department of the Environment and Natural Resources.[15]

At the same time, the judicial branch of government became increasingly involved in questions raised about the role of the federal government in environmental policy making. As a result of congressional and presidential action, the National Environmental Policy Act (NEPA) passed into law in 1970. This compelled both the federal courts and the Supreme Court to respond to issues related to the scope and nature of NEPA in general and the environmental impact statement (EIS) in particular.[16]

Furthermore, President Richard M. Nixon's New Federalism began a shift in responsibility for the implementation of federal environmental programs. When state and local governments had been responsible for environmental policy, priorities tended to favor development over preservation. As a result of changes at the federal level, states were becoming increasingly obligated to carry out environmental policy according to federal guidelines, which also encouraged governors and state legislators to establish new subnational environmental initiatives and state-level environmental bureaucracies.[17] By the end of the decade, the Superfund Act (1980), which addressed hazardous waste sites and established a National Priority List for the most hazardous sites, was passed, as was the Alaska Lands Act (1980), which set aside millions of acres of land in the forty-ninth state.

During the 1980s, environmental protection was less a priority for the United States when Ronald Reagan assumed power in the White House. The Reagan administration has generally been characterized as antienvironment, as it rejected previous bipartisan support for environmentalism and embraced instead a decidedly prodevelopment philosophy. Despite setbacks for several environmental issues including renewal of the Clean Air Act, which sat dormant since 1977, Congress passed several pieces of legislation important to environmental protection, either with the signature of the president or by overriding his veto. These include the Safe Drinking Water Act (1986), Superfund Amendments (1986), and Clean Water Act Amendments (1987).

During the last decade of the twentieth century, only a few important environmental proposals were passed into law despite former President George H.W. Bush declaring himself the "environmental" president and the fervent hope among environmentalists that Bill Clinton would be a "green" president. Namely, these were the Clean Air Act Amendments of 1990[18] and the California Desert Protection Act in 1994.[19] Bush used the powerful resources of the presidency to ensure passage of the clean air law. However, he disappointed environmentalists when he reversed his position on environmental issues, in response to pressure from fellow Republicans and business and industry interests. The California desert protection legislation was successful due to the efforts of California's senators, primarily Diane Feinstein. Still, those who supported and worked for the legislation were bolstered in their efforts, knowing that they had an ally in the Clinton White House who would at least sign rather than reject the legislation.

Moreover, given an obstructionist Republican Congress, Clinton used the 1906 Antiquities Act in order to set aside large tracts of public land. He did so in 1996 when he established the Grand Staircase-Escalante National Monument in Utah despite local opposition to his action. As he reached the end of his presidency, Clinton set aside millions of acres of land—an effort to bolster his environmental "legacy." (However, newly elected President George W. Bush has moved to block some of Clinton's actions.) Clinton was attempting to act as a "conservationist" president in the Theodore Roosevelt mold by setting aside public lands for future generations.

In the international arena in the twentieth century, the United States engaged in several major global initiatives. For example, ratification of the Limited Nuclear Test Ban Treaty with the Soviet Union in 1963 moved the two adversaries away from potential nuclear conflict and toward mutual nuclear arms control. This also reduced the public health and environmental risk posed by radioactive debris resulting from nuclear testing. In addition, the International Convention on Trade in Endangered Species of Wild Fauna and Flora (CITES) was a global effort to protect endangered animals and plants. The United States was the first nation to ratify this treaty in the mid-1970s, prohibiting international trade in and promoting conservation of wild plants and animals. The treaty was ratified by nearly one hundred nations by 1987.[20]

Also, in 1987, President Reagan signed the Montreal Protocol on Ozone Depletion. This accord was an important expression of the multilateral effort to address "new" global climate environmental issues. The North American Free Trade Act (NAFTA), signed into law in 1994 and geared toward enhancing free trade, was supported by President Bill Clinton. Because environmental groups voiced their concerns about the ecological impact of the treaty, Clinton stressed the importance of environmental protection via provisions added to the agreement.[21] President George W. Bush in early 2001 rejected the U.S. commitment to reduce greenhouse gases.

During the past several decades, the history of environmentalism in the United States has been characterized by conflict and compromise as the federal government increased its role in environmental management. Also during that period, the environmental policy-making process has involved a variety of old and newly emerging ecological issues. For example, environmental policy making was, during the late-nineteenth century, first concerned with the conservation of public lands. Since then, American citizens have been confronted with the changing nature of environmentalism and the evolution of environmental problems—namely, the first-generation problem of air and water pollution; second-tier issues including toxic and hazardous wastes; then new, third-tier issues involving stratospheric ozone depletion, global warming, and biodiversity.[22] Moreover, resolution of third-tier environmental problems is problematic due to their nature: less visible, imprecise measure of impact, and lack of consensus among experts.[23] In other words, where air and water pollution is a salient, direct issue for American citizens, the question of a global "greenhouse effect," for example, is difficult to grasp and quite remote from the typical person's realm of understanding.

The American Constitution, Public Policy, and the Environment

In the American political system, public policy is subject to a variety of political constraints including but not limited to the dispersion of power prescribed by the Madisonian model of separation of powers, and the system of checks and balances. The federal system of government divides political power between the national government and the fifty states. Moreover, as the framers of the Constitution were well aware as they argued in *Federalist #10*, the governmental system was subject to pressures exerted by organized interests. This motivated the framers to design a system that would moderate the actions of the myriad political actors within the sytem.

In the American political system, the three major national institutions (the executive, legislative, and judicial branches of government) have specific areas of political responsibility yet also exert their influence beyond their respective jurisdictions. Congress has the power to pass legislation, yet the framers of the Constitution gave to the president the ability to negate the efforts of those 535 legislators through the power of the veto. Then again, Congress can override the president's veto power if it can muster sufficient support (two-thirds of the congressional membership) to oppose the president's action. Although certain presidents have used the powerful resources available to them to take action on behalf of the environment—signing legislation, issuing executive orders, using the veto power—the environment has yet to assume a central place in their legislative agenda. As we will discuss later in this book, presidents can be classified as *activist* or *symbolic* in their behavior concerning the environment. As an activist, the president can take actions that promote environmental protection or support a developmental ethic over conservation efforts. Or the president can respond to environmental challenges in a symbolic way, exhibiting only modest to little attention to environmental issues.

Congress is a decentralized institution in which political power is fragmented among a variety of committees and subcommittees that can promote, delay, or oppose legislation as well as expand their jurisdiction. For example, eleven different committees in the House and the Senate have jurisdiction over environmental affairs.[24] Moreover, as former Speaker of the House Tip O'Neill asserted, "all politics is local."[25] Consequently, notwithstanding congressional responsibility for the national interest, members of the legislative branch of government remain committed to protecting state and local interests. In the process of so doing, important issues at the national level may become subverted to subnational pressure and interests. In addition to these considerations, Congress is also influenced by the partisan makeup of the legislative body. Although bipartisanship is evident on some legislation, partisan conflict over public policy is an integral feature of the legislative process.

The Supreme Court is the third pillar of the country's national institutional framework and has a role in influencing the actions of the other tiers—the presidency and Congress—as well as the states. As a result of the 1803 *Marbury v. Madison* decision, the Court has the power of judicial review, which underlies the Court's ability to interpret the actions of the executive and legislative branches of the federal government as well as events at the subnational level.

Just as the president sits atop the executive branch of government and sets the public agenda, executive agencies also play an important role in the policymaking process. The bureaucracy is similar to the legislative branch, in that it is a decentralized institution comprised of numerous agencies, departments, and bureaus sometimes having overlapping jurisdiction. As a public policy area, the environment is under the jurisdiction of a variety of regulatory agencies that either cooperate or engage in turf wars.[26]

Moreover, executive agencies, including major players like the Environmental Protection Agency (EPA) and the Department of the Interior, have been politicized as a result of presidential budget priorities and the appointment process. During the 1980s, for instance, both agencies received considerable media attention due to problems arising over political and personnel matters. Anne Gorsuch, head of the EPA, resigned and Rita Lavelle, Assistant Administrator for Hazardous Waste, was fired, due to allegations of mismanagement and lax enforcement of environmental regulations.[27] James Watt, Secretary of the Interior Department, had what Robert Durant called a "confrontational, arrogant, and badgering style" that "fanned the flames of conflict with congressional oversight committees . . . and the environmental community."[28] Watt eventually resigned as he faced mounting pressure from environmentalists, the public, and Congress.[29] Nonetheless, former President George H.W. Bush nominated his protegé Gale Norton to be Secretary of the Interior.

As far as the federal role in environmental management is concerned, jurisdiction for policy making is divided among the executive branch (president and executive agencies), legislative branch (Congress and its numerous committees and subcommittees), and the judicial system. Once legislation is passed by Congress and signed into law by the president, executive agencies establish regulations, and the lawmaking process places new responsibilities on the states for implementing federal guidelines. However, as power has shifted from Washington to the 50 states, the states have not necessarily acted consistently in the implementation process. While certain states have engaged in innovative efforts to improve environmental quality, others have opposed federal environmental guidelines or have not acted on federal legislation in a timely manner. Evan Ringquist reminds us that the states play an important role in environmental policy making, yet James Lester informs us that the actions of individual states are influenced by several factors including the state's wealth and the severity of its environmental problems, compared to other states.[30]

American citizens are linked to political institutions through political parties, the mass media, and interest groups. Political parties are noteworthy linkage institutions that provide cues for citizens because they "play an important role in translating issues into agenda items."[31] The extent to which the two major political parties have exhibited bipartisanship on environmental issues remains a topic for debate. While some studies have argued that the environment is a nonpartisan issue, others maintain that partisanship is indeed an integral feature of environmental politics and policy.[32] Recent research suggests that partisan differences about environmental issues separate Democrats and Republicans in Congress and in state legislatures.[33]

The U.S. political system was created to control factions, yet the fragmented system of government also provides numerous access points for interest groups to pursue their cause, supported by the First Amendment right of free expression. Similar to other public policy issues, conflict over management of the environment has resulted in proliferation of ecological interest groups. Nonetheless, although these groups share a common commitment to protect the environment, they are characterized by different sociodemographic attributes, size, budget, tactics, and strategies. Moreover, not all ecology groups conduct themselves in politically legitimate ways. For instance, whereas the National Wildlife Federation is considered a "mainstream" organization, Earth First! is characterized as a "radical" group due to its philosophy and the types of actions in which its members participate.

The broadcast and print media are traditional outlets for information dissemination and, along with the Internet, serve as the primary means by which American citizens receive political information. In recent years, the Internet has become an increasingly important source of information, as the number of political Web sites has exploded. Without a doubt, the Internet has altered the way citizens gain information. Individuals can go online to government Web sites at the national level (e.g., Congress, White House, Environmental Protection Agency) or at the state level (e.g., state legislatures, governor, state environmental and natural resource agencies). At the same time, Web sites exist for environmental, property rights, and business and industry groups.

As interest groups and the media link the public to the political system, public opinion remains an important yet problematic aspect of American politics.[34] On the one hand, in a democratic society, the public's preferences should be expressed in governmental action. Yet the extent to which this should be done is part of a long-standing debate in American politics. To what degree is the citizenry informed about political and environmental issues? Should policymakers rely on public opinion as a guide for action? While some observers have argued that the public is not an informed, rationally thinking body of individuals, others contend quite the opposite.[35] Although public opinion data indicate that Americans hold strong views about environmental protection, to what extent do policymakers take these into account? Policymakers must listen to their constituents but are also influenced by other political and economic interests regarding their participation in the environmental policy-making process.

In addition to the role played by a variety of actors in American domestic politics, the United States also has an international role to play. The United States is but one of some two-hundred countries whose actions affect the health of the global environment. As well, the United States is a member of numerous regional and international organizations that engage in environmental policy making. Similar to political conflict within the domestic policy arena due, in part, to differing interests, nation-states have shared, as well as distinct, interests that impact their orientation toward global environmental protection.

For example, the United States joined other countries and became a signatory to the 1987 protocol addressing ozone depletion. In contrast, at the Earth Summit in Rio in 1992, former President Bush didn't seek to unite the United States with other members of the international community, in their effort to secure a global commitment to environmental quality. Although global warming and biodiversity were salient environmental issues at the summit, President George H.W. Bush refused to sign the biodiversity treaty—the only participant to do so—and signed the global warming treaty only after it was revised to reflect voluntary rather than mandatory guidelines.[36]

The Role of Science and the Environment

"Rock superstar Sting," political scientist Dennis Soden reminds us "echoes the concerns of many who, 'you would say... [have] lost faith in science and progress.'"[37] While politicians and citizens debate environmental questions, what role should be played by scientists? According to Carl Sagan, Professor of Astronomy and Planetary Science, "Science, I maintain, is an absolutely essential tool for any society with a hope of surviving well into the next century with its fundamental values intact ... And if the scientists will not bring this about, who will?"[38] Should science play an important role regarding environmental politics and policy? What political or societal benefits might derive from input from the scientific community?

The environment is an area in which the well-being of the American people is being determined by public officials, who are by nature influenced by a variety of factors. In the process of decision making, policymakers are subject to numerous influences and, for example, are inclined to reject data that might be contrary to their self-interest. Also, they might disregard what they don't understand (such as complex scientific principles and findings) and hesitate to act when science lacks a consensus.[39] Consequently, while some in the scientific community argue that, when appropriately utilized, science can have a positive impact on policy making, others hold that, partly due to underutilization of science, environmental quality will continue to deteriorate, albeit at a slower rate.[40]

In 1997, a group of distinguished American environmental scientists argued in the journal *Science* that the earth's atmosphere, oceans, rivers, land, animals, and plants have been profoundly affected by human activity.[41] Some potential problems, among others, include increasing amounts of carbon dioxide released into the atmosphere, growing threats to biodiversity through destruction of natural habitats, reduced levels of clean water, and depleted supplies of ocean fish, all at a time when the human population is expanding. Moreover, surface areas have been negatively impacted through erosion, loss of timberlands, and the release of toxic substances.

Although researchers writing in *Science* proposed recommendations to redress the variety of global environmental problems, their arguments, together with their proposals, are subject to opposition by those who differ about the state of the planet in general and the American environment in particular. Namely: politicians harboring ideological or partisan differences; business and industry leaders worried about their economic interests; citizens concerned about taxes needed to resolve environmental problems; and state governments opposing continued intervention of "big" government in the environmental policy-making process or resentful at being forced to act due to "unfunded mandates."

The "politics and science" dilemma as it relates to the environment has been cogently described by Walter Rosenbaum:

> Public officials seek from scientists information accurate enough to indicate precisely where to establish environmental standards and credible enough to defend in the inevitable conflicts that follow. Scientists want government to act quickly and forcefully on ecological issues they believe to be critical.... The almost inevitable need to resolve scientific questions through the political process and the problems that arise in making scientific and political judgments compatible are two of the most troublesome characteristics of environmental politics.[42]

Lamont C. Hempel has argued that among those who fear that there will be an increasing role for technical expertise, there is also concern that "the growing complexity of economic, technological, and environmental problems will thrust experts more and more into public decision-making roles, thereby further eroding participation by uninformed or scientifically illiterate citizens."[43] As a researcher in U.S. water resource management recently framed the issue:

> It would be virtually impossible for those involved in the policy and lawmaking processes to be experts in all these fields. In fact, most are experts in none... lawmakers are, by virtue of our republican system of government, held accountable to those people whom they represent. Many of these people are equally uneducated in scientific matters, but can influence the votes of lawmakers on scientific issues nonetheless.[44]

In response, Professor Carl Sagan argues that it is imperative that science be conveyed to every citizen because it is dangerous to leave scientific understanding to only "the elite professionals." Moreover, the values of science and the values of democracy share common origins and characteristics including but not limited to the "free exchange of ideas."[45]

The technical dilemma regarding decision making has a more profound impact as one moves from the national to the global arena. According to Hempel, "Because attempts to solve global environmental problems invariably collide with the narrow self-interests of a state-centric system, few nations are prepared to follow the logic of collective environmental action to its political conclusion."[46] Nonetheless, efforts have been made at the regional and international levels to improve environmental quality. For example, member states of the European Union have engaged in collaborative efforts to improve the European environment.[47]

Accordingly, in the United States, more needs to be done to ensure that the American public has a better understanding of science, and scientists must improve their understanding of and communication with American citizens.[48] Also, this process needs to be expanded on a global level, to improve environmental management. Several approaches might be taken, the cumulative impact being improvement in environmental quality. Included among these approaches are advances in "research on environmental science," improved "monitoring of environmental conditions and trends," integrating "science (and scientists) in policy making," and advancements in green technology that have "fewer negative impacts."[49]

Environmental Beliefs and Value Orientation

When discussing politics of the environment, one is confronted with diverse perspectives. In many ways, disputes over how to address environmental issues are framed within value conflicts that occur between individuals and groups. During the late nineteenth/early twentieth century, the philosophical debate that occurred between John Muir and Gifford Pinchot—preservation versus conservation—set the stage for the future. For Muir, it was imperative to set aside land in its pristine state for future generations. He articulated his vision of environmental value in the following way: "Everybody needs beauty as well as bread, places to play in and pray in, where Nature may heal and cheer and give strength to body and soul alike."[50] Pinchot argued instead that land and natural resources could be used wisely and conserved for the future. By the time of FDR's administration, Aldo Leopold, founder of the Wilderness Society, challenged the prevailing conservationist philosophy by arguing in favor of a new environmental ethic. According to Leopold:

> A land ethic changes the role of *Homo sapiens* from conqueror of the land-community to plain member and citizen of it. It implies respect for his fellow-members, and also a respect for the community as such. . . . Conservation is a state of harmony between men and land. Despite nearly a century of propaganda, conservation still proceeds at a snail's pace; progress still consists largely of letterhead pieties and convention oratory.[51]

Where Aldo Leopold argued his case for an environmental ethic, three decades later, biologist Rachel Carson raised the issue of environmental consequences of new technology. In her book *Silent Spring* (1962), she described the threat to the public and environmental health posed by increasing use of pesticides. She argued that "future generations are unlikely to condone our lack of prudent concern for the integrity of the natural world that supports all life."[52]

In recent years, a number of analysts have set forth new explanations regarding the nature of values and value change in advanced industrial democracies including the United States. Samuel Hays, for example, has argued that as a result of post–World War II improvements in educational attainment and wider distribution of wealth in American society, new values took hold. According to Hays, "The driving force in the new interest in shaping improved levels of environmental quality were human and social values which took on an increasing level of importance in the second half of the twentieth century."[53] More important, Hays argues that "The expression of environmental values and the evolution of environmental culture can be understood only in terms of its engagement with opposing values associated with developmental rather than environmental objectives."[54] For instance, one can easily imagine the preservation/development debate staged between advocates of yet another hotel in a row of hotels along a tourist beach and preservationists demanding that green spaces be maintained for today and tomorrow.

For 30 years, Ronald Inglehart has conducted research about value change in advanced industrial (postindustrial) democracies.[55] Based upon cross-national survey data, Inglehart has reported that a new "postmaterialist" value orientation has emerged in which individuals put more emphasis on nonmaterial goals (e.g., a clean environment) rather than on materialist values (e.g., fighting rising prices). Inglehart built upon the work of Abraham Maslow's hierarchy of needs and determined that, as a result of postwar prosperity and world peace (economic and physical security), a greater concern for nonmaterial, postmaterialist values (including environmental protection) are an important aspect of postindustrial society.

Values and value change have an impact on political attitudes and behavior—that is, values serve as "standards that guide conduct in a variety of ways."[56] Consequently, values (preservation, conservation, development) and value conflict affect our social and political outlook and influence the priorities of political institutions and policy making.

Design of the Book

The environment as a public policy issue is the focus of this book. The purpose is to assess the role both of political institutions and the public in the making of environmental policy, and to offer the reader insight into how the American political system works. We use an institutional/behavioral approach—namely, how do institutions and the political actors functioning within them respond to environmental problems? Rather than focus on specific environmental issues in separate chapters, we instead turn our attention to politics and the political process.

Chapter 1 has discussed several aspects of environmental politics and policy, including ways in which government is important in shaping environmental policy, to provide a framework for topics discussed in subsequent chapters. Each chapter will focus on a single institution (or at times, two related institutions), examining major environmental decisions and contributions made.

Chapter 2 examines American federalism and intergovernmental relations. It will analyze the historical roots of relations between the national government and the 50 state governments generally and the contemporary dynamics of federal/state relations in the shaping of environmental policy in particular. This will be done against the backdrop of the devolution of power from Washington to the state capitals. Questions asked include: How important have states' actions been in shaping national policy? Which states have been most active in passing environmental policy? Regarding environmental policy, have certain states been more influential than others? Which states, if any, have initiated creative environmental policies? Why might some states be active in promotion of environmental policies while others have been resistant to the same? What are some of the complex trade-offs that exist between economic and environmental gains?

Chapter 3 evaluates the impact of public opinion and the mass media on environmental issues. Despite public opinion polls, which provide a portrait of American citizens' attitudes about a host of policy issues, governmental action does not always reflect public preference. Moreover, the scope and nature of the media's coverage of public policy issues has been questioned. How important has the public response to the environment as a policy issue been in the shaping of environmental policy? Regarding the environment, what has been the pattern of public opinion over time? To what extent has the media considered the environment to be an important public policy issue? Has media coverage of environmental concerns brought more attention to environmental issues among the public and policymakers?

In Chapter 4, the role of political parties and interest groups will be assessed. Parties and interest groups are important linkage institutions that tie the American public to the governmental process. Political parties are important because they aggregate public interests at the same time that interest groups, representing narrowly focused preferences, apply pressure on public officials. Have the two major political parties exhibited shared or distinct commitments with regard to the environment? How has the environment been addressed in the national party platforms of the Democrats and Republicans? To what extent have platform promises about the environment been translated into public policy? Which interest groups have been most influential over the years in shaping environmental policy? What are the characteristics of environmental groups? What kinds of tactics and strategies have environmental groups employed in the promotion of environmentalism? What role has been played by "wise use"/"property rights" groups in the political process and how do these groups differ from long-standing environmental groups such as the National Wildlife Federation and Sierra Club?

Chapter 5 addresses Congress, the legislative process, and the environment. As a deliberative body engaged in the process of bargaining and compromising among diverse interests, Congress can either work with the president or compete with the president's goals. Congressional efforts in environmental policy making have been characterized by bipartisanship and partisan differences. What is the nature of the legislative process in creating environmental policy? Which committees have been most important in shaping environmental policy? Which congressional leaders have had the most influence over environmental policy? Which Congresses have been most productive in producing environmental policy? How has either party united or divided members of Congress when voting on environmental measures? What are the key pieces of environmental legislation passed by the Congress?

The environmental presidency is the focus of Chapter 6. The president is the most visible political figure in American politics. Given the diversity of public policy issues, we can expect the president to become involved in environmental policy—but to what extent? Presidents will focus extensive attention on some issues and modest effort on others. The level of presidential action depends, of course, on a variety of factors. The roles played by the president (e.g., legislative leader, chief executive) help explain presidential involvement in environmental policy making. How has the presidency compared to Congress in the promotion of environmental protection? Has the environment been at the center of the president's public agenda? What contributions have presidents made in shaping environmental policies? Which presidents have been more protective of the environment and why? Which presidents, in contrast, have promoted a prodevelopment philosophy toward the environment? Have some presidents merely used the environment for their own legacy while caring little for its actual protection? Which presidents, if any, can be considered "environmental presidents"?

In Chapter 7 we examine the executive branch of government and the role played by executive agencies and environmental policy. The bureaucracy comprises numerous "executive institutions"—agencies, bureaus, departments, commissions—with jurisdiction over the environment. Which departments and agencies have been most influential in producing environmental policy? What has been the role of key personnel and/or heads within the executive bureaucracy in environmental policy making? What has been the interaction between agencies in the environmental policy process? Have the Environmental Protection Agency and the Department of the Interior dominated the creation of environmental policy, or have other departments and agencies been as important? What has been the role of presidential influence and the independence of executive agencies in the shaping of environmental policy?

In addition to Congress, the presidency, and executive agencies, the Supreme Court also plays an important role in the life of the nation. The role of the federal judiciary is the focus of Chapter 8. How important have Supreme Court decisions been in shaping environmental policy? How influential have individual justices been in particular cases involving environmental decision making? How important have the Court's decisions been in influencing other policymakers? How widespread has its impact been felt? How have other political actors in the polity responded to the Court's decisions?

Chapter 9 concentrates on global environmental politics and policy. While most of the discussion in this book concentrates on domestic politics, the United States also plays a role in the global environment. Regional and international treaties have been signed and are in force, and regional and international organizations have increasingly included the environment as a policy area demanding global attention and solutions. What have been the major environmental issues? What are the major international and regional organizations involved in the shaping of environmental policy? How successful have international treaties and agreements been in protecting the environment? What has been the impact of these organizations and agreements on U.S. environmental policy? What is the relationship between national security as practiced by nation-states and global environmental security?

The concluding chapter, Chapter 10, will evaluate the U.S. approach to environmentalism. The United States is but one of some 200 countries that share the global environment. We can assess how successful political institutions have been in environmental policy making both at home and abroad. How have U.S. political institutions addressed the environment as a public policy issue and which of these institutions played a more influential role in shaping environmental policy making? What can we expect as far as environmental decision making in coming decades? How interrelated will our environmental decisions be in the future? What impact will this have on the political institutions of government and the public?

The discussion that follows examines the environment from the perspective of the various policy units in the political system. As you examine the role played by each institution covered in the following chapters, keep in mind how political actors responded to environmentalism within the institutional setting.

How might the political behavior of the public and public officials be characterized in analyzing environmental policy making? What have been the major influences on political institutions and the political actors working within them? Why have certain political actors embraced environmentalism while others have resisted or delayed environmental initiatives? Finally, consider to what extent the environment, in comparison to other public policy issues, has been an important issue in American politics.

Endnotes

1 Scott Harper, "Being Green Will Be Profitable," *The Virginian Pilot*, January 20, 2000, M15.

2 George Gallup, Jr., *The Gallup Poll: Public Opinion 1995* (Wilmington, DE: Scholarly Resources Inc., 1996), 65–67.

3 Christopher J. Bosso, "Seizing Back the Day: The Challenge to Environmental Activism in the 1990s," in Norman J. Vig and Michael E. Kraft, eds. *Environmental Policy in the 1990s: Reform or Reaction?*, 3rd ed. (Washington, DC: CQ Press, 1997), 56.

4 Glen Sussman and Mark Andrew Kelso, "Environmental Priorities and the President as Legislative Leader," in Dennis L. Soden, ed. *The Environmental Presidency* (Albany, NY: State University of New York Press, 1999), 115–116.

5 Ibid., 116. See also Samuel P. Hays, *Conservation and the Gospel of Efficiency: The Progressive Conservation Movement, 1890–1920* (Cambridge, MA: Harvard University Press, 1959).

6 Gifford Pinchot, "Ends and Means," in Roderick Nash, ed. *The American Environment: Readings in The History of Conservation* (Reading, MA: Addison-Wesley Publishing Company, 1968), 59.

7 Jacqueline Vaughn Switzer with Gary Bryner, *Environmental Politics: Domestic and Global Dimensions*, 2nd ed. (New York: St. Martin's Press, 1998), 6.

8 Andrea Gerlak and Patrick J. McGovern, "The Twentieth Century: Progressivism, Prosperity, and Crisis," in Dennis L. Soden, *The Environmental Presidency* (Albany, NY: State University of New York Press, 1999), 67.

9 Ibid.

10 A.L. Owen, *Conservation Under FDR* (New York: Praeger, 1983), 146.

11 President Franklin D. Roosevelt quoted in "The Civilian Conservation Corps," in Roderick Nash, ed. *The American Environment: Readings in The History of Conservation* (Reading, MA: Addison-Wesley Publishing Company, 1968), 128.

12 Carolyn Long, Michael Cabral, Brooks Vandivort, "The Chief Environmental Diplomat," in Dennis L. Soden, ed. *The Environmental Presidency* (Albany, NY: State University of New York Press, 1999), 195.

13 President Dwight D. Eisenhower, *Public Papers of the Presidents of the United States: Dwight D. Eisenhower* (Washington, DC: U.S. Government Printing Office, 1954), 208–209.

14 James Sundquist, *Politics and Policy: The Eisenhower, Kennedy, and Johnson Years* (Washington, DC: The Brookings Institution, 1968), 323.

15 John Whitaker, *Striking a Balance: Environment and Natural Resources Policy in the Nixon-Ford Years* (Washington, DC: American Enterprise Institute for Public Policy Research, 1976), 52–56.

16 Lettie McSpadden, "The Courts and Environmental Policy," in James P. Lester, ed. *Environmental Politics and Policy: Theories and Evidence*, 2nd ed. (Durham and London: Duke University Press, 1995), 245–246.

17 Evan Ringquist, *Environmental Protection at the State Level: Politics and Progress in Controlling Pollution* (Armonk, NY: M.E. Sharpe, 1993), 43–45.

18 Recent news reports indicate that negative externalities have resulted from the Clean Air Act Amendments. While there has been progress in improving the quality of the air American citizens breathe, drinking water systems have been threatened due to the addition of methyl tertiary butyl ether (MTBE), an oxygenating agent added to gasoline. This agent, which is apparently leaking from underground fuel containers, is polluting community water supplies around the country, creating a new environmental problem for political leaders at all levels of government. Reported on the CBS news program *60 Minutes*, January 16, 2000.

19 Sussman and Kelso, "Environmental Priorities and the President as Legislative Leader," 119–131.

20 Nancy K. Kubakek and Gary S. Silverman, *Environmental Law*, 3rd ed. (Upper Saddle River, NJ: Prentice Hall, 2000), 335–336; Long, Cabral, Vandivort, "The Chief Environmental Diplomat," 207.

21 Long, Cabral, Vandivort, "The Chief Environmental Diplomat," 219–221.

22 Michael E. Kraft, *Environmental Policy and Politics: Toward the Twenty-First Century* (New York: HarperCollins College Publishers, 1996), 14.

23 Ibid.

24 Ibid., 62-63.

25 Tip O'Neill with William Novak, *Man of the House: The Life and Political Memoirs of Speaker Tip O'Neill* (New York: Random House, 1987), Chapter 1.

26 Kubasek and Silverman, *Environmental Law*, 97–108.

27 Mark Landy, Marc J. Roberts, Stephen R. Thomas, *The Environmental Protection Agency*, expanded ed. (New York and Oxford: Oxford University Press, 1994), 251.

28 Robert Durant, *The Administrative Presidency Revisited: Public Lands, the BLM, and the Reagan Revolution* (Albany, NY: State University of New York Press, 1992), 226–227.

29 Benjamin Kline, *First Along the River: A Brief History of the U.S. Environmental Movement* (San Francisco, Acada Books, 1997), 105.

30 Ringquist, *Environmental Protection at the State Level*; James Lester, "Federalism and State Environmental Policy," in James P. Lester, ed. *Environmental Politics and Policy: Theories and Evidence*, 2nd ed. (Durham and London, Duke University Press, 1995), 49–53.

31 Roger W. Cobb and Charles D. Elder, *Participation in American Politics: The Dynamics of Agenda-Building* (Baltimore: Johns Hopkins University Press, 1972), 91.

32 See, for instance, Riley, Dunlap, and Michael, "Partisan Differences on Environmental Issues: A Congressional Roll-Call Analysis," *Western Political Quarterly* 29, 384–397; Stahrl Edmunds and John Letey, *Environmental Administration* (New York: McGraw-Hill, 1973).

33 Sheldon Kamieniecki, "Political Parties and Environmental Policy," in James P. Lester, ed. *Environmental Politics and Policy: Theories and Evidence*, 2nd ed. (Durham and London: Duke University Press, 1995), 146–167.

34 Robert S. Erickson and Kent L. Tedin, *American Public Opinion: Its Origins, Content, and Impact*, 5th ed. (Boston: Allyn and Bacon, 1995),1–6.

35 See, for instance, Walter Lippman, *Public Opinion* (New York: Harcourt, 1922); George Gallup and Saul Rae, *The Pulse of Democracy* (New York: Simon, 1940).

36 Byron W. Daynes and Glen Sussman, *The American Presidency and the Social Agenda* (Upper Saddle River, NJ: Prentice Hall, 2001).

37 Dennis Soden, "At the Nexus: Science Policy," in Dennis L. Soden, *At the Nexus: Science Policy* (Commack, NY: Nova Science Publishers, 1996), 1.

[38] Carl Sagan, *The Demon-Haunted World: Science as a Candle in the Dark* (New York: Random House, 1995), 336.

[39] Switzer with Bryner, *Environmental Politics*, 300–301.

[40] See Kai N. Lee, *Compass and Gyroscope: Integrating Science and Politics for the Environment* (Washington, DC: Island Press, 1993); Lynton Keith Caldwell, *Between Two Worlds: Science, the Environmental Movement, and Policy Choice* (New York: Cambridge University Press, 1992), 20.

[41] Reported in Heather Dewar, "Focus: Our Threatened Planet," *The Virginian Pilot*, July 29, 1997, A4.

[42] Walter Rosenbaum, *Environmental Politics and Policy*, 3rd ed. (Washington, DC: CQ Press, 1995), 164–165.

[43] Lamont C. Hempel, *Environmental Governance. The Global Challenge* (Washington, DC: Island Press, 1996), 16–17.

[44] Sam Earman, "The Intersection of Science and the Law: Who Has the Right of Way," in Dennis L. Soden, ed. *At the Nexus: Science Policy* (Commack, NY: Nova Science Publishers, 1996), 13.

[45] Sagan, *The Demon-Haunted World*, 37–38.

[46] Hempel, *Environmental Governance*, 16.

[47] See, for instance, Regina S. Axelrod, "Environmental Policy and Management in the European Community," in Norman J. Vig and Michael E. Kraft, eds. *Environmental Policy in the 1990s: Toward a New Agenda*, 2nd ed. (Washington, DC: CQ Press, 1994), 253–273; Glen Sussman, "The European Union and Environmental Policy," in Brent S. Steel and Dennis L. Soden, eds. *Handbook of Global Environmental Policy and Administration* (New York: Marcel Dekker, Inc., 1999), 475–494.

[48] See Phyllis Starkey, "Using Science," in Michael Jacobs, ed. *Greening the Millennium? The New Politics of the Environment* (Oxford: Blackwell Publishers, 1997), 123–129.

[49] Kraft, *Environmental Policy and Politics*, 6.

[50] John Muir, "A Voice for Wilderness," in Roderick Nash, ed. *The American Environment: Readings in the History of Conservation* (Reading, MA: Addison-Wesley Publishing Company, 1968), 73.

[51] Aldo Leopold, "An Ethic for Man-land Relations," in Roderick Nash, *The American Environment: Readings in the History of Conservation* (Reading, MA: Addison-Wesley Publishing Company, 1968), 107.

[52] Rachel Carson, *Silent Spring* (Boston: Houghton Mifflin, 1962), 13.

[53] Samuel P. Hays, *Explorations in Environmental History* (Pittsburgh: University of Pittsburgh Press, 1998), 92.

[54] Ibid., 95.

[55] See, for example, the following works by Ronald Inglehart: *The Silent Revolution: Changing Values and Political Styles Among Western Publics* (Princeton: Princeton University Press, 1977) and *Culture Shift in Advanced Industrial Society* (Princeton: Princeton University Press, 1990).

[56] Milton Rokeach, *The Nature of Human Values* (New York: The Free Press, 1973), 13.

American Federalism and Environmental Politics

The U.S. Constitution separates powers among the executive, legislative, and judicial branches of government and also between the national government and the states. The term "federalism" is generally used to describe the constitutional division of powers between the national and the state governments. In a federal system, policy guidance may come from the president and Congress, but policy implementation must be responsive to input from the states and localities, as well as from national officials. Naturally, conflict is not unusual when different power centers are involved in policy making. This is especially true in the area of environmental politics, where there have been widespread calls for devolution of regulatory authority to state and local governments in recent years.[1] State and local governments as "laboratories of democracy" have been major sources of innovation in enviro-politics.

There is substantial disagreement among scholars on the meaning of the term "federalism." Krane has identified at least four categories of definition.[2] The "division-of-powers" approach mentioned above stresses the territorial division of power between a central government and several subnational (state and local) governments.[3] A second perspective emphasizes "bargaining and cooperation," a "dynamic human process" view in which negotiation is evident among competing "power centers" in order for power to be exercised "in a single political system."[4] A third view emphasizes diversity and competition in which a federal state is characterized by territorially based social and cultural diversity and conflict wherein federal governments manifest competing interests."[5] Finally, Krane notes the distinction between federalism and intergovernmental relations, with the latter denoting emphasis on the fragmentation of power among officials of various jurisdictions and tiers of government.[6]

American federalism is characterized by many of the elements defined above. Most students of American government are familiar with the division of powers that exists between the central and state governments as well as the bargaining, cooperation, and competition, that goes on between and within the levels of government. Watts provides a more precise analysis of U.S. federalism (or "federation") when he identifies 9 key attributes of this form: (1) two orders (not levels) of government, (2) a national government that deals directly with individual citizens, (3) formal distribution of legislative and executive authority, (4) revenue resources allocated between the two orders of government, (5) some autonomy for each order, (6) provision for the representation of regional views within the national policy-making institutions, (7) a constitution not unilaterally amendable and requiring the consent of all or a majority of the constituent units, (8) arbitrator courts or referendums to rule on disputes between governments, and (9) processes to facilitate intergovernmental relations.[7]

Federalism provides a prism through which to view environmental politics because policies (legislation, regulations) adopted at the national level are typically carried out by states and localities. DeWitt John, discussing the new civic environmentalism, has observed:

> In contrast to the traditional command-and-control model, the relationships that characterize civic environmentalism are not primarily hierarchical—orders do not come down from EPA to states to polluters. Rather, these key players relate to one another at almost the same level. . . . Most of the links involve nonregulatory "carrots" like information, education, subsidies, and economic incentives. However regulatory "sticks" are still important at times.[8]

In this chapter we examine environmental politics in the context of a federal system and intergovernmental relations. The historical and contemporary working relationships and linkages among key institutional players will be examined. Implementation strategies using regulatory "sticks" and nonregulatory "carrots" will also receive attention. We will focus primarily on the efforts of states and, to a lesser extent, localities in implementing environmental protection policies. The effort and innovative practices of various states in the area of environmental protection will be explored. Finally, individual case studies will highlight various dimensions and dynamics of federalism and environmental politics by focusing on controversial disputes arising in particular states.

Federal-State Relations: Historical Roots

The distribution of power between the national government and states and localities has shifted back and forth over the years. Given its extensive public land holdings, the federal government has had a long-standing interest in natural resource development policy but state and local governments were largely responsible for efforts to protect the environment. When states failed to adequately address problems that spilled across their boundaries, the national government stepped up its efforts. Most recently there has been a reverse trend, with a shift in power back to the states and localities for managing certain environmental programs. Six historical periods in the evolution of national environmental policy are briefly summarized below.[9]

The Common Law and Conservation Era: Pre-1945

The federal government's authority to regulate environmental matters rests primarily on four constitutional pillars: the commerce clause (concerning interstate flows of natural resources), the property clause (affecting disposition of public lands and water resources), the supremacy clause (holding that federal law prevails in federal-state conflicts), and the necessary and proper clause (requiring the government to act for the general welfare). Early in our nation's history, selling federal lands was a source of revenue, and federal land grants spurred states to pursue natural resource development projects. The Department of Interior was created in 1849, in part to oversee the transfer of federal lands to private interests. Laws such as the Homestead Act of 1862 and the Mining Act of 1872 stimulated development of public lands by private parties. Federal-state conflicts during this period were infrequent because federal development policy coincided with state preferences. The late 1800s witnessed a shift of emphasis from development to conservation with passage of the Forest Reserve Act in 1891. This shift led to growing discord because states and private parties, who were accustomed to federal policies promoting development and facilitating the transfer of public lands, were now subject to new constraints linked to conservation. Conservationists and preservationists were often at odds during this period, with the former believing in the sustainability of natural resources and the latter seeking to preserve wilderness areas from all but the most limited uses (e.g., education, recreation).[10]

Environmental regulation was limited in the pre–World War II era primarily to local policies protecting public health, and infrequently to state policies. Where such policies were adopted they dealt with air pollution, water quality, sanitation, waste disposal, and toxic chemicals. Federal regulatory policy was even less frequent, with the exception of laws that touched on environmental matters but principally addressed other concerns. Examples of such legislation include safety regulations for steamship boilers, permit requirements for discharging refuse in navigable waters, control of toxic substances, and a tax on matches containing white phosphorous. During this pre-1945 period there were other instances in which federal common law was used to protect state interests; for example, the Supreme Court used the common law "nuisance" standard to justify injunctions restraining pollution crossing state lines.

The inability of the states to respond to the demands of the Great Depression, and the increased regulatory role of the federal government with the advent of the New Deal, altered the conception of federalism. That is: national problems require national responses. Hence, in the post-1945 era, the federal role in environmental protection policy increased.

Federal Assistance for State Environmental Problems: 1945–1962

For almost 20 years after World War II, the federal government promoted environmental protection by providing research and financial assistance to states and localities. As industrial pollution crossed state lines, the federal government recognized the need to act, but actions were designed to encourage and assist the state's own ability to respond. In the 1950s and 1960s, congressional funding for state water pollution control, air pollution control, and municipal sewage treatment plants was predicated on the idea that state and local governments bore the responsibility for addressing environmental problems. Nonetheless, during this period, federal policymakers were becoming increasingly aware of the national scope of such pollution problems. At the same time, new environmental organizations emerged (African Wildlife Foundation, World Wildlife Fund) and existing ones (Sierra Club, Wilderness Society) expanded.

The Rise of the Modern Environmental Movement: 1962–1970

Publication of Rachel Carson's *Silent Spring*, warning the public about the dangers of pesticides, marked the beginning of a third era; a warning about the population explosion followed a few years later with the publication of Paul Ehrlich's *The Population Bomb*. Congressional policy debates pitted those supporting development of public resources against those favoring environmental protection, especially focusing on balancing recreation and economic interests against environmental concerns in areas such as national forests. Legislative initiatives during this period primarily targeted federal agency actions, rather than private-sector activities, seeking regulations to ensure that government projects took into account environmental concerns.

Three other important developments in this period include increased judicial attention to government agency actions regarding the environment, emergence of new environmental interest groups (Environmental Defense Fund, National Resources Defense Council, Council on Environmental Priorities), and passage of the Clean Air Act, Water Quality Act, Endangered Species Conservation Act, and the National Environmental Policy Act (NEPA) of 1969. NEPA mandated that federal agencies file environmental impact statements and assess environmental consequences of proposed actions. This era culminated with Earth Day on April 22, 1970.

Erecting the Federal Regulatory Infrastructure: 1970–1980

The decade of the 1970s witnessed a legislative explosion, with 20 important national environmental laws passed or significantly amended. This resulted in an expanded federal role in environmental protection, establishment of new federal standards and program requirements, continued attention to parks and wilderness, and enhanced access for citizen activists to voice their concerns via administrative procedures and litigation. Also, by executive order in 1970, President Nixon created the U.S. Environmental Protection Agency. Among the most important laws of this era are the Clean Air Act (amended in 1977), the Clean Water Act, the Marine Mammal Protection Act, the Federal Environmental Pesticides Control Act, the Safe Drinking Water Act, the Resource Conservation and Recovery Act (RCRA), the Surface Mining Act, and the Toxic Substances Control Act. While each of these laws imposed national standards and provided for substantial national regulation, most delegated significant authority to the states for program implementation and enforcement. For example, the Clean Air Act allowed states flexibility in implementing plans to achieve national air quality standards, and the Federal Water Pollution Control Act delegated authority to states to run a federal permit program controlling water pollution. The emerging partnership between the federal government and the states needed to be strengthened and fine-tuned to cope with the threat of what many were calling an "environmental crisis."

Extending and Refining Federal Regulatory Strategies: 1980–1990

The 1980s saw passage of additional legislation as well as augmentation of statutes passed earlier. Some of these laws relied heavily on states for implementation, but delegation by federal agencies, and therefore implementation of the legislation, was sometimes slow. For example, the Comprehensive Environmental Response, Compensation, and Liability Act ("Superfund") created a program for cleanup of hazardous substance releases, authorizing states to make decisions on cleanup; however, it took more than 10 years for the EPA to follow up and actually delegate cleanup decisions to the states.

Another example is the Low-Level Radioactive Waste Policy Act, which provided for states to develop interstate compacts to create area-wide disposal facilities for radioactive waste, but limited participation to states belonging to the compact. Rigid implementation guidelines with consequences for inaction were found also in amendments to such laws as the Resource Conservation and Recovery Act (1984), the Hazardous and Solid Waste Act (1984), the Superfund Act (1986), the Safe Drinking Water Act (1986), the Asbestos Hazardous Emergency Response Act (1986), the Clean Water Act (1987), and the Federal Insecticide, Fungicide, and Rodenticide Act (1988).

Other developments during this decade include mobilization by industry to curb the growth of environmental legislation, greater reliance on administrative decision making rather than legislative action, lax enforcement of federal environmental standards, and reduced federal funding to implement mandates. Nonetheless, more and more federal mandates and congressionally imposed deadlines were approved, incentives and "hammer clauses" to penalize noncompliant organizations were used, and information-disclosure requirements and market-based approaches to environmental protection were endorsed.[11]

Regulatory Recoil and Limits on Federal Power: 1991–Present

The early- to mid-1990s witnessed a decided change in the views of national environmental-protection policymakers, with Congress and the president seeking to reduce regulatory burdens on states and localities, and the Supreme Court questioning long-held views on national regulatory authority. For example, President Clinton's Executive Order 12875 in 1993 and congressional passage of the Unfunded Mandate Reform Act of 1995 both sought to make it harder to impose unfunded mandates on states and local governments. Court decisions in *New York v. United States* in 1992 and *United States v. Lopez* in 1995 addressed the question of constitutional limits on federal regulatory authority and indicated that the Court was reconsidering its long-standing views on federalism. Provisions in the "Contract with America," while not directly referring to the environment, sought to reduce regulatory burdens on business by requiring agencies to perform cost/benefit analyses on proposed regulations, cut paperwork, calculate compliance costs imposed on business, and reimburse landowners for expenses attributable to regulation. Furthermore, difficulties reauthorizing existing federal environmental laws (e.g., the Endangered Species Act), or efforts to weaken them, signaled a new and less favorable sentiment in Congress regarding environmental matters.

Contemporary Federal-State Interactions: Implementation and Enforcement

Legal relationships between federal and state governments take various forms. Scheberle identifies three types: "delegated" programs, "voluntary" programs, and "mandated" programs.[12] Delegated programs authorize a federal agency like the EPA to establish national standards but charge the states with primary implementation and enforcement responsibilities. Voluntary programs provide inducements ("carrots" such as more federal monies) to states without authorizing federal agencies to manage programs inside state jurisdictions. Mandated programs impose requirements, by federal laws, on states.

The Clean Water Act's national permitting program under Section 402 is a delegated program; the Indoor Radon Abatement Act's encouragement for states to establish radon programs is a voluntary program; and the Clean Air Act's requirement that states submit implementation plans specifying their efforts to meet national ambient air quality standards is a mandated program. These complex legal provisions and relationships influence the ways environmental policies are implemented and enforced.

In the process of implementation and enforcement, governments use a wide variety of regulatory "sticks" and nonregulatory "carrots." Examples of each of these inducements will be considered. Among the sticks are command-and-control regulation, oversight, technology-based requirements, permits and inspections, enforcement, and unfunded mandates. Each of these involves use of coercive powers of higher levels of government to influence the behavior of those at lower levels.

Sticks

Command-and-Control Conventional regulation relies on establishment of national environmental standards with substantive and procedural requirements, tight timetables, inspections, controls, penalties for noncompliance, and litigation. Federal enforcers of command-and-control regulations become what former EPA administrator William Ruckelshaus called the "gorilla in the closet," i.e., interpreting the law and telling firms what they should do to comply with it.[13] In the context of federalism, regulatory enforcement is better understood by considering the role of grants-in-aid, crossover sanctions, and partial preemptions.[14] Grants-in-aid are programs funded by the national government and given to state and local governments on the condition that the monies be used for purposes specified by the federal government. Crossover sanctions refer to actions by the federal government to withhold funding in a broad range of programs when lower governments fail to perform in any specific program. Partial preemption occurs when state or local actions are deemed inconsistent with federal requirements, leading the national government to override state or local actions in certain policy areas.

Critics of command-and-control regulation contend that it is costly, narrowly focused (e.g., on one pollutant or point source polluting activity), inefficient, inflexible, fragmented, concerned with remedial action rather than pollution prevention, adversarial, cumbersome, and slow to respond to changing conditions. It is also criticized for being inflexible by preventing subnational governments from tailoring programs that will achieve the greatest environmental benefit for their tax expenditure. As a result, in recent years alternatives to traditional command-and-control regulation have been advocated and tried in various jurisdictions.[15] Often these newer approaches involve collaboration with states and localities.

Oversight   After laws are passed and regulations are issued, legislative and bureaucratic oversight begins. Higher-level government routinely oversees the compliance activity of lower-level governments just as government at all levels oversees compliance activity of businesses and nonprofit organizations. Subnational administrators often follow orders and instructions from federal officials, although those sophisticated in bureaucratic politics have in some instances been able to successfully resist or modify policies and guidance from higher-level officials. Some effective methods of oversight include federal investigations, audits, and reviews of state action; reversion of certain decisions to federal officials in cases involving major impact; suspension of state action if federal authorities object to application of program guidelines; and revocation of state authority due to noncompliance with federal conditions.[16] The interaction of federal and state officials in the oversight and implementation of national environmental legislation has been examined regarding relations between those in the U.S. Department of the Interior and the Nevada Department of Wildlife,[17] and between federal regulators of the Low-Level Radioactive Waste Policy Act and state implementers in Michigan.[18] In both instances the dynamic interactions and strategic maneuvering by state-level bureaucrats altered the policy in question.

Technology-Based   Environmental laws often contain phrases regarding the required technology to be used in pursuit of national policy goals. For example, the 1990 Clear Air Act established very specific and precise standards for technology, while other laws include more ambiguous phrases such as "best available technology." Still others may have less stringent standards. Strict, precise mandates intentionally restrict the discretion and flexibility of those implementing the law and regulations. Also, these mandates have substantial cost implications for those subject to their statutory requirements. For example, compliance with a law requiring specific and stringent standards would likely entail significantly higher costs than with legislation having a less precise and demanding standard. The "stick" in this case helps to ensure that the intent of national policy is followed, but it imposes burdens on those charged with responsibility for carrying out or complying with the mandate.

Permits and Inspections   Alternative permitting systems and revamped inspection practices have been tried in various states. Certain states have strengthened penalties and sanctions, while others have loosened controls. For example, Georgia has increased penalties for water facilities that have poor environmental records by requiring privatization for noncompliant utilities and denying permits to water pollution control facilities that are in violation of state or federal environmental laws.[19] By contrast, Wisconsin has made its permitting system more flexible, with the understanding that participating firms will maintain the same level of environmental protection mandated under the old permits.[20] Similarly, Massachusetts has created clear industry-specific environmental performance standards to replace existing facility-specific permit requirements.[21] Accountability is maintained via annual reports certifying compliance, increased inspections and audits, vigorous enforcement against noncompliant firms, and other methods. Other state reforms have sought to help permit applicants by creating advocacy or permit-assistance offices, streamlining procedures, and encouraging prompt decisions. Also, comprehensive reforms have been implemented in Minnesota and New Jersey that introduced a more integrated, flexible approach to permitting as a trade-off for emissions reductions.[22]

Enforcement The federal government has traditionally relied heavily on enforcement mechanisms—and strong enforcement is thought to deter polluters.[23] State governments have taken steps to bolster enforcement of environmental laws as well. For example, New York has created a multifaceted plan that includes, among other things, a Comprehensive Enforcement Team, regional enforcement coordinators, heavy reliance on inspections, and a new air enforcement unit[24] and the EPA and the states have worked together to avoid creation of "safe havens" in states with lax enforcement efforts. However, states with more stringent environmental standards and companies that are more compliant would be at a competitive disadvantage.[25] Furthermore, the EPA's oversight and enforcement role is complicated by the variations in state organizational structure. For example, state environmental protection programs may be housed in public health agencies, mini-EPAs, environmental superagencies, or in separate boards or commissions. And most, but not all, are organized using a medium-based, pollution control framework.[26]

RON GATTO: ECO-COP

The safety of New York City's drinking water is protected by the Watershed Police, a division of the New York City Department of Environmental Protection (DEP). The Watershed Police are charged with guarding the city's water supply against polluters, vandals, or terrorists. Captain Ron Gatto is a DEP enforcement officer who was recognized by *Time* magazine as a "Hero for the Planet" in its thirtieth Anniversary of Earth Day issue.

New York City has had environmental police since 1905 and DEP has been in existence since 1978; however, no polluters had been arrested prior to 1989.[1] This inaction is attributable to city officials' reluctance to challenge powerful economic interests, resulting in persistent illegal pollution and increasing contamination of the city's water supply. Ron Gatto joined the DEP patrol in 1982 and sought to reverse this trend by aggressively pursuing DEP's environmental enforcement activities.[2] For example, in 1990 he made the first arrest in more than three

continued

decades in a case involving a hospital and correctional facility that had been discharging sewage into reservoirs that provided drinking water to New York City.[3] Two years later, Gatto assisted in creating DEP's Environmental Enforcement Division (EED) to investigate and enforce laws regarding watershed pollution.[4] In the past decade, Gatto has been personally responsible for hundreds of arrests for both environmental crimes and violations of penal law.[5]

The successful enforcement efforts of Ron Gatto and EED occurred despite allegations of DEP mismanagement, neglect, and harassment. Gatto has been personally investigated several times; denied promotions and raises; given inadequate equipment, office facilities, materials, and vehicles; and blocked from media appearances where his accomplishments were to receive public recognition.[6] This persistent pattern of persecution led other officers to resign from DEP, but Gatto was cleared of all charges and he continues to work tirelessly to implement DEP's environmental enforcement efforts.

Two specific cases highlight Ron Gatto's role as environmental champion. In 1990 he detected a restaurant owner who avoided paying costly sewer fees by emptying his septic tank into a storm drain that led to an area reservoir. Gatto arrested the owner who subsequently pled guilty and paid a hefty fine but avoided jail. In another case Gatto discovered that a developer had filled in a trout stream on a parcel of land near a reservoir. The developer was convicted of environmental crimes, paid thousands of dollars in fines, and was required by the courts to absorb the cost (about $1.5 million) to restore the stream to its previous condition.[7]

Ron Gatto is one eco-cop who has made a difference, but there are several others throughout the country who are encountering similar bureaucratic and political obstacles as they work to catch and punish polluters. In recent years they have taken collective action by creating the Public Employees for Environmental Responsibility (PEER) to defend environmental advocates against those who oppose their efforts. This Washington-based organization is now 10,000-members strong and growing, with members drawn from environmental enforcement agencies at all three levels of government.[8] Implementation and enforcement of environmental policies requires the vigilant efforts of environmental champions like Ron Gatto.

---

[1]Robert F. Kennedy, Jr., "Heroes for the Planet: Ron Gatto, Handcuffed Cop," *Time* (April–May, 2000), 70–71.

[2]Ibid.

[3]Robert F. Kennedy, Jr. "DEP's Watershed Policy: Cops in Cuffs: The Failure of Environmental Enforcement and Security in the New York City Watershed," **http://www.security-management.com/library/watershed.html**.

[4] Robert F. Kennedy, Jr., "Heroes for the Planet: Ron Gatto, Handcuffed Cop."

[5]Robert F. Kennedy, Jr., "DEP's Watershed Policy: Cops in Cuffs: The Failure of Environmental Enforcement and Security in the New York City Watershed."

[6]Robert F. Kennedy, Jr., "Heroes for the Planet: Ron Gatto, Handcuffed Cop"; Robert F. Kennedy, "DEP's Watershed Policy: Cops in Cuffs: The Failure of Environmental Enforcement and Security in the New York City Watershed"; Cat Lazaroff, "New York Cop Called Environmental Hero," **http://ens.lycos.com/ens/apr2000**.

[7]Cat Lazaroff, "New York Cop Called Environmental Hero."

[8]Robert F. Kennedy, Jr., "Heroes for the Planet: Ron Gatto, Handcuffed Cop."

Unfunded Mandates   Unfunded federal mandates involve obligations imposed on states by the federal government without monetary compensation. These costs can be considerable: in 1990 the EPA estimated that by the year 2000, state and local governments would expend $55 billion per year to maintain environmental quality, with the federal portion of these expenditures declining and the subnational share increasing. Furthermore, in 1993 it was estimated that complying with ten environmental mandates alone between 1994 and 1998 would cost cities $54 billion.[27]

As mentioned previously, congressional response to state and local government concerns about these escalating costs was passage of the Unfunded Mandate Relief Act of 1995. Under this law, unfunded mandates in excess of $50 million annually must be identified and separately voted upon. Costly regulatory requirements ($100 million or more annually) must be identified as well. Unfunded environmental mandates pose numerous problems for subnational governments, including ". . . fragmentation (institutional, scientific, legal and political), lack of information, and rigidity of laws and regulations."[28] The outcry from financially strapped state and local governments has altered the nation's approach to environmental protection.[29]

Carrots

Among the "carrots" or noncoercive strategies used to influence the behavior of subnational governments and firms are the following: voluntary compliance, public education, preventive efforts, technical assistance, market development, market-based approaches, privatization, partnerships, and user charges and tax policies. In many instances, federal funding provides the stimulus (carrot) for qualifying state programs to pursue such strategies. Together with the more coercive strategies discussed above, these tools are part of the strategic arsenal of higher levels of government.

Voluntary Compliance.   In some instances, regulatory "sticks" are not necessary; once organizations know what is required of them, they may willingly comply. In order for voluntary compliance to be effective, firms and other organizations must be aware of what is expected and have the incentives and resources to comply. In California, the Air Resources Board provided pollution-control district inspectors with technical manuals, and industries were given free simplified handbooks about air quality standards. In Minnesota, a voluntary program provided technical assistance for firms and people involved in aiding the cleanup of contaminated urban land. In Texas, volunteers were recruited to inventory likely sources of groundwater contamination. In each of these examples, innovative actions were undertaken without the threat of sanctions or litigation.[30] Similarly, tax credits are used in Alaska to reward firms that initiate voluntary water-quality monitoring projects, and likewise in California, to significantly reduce the cost of wind-generated electricity, making it more competitive with other energy sources.[31] And at the national level, the EPA's 33/50 program is an innovative example of a voluntary program to achieve targeted reductions in toxic chemical releases.[32]

Public Education   Public education, outreach, eco-information programs, energy efficiency labeling, and participation comprise strategies designed to improve environmental awareness and pollution prevention. An award-winning example of such an initiative is the State of Pennsylvania's *Greenworks* program. This is a half-hour-long cable television program shown monthly throughout the state. It highlights an environmental issue or problem, explores various facets of the issue, showcases innovative solutions, and suggests actions viewers can take to reduce the problem. Pennsylvania has established an online system whereby citizens can learn the extent to which individuals, firms, and local governments are obeying environmental laws. Putting inspection and compliance data on the Department of Environmental Protection's Web site enables interested parties to track the current enforcement status of all regulated entities. Online training focusing on environmental requirements and pollution prevention techniques are also available in Pennsylvania.[33]

Other states have developed innovative policies to keep the media informed about environmental matters (e.g., Maryland), created toll-free telephone lines to provide information and assistance regarding environmental regulations (e.g., Illinois), adopted eco-labeling programs with official recycling emblems (e.g., New York), and sought public input on development projects that impact water quality (e.g., Indiana).[34] California requires public disclosure in the form of an annually updated warning list of close to 500 cancer-causing or toxic chemicals.[35]

At the national level, the EPA plays a coordinating and clearinghouse role regarding state market-oriented eco-information. One example of the benefits of such activities is the information disclosure of toxic releases, which provides a measuring stick for stakeholders (interested parties) to assess the pollution records of various manufacturing firms.

Preventive Efforts   The federal government and several states have tried to refocus attention from regulating pollutants after they appear to preventing pollution before it occurs, but changing to this method has been slow.[36] Pennsylvania has used this approach by endorsing a zero-emissions concept that encourages organizations to incorporate environmental management objectives into their strategic plans. Individuals who substantially contribute to pollution prevention are profiled on Pennsylvania's cable television show, *Greenworks*.[37] Maine publishes successful case studies to highlight the advantages and reduced costs resulting from effective pollution prevention initiatives.[38] North Carolina funds pollution prevention projects through its Clean Water Management Trust Fund.[39] These preventive efforts are producing dividends by raising awareness and improving environmental protection. State prevention initiatives in Arizona, Minnesota, and New Jersey have benefited from federal grants. Under provisions of the 1991 New Jersey Pollution Prevention Act, for instance, close to 900 industrial facilities in that state must report their yearly chemical releases and their plans for preventing pollution.[40] Similarly, Minnesota's Toxic Pollution Control Act of 1990 requires approximately 350 businesses to report annual use and release of toxic pollutants along with goals for their reduction or elimination.[41]

Technical Assistance   Federal policymakers have broadened their concern in the past two decades from focusing primarily on environmental cleanup to efforts to minimize waste, conserve energy, and prevent pollution. This shift is evident in the passage of the Pollution Prevention Act of 1990. This law authorizes the EPA to give small grants to assist states in offering technical assistance in pollution prevention. The previously mentioned Minnesota law goes far beyond conventional technical assistance in its comprehensive toxic pollution prevention program. Nonetheless, provision of technical assistance by government is another of the noncoercive tools that can aid in the effort to reduce or prevent pollution.

Market Development   Some states are creating new markets that have positive environmental effects. In California, environmental protection was improved when an agreement between the state and Atlantic Richfield (ARCO) led ARCO to acquire land mitigating the impact of oil wells on endangered species in exchange for permits to drill additional wells. ARCO then can sell land-bank acreage to other developers with environmental obligations. In Florida, state and local water management districts run wetlands mitigation banks.[42] In Pennsylvania, a gubernatorial task force has created a market for recyclable materials by establishing an electronic bulletin board and hosting conferences of buyers and sellers of recyclable products. In Illinois, the Recycling Industry Modernization program decreased the volume of materials entering the solid waste stream and increased the use of recycled materials. Each of these innovative undertakings develops a new market.[43]

Market-Based Approaches   Market-based tools and strategies are advocated by some as an alternative to traditional command-and-control regulation. The conventional command-and-control approach sets uniform standards, typically in the form of technology or performance standards. The market-based approach seeks to influence behavior using pricing mechanisms instead of specific standards for levels or methods of pollution control. The most notable applications of market-based approaches at the federal or state level include: the EPA's emission trading program; a similar lead trading program to phase down the lead content of gasoline; water quality permit programs; a tradable permit system regulating sulfur dioxide emissions to reduce acid rain; a similar tradable permit program to reduce sulfur dioxide and nitrogen oxide emissions in Los Angeles (RECLAIM program); and a tradable allowance program to reduce the use of chlorofluorocarbon (CFC) to prevent stratospheric ozone depletion.[44]

AIR POLLUTION: RECLAIM— TRADING EMISSIONS ALLOWANCES

The ambitious RECLAIM program in Los Angeles, as noted in this chapter, involves the use of tradable permits to regulate sulfur dioxide (SO_2) and nitrogen oxide (NO_X) emissions to reduce acid rain and comply with ambient air standards for ozone. Other subnational governments (e.g., in Michigan, New Jersey, and Connecticut) and interstate commissions (e.g., in 12 northeastern and midatlantic states and the District of Columbia) have instituted emissions trading programs as well.[1] Federal policymakers have encouraged state and local governments to use market-based instruments of this type. Indeed, the Clean Air Act of 1990 authorizes tradable permit systems to meet federal requirements that SO_2 and NO_X emissions be cut by 10 million tons (from the 1980 base-line level) and by 2 million tons, respectively.[2] Using carrot (right to trade permits) and stick (hefty fines for emissions exceeding annual allowances), the federal government seeks to attack the cause of acid rain and other air pollutants.

Advocates of market-based instruments tout them as innovative tools and strategies to meet current and future environmental challenges. However, experience to date suggests that they have not lived up to expectations and that they have failed to become part of the mainstream of environmental policy.[3] This may be due to overly optimistic expectations, insufficient political will, unattractiveness to potential adopters, uncertainty about the program's future, and flaws in design.[4] Nonetheless, market-based environmental tools have not been without their benefits, and in some cases have produced attractive results.

A recent assessment of the RECLAIM program documents the mixed record of emissions trading as a tool for clean air management in this region.[5] The program was initiated in 1994 and sought to reduce selected pollutants by a fixed percentage annually. Firms that succeed in emissions reduction to the required level can sell pollution credits to firms that exceed the mandated level. Use of such economic incentives as an alternative to direct government intervention was supposed to be more effective and efficient in limiting emission of toxic pollutants. By allocating the pollution control burden among diverse polluting firms, it was expected that overall compliance costs would be reduced. Results to date are mixed. Kamieniecki and his associates examined this program in terms of its impacts on effectiveness, efficiency, equity, and democracy. In general they found that the RECLAIM program was modestly effective and efficient in meeting its goals, but that there are still questions about whether emissions trading programs of this type can adequately address environmental justice concerns and public participation objectives.[6]

Our federal system allows "laboratories of democracy" to experiment with programs such as RECLAIM to see if they work. Lessons from these experiments enable policymakers to profit from past experience, duplicating that which works well, and adjusting or abandoning failed experiments. While it is too early to proclaim RECLAIM an unqualified success, it is also premature to write it off as a failure. Subsequent experimentation with similar tools will provide a better basis for such judgments.

[1]Jeremy B. Hockenstein, Robert N. Stavins, and Bradley W. Whitehead, "Crafting the Next Generation of Market-Based Environmental Tools," *Environment* 39 (1997), 12–24.

[2]Anonymous, "The Use of Market-Based Instruments in the United States," *Environment* 39 (1997), 16–17.

[3]Jeremy B. Hockenstein, Robert N. Stavins, and Bradley W. Whitehead, "Crafting the Next Generation of Market-Based Environmental Tools."

[4]Ibid.

[5]Sheldon Kamieniecki, David Shafie, and Julie Silvers, "Forming Partnerships in Environmental Policy: The Business of Emissions Trading in Clean Air Management," in P.V. Rosenau (ed.) *Public Private Policy Partnerships* (Cambridge, MA: MIT Press, 2000):111–128. The region includes four California counties—Los Angeles, Orange, Riverside, and San Bernardino.

[6]Ibid., 123, 124.

Market incentives at the state level enable governments to meet environmental goals without complex legislation, especially in the areas of waste management, land use, and air quality. Examples include unit pricing for solid waste collection and disposal that establishes a direct connection between the amount of waste generated and prices charged, and land trading systems, or tradable permit programs, whereby governments license owners who preserve or upgrade their property and then authorize them to sell credits to developers. New Jersey, Florida, California, and other states have adopted such trading programs to encourage environmentally friendly land use. In addition, air emission trading programs, similar to RECLAIM in Los Angeles, have been launched in several other states. These programs allow firms that are in compliance with regulatory standards to sell emission credits to other businesses. Michigan, New Jersey, and Connecticut have approved such programs in recent years.[45]

Privatization   Government at all levels is increasingly contracting for services with the private and nonprofit sectors. A potential danger in privatizing government services is the loss or reduction of public accountability. Research by J.C. Morris distinguishes between "formal" and "informal" privatization and suggests that national policy objectives are more likely to be met under more formalized privatization arrangements.[46] Examples of privatization in the environmental protection area are somewhat limited. However, privatization initiatives are frequently found in the areas of solid and hazardous waste collection and disposal.[47]

Partnerships   Partnerships are encouraged as a means to link knowledge, experience, and resources to address environmental problems. The National Environmental Performance Partnership System (NEPPS) was an EPA initiative launched in the mid-1990s to facilitate identification of national, state, and local priorities and target resources to address them. The mechanisms to achieve this include partnership agreements and grants designed to enhance flexibility and reduce federal oversight. The EPA has established core performance measures to aid in implementing priorities and strategies, and to guide development of work plans and agreements. This has increased flexibility and reduced the reporting burden put on the states.

In addition to federal-state partnerships, states are negotiating public-private partnerships, multi-agency partnerships, multistate working groups, and agreements with professional associations, Native American nations, and local governments. Some partnerships have received innovation awards from the Council of State Governments. For example, the Missouri Department of Natural Resources partnered with the Missouri Department of Corrections and the University of Missouri-Columbia to remove unhealthy waste tire sites and convert the waste tires into energy for the University. Another example is the Cape May project in New Jersey, coordinated by the state environmental agency and involving the New Jersey Audubon Society, the Nature Conservancy, and the Association of New Jersey Environmental Commissioners. Its goal is to bring developers and city planning board members together to protect future endangered-species habitats and restore habitats destroyed by development.[48]

User Charges and Tax Policies   Charges to citizens and organizations that actually use a service are not uncommon in the energy and environmental policy area. One advantage of user fees and taxes is the heightened awareness that citizens gain regarding the cost of such matters as water usage and waste disposal. Minnesota relies on user fees from participating organizations to cover the administrative expenses of its Voluntary Investigation and Cleanup program of contaminated lands. Minnesota also taxes carbon emissions to control pollution and then uses the resulting revenues to offset other taxes.[49] Tax exemptions are available in Iowa and Louisiana for purchase of pollution control equipment.[50] Iowa also has used oil overcharge payments to fund its Agriculture-Energy-Environment Initiative; Georgia has used the same funding source to cover costs of both its Dry Hydrant Assistance program and its No-Tillage Assistance programs.[51] It is a common practice for local governments throughout the country to use unit pricing (by the bag or can) for trash pickup, sometimes called "pay-as-you-throw" garbage programs. Also, 10 states provide tax refunds on beverage containers.[52]

Effort and Performance of the States

State-by-state comparisons of effort and performance on environmentally related criteria are possible using data collected by the Council of State Governments (CSG) and others. One way of examining environmental effort is to consider state expenditures reported by CSG. While states vary considerably in the amount of money spent annually on environmental concerns, effort is better indicated by the percent of total expenditures allocated to protecting the environment. Table 2.1 reports FY 1996 data ranking states' spending on environmental matters in three ways: total expenditures, per capita expenditures, and percentage of total general expenditures. The top 10 states in terms of total environmental expenditures (left column) include: California, New York, Pennsylvania, Florida, Wisconsin, Texas, Michigan, Illinois, Washington, and Virginia. The top

TABLE 2.1

Rankings on State Environmental Spending, FY 1996

State	Expenditures	State	Per Capita	State	% of State Budget on Environment
California	$2,653,162,000.00	Alaska	$400.19	Wyoming	5.66%
New York	717,058,265.00	Wyoming	212.95	Alaska	4.74
Pennsylvania	617,291,000.00	Montana	107.93	Wisconsin	3.53
Florida	596,986,670.00	Wisconsin	104.74	Idaho	3.51
Wisconsin	539,031,722.00	Delaware	103.86	Montana	3.47
Texas	524,505,636.00	Idaho	91.12	Nevada	2.95
Michigan	441,527,908.00	Vermont	86.95	South Dakota	2.81
Illinois	364,145,763.00	Maine	84.07	Maine	2.79
Washington	316,409,628.00	California	83.28	California	2.69
Virginia	246,645,861.00	Nevada	74.26	Vermont	2.66
Alaska	242,101,100.00	South Dakota	70.92	Delaware	2.57
Minnesota	236,682,772.00	Utah	70.70	Utah	2.52
Missouri	228,146,449.00	West Virginia	70.48	Colorado	2.49
Colorado	221,265,613.00	Oregon	65.60	West Virginia	2.28
Louisiana	220,491,565.00	North Dakota	62.00	Oregon	2.18
Tennessee	216,501,118.00	Colorado	57.98	North Dakota	2.14
Maryland	214,455,328.00	Washington	57.33	Nebraska	2.06
Oregon	209,690,160.00	Nebraska	54.10	Arkansas	1.96
Georgia	209,157,929.00	Mississippi	52.17	Missouri	1.94
Ohio	208,065,538.00	Rhode Island	52.10	Mississippi	1.9
Indiana	206,269,139.00	Pennsylvania	51.27	Pennsylvania	1.86
New Jersey	202,060,759.00	Minnesota	50.91	Washington	1.8
Massachusetts	199,485,958.00	Louisiana	50.79	Florida	1.78
Kentucky	184,752,030.00	Arkansas	50.71	Louisiana	1.75
North Carolina	176,488,660.00	Connecticut	49.09	Kentucky	1.74
Connecticut	160,403,300.00	Kentucky	47.59	Tennessee	1.68
Utah	142,644,678.00	Hawaii	45.99	Oklahoma	1.63
Mississippi	141,431,794.00	Michigan	45.37	Maryland	1.61
South Carolina	139,175,226.00	Missouri	42.54	New Hampshire	1.6
Oklahoma	129,128,368.00	Maryland	42.38	Rhode Island	1.51
West Virginia	128,306,442.00	Florida	41.40	Virginia	1.51
Arkansas	127,082,040.00	Tennessee	40.79	Minnesota	1.5
Alabama	120,346,482.00	New York	39.54	Indiana	1.43
Nevada	118,874,908.00	Oklahoma	39.19	Michigan	1.4
Idaho	108,213,400.00	New Hampshire	39.18	Connecticut	1.37
Maine	104,131,285.00	New Mexico	38.66	South Carolina	1.3
Wyoming	102,216,274.00	South Carolina	37.45	Texas	1.26
Montana	94,616,585.00	Virginia	37.00	Kansas	1.23
Iowa	92,758,069.00	Indiana	35.39	Illinois	1.21
Nebraska	89,198,467.00	Massachusetts	32.78	Iowa	1.13
Kansas	82,250,299.00	Iowa	32.57	Georgia	1.13
Arizona	78,274,298.00	Kansas	31.89	Alabama	1.09
Delaware	75,139,946.00	Illinois	30.74	New Mexico	1.06
New Mexico	66,156,944.00	Georgia	28.52	Hawaii	1.04
Hawaii	54,404,175.00	Alabama	28.07	New York	1.04
South Dakota	52,306,010.00	Texas	27.47	North Carolina	0.91

continued

TABLE 2.1

(continued)

State	Expenditures	State	Per Capita	State	% of State Budget on Environment
Rhode Island	51,488,849.00	New Jersey	25.25	Massachusetts	0.88
Vermont	50,994,531.00	North Carolina	24.15	New Jersey	0.78
New Hampshire	45,459,837.00	Ohio	18.64	Ohio	0.73
North Dakota	39,842,139.00	Arizona	17.65	Arizona	0.72
Total	$12,587,222,917.00				

Source: Adapted from *Council of State Government Resource Guide to State Environmental Management,* 5th ed. (Lexington, KY: CSG, 1999), 33.

ten rankings are different when per capita expenditures (middle column) are examined: Alaska, Wyoming, Montana, Wisconsin, Delaware, Idaho, Vermont, Maine, California, and Nevada. Per capita expenditures range from a low of $17.65 (Arizona) to a high of $400.19 (Alaska). These rankings change again when the percentage of state budget spent on the environments is the basis for comparison (right column). Using this measure the leaders are: Wyoming, Alaska, Wisconsin, Idaho, Montana, Nevada, South Dakota, Maine, California, and Vermont. The percent spent on the environment in these states ranges from 2.66 percent to 5.66 percent. By contrast, five states spend less than one percent of their budget on the environment. These states include North Carolina, Massachusetts, New Jersey, Ohio, and Arizona.

Four other state-by-state rankings can be considered as well: two separate rankings by the Government Performance Project (GPP) of state management and capacity, James Lester's typology of state environmental innovation, and O'Leary and Yandle's assessments of state environmental dispute resolution (EDR) programs. Table 2.2 (pp. 38 and 39) reports each of these rankings.

First let's consider Lester. He classifies states based on environmental commitment and capacity for environmental management.[53] In his typology, Progressives are high in commitment and capacity, Regressives are low in commitment and capacity, Strugglers are high in commitment and low in capacity, and Delayers are low in commitment and high in capacity. He converts these categories into grades, with Progressives receiving an A, Strugglers receiving a B, Delayers receiving a C and Regressives receiving a D. These grades are listed in the first column of Table 2.2.

CASE STUDY: GRADING THE SKI RESORT INDUSTRY'S ENVIRONMENTAL RECORD

A dispute broke out recently between the ski industry and a coalition of environmental groups concerning the issuance of an environmental "Report Card." The group conducting the assessment, Ski Area Citizen's Coalition, graded 51 resorts in 10 Western states on their environmental policies.[1] The coalition consists of seven national environmental organizations from seven different states. Numerous other environmental groups endorsed the report.

The objective behind the rating scheme was to identify ski resorts that engage in environmentally sound environmental practices. Distribution of this report was intended to inform the public, reward those with high grades, and prod those with low grades into improving their environmental record. The grading criteria and the top- and bottom-rated ski resorts are shown below. Data providing the basis for grades were derived from public documents filed with government agencies (e.g., the National Forest Service, Army Corps of Engineers, EPA, U.S. Fish and Wildlife Service), scientific literature, ski industry documents, Internet Web sites, and other sources.[2] The overall grade distribution was: A (9), B (7), C (14), D (11) and F (10).[3] These grades were posted on the Internet.

Among those that received a failing grade were ski areas that expanded their terrain into national forests, or expressed plans to do so. The resort receiving the lowest grade, Copper Mountain, CO, was penalized primarily because it planned to build single-family residences at the bottom of the ski area on more than 100 acres of privately owned property.[4]

Not surprisingly, the ski industry vigorously attacked the ratings, claiming they are not objective but are instead based on incomplete or inaccurate data. For example, spokespersons for Copper Mountain claimed that the report omitted important information such as their recent partnership with environmental regulatory agencies and their efforts to restore fish habitats. Representatives from the ski industry pointed to their positive efforts at self-regulation, such as the National Ski Areas Association's environmental charter, which compiles environmental principles promoting effective stewardship. Fully 160 resorts in 31 states have joined this charter, which is used as a benchmark against which to assess progress. Ski industry officials also cite numerous awards granted to resorts that scored poorly on the coalition's report card and to the extensive study, analysis, and approvals that precede expansion activities.[5]

This issue points to the variations in environmental performance in one industry and region of the country. There is not only variation between the states, but also within the states (for example, three Colorado resorts received an A, four received a B, five got a C, three earned a D, and six flunked).[6] It also illustrates how contentious environmental assessments can be and shows the need for sound, objective data when distinguishing among high- and low-performing organizations.

Environmental Grade Reports for Ski Areas

Top Ten[7]

Ski Resort	State	Grade
Sundance Resort	Utah	A
Timberline Ski Area	Oregon	A

continued

Ski Resort	State	Grade
49 Degrees North Mountain Resort	Washington	A
Aspen Highlands Ski Resort	Colorado	A
Sun Valley Resort	Idaho	A
Wolf Creek Ski Area	Colorado	A
Silver Mountain Ski Resort	Idaho	A
Buttermilk Mountain Ski Resort	Colorado	A
Aspen Mountain Ski Resort	Colorado	B
Snowmass Ski Resort	Colorado	B

Bottom Ten[8]

Ski Resort	State	Grade
Copper Mountain Ski Resort	Colorado	F
Snowbasin Ski Resort	Utah	F
Keystone Ski Resort	Colorado	F
The Canyons	Utah	F
Breckenridge Ski Resort	Colorado	F
Deer Valley Ski Resort	Utah	F
Vail Ski Resort	Colorado	F
Telluride Ski and Golf Company	Colorado	F
Beaver Creek Ski Resort	Colorado	F
Crystal Mountain Ski Area	Washington	F

Criteria Summary[9]

Evaluation Criteria	Point Score
1. Avoiding expansion of developed skiing acreage into undisturbed forest	20
2. Avoiding commercial or residential development on undisturbed lands	20
3. Avoiding real estate development in conjunction with terrain expansion	10
4. Avoiding terrain alteration in environmentally sensitive areas	30
5. New snowmaking	15
6. Avoiding water degradation from ski area management activities	20
7. Environmental policy positions and public disclosure	15
8. Wildlife habitat and forest protection	15
9. Containing impacts within the ski area boundary	15
10. Recycling, water conservation, energy conservation, pollution reduction	28
11. Traffic and emissions reduction	8
12. Bonus criteria	5

[1]Michael Janofsky, "Environment Groups' Ratings Rile Ski Industry," *New York Times* (December 3, 2000), p. I.46.

[2]Jason Blevins, "Industry Blasts Coalition's Environmental 'Report Card.'" *The Denver Post* (November 30, 2000), C-01; **http://www.skiareacitizens.com/**.

[3]Michael Janofsky, "Environment Groups' Ratings Rile Ski Industry," p. I.46.

[4]Jason Blevins, "Industry Blasts Coalition's Environmental 'Report Card.'"

[5]Ibid.

[6]Ibid.

[7]http://www.skiareacitizens.com/.

[8]Ibid.

[9]Ibid.

Also in Table 2.2 are two rankings by the Government Performance Project (GPP). Their report card on each of the 50 states is based on five management functions: financial management, human resource management, information technology, capital management, and managing for results.[54] Ratings were given in each of these areas separately, along with an overall rating. These ratings of state management and capacity, in the form of grades, are reported in columns 2 and 3 of Table 2.2. While not specifically measuring environmental management and capacity, these two rankings provide different and more current indicators of state capacity than those provided in Lester's typology.

Finally, O'Leary and Yandle evaluated state environmental dispute resolution programs, and their state-by-state report card is found in column 5 of Table 2.2.[55] They discovered that 24 states had EDR programs and each was classified into one of four tiers. Their state-by-state classification of EDR programs is as follows: top tier (Florida, Kentucky, New Jersey, New York, Oregon, Pennsylvania, and Texas), second tier (Hawaii, Massachusetts, Michigan, Minnesota, North Carolina, Vermont, and Wisconsin), third tier (Maine, Montana, Nebraska, Ohio, Oklahoma, and Washington), and fourth tier (Alaska, Colorado, Connecticut, and Illinois). A majority of states (53%) do not have EDR programs.

These various state-by-state comparisons indicate the range in spending patterns, management and institutional capacity, state attitudes towards environmental regulation, and dispute resolution mechanisms devoted to the environment. The diversity of effort and performance related to environmental protection is evident, and some connections are no doubt present among these indicators. For example, O'Leary and Yandle note that "states with higher institutional capacity and management abilities appear to be slightly more likely to adopt EDR programs."[56]

Just as student grades convey feedback about course performance, the state report cards in Table 2.2 provide a big-picture view of overall performance. However, such broad grading schemes tell little about specific accomplishments of students or states. The Council of State Governments (CSG) annually identifies states that are engaged in specific best practices. Table 2.3 (pages 40–41) shows the 1998 CSG Innovation Award Winners. These innovative programs provide benchmarks of best practices in state environmental management. Successful experiments of the type profiled here provide models for other states to follow; to the extent that this is done, the notion of states as "laboratories of democracy" is validated.

A number of studies have sought to explain state commitment to such environmental policies as air pollution, water pollution, hazardous waste, and

TABLE 2.2

Grading the States

State	Lester Environmental Protection Grade	GPP Management Grade	GPP Capacity Grade	EDR Grade
Alabama	C	F	D	*
Alaska	C	C−	C	D
Arizona	D	B−	C−	*
Arkansas	C	D	C−	*
California	B	C−	C+	*
Colorado	B	C−	C−	D
Connecticut	B	B+	B	D
Delaware	B	B	C+	*
District of Columbia	*	*	*	*
Florida	A	B	C+	A−
Georgia	C	C+	C−	*
Hawaii	B	C−	C	B−
Idaho	B	C−	B−	*
Illinois	D	C−	C+	D−
Indiana	D	C	C+	*
Iowa	B	B+	B−	*
Kansas	D	C	B	*
Kentucky	D	B	B−	A−
Louisiana	C	B	B−	*
Maine	B	C	C	C
Maryland	A	B−	B	*
Massachusetts	A	C	B−	B−
Michigan	A	B	B+	B
Minnesota	B	B	B	B−
Mississippi	D	C	C+	*
Missouri	C	A−	A−	*
Montana	B	C	B−	C

groundwater quality. Explanations for variations in the extent of state commitment to environmental protection include such factors as state environmental conditions (e.g., severity of the problem), economic resources, political pressures (partisanship), the federal government's influence, managerial capacity, policy innovativeness, industrial disposition, elite ideology, and state government institutional characteristics.[57]

While states can be ranked and graded based on their particular performance in environmental protection, they have also engaged in collective efforts through the Environmental Council of the States (ECOS), a national association of state environmental agency directors, formed in 1993. ECOS has negotiated with the U.S. EPA to redefine partnerships and add flexibility for state agencies to focus on priorities that they identify as most important. Together with the EPA, the ECOS has developed statistical measures of pollution-control progress and accomplishment. ECOS has also worked with EPA to develop a comprehensive data inventory on ozone-forming pollutants.[58] Such

TABLE 2.2 (continued)

State	Lester Environmental Protection Grade	GPP Management Grade	GPP Capacity Grade	EDR Grade
Nebraska	D	B−	B	C-
Nevada	B	C	C+	*
New Hampshire	B	D+	C+	*
New Jersey	A	B-	B−	A−
New Mexico	D	D+	C−	*
New York	A	D+	C−	A−
North Carolina	B	B−	B	B
North Dakota	B	D	B−	*
Ohio	C	C+	B	C−
Oklahoma	C	D+	C	C
Oregon	A	B+	B−	A−
Pennsylvania	C	B−	B	A−
Rhode Island	B	C	C+	*
South Carolina	C	B−	B	*
South Dakota	D	D	B−	*
Tennessee	C	C	B−	*
Texas	C	B+	B	A−
Utah	D	B+	A−	*
Vermont	B	B−	B−	B−
Virginia	C	A−	A−	*
Washington	A	B+	A−	C
West Virginia	C	C	C+	*
Wisconsin	A	C	B	A−
Wyoming	D	C	C	*

Source: Adapted from Rosemary O'Leary and Tracy Yandle, "Environmental Management at the Millenium: The Use of Environmental Dispute Resolution by State Governments," *Journal of Public Administration Research and Theory* 10 (2000), 149.

collective action by state agencies indicates that states can take the lead without waiting for Congress or federal regulatory agencies to address complex environmental issues.

When states do interact with the federal government, their working relationships can be adversarial, cooperative, or a mix of the two. Sheberle has developed a four-element typology of federal-state relationships using two key variables: the level of trust and the extent of involvement between federal and state officials.[59] The four relationships emerging in her scheme include 1) high trust and high involvement (bodes well for successful policy implementation); 2) high trust and low involvement (suggests cooperative relations but limited resources, often needed for successful implementation); 3) low trust and high involvement (shared goals but disagreement regarding means to accomplish them); and 4) low trust and low involvement (a limited relationship, usually prescribed by legal mandate, with unlikely prospects for successful implementation). Prospects for successful implementation of environmental policy can obviously brighten or diminish, depending on the nature of the relationship between federal and state officials.

TABLE 2.3
Council of State Governments' Innovation Award Winners

State	Title	Description
California	Multistate Working Group on Environmental Management Systems	Regulatory agencies from 12 states, private firms, and nonprofit organizations work together to develop ISO 14001 and apply business systems or processes to assess total quality and environmental management. New models are being developed for managing environmental risk, measuring environmental performance, and reporting environmental data.
Delaware	Site Characterization Program	The Site Characterization Program provided for a full-service mobile laboratory to conduct chemical analysis of soil from sites suspected of contamination. In its four years of operation, the state has seen a 50% reduction in the costs of samples being tested for contamination. It also reduced turnaround time for lab results.
Florida	High Performance Building	The High Performance Building design concentrates on system improvements rather than architectural features or standard engineering requirements to cope with the problem of outgrowing office space. It has created more efficient state buildings and better served the public.
Illinois	Clean Break Project	The focus of the Clean Break Project was to eliminate fear and educate small businesses about environmental regulations. It provided a neutral agency where business could remain anonymous and evaluate possible fines and penalties.
Illinois	Recycling Industry Modernization (RIM) Program	This program's focus is to aid industry in modernization by allowing businesses the mobility to avert attention from waste management, by promoting practical and beneficial methods for the management of solid waste. The program is based on two strategies: decreasing the volume of materials targeted for the solid waste stream and increasing the use of recycled materials as manufacturing feedstock.

TABLE 2.3 *(continued)*

State	Title	Description
Massachusetts	The Environmental Results Program	This program moved from command-and-control to performance-based compliance by establishing environmental performance standards, replacing existing case-by-case permit requirements, and holding companies accountable to standards via certification of compliance, inspections, and audits.
Missouri	Special Area Land Treatment Program	This project involves a partnership among local, state, and federal organizations, a private foundation, and a local agribusiness to reduce and prevent agricultural nonpoint source water pollution.
Missouri	Waste Tire to Energy Program	The partnership program's focus is to clean up waste tire sites and develop a system to turn the waste tires into energy for the University of Missouri-Columbia. The project has saved $100,000 in tire disposal cost and the same amount annually in reduced fuel costs at UM-C.
Pennsylvania	*Greenworks* for Pennsylvania	This is a 30-minute television show, broadcast monthly on cable stations. It focuses on one topic at a time, with special segments for kids. Each segment introduces a problem, provides stories on innovative solutions, and offers viewers advice on what they can do to help.
Texas	Professional Engineer Development Program	This partnership program allows engineers to be certified as environmental engineers through the development of a course curriculum that includes organizational skills, test-taking tips, math and chemistry refreshers, toxicology and risk assessment, fluid mechanics, hydraulics and hydrology, water treatment, wastewater treatment, solid waste, hazardous waste, air issues, industrial hygiene, and occupational safety.
Washington	Habitat Conservation Plan	This is an extremely comprehensive plan, in terms of acreage covered and species protected, targeting overall species survival using an adaptive management style on state-owned forest lands.

Source: Adapted from Council of State Governments. *Resource Guide to State Environmental Management,* 5th ed. (Lexington, KY: CSG, 1999), 9–25.

Summary

The constitutional, legal, and historical context of federal-state relations has clearly influenced the formulation, implementation, and enforcement of environmental protection policies. The various inducements and tools available to federal decision makers enable them to vigorously pursue national environmental goals. Certain states have led while others have lagged in pursuit of environmental protection goals. Some success has been achieved by states acting in concert with each other, and there is considerable variation in the working relationships between the federal and state governments in the environmental arena. However, it is in the dynamics of implementation and enforcement that the political character of environmental policy is most evident, as illustrated below.

The Dynamics of Implementation and Enforcement I: Political Hardball and Sugar Tax Fight in Florida

The protracted war over restoration of the Florida Everglades pitted environmental groups against the powerful sugar industry. The Everglades ecosystem is a 50-mile wide "river of grass" and provides fresh water to 5 million Floridians. It is home to 600 animal species, more than 250 bird species, and 900 plant varieties, but it has been despoiled by years of draining, farming, pollution, and development. The estimated cost of restoration ranges from $700 million to $1.5 billion. The key issue is who pays more for the cleanup—the sugar growers or taxpayers? This battle highlights the role of federalism in environmental politics because each level and branch of government has been involved in efforts to successfully resolve the dispute. A more comprehensive recounting of the seemingly endless saga of efforts to restore the Everglades has been recorded elsewhere;[60] the fight over the sugar tax in Florida in the mid-1990s is the subject of the brief case that follows.

In 1994 the Supreme Court struck down a sugar tax amendment that the Court held had flawed wording and failed to meet the state's constitutional requirements. This was a victory for sugar growers, who claimed such a tax would drive them out of business and leave thousands of people jobless. It was a loss for environmentalists who backed the penny-per-pound tax on sugar growers to help fund the Everglades cleanup. Environmentalists argued that sugar growers gained profits while simultaneously harming the Everglades and polluting the water supply, largely by runoff from sugar cane fields, so they should help fund restoration efforts.[61]

A few years later, environmentalists pushed their case in Congress, seeking an amendment to farm legislation. This would impose a tax on Florida sugar growers of 2 cents per pound on sugar produced in the state. Such a tax would produce approximately $350 million over five years. This money could then be used to buy nearly 150,000 acres of sugar land that would no longer be used to produce sugar, but be converted to retention ponds for storing fresh water and cleansing marshes for filtering farm runoff.[62] For their part, sugar growers insisted that they were already paying their fair share as a result of a deal brokered by Florida Governor Lawton Chiles and Interior Secretary Bruce Babbitt. This followed the settling of a major federal lawsuit requiring sugar growers to pay up to $323 million over the next two decades for Everglades restoration.

Environmentalists pursued another legislative strategy as well. They were concerned about federal policies that encouraged sugar farmers to continue polluting the Everglades. Specifically, they sought to end the sugar price support system, which they insisted inflated U.S. prices, especially when coupled with policies restricting the amount of less-costly imported sugar. Environmentalists and their allies argued that such price supports continue to receive legislative support because of the millions of dollars of political contributions coming from the sugar industry. The General Accounting Office (GAO) estimates that price supports cost U.S. consumers $1.4 billion annually, with much of that money going to sugar growers, many of them in Florida.[63] Environmentalists were not successful in ending the federal government's sugar price support system. Spokesmen for the sugar industry argued that such supports were necessary for the industry to survive subsidized foreign competition and that they were already paying substantial amounts for ecological repair efforts.

The politics of Everglades restoration heated up when Republican presidential candidate and Senate Majority Leader Bob Dole added $200 million to the farm bill for Everglades protection. The Clinton administration countered with a proposal for buying 100,000 acres of farmland close to the Everglades to start restoring the degrading and shrinking ecosystem. The Clinton-Gore $1.5 billion program over a seven-year period would also create an Everglades Restoration Fund and add funding for federal Everglades science and management programs. It would include a penny-per-pound tax on Florida sugar (by cutting Florida sugar farmers' price guarantees) as well as relying on additional funds from state and local governments.[64]

Congress agreed to spend $200 million a year in federal monies for Everglades restoration and another $100 million if surplus federal land in Florida could be sold, but more funding was needed. Environmentalists were not optimistic that Florida lawmakers would approve legislation imposing a penny tax for restoration. They shifted tactics and started a campaign to put the tax on the November 1996 ballot for a constitutional amendment that would place a penny-per-pound tax on sugar for the next 25 years. Environmentalists estimated that the penny-per-pound tax on raw sugar from the Everglades farms would contribute about $37 million annually for 25 years (totaling $925 million) toward the estimated $1.5 billion needed for restoration.[65] The rest of the funding would come from taxpayers in formulas yet to be determined. To bring the issue to a vote required court approval of the initiative's language and 500,000 petition signatures. Both of these hurdles were met, setting the stage for the sugar tax battle—the most costly and bitterly fought campaign in Florida's history.[66]

Both sides waged costly mass-media campaigns to swing public opinion to their side. Indeed, the huge amount of money spent on both sides sets this conflict apart from other ballot fights over environmental issues. Television, radio, and newspaper advertisements saturated the state. Spending on advertising by environmentalists was estimated at $11 million, with $8 million coming from a single contributor, Paul Tudor Jones II, a commodities brokers from Connecticut with a second house in the Florida Keys. Spending by the sugar companies amounted to $18 million, with most of it coming from U.S. Sugar Corp., the Sugar Cane Growers Cooperative, and Flo-Sun Inc. Combined spending by the sugar industry ($23 million) and Save Our Everglades ($13 million) amounted to more than $36 million.[67] The spending of $36 million on this single campaign amounts to 24 percent of the spending nationwide in 1996 on all 90 ballot measures in 20 states.[68] It is estimated that the Florida campaign spent about $7 for every vote cast on the sugar tax measure.[69] The sugar companies went so far as to postpone the fall harvest, releasing thousands of employees from around the state to do precinct work. The sugar industry's campaign echoed arguments from disputes in previous years: that sugar taxes were unfair and would destroy the industry, and that the industry was already paying their fair share for restoration. A new argument was offered as well: an inefficient state bureaucracy would misspend the resources raised by the sugar tax.

There were multiple amendments on the ballot. Most of the attention focused on two amendments: Amendments 4 and 1. Amendment 4, the most controversial one, would have required sugar farmers to pay a penny-per-pound toward Everglades cleanup. It was defeated 54 percent to 46 percent on the statewide ballot. Amendment 1, bankrolled by Tax Cap, would have required a two-thirds vote to put any new tax in the state constitution, retroactive to 1994. It was supported by sugar representatives and approved by the voters. Amendment 5 passed by a 2–1 margin, requiring those who pollute Everglades waters to be primarily responsible for cleanup costs. Amendment 6 passed as well (57 percent support), creating an Everglades trust fund that could receive gifts as well as government revenues.[70] A postelection survey of those voting against Amendment 4 found that 3 in 10 believed that money would be wasted and not be spent on Everglades cleanup, while 1 in 4 believed the fee was a tax they would end up paying through property taxes or on consumer goods.[71]

A few months after the defeat of the tax on Florida's sugar growers, President Clinton revived the proposal as part of his plan to save the Everglades. With the antitax mood evident in the Republican-controlled Congress, it was unlikely to receive approval. In another aftermath of the sugar tax fight, each side of the bitter dispute filed lawsuits against the other. U.S. Sugar sued Save Our Everglades, claiming that SOE lied about its financial resources to get out of paying $150,000 in filing fees for the election. SOE sued the sugar company, claiming the firm lied to voters in their advertisements opposing the tax. Both parties subsequently dropped their lawsuits.[72]

Several months after the defeat of the sugar tax it became clear that the construction cost projections for Everglades cleanup were increasing. This troubled the sugar industry, especially in light of the newly passed constitutional provision requiring that polluters be "primarily responsible" for cleanup. The Florida attorney general informed the South Florida Water Management District that it was authorized to force the sugar industry to increase its payments. This set off a lobbying flurry by the industry to curb activities of the water district.[73]

These activities addressed the meaning of the recently approved Amendment 5. In March 1997, Governor Lawton Chiles requested an advisory opinion from the Florida Supreme Court regarding the interpretation of this amendment. Specifically, he asked whether the provision on Everglades pollution responsibility was self-executing, a position taken by both environmentalists and the state attorney general. He further asked whether "primarily responsible" meant that the polluters were required to pay all of the costs for abatement of water pollution.[74]

The court did not uphold the position of the environmentalists and the attorney general. Instead, it ruled unanimously that Amendment 5 was not "self-executing" and could not be implemented without the aid of "legislative enactment." Regarding the meaning of the term "primarily responsible" the court ruled that, in effect, the sugar industry was not responsible for 100 percent of the pollution in the Everglades protection area. It held that those within the area who are determined to be responsible must pay their share of the cost of abating that pollution. This decision throws the issue back into the state legislature because liability cannot be imposed now until the legislature establishes a procedure for determining whether, and to what extent, landowners are liable for the costs of cleaning up pollution. It is likely that the "bitter foes" in this controversy will continue their fight in the future over the issue of who pays for Everglades restoration.

This case is instructive because it shows how high the stakes are in environmental disputes and how fiercely the stakeholder combatants will battle over public policy issues. It also illustrates the interconnections between the branches and levels of American government. In this dispute the Florida Supreme Court was involved at the beginning and end of the controversy. Congressional and presidential politics were involved, as were state legislative politics. Interest groups and grass-roots mobilizing played a large role in the unfolding dispute, and each side spent considerable amounts of money in an effort to influence public opinion and prevail at the polls. The governor of Florida and other elected representatives had a role in the fray, as did voters, the media, and state administrative units. The case also shows how stakeholders often shift tactics and venues over time, so that a loss at one stage or in one arena of the policy process just moves the battleground to another stage or arena. Finally, issues of economic survival versus environmental protection were raised, a recurrent theme in environmental politics that is further explored in the case that follows.

The Dynamics of Implementation and Enforcement II: Mountaintop Removal in West Virginia

Environmentalists and coal mining interests in West Virginia recently became embroiled in a heated dispute related to a process called "mountaintop removal" strip-mining. West Virginia is a major supplier of the country's valuable, low-sulfur coal; as a nation we rely on coal for most of our electricity. Mountaintop removal is the method used to extract this coal. It involves use of explosives and huge equipment to blast away entire mountaintops, uncover the coal—which is then scooped up and hauled away—and, finally, dump the leftover rubble and dirt into the valleys, hollows, and streams below. Congress outlawed the practice in 1977, but it continued until recent action by a federal judge found that the West Virginia coal mining industry was breaking the law.

In the process of mining coal, the environment is adversely affected in numerous ways: by decapitating mountains, burying streams, destroying grasslands, and stripping off topsoil. Area residents have complained that flying debris has damaged their homes. Aggrieved parties have filed suit against the mining industry, contending that mines have violated state and federal laws and that regulators have been lax in enforcing these laws. A recent decision in the U.S. District Court bans coal mining companies from dumping waste into streams, but that decision is being appealed to the U.S. Court of Appeals. This case illustrates the intimate connection between state and national politics, and the ways various interests can seek to have their voices heard through different institutions in the political process. It also shows the potential conflict in many jurisdictions between economic concerns and environmental interests.

The key policy issue involved in this dispute is whether to allow coal companies to continue dumping excess rock and dirt into streams, in violation of the Clean Water Act and the 1977 Surface Mining Control and Reclamation Act. If they are prevented from doing so, some argue it will put the coal mines out of business. The major stakeholders in the controversy over mountaintop removal are the coal mining industry, environmentalists, area residents, state regulatory and elected officials, and federal officials in the legislative, executive, and judicial branches. Each stakeholder has a unique perspective on the issue and a role in the controversy. Examination of these conflicting interests highlights the issue, the power and salience of various actors in this particular microcosm of state-level environmental politics, and the intermeshing of these interests in the policy process.

The coal mining industry is king in West Virginia: It employs 3.3 percent of the state's work force, produces more than 170 million tons a year, and contributes $2.6 billion annually to the state's economy. It staunchly supports mountaintop removal. Strip-mining accounts for about one-third of the state's coal production. Spokespersons for the industry contend that an end to mountaintop removal, or "strip-mining on steroids" as some call it, would destroy the state's fragile economy and end all coal mining in the state.[75] The United Mine Workers of America are allied with the industry in opposing any efforts to curb the practice of mountaintop removal and the resulting layoffs of miners.[76] Mining proponents argue that this method allows the state's coal mining industry to remain competitive with cheaper coal imports from other parts of the United States and abroad. Further, they dispute the extent of environmental damage attributable to this practice, pointing to their successful efforts to recontour and reseed mountaintop project sites into rolling slopes with grass and shrubs.

Environmentalists sought to stop mountaintop removal to avoid further damage to the Appalachian ecosystem. Local as well as state and national environmental interest groups joined the fray. They were concerned that destruction of streams adversely affects fish migration and the ecosystem. Further, they felt that replacement of thousands of acres of hardwood forests with grasslands destroyed the original contours of the land. Mountain peaks are being demolished and whole communities are getting bulldozed. Groups such as the West Virginia Highlands Conservancy helped residents bring the case to the federal courts.

Area residents who live near the mountaintop removal sites share with environmentalists their unhappiness with the results of using this controversial technology, and they would like to see it stopped. They claim that their houses shake, that doors and windows have been damaged, that dust is a problem, and that Sheetrock and dry wall are falling down. Health problems from contaminated wells and groundwater, as well as accumulated dust, are also cited. Some residents have sold their homes, often at a reduced price, and relocated elsewhere. Others have refused to leave, and a few have stayed to fight the coal industry by filing a lawsuit.[77]

The West Virginia Division of Environmental Protection (DEP), along with the state and federal government, is the target of the lawsuit. The suit contends that the DEP has not met its statutory obligations to regulate the coal mines and that it has been too lax in enforcing the law and permitting the coal industry to illegally dump rubble into streams, valleys, and hollows. DEP permitted 38 new mountaintop removal mines over 27,000 acres in the three years from 1996 to 1998.[78] Critics claim that the DEP is controlled by the coal industry, pointing out that the last three directors came from the coal industry. The DEP claims they are doing their job—enforcing the law—and they deny destroying the streams.

State elected officials, many of whom depend on sizable contributions from the coal industry to finance their campaigns, overwhelmingly support the position of the coal industry, favoring mountaintop removal. An important exception is the secretary of state, Ken Hechler, an official elected statewide. Secretary Hechler is sympathetic to the position of the homeowners living in the mining areas and to environmentalists' concern for the Appalachian ecosystem. He is quick to speak out against continued use of mountaintop removal. Governor Cecil Underwood, a former coal company executive, sides with the coal industry and views efforts to stop mountaintop removal as "effectively closing coal mining," leading to widespread job loss and loss of tax revenues. Both the state legislature and Governor Underwood incurred the wrath of state regulators as well as the U.S. Environmental Protection Agency when they supported a law favored by the U.S. coal industry relaxing the rules for replacing streams destroyed by mining.

Elected officials, including Senator Robert Byrd and other members of West Virginia's congressional delegation, also sided with the coal industry. They lobbied Congress to undo actions halting mountaintop removal, but to no avail. Senator Byrd, powerful chair of the Senate Appropriations Committee, sought to permit the continued dumping of mine wastes in streams and valleys. He and his colleagues justify this position, arguing that it is necessary to protect the state's economy and miners' jobs. Their action came in the form of a rider attached to an FY2000 Senate appropriations bill. The Clinton administration initially supported this rider to accommodate Senator Byrd, but subsequently reversed itself under pressure from 20 national environmental groups to veto appropriations bills that contain antienvironmental provisions.[79]

Various federal executive agencies were involved in the issue. At one point, the U.S. EPA threatened to take over from the DEP the regulation of West Virginia coal mines.[80] The Office of Surface Mining (OSM) is the federal agency overseeing surface mines. Over the two decades of its existence it has moved from the principal regulator in most states, to the overseer of state government regulatory efforts. This delegation of responsibility from the federal government to the states was necessitated by recent congressional budget cuts and downsizing of the OSM. As a result, solo inspections by the OSM in West Virginia have stopped, and the number of joint federal-state investigations have diminished as well.[81] The EPA, OSM, the U.S. Army Corps of Engineers, and the West Virginia DEP all entered into a memorandum of understanding in 1999 specifying the conditions under which valley fills may be constructed in addition to the requirements for compliance with the Clean Water Act.

The courts were key actors on this issue. On October 20, 1999, U.S. District Court Judge Charles H. Haden II issued a 49-page ruling concluding that dumping mining waste from mountaintop removal into valley streams was a violation of the Clean Air Act and the Surface Mining Control Act. His decision stopped West Virginia's DEP from granting permits allowing such dumping in streams that run for half a year. It was this ruling that also prompted the coal companies to close mines and lay off workers. It also led to the vigorous opposition of Governor Underwood and the West Virginia congressional delegation. The delegation claimed the judge's interpretation of federal law was out of sync with congressional intent. The local media weighed in on the issue, with the *Charleston*

Gazette supporting the court ruling in an editorial saying the "decapitation method" makes ". . . West Virginia an international example of industrial ravages."[82] The issue also received national and international attention, with the appearance of numerous newspaper articles.[83] It was also the subject of a nationally televised CBS *60 Minutes* broadcast, which was sympathetic to both environmentalists and West Virginia homeowners affected by these mining methods.[84]

The Haden court ruling was subsequently stayed, pending appeal. It prevents the coal industry from dumping rubble within 100 feet of streams with year-round or half-year flows. The West Virginia delegation's attempt to pass a legislative rider overturning the court's decision passed in the Senate by a vote of 56–33, but was not taken up prior to adjournment of the House of Representatives. Most recently, in the wake of the stay of the District Court's ruling pending appeal, the West Virginia State DEP rescinded an order stopping the activities of valley fills downstream and halting new valley fill permits.

This dispute is ongoing and not likely to be resolved in the near term. It is unclear whether the final resolution will result from action by the federal courts or Congress. It does serve as another instructive example of environmental politics at the subnational level. As with the sugar tax case, the range of interests affected is extensive, stakes are high, interests conflict, players seek to prevail in different institutional settings and at different levels of government, and tactics change as the issue unfolds. The West Virginia case illustrates the interrelation between state-level interests and national interests as well as the interconnection between social, economic, political, technological, and ecological concerns. Controversial state environmental issues like this one cannot be resolved in isolation from conditions in the broader environment and from public officials at higher levels of government.

Conclusion

This chapter reviewed the meaning of environmental federalism, its historical context, regulatory and nonregulatory tools, the role and performance of the states, and political dynamics encountered in specific environmental disputes. While scholars disagree about the definition of federalism, they agree that government at all levels plays crucial roles in environmental protection. We showed how regulatory "sticks" in the form of command-and-control regulations are used to enforce national standards, and how states are expected to implement such directives, often lacking financial support from Washington. Recently, nonregulatory "carrots" have been used hand-in-hand with more coercive regulations. While policies in past decades were based on assumptions about the limited capability and commitment of state governments to effectively protect the environment, the 1990s reversed these assumptions as states demonstrated improved capacity and determination to achieve environmental goals. Today, relations between the federal and state governments in addressing environmental concerns reflect a mixture of cooperation, conflict, and strategic decision making.

The federal environmental regulatory structure was erected in the 1970s and extended in the 1980s, but the 1990s witnessed the diminished enthusiasm, and in some instances active hostility, of national policymakers for new federal environmental legislation. State and local policymakers now vigorously object to new federal mandates when resources do not accompany such directives. Yet when states have the will, resources, and capacity to act, they have achieved success. But state environmental initiatives remain uneven: some states take the lead and follow best practices, others lag behind, unwilling or unable to undertake innovative action to protect the environment. This substantial variation in effort and performance among the states is also evident in the extent of trust and involvement in federal-state relationships.

The two case studies in this chapter (Sugar Tax Fight and Mountaintop Removal) highlight the controversial nature of environmental politics and the complex trade-offs that often exist between economic and environmental gains. They show that political actors from all levels of government, citizens, organized interests, and the private sector have crucial stakes in the outcome of these contentious and often costly disputes. The strategic maneuvering of these key stakeholders is a political game that is shaped by legal, economic, social, technological, and ecological considerations. Environmental activists in Florida faced formidable adversaries in the sugar industry as they fought over the issue of who should pay for cleanup of the Everglades. In West Virginia the battle lines pitted environmentalists against powerful coal mining interests over "mountaintop removal" stripmining. In each case the "top down" influence of national government officials and the "bottom up" clout of state and local actors were critical in the political interplay that ensued. While the future of federal-state relations in environmental policy is still unfolding, as it is in these two cases, it is clear that successful solutions to environmental problems will require joint efforts by those at the top, middle, and bottom of the federal system.

**Web Sites
American Federalism and Environmental Politics:**

Council of State Governments: **www.statesnews.org**

International City/County Management Association: **www.icma.org**

National Association of Counties: **www.NACo.org**

National Conference of State Legislatures: **www.ncsl.org**

National League of Cities: **www.nlc.org**

National Governors Association: **www.nga.org**

State and Local Government on the Net:
  www.piperinfo.com/state/states.html

State Government Resources: **www.legal.gsa.gov/intro5.htm**

Meta-Indexes for State and Local Information:
  www.lcweb.loc.gov/global/state/stategov.html

The Local Government Home Page: **www.algov.org**

Source: Adapted from Project Vote Smart, Vote Smart Web (Yellow Pages), 2000 Edition, 174–176.

Endnotes

1   See, for example, David M. Hedge and Michael J. Scicchitano, "Regulating in Space and Time: The Case of Regulatory Federalism," *Journal of Politics* 56 (1994), 134–153; David Schoenbrod, "Why States, Not EPA, Should Set Pollution Standards," *Regulation* 19 (1996), 18–25; and A. Hunter Bacot and Roy A. Dawes, "Administration of State Environmental Policies," in John J. Gargan, ed. *Handbook of State Government Administration* (NY: Marcel Dekker, 1999), 591–612.

2   Dale Krane, "Federalism," in Jay M. Shafritz, ed. *International Encyclopedia of Public Policy and Administration*, vol. 2 (Boulder, CO: Westview, 1998), 865–877.

3   See K.C. Wheare, *Federal Government*, 3rd ed. (London: Oxford University Press, 1953); Arthur W. MacMahon, *Administering Federalism in a Democracy* (New York: Oxford University Press, 1972); and William H. Riker, "Federalism," in Fred Greenstein and Nelson Polsby, eds. *A Companion to Contemporary Political Philosophy* (Oxford: Blackwell Reference, 1975), 508–514. Samuel H. Beer, "Federalism and the Nation-State: What Can Be Learned from the American Experience?" in Karen Knop, et. al., eds. *Rethinking Federalism: Citizens, Markets, and Governments in a Changing World* (Vancouver, LIBC Press, 1995), 224–249.

4   Daniel J. Elazar, "Federalism," in David L. Sills, ed. *International Encyclopedia of the Social Sciences*. vol. 5 (New York: Macmillan and The Free Press, 1968), 353–367.

5   See Aaron Wildavsky, "A Bias Toward Federalism," in Aaron Wildavsky, *Speaking Truth to Power: The Art and Craft of Policy Analysis* (Boston: Little, Brown, 1979), 142–154; Thomas R. Dye, *American Federalism: Competition Among Governments* (Lexington, MA: D.C. Heath, 1990); and Vincent Ostrom, *The Meaning of American Federalism: Constituting a Self-Governing Society* (San Francisco: Institute for Contemporary Studies Press, 1991).

6   See Deil S. Wright, "Federalism, Intergovernmental Relations, and Intergovernmental Management: Historical Reflections and Conceptual Comparisons," *Public Administration Review* 50 (1990), 168–178.

7   Ronald Watts, "Contemporary Views on Federalism," Paper presented at the Centre for Constitutional Analysis, Republic of South Africa (August 2–6, 1993), as quoted in Douglas V. Verney, "Federalism, Federative Systems, and Federations: The United States, Canada, and India," *Publius: The Journal of Federalism* (Spring 1995), 84.

8   DeWitt John, *Civic Environmentalism: Alternatives to Regulation in States and Communities* (Washington, DC: Congressional Quarterly, 1994), 14.

9   R.V. Percival, "Environmental Federalism: Historical Roots and Contemporary Models," *Maryland Law Review* 54 (1995): 1141–1181. This historical summary relies heavily on Percival's framework and analysis supplemented by Jacqueline V. Switzer with Gary Bryner, *Environmental Politics: Domestic and Global Dimensions* (NY: St. Martin's Press, 1998) and Richard N.L. Andrews, *Managing the Environment, Managing Ourselves* (New Haven: Yale University Press, 1999).

10 Switzer with Bryner, *Environmental Politics: Domestic and Global Dimensions*, 5–6.

11 Andrews, *Managing the Environment, Managing Ourselves*, 227–228, 275–276, 282–283; Switzer with Bryner *Environmental Politics: Domestic and Global Dimensions*, 13–17; and Percival, "Environmental Federalism: Historical Roots and Contemporary Models, 1165–1171.

12 Denise Scheberle, *Federalism and Environmental Policy: Trust and the Politics of Implementation* (Washington, DC: Georgetown University Press, 1997),

13–14; and Denise Scheberle, "Partners in Policymaking: Forging Effective Federal-State Relations," *Environment* 40 (1998), 14–15.

[13] See John, *Civic Environmentalism: Alternatives to Regulation in States and Communities*, 5.

[14] See B. Dan Wood, "Federalism and Policy Responsiveness: The Clean Air Case," *Journal of Politics* 53 (1991), 851–859.

[15] See Margaret A. Reams, "Incentive Based vs. Command-and-Control Approaches to Improving Environmental Quality," *Spectrum* 68 (1995), 6–18.

[16] See Oliver A. Houck and Michael Roland, "Federalism in Wetlands Regulation: A Consideration of Delegation Under Section 404 and Related Programs to the States," *Maryland Law Review* 54 (1995), 1243–1313; and Hedge and Scicchitano, "Regulating in Space and Time: The Case of Regulatory Federalism," 134–153.

[17] See Rosemary O'Leary, "The Bureaucratic Politics Paradox: The Case of Wetlands Legislation in Nevada," *Journal of Public Administration Research and Theory* 4 (1994), 443–467.

[18] See Jeffrey S. Hill and Carol S. Weissert, "Implementation and the Irony of Delegation: the Politics of Low-Level Radioactive Waste Disposal," *Journal of Politics* 57 (1995), 344–369.

[19] Council of State Governments, *Resource Guide to State Environmental Management*, 5th ed. (Lexington, KY: Council of State Governments, 1999), 23.

[20] Ibid., 24.

[21] Ibid., 9.

[22] See Barry G. Rabe, "Integrating Environmental Regulation: Permitting Innovation at the State Level," *Journal of Policy Analysis and Management* 14 (1995), 467–472; and Barry G. Rabe, "Integrated Environmental Permitting: Experience and Innovation at the State Level," *State and Local Government Review* 27 (1995), 209–220.

[23] See Raymond J. Burby and Robert G. Patterson, "Improving Compliance with State Environmental Regulations," *Journal of Public Policy Analysis and Management* 12 (1993), 753–772.

[24] Council of State Governments, 13.

[25] Steven A. Herman, "It Takes a Partnership," *The Environmental Forum* 14 (1997), 26; see also David R. Hodas, "Enforcement of Environmental Law in a Triangular Federal System: Can Three Not Be a Crown When Enforcement Authority Is Shared by the United States, the States, and Their Citizens," *Maryland Law Review* 54 (1995), 1552–1657.

[26] See Hodas, "Enforcement of Environmental Law in a Triangular Federal System," 1580; and Barry G. Rabe, "Power to the States: Promise and Pitfalls," in Norman J. Vig and Michael E. Kraft, eds. *Environmental Policy* (Washington, DC: CQ Press, 2000), 42.

[27] Scheberle, "Partners in Policymaking: Forging Effective Federal-State Relations," 17–18.

[28] See Carole J. Cimitile, Victoria S. Kennedy, Henry W. Lambright, Rosemary O'Leary, and Paul Weiland, "Balancing Rise and Finance: The Challenge of Implementing Unfunded Environmental Mandates," *Public Administration Review* 57 (1997), 65–74.

[29] See Michael J. Pompili, "The Rising Impact of Environmental Mandates on Local Government," *Regulation* 18 (1995), 76–84.

[30] Sanford F. Borins, *Innovating with Integrity* (Washington, DC: Georgetown University Press, 1998), 190–193.

[31] Council of State Governments, p. 23.

32   See Laurence O'Toole, Jr., Chilik Yu, James Cooley, and Gail Cowie, "Reducing Toxic Chemical Releases and Transfers: Explaining Outcomes for a Voluntary Program," *Policy Studies Journal* 25 (1997), 11–26.

33   Council of State Governments, p. 21.

34   Ibid, 12, 21; and Peter S. Menell, "Structuring a Market-Oriented Federal Eco-Information Policy," *Maryland Law Review* 54 (1995), 1439.

35   See Rabe, "Power to the States: Promise and Pitfalls," 39.

36   See Mary Durfee, "Diffusion of Pollution Prevention Policy," *Annals of the American Academy of Political and Social Science* 566 (November 1999), 108–119; and Barry G. Rabe "Federalism and Entrepreneurship: Explaining American and Canadian Innovation in Pollution Prevention and Regulatory Integration," *Policy Studies Journal* 27 (1999), 27–43.

37   Council of State Governments, 21.

38   Ibid., 12.

39   Ibid., 24.

40   Rabe, "Federalism and Entrepreneurship: Explaining American and Canadian Innovation in Pollution Prevention and Regulatory Integration," 293.

41   Rabe, "Power to the States: Promise and Pitfalls," 36.

42   Borins, *Innovating with Integrity*, 193. See also Jeremy B. Hockenstein, Robert N. Stavins, and Bradley W. Whitehead, "Crafting the Next Generation of Market-Based Environmental Tools," *Environment* 39 (1997), 12.

43   See also Marian R. Chertow and Daniel C. Esty, "Environmental Policy: The Next Generation," *Issues in Science and Technology* 14 (1997), 79.

44   "The Use of Market-Based Instruments in the United States," *Environment* 39 (4), 16–17.

45   Hockenstein, Stavins, and Whitehead, "Crafting the Next Generation of Market-Based Environmental Tools," 12–15.

46   J.C. Morris, "The Distributional Impacts of Privatization in National Water-Quality Policy," *Journal of Politics* 59 (1997), 56–72.

47   E.S. Savas, "Privatization and Productivity," In Marc Holzer, ed. *Public Productivity Handbook.* (New York: Marcel Dekker, 1992), 79–98.

48   Council of State Governments, 18.

49   Michael Alexander and George Backus, "The Effect of Green Taxes and Carbon Tax Shifting on the State of Minnesota," *International Journal of Public Administration* 22 (1999), 975–996.

50   Rabe, "Power to the States: Promise and Pitfalls," 37.

51   Borins, *Innovating with Integrity*, 194.

52   Rabe, "Power to the States: Promise and Pitfalls," 37.

53   James P. Lester, "A New Federalism? Environmental Policy in the States," in Norman M. Vig and Michael E. Kraft, eds. *Environmental Policy in the 1990s* (Washington, DC: CQ Press, 1994), 51–68; and James P. Lester, "Federalism and State Environmental Policy," in James P. Lester, ed. *Environmental Politics and Policy* (Durham, NC: Duke University Press, 1995), 39–60.

54   Katherine Barrett and Richard Greene, "Grading the States," *Governing* (February 1999), **www.governing.com/gp9intro.htm**. Retrieved on June 27, 2000. Researchers from the Maxwell School of Citizenship and Public Affairs at Syracuse University developed the GPP ratings supported by a grant from the Pew Charitable Fund.

55   Rosemary O'Leary and Tracy Yandle, "Environmental Management at the Millennium: The Use of Environmental Dispute Resolution by State Governments," *Journal of Public Administration Research and Theory* 10 (2000), 149. Alternative dispute-resolution programs involve independent, third-party neutrals con-

vening, seeking consensus, and mediating among disputing parties to seek voluntary settlement. The authors' grading criteria included the existence of a legislatively supported ADR program, presence of full-time staff and funding, top-level support, and neutrality and independence of the office.

56 Ibid., 150.

57 See, for example, Scott P. Hays, Michael Esler, and Carol E. Hays, "Environmental Commitment Among the States: Integrating Alternative Approaches to State Environmental Policy," *Publius* 26 (1996), 41–59; A. Hunter Bacot and Roy A. Dawes, "Responses to Federal Devolution: Measuring State Environmental Efforts," *State and Local Government Review* 28 (1996), 124–135; A. Hunter Bacot and Roy A. Dawes, "State Expenditures and Policy Outcomes in Environmental Program Management," *Policy Studies Journal* 25 (1997), 355–370; A. Hunter Bacot, Roy A. Dawes, and Ann Sawtelle, "A Preliminary Analysis of Environmental Management in the Southern States," *Public Administration Quarterly* 19 (1996), 389–403; Lester, "A New Federalism? Environmental Policy in the States," 51–68; Lester, "Federalism and State Environmental Policy," 39–60; Emmett N. Lombard, "Determinants of State Air Quality Management," *American Review of Public Administration* 23 (1993), 57–74; L.L. Malysa, "A Comparative Assessment of State Planning and Management Capacity: Tidal Wetlands Protection in Virginia and Maryland," *State and Local Government Review* 28 (1996), 205–218; and Evan J. Ringquist, "Policy Influence and Policy Responsiveness in State Pollution Control," *Policy Studies Journal* 22 (1994), 25–41.

58 "Teaching the Feds Respect," *Governing*, **http://www.governing.com/poy/ptrob.htm**. Retrieved March 9, 2000; "Pathbreaking a Pollution Pact," *Governing*, **http://www.governing.com/poy/ptgade.htm**. Retrieved March 9, 2000.

59 Scheberle, *Federalism and Environmental Policy: Trust and the Politics of Implementation*, 18.

60 See John, *Civic Environmentalism*, 125–201.

61 See Greenwire, "Everglades: FL High Court Strikes Down Sugar Tax Amendment," American Political Network (May 31, 1994), **http://web.lexis-nexis.com/universe**. Retrieved June 28, 2000; and National Association of Attorneys General, "Florida Strikes Constitutional Amendment to Finance Everglades Restoration with Sugar Tax," *State Constitutional Law Bulletin* 81 (October 1994).

62 William Booth, "Sugar Growers Stuck in Everglades Battle; Opposition Pushing Tax to Pay for Cleanup," *The Washington Post* (January 12, 1996), A03; "Everglades Restoration," United Press International (January 18, 1996).

63 Booth, "Sugar Growers Stuck in Everglades Battle, A03.

64 Greenwire, "Everglades: White House Chews Over a New Sugar Tax Plan," American Political Network (February 16, 1996), **http://www.web.lexis-nexis.com/universe**. Retrieved June 28, 2000; John A.Baden, "More Subsidies in the Age of Corruption Entitlements," *The Seattle Times* (February 28, 1996), B5; Amy Moritz, "Commentary on the Administration's Penny-per-Pound Sugar Tax Proposal," **http://www.nationalcenter.org/Nosugar.html**.

65 Greenwire, "Everglades: White House Chews Over a New Sugar Tax Plan," **http://www.web.lexis-nexis.com/universe**. Retrieved June 28, 2000; John H. Cushman, Jr., "Noisy Fight Over a Tax on Sugar," *New York Times* (November 2, 1996), A12; David Olinger, "Everglades Fight Enters Next Round," *St. Petersburg Times* (November 7, 1996), 4B.

66 Jan Hollingsworth, "Voters Reject Penny Tax on Sugar," *Tampa Tribune* (November 6, 1996), 1.

[67] R. Chebium, "Penny Per Pound Tax Proposed to Help Heal Everglades," *Business News* (October 27, 1996).

[68] Eric Schine, E. "Let's Put a Lid on Ballot Propositions," *Business Week* (November 18, 1996), 50.

[69] David Olinger, "Two Sides Pour $36-million into a Sugar Tax Feud," *St. Petersburg Times* (November 9, 1996), 1B; Greenwire, "Everglades: Sugar Firm, Enviro Group Drop Lawsuits," The National Journal Group (November 3, 1997), **http://www.lexis-nexis.com/universe**. Retrieved June 28, 2000.

[70] David Olinger, "Sugar Growers Beat Penny-a-Pound Tax," *St. Petersburg Times* (November 6, 1996), 1A.

[71] Jan Hollingsworth, "Opponents Feared Waste of Tax Revenue," *Tampa Tribune* (November 7, 1996), 1.

[72] Greenwire, "Everglades: Sugar Firm, Enviro Group Drop Lawsuits," **http://www.lexis-nexis.com/universe.** Retrieved June 28, 2000.

[73] "Sugar's Aim Is Off," *St. Petersburg Times* (April 6, 1997), 2D.

[74] M. Rosen, "Everglades Pollution Responsibility Amendment Not 'Self-Executing,' *Florida Environmental Compliance Update* (Brentwood, TN: M. Lee Smith Publisher), February 1998.

[75] Ken Ward, Jr., "A Controversial Ruling Pits Miners Against Environmentalists in West Virginia," *In These Times* (December 12, 1999), 24.

[76] Martha Bryson Hodel, "Union President Sees Mining 'Under Assault as Never Before,'" *The Courier-Journal* (April 2, 1999), **http://www.mountaintopmining. com/newsarchive/union.htm**. Retrieved March 6, 2000.

[77] CBS News, "King Coal; Debate Over Whether a Lawsuit Against a Form of Coal Mining Has Devastated the West Virginia Mining Industry as Much as Coal Companies Contend," *60 Minutes* (February 27, 2000), **http://web.lexis-nexis. com/universe/printdoc**. Retrieved February 29, 2000.

[78] Mark Tran, "Ex-Coal Worker with Mountain to Climb to Save Valley," *The Guardian* (London: August 14, 1998), 22.

[79] Peter Slavin, "A Rumble in the Hills," *Financial Times* (London: November 20, 1999), A–24.

[80] Martha Bryson Hodel, "Virginians Resist Mountaintop-Removal Mines," *Milwaukee Journal Sentinel* (October 11, 1998), 8.

[81] Joby Warwick, "'Mountaintop Removal' Shakes Coal State; Cost of Prosperity Hits Close to Home," *The Washington Post* (April 31, 1998), A01.

[82] Mark Tran, "Ex-Coal Worker with Mountain to Climb to Save Valley," 22.

[83] Ward, "A Controversial Ruling Pits Miners Against Environmentalists in West Virginia," 24; Ken Ward, Jr.,"Haden Suspends Mining Rule," *Charleston Gazette Online* (October 30, 1999). **http://www.wvgazette.com/news/News/1999103937/**; Tom Kenworthy and Juliet Eilperin, "White House Backs W. Va. on Mine Dumping," *Washington Post* (October 30, 1999), A02; Mark Tran, "Ex-Coal Worker with Mountain to Climb to Save Valley," 22; Hodel, "Union President Sees Mining 'Under Assault as Never Before,'" **http://www.mountaintopmining.com/newsarchive/ union.htm**; Hodel, "Virginians Resist Mountaintop-Removal Mines," 8; and Slavin, "A Rumble in the Hills," A–24.

[84] CBS News, "King Coal; Debate Over Whether a Lawsuit Against a Form of Coal Mining Has Devastated the West Virginia Mining Industry as Much as Coal Companies Contend," **http://web.lexis-nexis.com/universe/printdoc.** Retrieved February 29, 2000.

CHAPTER 3

Public Opinion, the Media, and Environmental Issues

Public attitudes about political and social issues are important considerations for government officials engaged in the process of policy making. The president and members of Congress or governors and state legislators are very likely to give some attention to the public's orientation toward the important issues of the day. At the same time, the mass media serve as both a means of information dissemination and a potential vehicle for persuading an audience. Moreover, the news media are the primary outlet for publicizing public opinion polls. As one political observer has noted, "One of the major functions of the news media has always been to keep the public informed about public debate on political issues as well as on events of the day."[1]

In democratic societies, governmental leaders are theoretically obligated to take into consideration the views held by the public. The extent to which they do so remains problematic, however. Majority opinion on numerous issues does not necessarily translate into public policy. For example, although 61 percent of the public supports strict laws governing the sale of firearms, with 90 percent supporting a waiting period prior to the purchase of firearms,[2] the Republican-controlled Congress of the 1990s has been recalcitrant in debating, let alone implementing, new gun control measures.

The notion of public opinion spans 2,000 years of political history. As Erickson and Tedin observe, Plato, Aristotle, Hobbes, Locke, and Rousseau all spoke about the "group mind" or the "general will."[3] Serious consideration of the opinions of the public is another story. Should government leaders base their decisions on the judgment of the masses of citizens? Early American political thinkers differed on this issue. For example, Alexander Hamilton reflected the views of many of the founding fathers when he asserted:

> The voice of the people has been said to be the voice of God; and however generally this maxim has been quoted and believed, it is not true in fact. The people are turbulent and changing; they seldom judge or determine right.[4]

As the process of democratization in the United States evolved, the public increasingly demanded input into the political system. Yet the acquisition of a solid basis for determining the views of the public in a reliable and valid way did not occur until the twentieth century. At the time of Franklin D. Roosevelt's reelection campaign in 1936, two major polls were conducted, each with the goal of determining who would be elected the next president of the United States.[5] *The Literary Digest* magazine's nonscientific poll drawn from a biased sample of respondents from automobile registrations and telephone books (at a time when the country was suffering during the Great Depression) resulted in an incorrect assessment of the presidential campaign—suggesting that Alf Landon would be the next president. The modern-day Gallup poll was born at this time when George Gallup, Jr., predicted correctly that Franklin Roosevelt would be reelected. Unlike *The Literary Digest* approach, Gallup measured the distribution of opinion regarding the presidential candidates by using scientific methodology.

Today numerous polls are conducted by a variety of sources, from television networks and national newspapers to ideologically based interest groups, from the White House to academics conducting research. Polls are conducted to learn about the public's attitudes about specific issues and candidates for public office, among others. The point is that while public opinion can fluctuate or remain stable it is important to determine what the public thinks at a given time or over a certain period.

The difficulty lies in the extent to which the public's views about political issues, for instance, should be taken into account when lawmakers are in the process of public policy making. In describing the role of public opinion in democratic societies, two researchers explain:

> Most political theorists have assigned an important role to public opinion in democracies such as the United States, not because it exists only in democracies but only in a democratic society is it regarded as a legitimate expression of the will of the people. In a democracy public opinion is actively sought because it provides a means by which citizens' views can be presented to their leaders.[6]

The American public has access to the world through a wide variety of news sources. Citizens can acquire information from television networks, newspapers, radio, and magazines. But how often have the major television networks broadcast news stories about environmental affairs? Figure 3.1 shows the frequency of early evening news stories about two environmental issues—namely, pollution and endangered species during the 20-year period 1978–1998.[7] From 1978 onward, environmental pollution received much more televised coverage than did endangered species. However, by 1998, the issue of biodiversity became a much more visible issue—television networks broadcast more stories about endangered species than in prior years and the issue received almost as many stories as pollution did, which had had a higher frequency of stories in the past. It is also noteworthy that as television broadcasts about pollution declined, stories about endangered species rose in the late 1990s, indicating that the issue became more newsworthy.

While Americans tend to receive most of their political information from television, it is primarily from the traditional (noncable) networks.[8] Nonetheless,

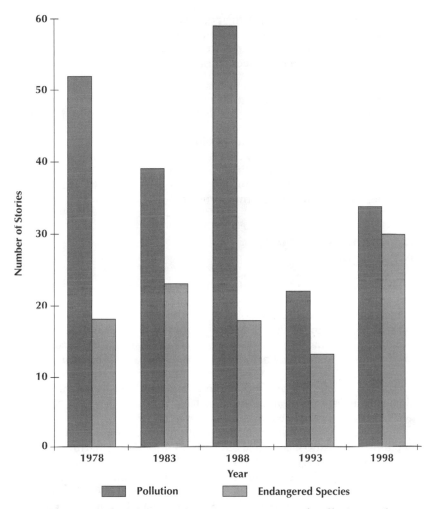

FIGURE 3.1 *Television Evening News Coverage of Pollution and Endangered Species.*

technological advances in the distribution of information has not only offered additional sources of information for citizens but also has fragmented the viewing public. Cable television, which was linked to about 20 percent of American households in the mid-1980s, reached about 6 in 10 homes by the early 1990s.[9] Beginning about 20 years ago, Cable News Network (CNN) and C-SPAN (the public affairs broadcasting system) have provided citizens with a viable alternative to traditional network news broadcasts. Moreover, while CNN broadcasts news around the clock, C-SPAN offers direct access to political and governmental affairs so viewers can watch "gavel-to-gavel" programming. In recent years additional specialized cable programming (e.g., MS-NBC) has challenged both the traditional media outlets as well as existing cable news sources.

The Internet is yet another contemporary means by which citizens can access political information. Organized interests as well as governments (among others) have established Web sites to provide the political consumer with information, data, and statistics. However, the proliferation of Web sites and the international scope of the Internet raises serious questions regarding the validity and reliability of the Web. As one political analyst recently observed:

> Citizens who extend themselves into cyberspace need to be aware of the differences between the types of information and services available. They should demand accuracy from those who govern and they should be aware of being misled by those who seek to persuade. When citizens access public affairs information on the World Wide Web, the current dominant form of accessing cyberspace, they should note whether they are referencing an official source, or not. They should also take careful note of the content, no matter what the source; for even official sources may contain some political information that has slipped through the thin lines that form its border.[10]

Public Opinion, the Media, and the Environment

From the early Gallup polls of the 1930s to the contemporary election polls regarding the year 2000 race for the presidency, public opinion polls have become an integral part of modern American politics. For the interested citizen or policymaker, the attitudes of Americans are readily available, from local libraries to Internet sources. At the same time, some researchers suggest that the media plays an agenda-setting role, deciding what issues to cover and how much time to devote to these issues. How important is the environment to the American public? How prominent has the environment been in public opinion polls? While a vast array of domestic and international issues has been the focus of media coverage, how salient has the coverage been on the environment?

For more than 30 years, public opinion polls have demonstrated that the American public has been concerned about the condition of the natural environment. Early on, policymakers as well as citizens were most concerned about pollution issues, i.e., the quality of the air and the water. By the early 1960s, public health and environmental problems associated with chemical pesticides become a public issue when the book *Silent Spring* was published by biologist Rachel Carson. Moreover, the environment was clearly shown to be an issue of major concern to the American public as a result of the tremendous response to the first Earth Day in April 1970.

Political communication is important to all societies. In the American democratic system, the media are protected by the First Amendment in order to ensure the free flow of information to the American public. Nonetheless, having access to political information disseminated by the media is one thing; using it is quite another. Over the last seven decades, Americans have witnessed the evolution of the media, from the printed page to the rise of radio to traditional television broadcasting to cable television to the Internet. Polls have shown that for quite some time, citizens have used television more than the other traditional sources of political information (e.g., newspapers and magazines). However, in recent years, the traditional news sources, including television, have been losing their audience to the Internet as online news has become more easily accessible.[11] The benefit of this transformation in the dissemination of political information is that one out of four Internet customers who generally don't pay much attention to the traditional news sources consult the Internet for news.[12] The potential drawback is, as noted earlier, the proliferation of Web sites and the questionable reliability of their information.

The following analysis of public opinion and the mass media examines their role as they relate to the environment. As far as public opinion is concerned, we will examine the role of public opinion in the American political setting in general and with regard to environmentalism in particular. In doing so, we will also assess several demographic variables including gender, race, and generation, among others. In the case of the media, our goal is to describe and explain the role of the media in American politics and the coverage given to the environment as an important public policy issue.

The Study of American Public Opinion

Public opinion polls are conducted in order to obtain a portrait of the political orientations of American citizens, usually at a given point in time. Questions in national polls might range from the public's level of satisfaction with the president's job performance to attitudes about a multitude of public policy issues to the electorate's preference for presidential candidates during the campaign season. The public's opinion about politics can be obtained in several ways, including personal visits to a household, mail surveys, and telephone interviewing. In an effort to gauge public opinion, a random sample of the national population is selected and surveyed on given political items to collect aggregate level data comprised of individual opinions.[13]

There are a variety of methodological concerns involved in the collection of public opinion data. These include but are not limited to the saliency, intensity, and stability of opinions, as well as the knowledge level of survey respondents about public issues. Perhaps a given issue is important (salient) to one group but not so important to another group, which affects aggregate opinion about the issue. While some survey respondents might have strong feelings (intensity) about an issue, others might agree or disagree but do so moderately rather than strongly. Does the public feel the same way about an issue over time (stability) or is there fluctuation (instability) in the public's attitudes about issues? Moreover, considerable research has indicated that, sadly, Americans are not well informed (knowledge level) about politics and can be volatile when it comes to specific issues. For example, many citizens have problems answering questions about the president's term in office, how many senators represent each state, or what the name is of specific public figures.[14] Nonetheless, the typical citizen who is unable to explain how a nuclear power plant functions may still have strong opinions about whether he or she wants that kind of energy source used in the country. Moreover, issues such as abortion, gun control, and the environment/property rights debate can turn a usually quiet person into a strongly voiced partisan!

Ultimately, in a democratic society, the purpose of gaining a better understanding of public opinion is to determine the extent to which there is linkage between opinion and policy making. As Elaine Sharp stated in her study of public opinion and social policy, "Because so many social policies have direct personal impacts and have implications for citizens' fundamental values, if we cannot find a close connection between public opinion and policy development in this realm, there is little reason to be sanguine about public knowledge and governmental responsiveness in other areas of public affairs."[15] In this chapter, as we examine public opinion and environmentalism, our goal is to gain a better appreciation of the public's attitudes toward the environment. This will provide a foundation upon which to assess the role of political institutions and the behavior of political actors involved in the environmental policy process.

Public Opinion and the Environment

One of the interesting aspects of the American public's consideration of environmental issues has been the general consistency in the public's attitudes about protecting the environment. Almost 30 years ago, Anthony Downs presented an "issue attention" model to explain the evolution of public policy problems.[16] The model developed by Downs suggested that all public policy problems, including the environment, emerge, evolve, mature, and decline in a five-stage process. Namely, the preproblem stage; the alarmed discovery and public desire for the government to do something about it stage; the realization of the costs of progress stage, the decline in public interest in the problem stage; and finally the postproblem stage in which new problems arise, displacing the original issue. Nevertheless, the public's interest in the environment as a public policy problem does not necessarily end with the final postproblem stage. Rather than declining in salience, the American public has remained very concerned about environmental quality.

Environmental Protection and Government Performance

A quarter century ago, when asked in a Roper national survey their opinion about whether environmental protection laws have gone too far or not far enough, 31 percent of the survey's respondents indicated "not far enough" while 20 percent said "too far."[17] Four years later, in 1980, the public's views had not changed much. However, by 1990, more than half of the American public (54 percent) held the view that environmental laws and regulations had not gone far enough.[18] By the end of the decade of the 1990s, almost 8 out of 10 voters indicated that "tougher environmental laws" and "stricter enforcement" of those laws were needed.[19]

Another way to assess the public's concern about the environment is to examine their views about the government's and their fellow citizens' level of concern about environmental protection. For example, in 1990, approximately 75 percent of Gallup poll respondents believed that both the American government and the public were not seriously worried about the quality of the environment; by 1999, this belief had dropped to 57 percent.[20]

During the period 1984–2000, when asked to choose between two very important societal goals—environmental protection and economic growth—fully two-thirds of Americans have supported environmental protection while one-quarter preferred growing the economy.[21] Support for environmental protection reached a high of 71 percent in 1990 and 1991 and a low of 58 percent in 1992. Preference for economic growth attained a high of 32 percent in 1995 and a low of 19 percent in 1990. In the year 2000, when asked to choose between protecting the environment and economic growth, once again, a majority of Americans (almost 7 out of 10) preferred environmental protection over growing the economy.[22] Although there has been some fluctuation in the public's societal priorities (protecting the environment versus economic growth), Americans overall have shown a strong concern for securing a healthy environment.

One way to describe the public's orientation toward the level of government progress in the environmental policy arena is the extent to which the government has made a "great deal" of progress which, in effect, assesses intense feelings among the public.[23] A decade ago, during the midpoint of the George H.W. Bush administration (1990), only 14 percent of Americans held the view that the federal government was making a "great deal" of progress in protecting the environment. By the last year of the Clinton administration (2000), 26 percent felt that "a great deal" of progress had occurred regarding the health of the environment.[24] In this regard, a 12-point gap separates the public's assessment of the government's role at the beginning and at the end of the decade of the 1990s. Still, the American public has revealed in poll data that it feels that the federal government should be doing more to assure protection of the environment.[25] In 1990, 71 percent of Americans indicated that the U.S. government was spending "too little" to improve the environment, up from 48 percent in 1980 and 61 percent in 1973.[26] At about the same time, in 1992 (the last year of the George H.W. Bush administration), 68 percent of the American public indicated that the U.S. government was doing "too little" regarding environmental protection. By April 2000 (the last year of the Clinton administration), another change in the public's assessment of the role of the federal government in protecting the environment occurred. As Americans were preparing to begin a new century, 58 percent of them felt that the government was doing "too little"—a 10 percent decline from 1992. This suggests that during the period 1992–2000, the American public saw the federal government playing a positive role in environmental protection.

As we will note in Chapter 4, the environmental movement is one among many social movements in the country. Given the important role of environmental groups in American politics, the public's view of their legitimacy is an important consideration. In a recent Gallup poll to discover the public's view of the environmental movement, Riley Dunlap reports that not only are the goals of the environmental movement endorsed by a majority of the American public, but also the movement retains the public's confidence to do what is necessary to protect the environment.[27] Moreover, as Dunlap states:

> Ironically, many social movements find it difficult to survive once their goals are adopted by government (most social movements never manage to achieve such success in the first place). But while the environmental movement has had its ups and downs over the past 30 years, it continues to remain a vital force in American society.[28]

Public Trust in Government, Business and Industry, and Environmental Groups

The question of trust between the public, government, business, and environmental groups is important when analyzing American politics and the environment. In 1995, when asked about which societal interest could best be trusted to protect the environment, the American public chose the federal government over business and industry.[29] Five years later, how did government and business as well as environmental groups, fare in terms of the public's level of trust relative to protecting the environment? An April 2000 Gallup poll of the American public's level of trust in ten different institutions revealed that large environmental organizations and environmental agencies at the national level ranked near the top of the list.[30] Small businesses ranked seventh and large corporations were located at the bottom of the list. The American public ranked the U.S. Congress 8 out of 10, which reflects the public's low estimation of Congress overall. Democrats were ranked higher (sixth) than Republicans (ninth) regarding trust and environmental protection.[31]

Given this view by the American public, business and industry should be encouraged to change how it operates, and conduct business in a more environmentally friendly way. In 1970, only 14 percent of the public felt that business and industry would act on its own to improve its contribution to solving the pollution problem, while 72 percent held the view that business and industry would take action only if the government forced them to.[32] By 1990, only 9 percent of American citizens thought that business and industry would act voluntarily, while 82 percent saw industry taking action as a result of government force.[33] All in all, the public had become increasingly more skeptical that business and industry would engage in practices geared toward improving the environment. By the end of the 1990s, where less than 6 out of 10 Americans believed that the federal government and American citizens were "not worried enough" about the environment, 75 percent felt that business and industry were "not worried enough," down only 10+ points from 85 percent in 1990.[34]

AIR POLLUTION: PUBLIC OPINION AND AIR QUALITY

Pollution comes in many forms—air, water, toxic substances, nuclear fallout. The debate over air pollution centers not only on the conflict between environmentalists and business and industry but also between regions in the United States, because one region blames another for air pollution problems.[1] Although the first air pollution regulation was passed as a city ordinance in Chicago in 1881, air pollution did not assume national importance until smog control became an issue in Los Angeles in 1948 and thousands of citizens in Donora, Pennsylvania, fell ill to the effects of smog that same year.[2] As a result, and after much political conflict and lobbying by environmental groups and business and industry, from the 1960s to 1990 several important pieces of air quality legislation were passed into law. Included among these important bills are the 1963 Clean Air Act, the 1965 Motor Vehicle Air Pollution Control Act, the 1967 Air Quality Act, the 1970 Clean Air Act, the 1977 Clean Air Act Amendments, and 1990 Clean Air Act Amendments. How has the public addressed air pollution as an important public policy problem?

Several polling agencies have included questions about the environment for the last three decades or so, which allows us to assess the public's opinions about the quality of the environment in general and air pollution in particular. More than three decades ago, in 1965, the Opinion Research Corporation reported that only 28 percent of the public viewed air pollution as a "very or somewhat serious" problem (and 35 percent held the same view about water pollution).[3] Just five years later, 69 percent of Americans viewed air pollution as a "very or somewhat serious" problem (while 74 percent felt the same way about water pollution).[4]

In a Roper poll in the mid- to late-1970s, survey respondents were asked whether air and water pollution will be a serious problem in 25 to 50 years. About 7 out of 10 Americans felt that air and water pollution would be a "serious problem" in the future.[5] By the late 1980s, the proportion of Americans who saw air and water pollution as a "serious problem" jumped to 82 percent.[6] According to several Gallup polls taken regarding the public's concern about air pollution, in particular, there has been some fluctuation in American citizens' assessment of air quality in recent years.[7] The proportion of American citizens who worried "a great deal" about air pollution was 63 percent in 1989 but declined to 59 percent in 1991 and declined further to 42 percent in 1997. By 1999, the percentage of Americans who felt this way increased 10 points, to 52 percent, and rose again to 59 percent in mid-2000. Moreover, when asked what is the most important environmental problem, Americans are likely to include air and water pollution.[8]

Despite the up-and-down pattern in the American public's attitudes about air pollution, taking into consideration the data from both the Roper and Gallup polls, one can say that a majority of Americans have expressed serious concern about air and water quality in the United States, particularly over the past decade or two. At the same time, efforts to promote conservation among citizens (including, for instance, alternative energy sources and car-pooling) have been difficult, as Americans have been socialized in a mobile, automobile-oriented society. Moreover, the oil, coal, and automobile industries have lobbied heavily and spent millions of dollars to promote their views and influence public policy.

---

[1]See Gary C. Bryner, *Blue Skies, Green Politics: The Clean Air Act of 1990* (Washington, DC: CQ Press, 1993), 79-80.

[2]See J. Clarence Davies, *The Politics of Pollution* (New York: Pegasus, 1970), 33–34, 49.

[3]Riley E. Dunlap, "Trends in Public Opinion Toward Environmental Issues: 1965–1990," in Riley E. Dunlap and Angela G. Mertig, eds. *American Environmentalism: The U.S. Environmental Movement, 1970–1990* (New York: Taylor & Francis, 1992), 93.

[4]Ibid.

[5]Ibid., 98.

[6]Ibid., 108.

[7]See George Gallup, Jr., *The Gallup Poll: Public Opinion 1991* (Wilmington, DE: Scholarly Resources Inc., 1992), 87; see also **http://www.gallup.com/poll/releases/pr990422.asp.** Retrieved June 6, 2000.

[8]See George Gallup, Jr., *The Gallup Poll: Public Opinion 1999* (Wilmington, DE: Scholarly Resources, 2000), 167.

Public Opinion and Environmental Issues

What has been the public's level of concern with ten major environmental issues during the period 1980–2000 (Table 3.1 and Table 3.2)? On the one hand, as the data indicate, there has been an overall decline in the public's level of concern about the environment. On the other hand, however, a majority still remains concerned "a great deal" about seven of these issues and a significant proportion of the public is still concerned "a great deal" about the remaining three issues.

In the year 2000, as well as in 1989, most people expressed "a great deal" of concern about water quality. Fewer people expressed "a great deal" of concern about global warming in 1989 and acid rain in 2000.

During the 1990s, several fundamental changes occurred. First, when assessing the public's attitude expressed as "a great deal" of concern, where air and water quality, toxic waste, and ocean pollution ranked at the top of the list of environmental issues in 1989, only water quality, toxic waste, and air quality (barely) ranked near the top (at the 60-percent level) in 2000. Second, the loss of wildlife habitat, ozone depletion, and acid rain declined on the list of the 10 environmental issues. At the same time, however, public concern about global warming and the loss of rain forests increased.

TABLE 3.1

Ranking Environmental Issues, 1989 and 2000

1989		2000	
Water quality	72%	Water quality	66%
Toxic waste	69	Toxic waste	64
Air quality	63	Air quality	59
Ocean pollution	60	Ocean pollution	54
Loss of wildlife habitat	58	Radioactive contamination	52
Radioactive contamination	54	Loss of rain forests	51
Ozone depletion	51	Loss of wildlife habitat	51
Loss of rain forests	42	Ozone depletion	49
Acid rain	41	Global warming	40
Global warming	35	Acid rain	34

Source: Adapted from Lydia Saad and Riley E. Dunlap, "Americans Are Environmentally Friendly, but Issue Not Seen as Urgent Problem." **http://www.gallup.com/poll/releases/pr000417.asp.** Retrieved July 22, 2000.

Note: Percentages based upon survey respondent's "great deal of concern" about the issue.

TABLE 3.2

Change in Public Concern for Environmental Issues, 1989 and 2000

	Increase in Concern	*Decrease in Concern*
First-tier issues	None	Air pollution, water pollution
Second-tier issues	None	Radioactive contamination, toxic waste
Third-tier issues	Loss of rain forests, global warming	Ozone layer depletion, ocean pollution, loss of biodiversity, acid rain

Sociodemographic Characteristics and the Environment

Up to this point we have evaluated public opinion about environmental issues in terms of aggregate opinion. Given that the United States is a diverse society, are American citizens unified or divided when asked to identify themselves as "environmentalist"? Twenty years ago, survey data collected by Van Liere and Dunlap in order to determine the social bases of concern about the environment produced the following results.[35] These researchers found that concern about the environment was more closely identified with the young rather than the old, the well educated as opposed to those with a lower level of education, and liberals more so than conservatives.

Recent survey data collected by the Gallup polling organization shows that small demographic variation is again evident among the American public.[36] Although differences are negligible regarding gender, age, and political ideology, small but perceptible variation is noticeable regarding race, education, and party identification. Citizens with an advanced degree or education beyond the bachelor's degree, nonwhites, and Democrats are more likely to identify as environmentalists. However, the demographic differences are, overall, rather small. In the earlier study by Van Liere and Dunlap, the researchers had suggested, on the basis of their findings, that differences were moderate and that there was "widespread distribution of such concern in our society."[37] Although the more recent poll data differ somewhat from the earlier Van Liere and Dunlap study of the sociodemographic differences associated with concern about the environment, their conclusion stands until further research shows otherwise.

Poll data released during spring 2000 added an intriguing demographic perspective on the American public and the environment, by comparing political generations rather than examining citizens based on their age cohort.[38] The poll investigated the extent to which members of the Baby Boom generation (45–55-year-olds) and young adults or Internet generation (18–25-year-olds) exhibited shared or distinct attitudes about the environment.

One of several interesting findings in the poll concerned attitudes about progress made regarding environmental protection. A majority of both generations hold the view that the quality of the environment has not increased much over the past three decades—a very skeptical attitude, indeed. In fact, the younger generation is less sanguine about environmental conditions, as 62 percent feel this way, opposed to 52 percent of the Baby Boom generation. On the issue of air and water quality, in particular, once again, the Internet generation (71 percent) views the quality of the air and water as getting worse rather than better, compared to the Baby Boomers (62 percent).

As mentioned in Chapter 1, environmental issues can be categorized into first, second-, and third-tier issues. Table 3.3 compares the environmental concerns of Baby Boomers and young adults in terms of this classification. Taken as a whole, a majority of both generations are concerned about all of the environmental issues. While both groups rank first-tier pollution issues near the top (only a slight difference—5 percent—separates the two groups), Baby Boomers are much more inclined to be concerned about the consequences of toxic waste, a second-tier environmental issue. The two generational groups are rather similar in their overall level of concern about third-tier issues. Nonetheless, if we disaggregate third-tier issues into individual components, we find that the Baby

TABLE 3.3

Comparing Generational Concern About Environmental Issues

	Young Adults	Baby Boomers	Percentage Difference Index
First-tier issues	69%	74%	+ 5
Second-tier issues	60%	78%	+18
Third-tier issues	54%	54%	0

Source: Adapted from Margot Higgins, "Generations agree on green issues, poll shows, Thursday, April 2000" at **http://www.enn.com/news/ennstories/2000/04/04132000/boompoll_11962.asp.**

(+) indicates more concern by Baby Boomers

Note: First-tier issues include air and water pollution; second-tier issues reflect concern with toxic waste; third-tier issues concern rain forest depletion, endangered species, fisheries depletion, and global warming.

Boomers express more concern about global warming and fisheries depletion compared to the Internet generation, which ranked endangered species ahead of global warming and fisheries depletion. It is interesting to note that both groups were most concerned about the diminishing rain forests as their primary third-tier environmental issue.

Finally, what is fundamental to both groups is the continuing importance of first- and second-tier issues—namely, air and water pollution, and the threat posed by toxic waste. Third-tier issues rank lower due, perhaps, to the nature of these issues, the fact that they are more remote and complex, and because they lack political and/or scientific consensus about the threat and potential consequences.

Although there is an expanding literature about public opinion and the environment, the research debate continues regarding the role of the media and its coverage of politics and public opinion, and whether and to what degree the media might influence public opinion about public policies in general and the environment in particular. Moreover, to what extent does media coverage of public affairs correlate with the public's level of interest in specific issues, including the environment? The remainder of this chapter will address these questions.

The Role and Function of the Media

We noted earlier in this chapter that Americans have access to a variety of news outlets but have relied on television more than other news sources. In recent years, however, traditional broadcast networks have been challenged by cable television and by the Internet. What are the roles and functions of the news media?

According to Doris Graber, the mass media have several important functions.[39] The media provide information to viewers about "selected people, organizations, and events." The media help the viewer understand the political world by interpreting and putting into context news items of the day. The media also serve as an agent of political socialization by focusing on American cultural values and the public's belief system. Finally, the media might practice "manipulation" represented on the one hand by investigative journalism or on the other hand by sensationalizing the news.

If the role of the media is to be neutral and dispassionate in disseminating information to viewers, to help them be better informed, it certainly has its critics. For example, some argue that the mass media serve solely as a means for political elites to disseminate their ideas to the public.[40] Others argue that the media is subject to the "economic imperative"—namely, it is profit driven, which takes precedence over suitably informing the public or containing costs.[41] Still others suggest that not only is the media's function to make money rather than to inform the public but also that large financial institutions control the media, its operation, and its message.[42]

As we will see in subsequent chapters, the major institutions of the federal government, each in their own way, play an important part in the environmental policy-making process. As the key political figure in the country, the president receives the preponderance of media coverage. The president, through the State of the Union message or news conferences, for example, can highlight specific public policies, including environmental protection. Doris Graber informs us that the media serve as a source of information for the president about events and public opinion, and also provide the means to communicate with the public, constituent groups, and fellow policymakers, and to remain in the public eye.[43]

Although the United States Congress receives less media coverage than the president, lawmakers can make news in a variety of ways, including introducing environmental legislation as well as publicizing results of a public opinion poll of constituents, among others. At the same time, as Timothy Cook reports:

> Members of Congress and their staffs are part of the audience for national news: it is the way they discover what the rest of the country is finding out. And while the media lag behind other cues, such as voters, committee leaders, or party colleagues, members themselves estimate the news to be as influential as presidents and bureaucrats.[44]

Moreover, a revolution in political communication occurred when the Cable-Satellite Public Affairs Network (C-SPAN) began gavel-to-gavel broadcasting of congressional affairs. For the first time, the American electorate could watch House and Senate proceedings beginning in 1979 and 1986, respectively. For the interested citizen who wanted to know more about the legislative process and current affairs than was covered in the traditional news outlets, C-SPAN brought the audience into the halls of government. This technological innovation provided the opportunity for viewers to watch speeches, debates, and committee hearings firsthand about a variety of public policy issues.

Finally, two institutions that have maintained relative anonymity from the news media are the Supreme Court and the executive branch agencies, departments, and bureaus. Although state level courts have opened up the judicial process to television cameras, the Supreme Court retains a protective distance from the media and the public.[45] Accordingly, "The judges still control much of the information reported about themselves and their work."[46] The bureaucratic units that constitute the executive branch of our political system are vital to the governmental process. The Environmental Protection Agency and the Department of the Interior, for example, play significant roles in environmental policy making. Yet, as Richard Davis explains, executive agencies are "underreported" because much of what they do is considered by the media to be "unnewsworthy" and lacking "visual or dramatic events," and also viewers who "simply aren't interested" in what they do.[47]

The Environment as a Mediated Issue

Although the notion of environmentalism can be traced to the founding of the United States, when most people think about environmental protection they think about Rachel Carson's *Silent Spring* published in 1962 and the political activism beginning in the mid-1960s and continuing afterward. Moreover, the role of the media changed at about the same time as television assumed a prominent place in American households. Television coverage changed the dynamics of environmental activism and events as they were portrayed to a growing American audience. Nonetheless, media coverage of the environment predates television, as the issue has been covered for some two centuries. As a matter of fact, in the mid-eighteenth century, in an effort lost to economic and development interests, Benjamin Franklin used his newspaper, the *Pennsylvania Gazette*, to try to persuade members of the Pennsylvania Assembly to do something about water pollution in Philadelphia.[48]

Neuzil and Kovarik characterize the mass media of the pre-1960s period in the following way:

> Journalists have been made conscious of local and regional environmental controversies from the early 18th century to the 1950s, when a national dialogue about air and water pollution emerged. Long before the 1960s, serious concerns about environmental issues were closely and hotly debated, with the media involved. From the muckrakers' work in the public health reform movements to scientific and political fights to conserve western lands and resources, journalists participated in many environmental controversies of their era.[49]

For example, subsequent to the 1948 "killer smog" tragedy where almost two dozen people died and the health of thousands was threatened in Donora, Pennsylvania, the media began to give regular attention to air pollution (and "killer smog") problems in cities in the United States and abroad.[50]

Both the media and environmental groups have played an important role in drawing attention to the environment. As we will see in Chapter 4, the emergence of environmental groups in the United States can be traced to the beginning of the twentieth century. Since then, organized interests concerned about environmental protection have proliferated both in number and in membership. Moreover, during the same period of time we have witnessed the evolution of the mass media, from the dominance of the print media to the development of radio and then television and, more recently, the Internet. Both the media and environmental groups constitute private interests engaged in an effort to disseminate information about a selected policy area. Samuel Hays characterizes their role in political communication in the following way:

> Thus far there have been two levels of public environmental information, publications of membership organizations and the mass media. Both tend to identify environmental matters as peripheral to the nation's information system. Publications of environmental organizations focus on the limited issues in which they are interested to rally their members to action. The mass media, on the other hand, prefer only the dramatic and the sensational and hence miss more mundane news that is often far more important. One can obtain much information from a variety of specialized publications as scientific and technical journals, trade association magazines, and newsletters. But environmental affairs

will arrive in the mainstream of American society only when environmental information becomes more central in the mainstream media.[51]

For example, there are thousands of radio stations in the United States. The Environmental News Network (ENN) Web site recently highlighted the salience of the environment as a policy issue in a variety of radio broadcast formats.[52] Included in radio programming are *The Environment Show* broadcast on National Public Radio and ABC Radio, Los Angeles-based *The Green Scene*, Wisconsin Public Radio's *Earthwatch Radio*, and the Web-based radio program *Zero 24-7*, among others.

Although our discussion about the media and the environment is concerned primarily with political matters, it is also interesting to ask whether and to what extent environmental issues are given coverage in entertainment broadcasting. In other words, how likely is it that we might find environmental messages delivered to the audience? On the one hand, several researchers in the area of the mass media find that ecological issues and environmental matters are conspicuously missing from entertainment programming.[53] On the other hand, the Environmental Media Association (EMA) reports that its mobilization efforts "keep the entertainment industry informed and involved," which has resulted in "feature films and television programs that have expanded awareness of environmental issues across the globe."[54] The EMA has given awards to *The American President*, *X-Files*, *Dances with Wolves*, *Free Willy*, *A Civil Action*, and *Erin Brockovich*, for including attention to environmental issues.[55]

Media Coverage of the Environment

There are several useful approaches in addressing media coverage of environmental affairs.[56] In the following section we will examine the debate regarding the agenda-setting function, the problem of science and risk as it relates to media coverage of the environment, and what factors might account for how journalists cover environmental issues, given the structure and norms of the mass media.

The Agenda-Setting Function

One of the important issues concerning the role of the media and politics is the question of agenda-setting. According to Bernard Cohen, the press "may not be successful in telling its readers what to think, but it is stunningly successful in telling its readers what to think about . . . ."[57] Christine Ader describes agenda-setting as the "relationship between the relative emphasis given by the media to various topics and the degree of salience these topics have for the general public."[58] Or, as Ansolabehere, Behr, and Iyengar characterize it, "The idea of agenda-setting is that the public's social and political priorities and concerns— their beliefs about what is a significant issue or event—are determined by the amount of news coverage accorded various issues and events."[59] In other words, is there a correlation between what the media covers and the public's agenda?

The first issue we will address, then, involves the question of an agenda-setting function where the media has influence over the public's agenda. Over a quarter century ago, Funkhouser's study of the relationship between the public's interest in 14 major issues and media coverage of these issues suggested that campaigns and mobilization efforts had an impact on gaining media attention.

As Funkhouser stated, "Rather than mirroring the realities of the times, the media seem to have attended to persons or agencies with the ability and motivation to call attention to particular issues by creating 'news,' and to decrease their attention to other issues . . . ."[60]

While referring to the low but consistent correlation between media coverage of issues and the public's agenda, Atwater, Saliven, and Anderson argue that, based on their study of the media and environmental issues, a "moderate relationship between media salience and audience intra-personal salience" was found, suggesting that the "media may be able to transfer detailed levels of information about a single issue to the audience."[61] Studies by Behr and Iyengar in 1985 and Ader in 1995 tend to confirm the notion of an agenda-setting function. As Behr and Iyengar argue, "television news coverage is at least partially determined by real-world conditions and events. . . . News coverage is for the most part unaffected by public opinion and the assumption that agenda-setting is a recursive process is on solid ground."[62] Ader's study to determine the impact of the media and real-world conditions on the public during the period 1970–1990 found that "the amount of media attention devoted to pollution influenced the degree of public salience for the issue" while at the same time "real-world conditions and the public agenda for pollution were not correlated."[63]

Some researchers, however, are critical of the agenda-setting function of the media. They are cautious in making the argument that there is a direct relationship between media coverage of public and environmental affairs and what the public thinks about those affairs. Two studies—one in the United States and the other in Sweden—have challenged the basic assumption of the agenda-setting function of the media. In the U.S. study, the public was actually less inclined to be influenced by television coverage of a hazardous waste problem; instead, public officials rather than citizens were more likely to respond to the news coverage and take action to resolve the problem.[64] In contrast to this study of televised coverage of the hazardous waste problem in the United States, a decade later, the Swedish study focused on newspaper coverage of ecological risks and the potential impact on public opinion. The findings from this research indicated that citizens' attitudes about several environmental problems were not correlated with the amount of press coverage.[65]

Is there an agenda-setting function? A group of researchers comparing American and Canadian citizens argues that the public's perceptions and knowledge about environmental issues depends on the type of media used by the public.[66] It is suggested that television and newspaper use might have a differential effect on the audience. Or as Richard Davis suggests, "The media agenda is more likely to be adopted for issues where the media are the primary source of information on the topic."[67]

Media Coverage, Science, and Risk

A second concern about the media and politics involves which stories are covered, how, and why. A multitude of events occur each day, and network anchors and newspaper editors have to prioritize the importance of these events while taking into consideration the limited time to process the news as well as what they think will interest the audience. For example, consider a story broadcast on the evening news or printed in the daily newspaper: Is this discussion made because of the serious risk posed by an event or because of good pictures?

Moreover, which factors might account for the selection of the stories and how they are covered regarding environmental affairs? Network anchors and newspaper editors are very likely to rely on traditional principles and cues, and in recent years have been confronted with financial considerations and ratings wars. In assessing public opinion polls about environmental protection, Gillroy and Shapiro argued that due to a plethora of dramatic events, the "environment has been a persistent concern, prominent in the media and magnified by worldwide environmental groups."[68] On the other hand, a case can be made that, compared to media coverage of other public policy issues, the environment might not be considered as newsworthy as some might suggest.

One of the fundamental issues concerning news coverage of environmental affairs involves the scientific understanding of the issue. As journalists cover public affairs issues, the norms and principles underlying their news-gathering approach may be at odds with the actual science or risk associated with the problem. According to one environmental journalist:

> Scientific education is vital, and this is one of my favorite sermons. I never cease to be amazed by the gulf between scientists and the rest of us, and can't but help believe a lot of our political problems could be solved by narrowing that gulf. The scientists, especially the new breed under the banner of conservation biologists, have many of the answers the political debate needs, but I think they've simply grown impatient with our ignoring them. That needs to stop.[69]

CARL SAGAN: LOOKING BACK FROM THE COSMOS

When astronomer Carl Sagan died in 1996 at the age of 62, he left behind a body of work that focused on reaching out beyond the borders of the earth as well as his commitment to enhancing the quality of life on planet Earth.[1] Sagan spent decades of his life searching for intelligent life in the cosmos, partly a reflection of his passion for scientific inquiry but also because of his concern about the human impact on our planet. While patiently waiting for a signal from across the "billions and billions" of stars in the universe, Sagan lamented that "It says something about the rarity and preciousness of life on this planet. The flip side of not finding life on another planet is appreciating life on Earth." Wondered Carl Sagan, who was committed to reversing the nuclear arms race, are human beings so ignorant that they would destroy the planet upon which they lived in a nuclear war or perhaps subject its population to a "nuclear winter"?[2] At the same time, he was committed to reversing the effects of human-made technologies that were polluting the atmosphere, creating the dual problem of global warming and stratospheric ozone depletion.

Carl Sagan was a scientist first, yet he was able to establish a connection between the general population and the expansive universe through his writings, speeches, guest spots on popular television programs, and most brilliantly, through his award-winning television series *Cosmos*. For Sagan, by making science intelligible to the average citizen, he was

continued

fulfilling several important tasks—namely, enhancing democracy, improving the level of knowledge about the population, and broadening awareness of the fragile global environment, as well as raising the possibility of intelligent life on other planets. As Sagan once stated, "We've arranged a global civilization in which most crucial elements . . . [including protecting the environment] . . . profoundly depend on science and technology. We have also arranged things so that almost no one understands science and technology. This is a prescription for disaster."[3]

So, how to expand the level of knowledge about science and technology, which have such enormous impact on citizens of the world? For Sagan, the best way to broaden the public's understanding of the global impact of science and technology was through the mass media. This would have a salutary result by creating a knowledgeable citizenry who would not be at the mercy of political or scientific elites and who at the same time could make informed judgments about important global issues, including the health of the global environment.

In the fascinating 13-part television series *Cosmos*, Carl Sagan brought the Earth and the planets and the stars into living rooms around the world. At the same time that he described the vast universe, the cosmos, within which the Earth occupied its place, he also emphasized the role of human beings and their impact on the planet. For example, he inquired about whether we are raising the atmospheric temperature through the burning of oil, coal, natural gas, and wood or whether we are having a cooling effect on the planet through the decimation of the world's forests and tropical rain forests and grasslands, resulting in less solar radiation being absorbed by the earth. In raising these questions in *Cosmos* to a global audience, Sagan argued that "In our ignorance, we continue to push and pull, to pollute the atmosphere and blighten the land, oblivious of the fact that the long-term consequences are largely unknown. . . . The Earth is a tiny and fragile world. It needs to be cherished."[4]

While observing the vast cosmos from Earth, Carl Sagan also looked back at the third planet from the sun, providing us with a different and ecologically important view of a small, blue-green sphere.

[1]Norma Quarles, "Carl Sagan dies at 62," at **http://www.cnn.com/US/9612/20/sagan/ index.html.** Retrieved December 28, 2000.

[2]Nuclear winter is a condition that would exist as a result of simultaneous nuclear explosions employed in a nuclear war. The resulting soot and debris in the atmosphere due to these explosions would, in effect, block sunlight and decrease the temperature on the planet for the remaining inhabitants. See Paul R. Ehrlich, Carl Sagan, Donald Kennedy, Walter Orr Roberts, *The Cold and the Dark: The World After Nuclear War* (New York: W.W. Norton & Company, 1984).

[3]Carl Sagan, *The Demon-Haunted World: Science as a Candle in the Dark* (New York: Random House, 1995), 26.

[4]Carl Sagan, *Cosmos* (New York: Random House, 1980), 103.

It is not surprising to say that each of us views an event from our own particular professional vantage point. Our professional experience provides us with the tools to assess political phenomena from our specific perspective. Nonetheless, the cross-fertilization of ideas in pursuit of solutions to environmental problems appears to be an urgent need. Although it is the responsibility of the media to inform us about public and environmental affairs in an intelligible way, such is not always the case. As Wilson stated in a study of global climate change, "Often what are portrayed in the media are not carefully worded scientific findings, but rather dramatic, eye-catching, entertaining stories that attract audiences but do little to enlighten them about the risks associated with climate change."[70] Greenberg, et. al., tend to confirm this characterization of the media in their study of network coverage of environmental risks.[71] In the course of their research about the media and environmental risks, these researchers found that news coverage tends to be influenced less by the scientific risks involving the issue and more by the visual effects and drama of the event. What becomes conspicuously important on the basis of their study's findings is that the public may get the idea that one event is more serious than another (whether true or false), based upon the amount of media coverage it receives as well as how it was covered.

News Coverage Criteria

A third serious consideration about the role of the media in presenting news to the public is the question of the understanding that journalists have about the story they are covering. As Allan, Adam, and Carter put it:

> Confronted by scientific uncertainty, the lay public is likely to turn to the mass media for a greater understanding of what is at stake. Journalists, in particular, are charged with the responsibility of imposing meaning upon uncertainties, that is, it is expected that they will render intelligible the underlying significance of uncertainties for their audience's everyday experiences of modern day life.[72]

Given the pervasiveness of the media in this country and the increasing access available to citizens as a result of new communication technology, why might it be the case that the public and journalists lack a greater understanding of environmental affairs? Given the public's interest in environmental affairs (discussed earlier in this chapter), one might assume that media coverage would provide a product that meets the public's needs. One explanation might lie in the factors associated with media coverage of environmental issues. Anderson suggests that three factors—event-centered, visual component, 24-hour daily cycle—govern whether and to what extent environmental issues might be covered.[73] Whether it is an abandoned toxic dump site, a large-scale oil spill, or a stranded whale, these kinds of events gain the attention of journalists. Herein lies a fundamental problem for environmental journalism. Certain issues do not fall neatly into an "event-centered" framework. Some environmental problems evolve over time and are complex and difficult to understand. For example, when addressing the problem of global warming, "How do you take a picture of the earth getting hotter?"[74]

Moreover, the visual image is very important and defines the difference between television, newspapers, and radio. The impact of watching the space shuttle explode on television had much more impact on the audience than reading about it in the newspaper or hearing about it on the radio. Compare the difference between television pictures of oil-covered baby ducks as opposed to photographs of them in the newspaper. More important, it is easier for the audience to be captivated by the visual component regarding, for instance, the threat of oil sludge to marine animals versus newspaper stories that require "effort" but are also more likely to provide additional background coverage and analysis of the problem of oil spills.

CASE STUDY: THE 1989 *EXXON VALDEZ* OIL SPILL

On March 23, 1989, the *Exxon Valdez* oil tanker under the command of Captain John Hazlewood ran aground. This resulted in the worst oil spill in the history of the United States. Eleven million gallons of oil poured into Prince William Sound in Alaska. Only two months earlier, 72,000 gallons of oil had leaked into Port Valdez in Alaska by the oil tanker *Thompson Pass*. The impact of the *Exxon Valdez* oil spill had multiple effects—tremendous damage to biodiversity, the fishing industry, and the social life of the region's people. Eventually, a lawsuit was filed against Exxon Corporation.

The Prince William Sound ecosystem was devastated. According to one report, "Over 16,000 dead birds and nearly 700 dead otters had been recovered, and thousands more dead animals had been sighted on and near the oiled beaches. Because of the rugged conditions and the difficulty of spotting oiled animals in an oiled terrain, or on oiled water, however, it had become apparent that the majority of the dead animals would never be recovered or counted."[1]

The *Exxon Valdez* oil spill became a media event. It was one of the major stories of 1989, reflected by hundreds of stories in the broadcast and print media and the top story numerous times on the three major networks for almost two weeks after the spill.[2] Although the accident received considerable media coverage, the question arose as to the context of coverage.

In other words, how was the accident being covered and to what extent was the public being fully informed about the issue of the safe transport of oil? According to a study of press coverage of the oil spill, mainstream media coverage focused on Captain Hazlewood, an alcoholic, as personally responsible for the oil disaster.[3] It is easier to simplify disasters for the public; yet, did the accident require more in-depth analysis? What was ignored in the media coverage of the oil spill was substantive discussion and debate about more important issues, including production and distribution systems and corporate responsibility.[4] For example, to what extent were discussions included about the use of double-hulled oil tankers or the difficulties associated with the shipping lanes in southern Alaskan waters?

Attitudes About the *Exxon Valdez* Oil Spill

	Reporters	Bush Administration	Oil Industry
Oil spill a major disaster	5	7	3
Effective cleanup by Exxon	4	8	7
Congress should not approve oil exploration in Alaska Arctic National Wildlife Refuge	4	2	1

Source: Adapted from Conrad Smith, *Media and Apocalypse: News Coverage of the Yellowstone Forest Fires,* Exxon Valdez *Oil Spill, and Loma Prieta Earthquake* (Westport, CT: Greenwood Press, 1992), 98.

Note: Attitude scale: 1—strongly disagree, 9—strongly agree

Three major participants in the oil spill tragedy include reporters, the oil industry, and the Bush administration. It is interesting to note that distinct differences existed, in particular, between the attitudes of journalists covering the accident and the oil industry.

The oil industry differed considerably from journalists and the Bush administration concerning the extent to which the accident was regarded as a major disaster. First, where the reporters and government officials were more inclined to see the accident as a major disaster, it appeared that oil industry representatives viewed it as a routine and acceptable part of the oil transportation business. Second, Exxon Corporation spent millions of dollars in its cleanup effort and the oil industry, along with the Bush administration, held the view that Exxon had engaged in an effective effort to clean up the oil. However, reporters were more inclined to argue that more could have been done. Third, regarding the quest for oil, both the Bush administration and the oil industry supported oil exploration drilling in the fragile ecosystem of the Alaska National Wildlife Refuge. Journalists were less likely than the oil industry and President Bush to support opening up a pristine area of Alaska to oil drilling.

Although to a lesser extent, while the oil spill became a media event, so did the lawsuit filed against Exxon Corporation. Major media publications sounded off regarding the $5 billion jury award to the people of Prince William Sound. For instance, the *New York Times* argued that "Despite its size, the penalty is appropriate to the scale of the ecological havoc wrought by the spill and the wreckless behavior that caused it."[5] In support of Exxon and the oil industry, *Forbes* magazine countered that "This is one giant deep-pockets-lawsuit. It is an opportunity to gouge money out of someone so rich and

continued

so unpopular that no one will sympathize with the victim."[6] In a retrospective ten years after the oil spill, the CBS news magazine *60 Minutes* broadcast that the oil spill is still affecting Prince William Sound. Correspondent Ed Bradley interviewed residents of the area who indicated that the environment, the fishing industry, and social life were still suffering due to the oil spill. Moreover, residents were still waiting for the $5 billion jury award because Exxon appealed the decision in court.

What have we learned from media coverage and public opinion polls about the *Exxon Valdez* oil spill? Nine out of ten Americans believe that an *Exxon Valdez*–type oil spill will happen again.[7] In numerous press accounts, newly elected president George W. Bush and his Secretary of the Interior both have advocated opening up the pristine Alaska Arctic National Wildlife Refuge to oil drilling.

[1]John Keeble, *Out of the Channel: The* Exxon Valdez *Oil Spill in Prince William Sound* (Cheney, WA: Eastern Washington University Press, 1999), 185.

[2]See Conrad Smith, *Media and Apocalypse: News Coverage of the Yellowstone Forest Fires,* Exxon Valdez *Oil Spill, and Loma Prieta Earthquake* (Westport, CT: Greenwood Press, 1992), 78.

[3]See Patrick Daley with Dan O'Neill, "Sad Is Too Mild A Word: Press Coverage of the *Exxon Valdez* Oil Spill," *Journal of Communication* 41 (Autumn 1991), 42–57.

[4]Ibid. Ten years after the *Exxon Valdez* oil spill, a BBC-TV news report argued that the mass media focused on a drunken ship captain as responsible for the disaster while ignoring the problems associated with the oil transport system. See Julian Darley, "Making the Environment News on the *Today Programme*" in Joe Smith, ed. *The Daily Globe: Environmental Change, the Public, and the Media* (London: Earthscan Publications Ltd., 2000), 155.

[5]See David Lebedoff, *Cleaning Up: The Story Behind the Biggest Legal Bonanza of Our Time* (New York: The Free Press, 1997), 300.

[6]Ibid.

[7]See George Gallup, Jr., *The Gallup Poll: Public Opinion 1999* (Wilmington, DE: Scholarly Resources, 2000), 166.

Hansen directs our attention to the 24-hour news cycle and how environmental problems do not necessarily fall easily into this cycle, since they tend to be lengthy events. Television news must be prepared for the early evening broadcast. Newspapers have a morning delivery deadline. Although she suggests that this might not be as great a problem today as in the past, other factors still play a role regarding this cycle. For example, according to one observer of media coverage of the environment, "To many editors, the environment is one of many important and compelling topics the public needs to know about."[75] At one time, the deadly health risk posed by AIDS was front page news but was eventually turned aside as new issues arose. Television coverage of starving children in Africa becomes obsolete in the face of concerns about the future of social security, the status of Elian Gonzalez, or an outbreak of *E. coli* in hamburgers in middle America. Yet according to opinion polls, Americans' concern about the environment is not a passing fad but one that is considered very important to the public. A researcher of the media and the environment asks and answers his own question:

> If it is all so simple, why don't the news media simply develop a strategic plan and make it happen? The answer is simpler still: The environment, while profoundly important, is seen by the media as one of many topics worthy of coverage, but at the same time one that is all too often what *The Economist* calls "a snore." What the various news media decide to cover is at one level a daily bargaining game between and among competing interests and topics. That bargaining game is guided partly by tradition, but also by structural patterns within the press that value certain subjects and situations more than others.[76]

Related to this last point is the source of information used by journalists. Are those who gather and report the news more or less likely to use certain sources to the exclusion of others? According to one study, which assessed the information sources employed in covering environmental affairs, government officials accounted for over half of the "attributable quotes," compared to environmentalists, who comprised less than 4 percent.[77]

The Public's News Interest and Its Assessment of Media Coverage

Over the last six or seven decades, mass media technology has changed considerably. Where the print media were dominant due to the monopoly over communication, the broadcast media emerged as a powerful force in the communication industry, transmitting information to the public via radio and television. The Internet has the potential for transforming the entire communication system impacting both the news process and the information-gathering behavior of the audience. As Table 3.4 shows, Americans have a diverse choice when seeking to learn about the political world around them. If we examine media use on a daily basis, we find that television remains the primary means by which Americans gather political news, although more people watch local news than national news. The print media are important but more so at the local level. Moreover, almost half of American citizens listen to the radio for news. While gaining popularity among the general public, the Internet is apparently being used for a variety of purposes but not necessarily for news acquisition. While Americans might be purchasing airline tickets, communicating with their relatives and friends via e-mail, and doing other sundry activities on the Web, fewer are using the Internet for obtaining political information. It is interesting to note that as recently as 1995 only 5 million people had access to the Internet, yet by 1999 some 50 million were connected.[78] Two-thirds of Baby Boomers and

TABLE 3.4

Percentage of Public Using Media for Political News

	Every Day	Never
Broadcast		
National television news	39%	6%
Local television news	54	4
Radio	49	18
Newspaper		
National	9	47
Local	52	6
Internet	7*	75

Source: Adapted from "How Americans Use the News and What They Think About It," **http://www.newseum.org/survey/index.html.** Retrieved January 5, 1999.

*Percentage is low because it is "news usage" rather than "other activities."

more than 8 out of 10 Americans aged 18–25 were online by the end of the decade.[79] However, the Internet was used as a research tool about environmental affairs by less than one-third of the members of both groups.[80]

Earlier in this chapter we discussed several important factors associated with media coverage of public affairs generally and the environment in particular, while raising the question about the relationship between the media and the public. One of these factors, for example, was agenda-setting, which suggests that public opinion is influenced by the media. In an effort to learn more about the linkage between media coverage and public affairs, we will examine two factors and the degree to which there is correlation between the two—namely, the public's interest in different kinds of news and the public's assessment of news coverage of these various topics, including the environment. Are the media meeting the needs of citizens regarding their news preferences? In other words, is there a uniform level of media performance when covering different news topics? Are the media doing a better or worse job when covering certain news stories as opposed to others?

Table 3.5A presents the public's level of interest in 11 different news topics and its assessment of the media's coverage of these topics. According to the data in the table, a large majority of the public is most interested in local news, crime, and the environment and is least interested in sports, the arts, and political campaigns. The question remains: To what extent have the media provided sufficient coverage to meet the needs of the public?

We have created a typology in Table 3.5B based upon the data in Table 3.5A. The purpose is to determine if there is some correlation between the public's news interest and the media's coverage of the news topic. News interest ranges from high to moderate to low. The public's assessment of media coverage ranges from good to average to poor. Using this scale, we find that the media has conducted itself quite well in meeting the needs of the public regarding local news and crime and has performed well in two areas of moderate to low public interest—namely, coverage of national affairs and sports. Sadly, the media has performed only moderately or poorly in 7 of the 11 cases.

TABLE 3.5A

Comparing News Interest and Assessment of Media Coverage

	Interest	Assessment
Local news	69%*	67%**
Crime	68	64
Environment	59	44
Local government	54	52
National affairs	52	62
Federal government	48	53
World affairs	39	54
Business and financial	36	51
Sports	33	75
Arts	25	41
Political campaigns	20	50

Source: Adapted from "How Americans Use the News and What They Think About It," **http://www.newseum.org/survey/index.html.** Retrieved January 5, 1999.

*Extremely interested and very interested combined

**Excellent and good combined

TABLE 3.5B

Typology of News Interest and Assessment of Media Coverage

	Interest	Assessment
Local news	High	Good
Crime	High	Good
Environment	High	Poor
National affairs	Moderate	Good
Local government	Moderate	Average
Federal government	Moderate	Average
Sports	Low	Good
World affairs	Low	Average
Business and financial	Low	Average
Political campaigns	Low	Average
Arts	Low	Poor

Scale:	Interest		Assessment	
	High:	59%–69%	Good:	62%–75%
	Moderate:	48–54	Average:	50–54
	Low:	20–39	Poor:	41–44

As far as the environment is concerned, the public retains a high news interest in this important public policy domain. However, according to the public's assessment, the media are doing a poor job in covering environmental affairs. As one observer has stated:

> . . . it is a minority of news media leaders in America who have given "the environment" their seal of approval as a news story of the very highest priority. While many will say it is, a look at their news choices suggests otherwise. One

of the reasons is that the media still value people and ideas in conflict more than conditions and trends that are omnipresent. While a great environmental disaster will attract attention, scientific reports on acid rain or air quality will get only fleeting notice, mainly because the human interest factor is thought to be limited and ephemeral.[81]

Politics, Organized Interests, the Media, and the Environment

For both the public and environmentalists, the appropriate stewardship of the environment is a fundamental issue in American politics. For public officials, however, the question of a commitment to environmental protection can be substantive or symbolic, activist or passive. As we will see in subsequent chapters, for instance, environmental legislation was embraced by Congress in the 1970s while other years (e.g., the 104th Congress 1995–1996) were unlikely to support an environmental agenda. Some presidents (e.g., Franklin D. Roosevelt, Lyndon Johnson, and Richard Nixon) have used the resources of their office in an effort to promote and protect the environment. Lyndon Johnson, Richard Nixon, and George H.W. Bush included the environment in many speeches that were covered by the news media.[82] By contrast, Ronald Reagan pursued an anti-environment agenda through his appointees and management of the budget.

Certain presidents have used the media in general and photo opportunities in particular to demonstrate their purported support for the environment. For example, during the 1988 presidential campaign, George H.W. Bush exclaimed that he would be an "environmental president." His message quickly became a media sound bite, as television and newspapers around the country carried it to the American electorate. Moreover, during the campaign, former Massachusetts governor Michael Dukakis, the Democratic presidential candidate, was criticized in a negative television ad that showed a polluted harbor. This suggested to the audience that Dukakis was directly responsible for not attending to the environmental health of Boston Harbor.

As Bill Clinton was confronted with an adversarial Republican-controlled Congress subsequent to the 1994 congressional elections, he made use of his executive powers to promote environmentalism. Although Clinton signed into law the 1994 California Desert Protection Act, it was unlikely that the new Republican-controlled Congress would send him major environmental legislation. One approach employed by Clinton was using the 1906 Antiquities Act and the power of the chief executive to promote public land conservation. Clinton's creation of the Grand Staircase-Escalante National Monument in Utah in 1996 was an example of both federal-state conflict and creation of a media event. Utah has not been a friendly state to Democrats in general and Bill Clinton in particular. When he used the powerful resources of his office to establish the new monument, rather than making the announcement in Utah (where 1.7 million acres of resource-rich public lands would be protected from private interests), Clinton led a public, televised ceremony in Arizona with the Grand Canyon in the background. The fact that Clinton was making the announcement in Arizona rather than Utah was probably missed by the television and newspaper audience. What was important was the image—a president engaging in a public land legacy against the backdrop of a well-known national park. The scene was perfect for television and made a great photo opportunity for newspapers.

The mass media constitute an important means by which to disseminate public service messages about the environment. Corporate America has also used the media to respond to criticisms that it is more interested in making profits than in environmental protection. For example, Benjamin Kline reports:

> In the 1960s television was used for the first time to bring public attention to an environmental issue. The National Advertising Council released a commercial that showed a Native American dressed in traditional garb staring at a littered landscape while a tear rolls slowly down his cheek. This powerful image helped raise the public's awareness of the problem of litter.[83]

In the private domain, millions of dollars have been spent by a variety of companies in order to disseminate a "green" message to the public that they are, for example, committed to clean air and water and protection of marine mammals. Moreover, corporations in the United States and in other countries use animals, some of which are endangered, as logos in their advertising.[84] The point is that using animals as logos might be good for sales; however, to what extent is the consumer being informed about the status of these animals (threatened, endangered) other than the positive image they convey for business?

As the most recent expression of new media technology, the Internet has provided the means for governmental and nongovernmental organizations to publicize their activities to the information consumer. The United States government as well as state governments, for instance, have Web sites for their respective environmental agencies. At the national level, we can find the Environmental Protection Agency and the Department of the Interior, among others, while at the subnational level, the respective state environmental or natural resource agency can be accessed by the interested citizen. Nongovernmental organizations, including environmental groups and wise-use and property-rights groups also have Web sites, which provide information about the organization including its philosophy, background, activities, chronology of victories, and more.

Conclusion

For six decades, surveys have been conducted to ascertain what the public thinks about politics, public issues, and political celebrities. Poll data enables citizens, public officials, academics, business and industry, and organized interests to learn more about Americans' political orientations. At the same time, most Americans experience political reality through the prism of the mass media. Political information is disseminated in a variety of mass media outlets including newspapers, television, radio, magazines, and the Internet. This chapter examined public opinion about environmental matters and the role of media coverage of this most important public policy issue. We assessed the public's political attitudes toward a variety of environmental issues. Moreover, survey data were analyzed in order to ascertain whether the news media is providing sufficient coverage of public issues, including the environment, important to American citizens.

Public opinion polls have informed us that the environment is an important public policy area that should not be neglected by the government or business and industry. American citizens have indicated to policymakers through opinion polls that air and water quality among other environmental concerns need to be addressed. Policymakers are encouraged to make a stronger political commitment to environmental protection and also provide more funds to be allocated for the environment. Moreover, Americans have exhibited a consistent pro-environment position by affirming in one national poll after another that environmental protection is *more* important than economic growth. Although public opinion about environmental matters has fluctuated over the years, the American people have maintained, overall, strong support for environmental protection. At the same time, the media could improve its performance regarding coverage of environmental matters.

Evaluating government performance and the importance of the environment during routine times as opposed to periods of electoral campaigns are two entirely different matters. While the American public has clearly indicated that it is concerned about the quality of the environment (though not as concerned as a decade ago), the extent to which the environment as an important policy issue influences one's vote is problematic. As Al Gore (who published his pro-environment book, *Earth in the Balance*, in 1992) and George W. Bush contended for the presidency in 2000, the environment was one among several important public policy issues involved in the campaign. Saad and Dunlap gathered survey data that indicated that the environment was a "mid-level" political issue in the 2000 presidential campaign.[85] Assessing the public policy issues (e.g., education, health care, crime, foreign affairs, abortion) in the Gallup poll conducted by Saad and Dunlap, the environment ranked eighth out of twelve. Nonetheless, two-thirds of the public still considered environmental protection "extremely" or "very important" as far as their choice for president was concerned. At the same time, the degree to which the environment or any other issue, taken alone, plays a major factor in a voter's choice for president remains a question for further investigation.

It is very likely that the American public and the news media will face more challenges as they are confronted with new environmental problems. What can the media do to improve coverage of environmental affairs? How will the news media cover the environment compared to other important policy issues throughout future presidential campaigns and during routine times? As James Shanahan put it:

> . . . the environmental role of mass media is to make us aware of problems. Media should report on environmental harms and should tell us about progress being made in the environmental struggle. In short, environmental news must find a regular and prominent place in the flow of the world's news, and the presentation of this news would hopefully avoid much of the inequity that has been observed in the general flow of news worldwide.[86]

Given the positive orientation of Americans toward the environment, what is the value of public opinion? Riley Dunlap points out that "broad public support in favor of environmental protection provides legitimacy for those working on its behalf," which underscores the significance of American public opinion about the environment as an important public policy issue.[87]

Web Sites
Public Opinion, the Media, and Environmental Issues:

Public Opinion

Gallup Poll: **www.gallup.com**

Roper Center: **www.ropercenter.uconn.edu**

National Opinion Research Center: **www.norc.uchicago.edu**

Public Agenda: **www.publicagenda.org**

Louis Harris Center: **www.irss.unc.edu/data_archive/pollsearch.html**

The Media

ABC News: **www.abc.com**

CBS News: **www.cbs.com**

NBC News: **www.nbc.com**

Cable News Network: **www.cnn.com**

Cable-Satellite Public Affairs Network: **www.c-span.com**

Environmental News Network: **www.enn.com**

Environmental News Service: **www.ens.lycos.com**

The Washington Post: **www.washingtonpost.com**

The New York Times: **www.nytimes.com**

World Resources Institute: **www.wri.org**

Public Broadcasting System: **www.pbs.org/neighborhoods/nature**

Endnotes

[1] Irving Crespi, *Public Opinion, Polls, and Democracy* (Boulder, CO: Westview Press, 1989), 108.

[2] See Samuel C. Patterson and Keith R. Eakins, "Congress and Gun Control," in John M. Bruce and Clyde Wilcox, eds. *The Changing Politics of Gun Control* (Lanham, MD: Rowman & Littlefield Publishers, Inc., 1998), 63–64; and David R. Harding Jr., "Public Opinion and Gun Control: Appearance and Transparence in Support and Opposition," in John M. Bruce and Clyde Wilcox, eds. *The Changing Politics of Gun Control* (Lanham, MD: Littlefield Publishers, Inc., 1998), 209.

[3] Robert S. Erickson and Kent L. Tedin, *American Public Opinion: Its Origins, Content, and Impact*, 5th ed. (Boston: Allyn and Bacon, 1995), 1.

[4] Alexander Hamilton quoted in Ibid., 2.

[5] See Benjamin Ginsburg, *The Captive Public* (New York: Basic Books, 1986).

6   Jerry L. Yetic and John R. Todd, *Public Opinion: The Visible Politics*, 2nd ed. (Itasca, IL: F.E. Peacock Publishers, Inc., 1989), 14.

7   Vanderbilt University's *Television News Archive* is a collection of evening news abstracts beginning in 1968. We used the archive to collect data to compare the number of stories broadcast about air and water pollution and endangered species. See **http://tvnews.vanderbilt.edu/cgi-bin/nph-abstracts.cgi.** Retrieved April 13, 2000.

8   Stephen Ansolabehere, Roy Behr, Shanto Iyengar, *The Media Game: American Politics in the Television Age* (New York: Macmillan Publishing Company, 1993), 2.

9   Ibid., 26; Calvin Exoo, *The Politics of the Mass Media* (St. Paul, MN: West Publishing Company, 1994), 227.

10 Alan J. Rosenblatt, "The Internet as a Governmental and Political Resource." In Quentin Kidd, ed. *Government and Politics in Virginia: The Old Dominion at the 21st Century* (Needham Heights, MA: Simon & Schuster Custom Publishing, 1999), 124–125.

11 Richard Morin, "It's No Longer About All the News That Fits," *The Washington Post National Weekly Edition*, June 19, 2000, 34.

12 Ibid.

13 It is beyond the scope of this discussion to describe the appropriate methodological procedures involved in polling in order to ensure reliability and validity. We note, however, for the reader that a representative, random sample of the population is the basis for obtaining information about the public's sentiment on political issues.

14 See, for instance, Robert Erickson, Norman Luttbeg, Kent L. Tedin, *American Public Opinion*, 2nd ed. (New York: Wiley, 1980), 19; Don D. Smith, "Dark Arenas of Ignorance Revisited," in Dan D. Nimmo and Charles Bonjean, eds. *Political Attitudes and Public Opinion* (New York: McKay, 1972), 271; Robert Weissberg, *Public Opinion and Popular Government* (Englewood Cliffs, NJ: Prentice-Hall, 1976), 33.

15 Elaine Sharp, *The Sometime Connection: Public Opinion and Social Policy* (Albany: State University of New York Press, 1999), 3.

16 Anthony Downs, "Up and Down with Ecology—The 'Issue-Attention Cycle,'" *The Public Interest*, 28, 38–50.

17 Ibid., 98

18 Ibid., 104

19 See Robinson Shaw, "Environment Is Crucial Issue for Voters," April 9, 2000 at **http://www.enn.com/enn-news-archive/2000/04/04092000/lcvpoll_11800.asp.** Retrieved June 22, 2000.

20 See Lydia Saad, "Environmental Concern Wanes in 1999 Earth Day Poll," April 22, 2000 at **http://www.gallup.com/poll/releases/pr990422.asp.** Retrieved June 6, 2000; Lydia Saad and Riley E. Dunlap, "Americans are Environmentally Friendly, but Issue Not Seen as Urgent Problem," April 17, 2000 at **http://www.gallup.com/poll/releases/pr000417.asp.** Retrieved July 22, 2000.

21 See Saad, "Environmental Concern Wanes in 1999 Earth Day Poll."

22 Saad and Dunlap, "Americans are Environmentally Friendly, but Issue Not Seen as Urgent Problem."

23 See Saad, "Environmental Concern Wanes in 1999 Earth Day Poll;" Saad and Dunlap, "Americans are Environmentally Friendly, but Issue Not Seen as Urgent Problem."

24 Saad and Dunlap, "Americans are Environmentally Friendly, but Issue Not Seen as Urgent Problem."

25 See Saad, "Environmental Concern Wanes in 1999 Earth Day Poll"; Saad and Dunlap, "Americans are Environmentally Friendly, but Issue Not Seen as Urgent Problem."

26 Ibid., 98, 104.

27 Riley E. Dunlap, "Guest Scholar Poll Review," April 18, 2000 at **http://gallup. com/poll/guest_scholar/gs000418.asp.** Retrieved June 22, 2000.

28 Ibid.

29 George Gallup, Jr., *The Gallup Poll: Public Opinion 1995* (Wilmington, DE: Scholarly Resources, Inc., 1996), 66.

30 Dunlap, "Guest Scholar Poll Review." A survey conducted by the environmental group Environmental Defense (formerly Environmental Defense Fund) also revealed that Americans had more confidence in environmental groups than in industry to protect the environment. Moreover, there were no statistically significant differences between the survey generations (18–25 and 45–55) on this issue. See "Environmental Poll Compares Attitudes Of Boomers & Internet Generation," April 12, 2000 at **http://edf.org/pubs/newsreleases/2000/apr/f_earthday.html.** Retrieved April 13, 2000.

31 Similar results about public opinion and partisan differences have been found in other national surveys. See "Environmental Poll Compares Attitudes Of Boomers & Internet Generation."

32 Ibid.

33 Ibid.

34 Saad, "Environmental Concern Wanes in 1999 Earth Day Poll."

35 See Kent D. Van Liere and Riley E. Dunlap, "The Social Bases of Environmental Concern: A Review of Hypotheses, Explanations and Empirical Evidence," *Public Opinion Quarterly* 44 (Summer 1980), 181–197.

36 See Saad, "Environmental Concern Wanes in 1999 Earth Day Poll."

37 Van Liere and Dunlap, "The Social Bases of Environmental Concern," 193.

38 See "Environmental Poll Compares Attitudes of Boomers & Internet Generation."

39 See Doris Graber, *Mass Media and American Politics*, 3rd ed. (Washington, DC: CQ Press, 1989), 5–12.

40 See, for example, Theodore Draper, *The Dominican Revolt* (New York: Commentary, 1968).

41 The concept "economic imperative" is attributed to professor Paul Hagner although it is unknown whether he or someone else originated it. See, for instance, Kathleen Hall Jamieson and Karlyn Kohrs Campbell, *The Interplay of Influence: News, Advertising, Politics, and the Mass Media*, 3rd ed. (Belmont, CA: Wadsworth Publishing Company, 1992), 114–118.

42 See Michael Parenti, *Democracy for the Few*, 3rd ed. (New York: St. Martin's Press, 1980), Chapter 10.

43 Graber, *Mass Media and American Politics*, 237–238.

44 Timothy E. Cook, *Making Laws and Making News: Media Strategies in the U.S. House of Representatives* (Washington, DC: The Brookings Institution, 1989), 122.

45 See Nicholas P. Lovrich, et. al., "Cameras in the Courtroom" in Steven W. Hays and Cole Blease Graham, eds. *Handbook of Court Administration and Management* (New York: Marcel Dekker, Inc., 1993), 439–460.

46 Charles Press and Kenneth Verburg, *American Politicians and Journalists* (Glenville, IL: Scott, Foresman and Company, 1988), 250.

47 See Richard Davis, *The Press and American Politics: The New Mediator* (New York: Longman, 1992), 203.

[48] Mark Neuzil and William Kovarik, *Mass Media and Environmental Conflict: America's Green Crusades* (Thousand Oaks, CA: Sage Publications, 1996), 196–197.

[49] Ibid., xx–xxi.

[50] Neuzil and Kovarik, *Mass Media and Environmental Conflict*, Chapter 7.

[51] Samuel P. Hays, *Explorations in Environmental History* (Pittsburgh: University of Pittsburgh Press, 1998), 384.

[52] See Chris Hayhurst, "Sound Ideas: Environmental Radio Does the Unexpected" at **http://enn.com/features/2000/03/03082000/radio_10414.asp.** Retrieved June 22, 2000.

[53] See Allan Schnaiberg and Kenneth Alan Gould, *Environment and Society: The Enduring Conflict* (New York: St. Martin's Press, 1994), 102; James Shanahan, "Television and the Cultivation of Environmental Concern: 1988–1992," in Anders Hansen, *The Mass Media and Environmental Issues* (Leicester: Leicester University Press, 1993), 186.

[54] See "What EMA Does," at **http://www.ema-online.org/WhatEMADoes.html.** Retrieved June 22, 2000.

[55] Ibid.

[56] It is not our intention to neglect the valuable literature that has been produced about the media and politics. We encourage the reader to investigate the subject matter thoroughly.

[57] Bernard Cohen, *The Press and Foreign Policy* (Princeton, NJ: Princeton University Press, 1963), 13.

[58] Christine R. Ader, "A Longitudinal Study of Agenda Setting for the Issue of Environmental Pollution," *Journalism and Mass Communication Quarterly* 72 (Summer 1995), 300.

[59] Stephen Ansolabehere, Roy Behr, Shanto Iyengar, *The Media Game: American Politics in the Television Age* (New York: Macmillan Publishing Company, 1993), 142.

[60] Ray Funkhouser, "The Issues of the Sixties: An Exploratory Study in the Dynamics of Public Opinion," *Public Opinion Quarterly* 37 (Spring 1973), 73.

[61] Tony Atwater, Michael B. Saliven, Ronald B. Anderson, "Media Agenda-Setting with Environmental Issues," *Journalism Quarterly* 62 (Summer 1985), 397.

[62] Roy L. Behr and Shanto Iyengar, "Television News, Real-World Cues, and Changes in the Public Agenda," *Public Opinion Quarterly* 49 (Spring 1985), 47.

[63] Ader, "A Longitudinal Study of Agenda Setting for the Issue of Environmental Pollution," 309.

[64] David L. Protess, et. al., "The Impact of Investigative Reporting on Public Opinion and Policy Making: Targeting Toxic Waste," *Public Opinion Quarterly* 51 (Summer 1987), 166–185.

[65] See Alison Anderson, *Media, Culture and the Environment* (New Brunswick, NJ: Rutgers University Press, 1997), 179.

[66] See John C. Pierce, Lynette Lee-Sammons, Mary Ann E. Steger, Nicholas P. Lovrich, Jr. "Media Reliance and Public Images of Environmental Politics in Ontario and Michigan," *Journalism Quarterly* 67 (Winter 1990), 838–842.

[67] Richard Davis, *The Press and American Politics* (New York: Longman, 1992), 243.

[68] John M. Gillroy and Robert Y. Shapiro, "The Polls: Environmental Protection," *Public Opinion Quarterly* 50 (Summer 1986), 270.

[69] Richard Manning quoted in Michael Frome, *Green Ink: An Introduction to Environmental Journalism* (Salt Lake City, UT: University of Utah Press, 1998), 125.

[70] Kris M. Wilson, "Communicating Climate Change Through the Media: Predictions, Politics and the Perceptions of Risk," in Stuart Allan, Barbara Adam, Cynthia Carter, eds. *Environmental Risks and the Media* (London and New York: Routledge, 2000), 201.

[71] Michael R. Greenberg, et. al., "Risk, Drama and Geography in Coverage of Environmental Risk by Network TV," *Journalism Quarterly* 66 (Summer 1989), 267–276.

[72] Stuart Allan, Barbara Adam, Cynthia Carter, "Introduction: The Media Politics of Environmental Risk," in Stuart Allan, Barbara Adam, Cynthia Carter, eds. *Environmental Risks and the Media* (London and New York: Routledge, 2000), 12.

[73] Anderson, *Media, Culture and the Environment*, 121–123.

[74] Quotation attributed to media critic Mark Hertsgaard in Kevin Michael DeLuca, *Image Politics: The New Rhetoric of Environmental Activism* (New York: The Guilford Press, 1999), 92.

[75] Everett E. Dennis, "In Context: Environmentalism in the System of News," in Craig L. LaMay and Everett E. Dennis, *Media and the Environment* (Washington, DC: Island Press, 1991), 59.

[76] Ibid., 55.

[77] See DeLuca, *Image Politics*, 91.

[78] Guido H. Stempel III, Thomas Hargrove, Joseph B. Bernt, "Relation of Growth of Use of the Internet to Changes in Media Use from 1995 to 1999," *Journalism and Mass Communication Quarterly* 77 (Spring 2000), 71.

[79] See "Environmental Poll Compares Attitudes of Boomers & Internet Generation."

[80] Ibid.

[81] Dennis, "In Context: Environmentalism in the System of News," 60.

[82] See Byron W. Daynes and Glen Sussman, *The American Presidency and the Social Agenda* (Upper Saddle River, NJ: Prentice Hall, 2001), Chapter 2.

[83] Benjamin Kline, *First Along the River: A Brief History of the U.S. Environmental Movement*, 2nd ed. (San Francisco: Acada Books, 2000), 78.

[84] See, for example, Doug Harbrecht, "Animals in the Ad Game," *International Wildlife* 23 (November–December 1993), 38–43.

[85] See Saad and Dunlap, "Americans are Environmentally Friendly, but Issue Not Seen as Urgent Problem."

[86] Shanahan, "Television and the Cultivation of Environmental Concern," 183.

[87] See Riley E. Dunlap, "Public Opinion and Environmental Policy," in James P. Lester, ed. *Environmental Politics and Policy*, 2nd ed. (Durham: Duke University Press, 1995), 108.

Environmental Activism:
Political Parties and Interest Groups

Political parties and interest groups serve as linkage institutions tying citizens to their representatives in government. As linkage institutions, a formal relationship between the public and political institutions ensures, at least theoretically, that public preferences will be taken into account when public officials are involved in the process of making public policy.

Political parties are important because they formally aggregate policy preferences that represent the interests of the party faithful. Moreover, they act as a cue for the larger mass of citizens who look to the parties as a way to carry out their interests on matters of public policy. In contrast, interest groups articulate the views of citizens with shared interests and try to influence those in power. While parties try to control the institutional arrangements of the government, interest groups mobilize in a variety of ways to influence the behavior of politicians who control the apparatus of government.

Political parties were not a formal part of the foundation of the United States. As a matter of fact, nowhere in the U.S. Constitution is there any mention of political parties. In the American political experience, political parties evolved over time, beginning with the initial political divisions between federalists and antifederalists during the late eighteenth century and later represented in modern American politics by two dominant parties—namely, the Democrats and Republicans. Although minor parties have been a feature of party politics in the United States, the country has been dominated primarily by the two major parties.

Interest groups are a voluntary mode of participation in U.S. politics. Yet during the founding of the country, the framers of the Constitution were aware of the problems associated with separate and conflicting interests, and their impact on the government. In *Federalist #10* James Madison raised this issue when he argued that governments are threatened by "factions" and the potential and undue influence they might wield. Consequently, the framers of the Constitution designed a political system that we call the Madison model of democracy— namely, a system based upon the separation of powers and checks and balances.

In an effort to impose constraints on the influence of organized interests, the founders sought to create a system in which political power was fragmented and dispersed among several constituent parts. Consequently, the system was set up in an effort to maintain stability and reduce the possibility of becoming dominated by any one power center. At the same time, however, the system created numerous *access* points where organized interests could lobby and pursue their cause, e.g., executive branch agencies, bureaus and departments, the legislative process with its committee and subcommittee system, and the judiciary.

Political Parties, Interest Groups, and the Environment

Political parties and interest groups are central to the operation of the political system. The environment is one among numerous public policy issues that poses challenges for parties and mobilizes organized interests. Although the environment has been a salient aspect of modern American politics for quite some time, has this always been the case? Has the environment been a central feature of party politics? When and to what extent have citizens organized into formal groups to express their concerns about environmental protection?

Some political observers have argued that parties are not divided on environmentalism.[1] They claim that the parties have demonstrated shared attitudes in support of environmental protection as a policy issue. Others have suggested that the parties have been found to diverge on policy matters related to the environment.[2] Recent research into the role of the parties and environmental politics has indicated that partisan differences are evident, and that Democrats tend to be more supportive of environmentalism, while Republicans practice caution.[3]

Although environmental interest groups are very active in American politics, "green" politics is not necessarily united in its tactics, strategies, and goals. To the contrary, organized environmental interests have shared interests in the overall objective of environmental protection but differ in many ways. For example, large organizations like the National Wildlife Federation have a membership and resources that dwarf smaller groups like Friends of the Earth. Certain groups have broad concerns while others are much narrower in their focus. Some groups are primarily mainstream and legitimate in their political activities, while the actions of other groups might be considered extreme or even radical. Some environmental organizations are characterized by formal, legitimate practices while other groups exhibit what is referred to as unconventional, direct-action techniques.

The discussion that follows addresses the role played by political parties and interest groups vis-á-vis environmentalism. We will examine the role of the two major political parties and the characteristics and activities of major environmental organizations. In doing so, our purpose is twofold. First, we want to expand our knowledge about the major parties regarding environmental protection, including the extent to which they exhibit a shared or distinct orientation toward environmentalism. Second, in our examination of environmental groups, our goal is to improve our understanding of the nature of interest group activism as it relates to environmental and ecological issues.

The Role and Function of Political Parties

Political parties serve various functions, including recruiting and nominating candidates for office and putting their candidates into office at various levels of government. As Richard Rose argues, "the party winning an election will carry out its intentions in practice" and that "voters will not only be offered a choice but also that their choice makes a real difference in how society is governed."[4]

In order to better understand the role played by political parties in environmental politics and policy, we will examine three different institutions— namely, presidential performance in fulfilling party platform pledges, congressional partisanship, and state legislative party politics. To what extent do presidents fulfill the promises made by the major parties during their national conventions? Are partisan differences evident in the level of support for environmental legislation by Democratic and Republican members of Congress? Is support for environmental legislation in state legislatures characterized by partisanship or bipartisanship? These are important questions, given the fact that parties "attempt to guide the elected officeholders of government to provide particular policy or patronage benefits."[5]

Party Platforms and Presidential Performance

Gerald Pomper and Susan Lederman have argued that "the platform indicates the party's future intentions. If victorious, the party coalition will pursue its programs. Endorsement of a proposal in the platform provides evidence of its suitability for governmental action and an argument in its behalf."[6] Moreover, Woodrow Wilson characterized the president as party leader: "He is the party's choice and is responsible for carrying out the party platform."[7]

The relationship between party platform pledges and actions taken by the president as party leader is important for several reasons. First, party platforms serve as instruments for public policy. Platforms indicate to the electorate the party's commitment to public policy issues. Second, platforms are an expression of the party's agenda during the electoral campaign by showing its commitment to policy goals and showing partisan differences on issues. Third, party platforms exhibit a symbolic role by defining the importance the party attaches to specific policy issues. Fourth, party platforms serve an important function for democratic politics by offering the voters distinct choices regarding public policy.

The American electorate is presented a new party platform every four years by the major parties and their candidate for the presidency. Thirty years of research has demonstrated that, overall, presidents have used the powerful resources of their office to fulfill the promises made in their party's platform.[8] Although presidents might be more or less assertive on certain public policy issues over others, in a majority of cases they redeem the promises made to the public in the party's platform.

Presidents have a range of resources they can employ to carry out public policy. For example, they can sign legislation and issue executive orders to fulfill party pledges. On the basis of these two methods of presidential action, and after examining the first term in office of President Kennedy through President Reagan, Fishel asserted "when presidential candidates make reasonably specific promises about future domestic policy, take those promises seriously!"[9]

Moreover, party platforms are important in that they have "produced different policies because elected officials of both parties have a relatively good record of meeting their pledges."[10] Although the success rate of presidents in meeting their party's goals as outlined in the national convention party platforms is impressive, party differences in the completion of party commitments remain. According to a study of party platforms and presidential action during the period 1912–1976, one researcher has argued that electoral promises were more likely to be fulfilled by Democratic rather than Republican presidents.[11]

What is the relationship between party platform pledges regarding the environment and presidential action in achieving these goals? How have occupants of the White House used their office to redeem party pledges? To what extent have presidential administrations exhibited shared or distinct behavior regarding their party's commitment to environmental goals?

Measuring Party Platforms and Presidential Action

In order to gain a better appreciation of the role played by the environment in national party politics, we examined the platforms of the two major parties. Since we are examining the extent to which presidents have acted to fulfill party commitments to the environment, we only examined the party platforms of the winning presidential contender. In making our assessment, *party pledges* were considered statements made in the party platform about a commitment to fulfill a party goal, while *presidential performance* was measured by the correspondence between a promise and a specific presidential act. Promises were considered *fulfilled* if a presidential action was closely associated with or responded to a pledge in a substantial way.

For example, in 1988 the Republicans promised in their party platform to work toward the goal of improving air quality. The Clean Air Act Amendments of 1990 were signed into law by President George H.W. Bush, who fulfilled his party's goal. In the 1992 Democratic party platform, the Democrats pledged to "support a reasonable waiting period to permit background checks for purchases of handguns." The pledge was fulfilled in 1993 when President Clinton signed into law the Brady Bill.

Evaluating Presidential Performance in Fulfilling Party Commitments to the Environment

Every four years, the parties make commitments to the American public in the platforms presented at their respective national conventions. While some issues are salient features of the platform, others receive scant attention or are neglected altogether. The environment as a public issue is but one policy area that may or may not receive specific party attention in the form of promises to be fulfilled by the party's candidates for Congress and the presidency. One way to assess the extent to which the parties have focused on the environment, and if so, how successful the presidents as leaders of the party have been in completing the party promise, is to examine the party platforms and presidential actions, if any, in response to these promises. After all, "As the only independently elected candidate of the national party, the president . . . assumes the role of party leader. . . ."[12]

We examined party platforms to determine which platforms included party pledges about the environment, beginning with the administration of Franklin D. Roosevelt (FDR) in 1932 and continuing through 1996 (Table 4.1).[13] In 14 out of the 17 election years, both parties made commitments to the environment. Democrats did not include the environment in their party platforms in 1936 and 1944, while Republicans excluded the environment from their platform in 1964.

In order to explain the exclusion of the environment from the party platforms one might consider the nature of the times and/or political ideology. In the case of the Democratic platforms of 1936 and 1944, FDR was arguably most concerned about addressing domestic economic problems during the Great Depression of the 1930s, and during the 1940s he was serving as commander in chief during World War II against Germany and Japan. In 1964 the Republican party nominated a candidate who was decidedly conservative in his political orientation and the environment was not at the top of the party's agenda. Moreover, during the 1980 presidential election, despite a few references to the environment, Ronald Reagan spent most of his time discussing taxing and spending issues and the military budget, along with several moral issues including abortion and school prayer.[14] Inclusion of the environment in the party platform did not dissuade Reagan from emphasizing what he considered to be more important social policy issues.

When the environment was included in the party platform of the winning candidate for the presidency, to what extent did the new occupant of the White House use the power resources of the office to fulfill party pledges about the environment? We can assess this question in three ways—namely, the overall success rate of presidents in fulfilling party promises in general, the success rate of Democratic and Republican presidents in particular, and pro- or anti-environment orientation of presidential action.

Research by Daynes and Sussman about party platforms, presidential performance, and social issues indicated that, overall, presidents have used their office to fulfill party promises.[15] In their research, which included six social issues, these researchers found that 64 percent of party pledges made about the environment, in particular, were redeemed by the president regardless of their party affiliation. In an examination of presidential action in fulfilling party commitments, there were no significant differences between Democrats and Republicans—Democrats fulfilled 65 percent of their party's pledges while Republicans completed 64 percent of their party's pledges.

Finally, were ideological differences evident in the actions of the presidents? In most cases, party promises about the environment tended to be "pro-environment" in orientation (e.g., the party would work for clean air, clean water). Generally, both Democratic and Republican presidents supported their party in fulfilling the party's "pro-environment" goals. The major anomaly was Ronald Reagan, who took a decidedly "prodevelopment" approach to the environment and was not personally committed to fulfilling pro-environmental goals during his term in office.

On the basis of our examination of major party platforms, we have seen that in most cases bipartisanship has characterized American presidents when they have addressed environmental issues. Parties have made numerous commitments to ensure environmental quality and the president has used the powerful

TABLE 4.1
Party Platforms and the Environment

Year	Party	Party Platform
1932	Democrat	+
	Republican	+
1936	Democrat	−
	Republican	+
1940	Democrat	+
	Republican	+
1944	Democrat	−
	Republican	+
1948	Democrat	+
	Republican	+
1952	Democrat	+
	Republican	+
1956	Democrat	+
	Republican	+
1960	Democrat	+
	Republican	+
1964	Democrat	+
	Republican	−
1968	Democrat	+
	Republican	+
1972	Democrat	+
	Republican	+
1976	Democrat	+
	Republican	+
1980	Democrat	+
	Republican	+
1984	Democrat	+
	Republican	+
1988	Democrat	+
	Republican	+
1992	Democrat	+
	Republican	+
1996	Democrat	+
	Republican	+

Source: Adapted from Byron W. Daynes and Glen Sussman, *The American Presidency and the Social Agenda* (Upper Saddle River, NJ: Prentice Hall, 2001.).

(+) Indicates that the environment was included in the party platform

(−) Indicates that the environment was not included in the party platform

resources available to the White House to put these promises into effect. In fact, nearly two-thirds of Democratic and Republican party platform promises about the environment were fulfilled and, more often than not, the parties exhibited shared characteristics in their efforts. All in all, American presidents have taken a pro-environment, bipartisan stance in fulfilling party platform pledges regarding the environment as a public policy issue.

Parties, Legislatures, and Environmental Politics

The preceding discussion has demonstrated that in most instances the president has supported the environmental commitments made by the party. We now turn our attention to political parties in the legislative branch of government. We first examine partisanship in Congress. According to a study of political parties in the United States, "In no segment of American government is the party more visible or vital than in the Congress."[16] To what extent are Democrats and Republicans in agreement over environmentalism? Are partisan differences more noticeable in the House or in the Senate?

Second, our intention is to ascertain the degree to which bipartisanship is evident in state legislatures. Do state legislatures reflect similar trends found in Congress? Do Democrats and Republicans in state legislatures tend to support or oppose environmental legislation?

Third, we give a brief account of one environmental policy area—public land policy—at the national and state level, in order to better understand legislative parties and environmental issues.

AIR POLLUTION: POLITICAL PARTIES AND THE CLEAN AIR ACTS OF 1970 AND 1990

Air pollution is not a contemporary environmental problem. In fact, references to it can be traced back almost 3,000 years ago "to the fumes produced at the asphalt mining town of Hit, about one hundred miles west of Babylon in the writings of King Tukulti."[1] Federal policy regarding air pollution dates back about four decades or so, when President Kennedy argued in a special message to Congress that "We need an effective federal air pollution control program now."[2] Two years later, Congress passed and President Johnson signed into law the Clean Air Act of 1963. Seven years later, President Nixon supported passage of the 1970 Clean Air Act. President Carter signed the Clean Air Act of 1977 and President Bush used the power of his office to secure passage of the Clean Air Act of 1990. Clean air legislation has been characterized as "one of the longest, most complex, and most technically detailed regulatory programs ever enacted on a federal level."[3]

In 1970 and again in 1990 the president was instrumental in securing passage of a clean air act in Congress. What role did the political parties play in support of air quality legislation? Did legislative behavior reflect bipartisanship or major divisions in the final outcome of air quality legislation?

Passage of clean air acts in 1970 and again in 1990 would not have been possible without the strong support of the president but also the willingness of Democrats and Republicans to work together. Congress was almost unanimous in its support for the clean air legislation in 1970. This was a time when the president embraced environmentalism

Party Voting on Clean Air Legislation

	1970 Clean Air Act		
	Democrats	Republicans	Total
House			
Support	210	165	375
Oppose	0	1	1
Senate			
Support	43	30	73
Oppose	0	0	0

	1990 Clean Air Act		
	Democrats	Republicans	Total
House			
Support	247	154	401
Oppose	5	16	21
Senate			
Support	50	39	89
Oppose	5	6	11

Source: Roll call votes compiled from Congressional Quarterly, Congressional Quarterly Almanac 1970 (Washington, DC: Congressional Quarterly Inc., 1970), 34H, 472; Congressional Quarterly, Congressional Quarterly Almanac 1990 (Washington, DC: Congressional Quarterly Inc., 1991), 135, 48H.

(albeit for political reasons)[4] and Earth Day was born. Twenty years later, George Bush campaigned to be the "environmental president." Although he disappointed environmentalists, he was instrumental in building a working coalition to ensure passage of the 1990 Clean Air Act. Once again, Democrats and Republicans joined together in the spirit of bipartisanship in working with the president on this legislation.

The political parties have been characterized as having different orientations toward environmental protection. Yet an empirical examination of the record indicates that, in contrast to other environment and social issues, air pollution legislation received bipartisanship support in Congress (and among Democratic and Republican presidents). However, recently Congress has had a large Republican membership with a decidedly less friendly attitude toward the environment than in previous years. Given the new Republican president and a Congress that is, more or less, evenly split between Democrats and Republicans, it remains to be seen if partisanship or bipartisanship will be the order of the day regarding environmental protection in general and air quality in particular.

continued

[1] Jacqueline Vaughn Switzer, *Environmental Politics: Domestic and International Dimensions,* 3rd ed. (New York: Bedford/St. Martin's, 2001), 190.

[2] John F. Kennedy, *Public Papers of the Presidents of the United States: John F. Kennedy, 1963* (Washington, DC: United States Government Printing Office, 1962), 117.

[3] Walter A. Rosenbaum, *Environmental Politics and Policy,* 3rd ed. (Washington, DC: CQ Press, 1995), 202.

[4] See Glen Sussman and Mark Kelso, "Environmental Priorities and the President as Legislative Leader," in Dennis L. Soden, ed. *The Environmental Presidency* (Albany, NY: State University of New York Press, 1999), 135.

Congressional Voting and Environmental Legislation

The environment is but one among many public policy areas that provide an opportunity to assess partisanship among legislators at the national level of government. What role has partisanship played over the last quarter century or so? Congressional voting on legislative measures provides one means to understand the role played by partisanship.

For example, a quarter century ago, Matthews and Stimson argued in their classic study of decision making in the United States House of Representatives that if roll call voting was not important "there would be little point in reading a book—or writing one—on roll call voting" in Congress.[17] Roll call voting takes on increasing importance for this study because partisanship has a major impact on legislative voting.[18] Moreover, as Barbara Hinckley points out, "The tendency to vote on the liberal or conservative sides on a wide range of issues can be clearly differentiated by party. Democrats are skewed toward the liberal, Republicans toward the conservative side."[19] Given this trend in congressional voting in general, to what extent has partisanship characterized voting on environmental legislation in particular?

Parties do indeed differ in their approach to environmental legislation (Table 4.2). During the mid-to-late 1970s, Democrats were more closely associated with environmental legislation than their Republican counterparts. In fact, by the late 1970s, only about one-third of Republicans could be considered to have a "green" voting record. By the 1990s, Democrats and Republicans were moving in the opposite direction, as support for environmental legislation among Democrats in the House and Senate increased and support among Republican legislators in both houses of Congress decreased. Moreover, by the late 1990s, "green" voting among Republicans was becoming a rare event.

Using the data in Table 4.2 we can create a percentage difference index to determine the gap between Democrats and Republicans in the House and Senate with regard to voting on environmental legislation. Table 4.3 provides a different perspective of congressional roll call voting on environmental legislation by showing the partisan differences among the members of Congress. The table confirms that Democrats are more supportive of environmental legislation than are Republican legislators. In every case, there is a Democratic advantage in "green" voting. Moreover, two important findings are evident. First, the gap in "green" voting favoring

TABLE 4.2

Party Support for Environmental Legislation in Congress

	Democrat		Republican	
	House	*Senate*	*House*	*Senate*
1974	57.9%	57.2%	39.4%	41.2%
1978	57.2	63.6	30.3	31.9
1990	73.5	67.3	37.1	29.9
1999	78.0	76.0	16.0	13.0

Source: Data for 1974, 1978, and 1990 adapted from Sheldon Kamieniecki, "Political Parties and Environmental Policy," in James P. Lester, ed. *Environmental Politics and Policy,* 2nd ed. (Durham: Duke University Press, 1995), 156. Data for 1999 from the League of Conservation Voters at **http://www.scorecard.lcv.org/analysis_results.cfm**. Retrieved March 9, 2000. Calculations by the authors.

TABLE 4.3

Party Differences, Congress, and the Environment

	House	*Senate*
1974	+18.5%	+16.0%
1978	+26.9	+31.4
1990	+36.4	+37.4
1999	+62.0	+63.0

Source: The data for 1974, 1978, and 1990 adapted from Sheldon Kamieniecki, "Political Parties and Environmental Policy," in James P. Lester, ed. *Environmental Politics and Policy,* 2nd ed. (Durham: Duke University Press, 1995), 156. Data for 1999 from the League of Conservation Voters at **http://www.scorecard.lcv.org/analysis_results.cfm**. Retrieved March 9, 2000. Calculations by the authors.

Note: (+) represents more support for environmental legislation by Democrats

Democrats has increased over time. Second, partisan differences are not limited to only one chamber of Congress. In fact, the variation in "green" voting between Democrats and Republicans has widened in both chambers of Congress.

State Legislatures and Environmental Legislation

On the basis of the Constitutional division of power in the United States, state governments engage in a myriad of activities that impact citizens' lives. Moreover, given the increasing devolution of power from the federal to state governments, "Programs promoting the quality of the environment . . . are good examples of federal initiatives where the states are also playing a vital role."[20] We have seen that partisan differences separate Democrats and Republicans in Congress when it comes to voting on environmental legislation. Yet we also know that partisanship may play an even greater role in legislative voting in state legislatures.[21] We now turn our attention to subnational legislative politics in order to determine if a similar pattern of partisan differences regarding the environment is evident among state legislators. Table 4.4 presents a percentage difference index based upon a sample of states where the mean environmental support scores were collected in order to assess partisanship in state legislative roll call voting.[22]

TABLE 4.4

Party Differences, State Legislative Politics, and the Environment

Region	Year	House	Senate
Northeast			
Maine	1992	+28.2%	+30.8%
New York	1982	+46.5	+51.0
	1992	+17.8	+27.5
Pennsylvania	1990	+34.0	− 6.6
Vermont	1992	+49.4	+39.7
South			
Florida	1992	+ 7.0	+4.0
Missouri	1992	+14.1	+1.2
North Carolina	1991	+27.7	+2.8
South Carolina	1992	+44.5	N/A
Tennessee	1992	+ 2.8	+3.6
Virginia	1992	+27.0	+8.0
Midwest			
Illinois	1981	+21.6	+36.2
	1992	+ 9.2	+38.5
Kansas	1992	+38.2	+23.9
Michigan	1992	+49.0	N/A
Minnesota	1992	+38.2	+23.2
Wisconsin	1983	+39.7	+33.4
	1992	+55.3	+36.8
West			
Alaska	1983	+38.0	+14.0
	1992	+55.9	+39.7
Arizona	1992	+36.5	+59.1
California	1983	+45.1	+26.4
	1991	+75.4	+44.7
Colorado	1992	+42.8	+53.2
Idaho	1983	+29.9	+47.7
	1992	+49.3	+49.7
Montana	1983	+39.3	+53.7
	1991	+48.6	+70.8
Oregon	1983	+38.1	+38.7
	1991	+50.0	+50.0
Utah	1992	+18.5	+16.5
Washington	1984	+66.4	+41.0
	1992	+60.0	+42.2
Wyoming	1983	+24.2	+45.4
	1992	+34.7	+23.7

Source: Adapted from Sheldon Kamieniecki, "Political Parties and Environmental Policy," in James P. Lester, ed. *Environmental Politics and Policy: Theories and Evidence*, 2nd ed. (Durham: Duke University Press, 1995), 159–161.

Note: (+) represents more support for environmental legislation by Democrats
        (–) represents more support for environmental legislation by Republicans

Our analysis focuses on three concerns about environmental voting in the state legislatures—namely, a comparison of the four major regions of the country, partisan differences in the house and the senate generally, and partisan differences in the house and senate over time. First, we aggregated the sample of 25 states into the four major regions of the country.[23] In every region, partisanship is evident in "green" voting; the only instance where Republicans were associated with "green" voting more than their Democratic colleagues was in the Pennsylvania Senate. The gap between Democrats and Republicans was greatest in the West and less significant in the South. A regional comparison indicates that state legislators in the South were the least likely to demonstrate "green" voting. A closer investigation of the southern region of the country also indicates that House Republicans were even less likely to vote in favor of environmental legislation than their colleagues in the senate, indicating interchamber variation in state legislative voting on the environment.

Second, if we look at environmental voting by state legislators in general rather than on a regional basis, we find that Democrats, across the board, voted "green" more often than Republican state lawmakers. In the states where data from the 1980s is available, the partisan gap is not limited to either chamber. In some cases, the partisan gap in "green" voting was greater in the house while in other cases, a similar "green" voting gap was evident in the senate. In other words, the gap in "green" voting was not overtly identified with one chamber or the other. Consequently, environmental lobbyists have been compelled to be vigilant in their lobbying efforts in both chambers of the state legislature.

Third, to what degree were partisan differences evident *over time* in the house and the senate in state legislatures? By the early 1990s, the partisan gap in "green" voting was larger, more often than not, in the house rather than in the senate. In other words, house Democrats were more likely to vote in support of environmental legislation than Democrats in the senate. Nonetheless, an examination of the roll call data in 1991 and 1992 indicates quite clearly that partisanship in state legislatures reflected that which was occurring in the Congress—namely, Democrats were more closely identified with voting in support of environmental legislation compared to their Republican counterparts. However, having said this, we also note that the partisan gap in "green" voting was rather narrow in several cases including Florida , Missouri (senate), North Carolina (senate), Tennessee, Virginia (senate), Illinois (house). In these states, Democrats and Republicans were more alike than different when it came to voting on environmental legislation.

California as a Case Study in State Legislative Partisanship and the Environment

In our assessment of partisanship in legislative politics we have found that, overall, Democrats have been more supportive of environmental legislation than Republicans in the House and in the Senate both in national and state politics. We briefly turn our attention to the state of California in order to undertake a similar investigation.

California is the largest state in the country, with a diverse geography and terrain, economy, and population. Given the importance of California in both state and national politics, we decided to take a closer look at party politics in California and the orientation toward the environment.[24] We will assess state-level party support for environmentalism in general, followed by analysis of the California Desert Protection Act of 1994—an important public lands issue. We will examine the roll call votes of both Congress and the California house delegation for the purpose of analysis and comparison of party politics.

During the last two decades, California Democrats voted in support of environmental legislation more so than their Republican colleagues in the legislature (Table 4.5A). Moreover, the partisan gap in "green" voting between Democrats and Republicans in the California house and senate was fairly large in the early 1980s and grew considerably over time. By the end of the 1990s, "green" voting was closely identified with Democrats, as Republican legislators strongly rejected environmental initiatives. Partisanship in environmental voting is indeed evident in the largest state in the country.

Although the 1994 California Desert Protection Act, which set aside millions of acres of public land, was signed into law by President Clinton, it was California's senators, especially Diane Feinstein, who were instrumental in the successful passage of the legislation into law. Senator Feinstein fought for the legislation because it "would take most of the beautiful areas in our state and preserve them for our children and our grandchildren for all time" and protect public lands from anticipated population growth and development.[25] The act is a good case study of the problems associated with many western states' view that the federal government has been waging a "war on the West."[26] Despite a contentious and divisive debate in both Congress and the California legislature, the bill passed (Table 4.5B).

Consideration of party politics and the legislation is important for two reasons. First, it is a significant part of the public lands controversy in the United

TABLE 4.5A

Party Support for Environmental Legislation in California

| | Support Score | | | |
| | Democrats | | Republicans | |
	House	Senate	House	Senate
1980	74.8%	64.1%	38.8%	46.0%
1991	90.7	80.6	15.3	35.9
1999	92.0	98.0	13.0	11.0
	Partisan Gap			
	House	Senate		
1983	+45.1%	+26.4%		
1991	+75.4	+44.7		
1999	+79.0	+87.0		

Source: Data for 1980, 1983 and 1991 adapted from Sheldon Kamieniecki, "Political Parties and Environmental Policy," in James P. Lester, ed. *Environmental Politics and Policy*, 2nd ed. (Durham: Duke University Press, 1995), 159. Data for 1999 from the California League of Conservation Voters at **http://www.ecovote.org/99clcv.pdf**. Retrieved March 9, 2000. Calculations by the authors.

Note: (+) represents more support for environmental legislation by Democrats

TABLE 4.5B

Party Support for the California Desert Protection Act of 1994: A Comparison of Congress and the California Delegation*

	Support	Oppose	Total
Congress			
House			
Democrats	244	6	250
Republicans	53	122	175
Independents	1	0	1
Senate			
Democrats	53	1	54
Republicans	16	28	44
California House Delegation			
Democrats	29	0	29
Republicans	0	21	21

Source: Roll call votes for Congress compiled from *Congressional Quarterly Weekly Report,* April 16, 1994, 915; *Congressional Quarterly Weekly Report,* July 30, 1994, 2182. Roll call votes for the California Delegation compiled from *Congressional Quarterly Weekly Report,* July 30, 1994, 2182.

*Note: California Senate vote was excluded as there are only two members

States and a central topic of divisive debates in the country. After all, the California act set aside some 8 million acres of public land and created two national parks. Second, it was the only major piece of environmental legislation passed during the first term of the Clinton administration.

How did party politics play regarding the California Desert Protection Act? According to the roll call votes for both Congress and the California delegation, partisan differences were quite evident in legislative voting on the act. In both the House and the Senate, Democrats were strongly in favor of it while Republican legislators voted in large numbers against it. Among California's delegation in Congress, variation in party voting was similar to the congressional vote. In fact, differences between the parties were greater among Californians than in Congress as a whole. Other than one abstention, every California Democrat supported the legislation while every Republican except one opposed it.

The California Desert Protection Act of 1994 is an important example of partisan politics in general. It is also a reflection of the divisions over public lands issues in our country, epitomized by the Sagebrush Rebellion, which became a salient issue in the country in the late 1970s. This event colored political debates involving contemporary public lands, wise use, and property-rights issues.

The Role and Function of Interest Groups

Interest groups have become a central feature of American politics. In the process of seeking to influence public policy, organized interests have been active at all levels of government. The distinct relationship between government decision making and public action has been characterized by Cortner and Moote in the following way:

> Public problems arise when the consequences of people's actions are on such a scale that collective rather than individual action may be necessary to provide relief and repair. Government is that set of institutions established to allow collective action and make decisions binding on the whole of society. Inevitably conflicts are generated as people explore the causes of public problems and organize to deal with them.[27]

As such, "interest groups urge people to take part in governmental politics because they want to accomplish something. . . . By participating, they hope to bring about policies that benefit them."[28]

The underlying rationale for public involvement in interest group behavior has been debated over the years. For some, the interest group process serves an important function because the variety of interests in American society are aligned in a competitive system characterized by multiple access points to the American governmental system and numerous political actors rather than one dominant player.[29] For others, government has actually been captured by organized interests—*interest group liberalism*—where "the role of government is one of insuring access to the most effectively organized, and of ratifying the agreements and adjustments worked out among the competing leaders."[30] Still others raise the concern about the core value of representation. As Loomis and Ciglar argue:

> the "problem" of contemporary interest group politics is one of representation. For particular interests, especially those that are well defined and adequately funded, the government is responsive on the issues of their greatest concern. But representation is not just a matter of responding to special interests or citizens; the government also must respond to the collective needs of a society, and here the success of individual interests may foreclose the possibility of overall responsiveness. The very vibrancy and success of contemporary groups help contribute to a society that finds it increasingly difficult to formulate solutions to complex policy questions.[31]

What motivates individuals to become involved in and contribute to the activities of organized interests? Are individuals motivated by economic incentives or by other noneconomic factors? Terry Moe has argued that "economic self-interest and economic selective incentives are not major motivational factors, that the crucial roles are played instead by . . . nonmaterial values and incentives . . . ."[32] Nonmaterial values and incentives might include "belief in a cause or ideology," "status," "prestige," "power," among others.[33] Does the fact that members of interest groups obtain "selective benefits" ensure that other individuals in the larger society who share common interests will also join the group? Mancur Olson informs us that interest groups are subject to what he refers to as the "free rider" problem whereby nongroup members receive the benefits of interest group activism but fail to contribute, directly or indirectly, to the group.[34] As Olson put it, why should an individual become involved in the activities of an organized interest when he or she would receive tangible benefits from the group's action without his or her contribution?

Finally, it is important to note that the role and scope of the federal government has also had an impact on interest group formation and action. Loomis and Ciglar argue that the New Deal programs of the 1930s encouraged "group formation" and later the "expansion of federal programs . . . since 1960," which resulted in "proliferation of government activities" and in turn "led to a mush-rooming of groups around the affected policy areas."[35] The point is that since the era of FDR, the federal government has expanded its involvement in the social, political, and economic life of the United States. In turn, the public has become increasingly politicized, resulting in interest group formation or expanded group membership, as citizens sought to influence or shape public policy.

CASE STUDY: GROUP ACTIVISM AND WOLF REINTRODUCTION INTO YELLOWSTONE NATIONAL PARK AND THE NORTHERN ROCKY MOUNTAINS

The reintroduction of wolves into Yellowstone National Park has been a most controversial issue facing environmentalists, citizens, western states, and the federal government. While seemingly appearing as a narrow environmental issue, the debate over wolf repopulation is a good example of the contemporary preservation versus property rights controversy.

On the one hand, cattle and livestock interests have long supported removal (by death or relocation) of the wolf due to the alleged threat posed to cattle and livestock. On the other hand, environmental groups and wildlife biologists have argued that the wolf is part and parcel of the western states' legacy and does not pose the kind of threat suggested by wolf recovery opponents.

Wolves are a natural part of the ecosystem yet they have all too often been viewed with fear rather than interest and a desire for understanding of their behavior. Although wolves roamed freely in the northern Rocky Mountains, in 1926 the U.S. government sponsored an eradication program that resulted in removal of wolves from Yellowstone National Park.[1] After nearly seven decades, the U.S. Fish and Wildlife Service (FWS) issued and the Department of the Interior adopted a wolf recovery program. Based upon the FWS environmental impact statement "The Reintroduction of Wolves to Yellowstone National Park and Central Idaho," the stage was set for wolf recovery in 1994.[2]

The process involved introducing Canadian wolves into Yellowstone National Park and Idaho. However, although wolves were reintroduced into Yellowstone National Park in 1995, cattle and livestock interests represented by the American Farm Bureau filed a lawsuit against the Department of the Interior to reverse the program. The American Farm Bureau argued against the federal government's interference in state affairs. Moreover, the organization suggested that the interests of the wolf were being placed above those of ranchers and farmers.

In December 1997, William Downes, a Wyoming federal judge, ruled that the wolf reintroduction program was illegal and therefore

continued

the Canadian wolves were to be removed from Yellowstone and Idaho. Environmental groups stepped forward to appeal Judge Downes's decision. Included in the judicial appeal process were the National Wildlife Federation (NWF), the Defenders of Wildlife, and the National Audubon Society. Moreover, the Interior Department had joined with environmental groups in opposing the American Farm Bureau and the decision by Judge Downes. These groups argued that wolves, as predators, have an important role to play in maintaining the natural balance in the Rocky Mountain ecosystem and did not pose a threat to livestock interests.

Oral arguments were heard by the 10th Circuit Court of Appeals. After a long court battle in which environmental groups opposed livestock interests, in early 2000, the Court of Appeals ruled, in effect, that wolf reintroduction in the Rocky Mountain region was acceptable. This resulted in Mark Van Putten, president of the NWF to remark, "The court has upheld a balanced approach to wolf recovery that has returned a part of America's wild heritage. . . . The Endangered Species Act has worked to restore a very special part of America's wildlife heritage and now that success will stand."[3]

The NWF considered the wolf recovery program important not only for its impact on the survival of wolves but also because of its spillover effect. The plight of the wolf in western states is but one of many instances of the divisive debate over the Endangered Species Act. Livestock and property rights interests argue that the act poses economic burdens on them. In contrast, the act is viewed by environmental groups as an important mechanism to protect animal species as well as to help them flourish.

For example, according to one NWF attorney involved in the wolf recovery program, "The 10th Circuit decision means that the Endangered Species Act can be used to restore other species in ways that meet local needs. It can help us unite people to bring back species like the grizzly bear and to stop the decline of others. That's a win for everyone."[4] Moreover, in addition to the efforts promoted by environmental groups, the U.S. Fish and Wildlife Service predicted an increase in park attendance due to the wolf reintroduction plan.[5]

As he neared the end of his term, Secretary of the Interior Bruce Babbit stated that he was "looking forward to visiting Yellowstone one last time to see for myself this program which has been so popular with the public."[6] As to what was accomplished with the program, Babbitt happily stated that "We introduced wolves back into Yellowstone six years ago and it has been one of the most successful actions during my tenure."[7]

---

[1]See "Restoring Wolves" at **http://www.defenders.org/wildlife/wolf/ynpfact.html.** Retrieved January 14, 2001.

[2]Ibid.

³Mark Van Putten quoted in "Court Reversal of Wolf Removal Order: Victory for Common Sense Conservation," at **http://www.nwf.org/wolves/court_reversal.html.** Retrieved March 9, 2000.

⁴ Ibid.

⁵ See "Restoring Wolves."

⁶ See Office of the Secretary, U.S. Department of the Interior, "Media Advisory: Babbitt Will Visit Yellowstone to Discuss Successful Wolf Re-Introduction" at **http://www.doi. gov/news/010105a.html.** Retrieved January 14, 2001.

⁷ Ibid.

Types and Characteristics of Environmental Groups

We live in an age in which interest groups have proliferated in American politics. Environmental interest groups are but one subset of a variety of interests, each seeking to influence public policy in the nation's capital as well as in the 50 states and at the local level. While most environmental groups engage in what one might call legitimate political action (e.g., lobbying), other groups prefer alternative participatory avenues to publicize their cause and influence policy (e.g., direct action). In an analysis of national environmental groups, Christopher Bosso suggests that environmental organizations can be classified into five basic types—namely, large groups that focus on many issues; small groups with a more narrowly defined focus; nonpartisan groups that emphasize education and research; groups that promote solutions based upon a legal and/or scientific basis; and groups that protect land and ecosystems through its purchase and eventual preservation.[36] What these groups have in common is their emphasis on legitimate, conventional political action. Conventional political action includes a multitude of avenues of political expression whereby organized interests seek to influence public policy. These methods of political action include but are not limited to traditional activities such as coalition formation, legislative testimony, grassroots organizing, litigation, use of the media, polling, and modern communication techniques including the Internet.

However, research also shows that alternative means of political expression are also either supported or put into practice by segments of the public, both in the United States and in other countries.[37] These types of actions are considered "unconventional" because they are considered outside the mainstream of typical political expression and include direct action techniques that might be considered radical or in some cases unlawful. In contrasting "ordinary" and "extraordinary" politics, Charles Euchner argues that, while the former provides a "system of competition" but fails to provide "an effective means to challenge dominant values," the latter "aims to force the political establishment to address issues that it would rather ignore."[38] Nonetheless, members of certain environmental groups see these kinds of actions as an appropriate means by which to engage in the promotion of environmental protection.

Membership, Tactics, and Strategy of National Environmental Groups

Disagreements are evident in the debate over the extent to which the public should have input into public policy making.[39] For example, should public officials and civil servants be entrusted to make policy for the public good or should citizens, rather than their elected representatives, have direct influence over the policy-making process? Although the government itself has initiated numerous citizen advisory groups to promote public input into environmental policy making,[40] the proliferation of environmental groups and increase in membership over the years is a clear indication of the level of public concern about the quality of the environment.

Moreover, to what extent do citizens contribute financially to support organized interests? It is not surprising to find that when citizens feel that the environment is receiving due consideration from government, the level of financial contributions to organized interests levels off. Nonetheless, research shows that while donations to environmental groups decline during times of unemployment, partisanship still matters to the public—namely, when the Republican party is in control of the White House, financial contributions to environmental groups increases.[41]

In Table 4.6 several characteristics of a select group of national environmental organizations are presented, beginning with one of the oldest groups, the Sierra Club, and ending with one of the newest, NRDC. The earliest groups, dating from the turn of the century through the administration of Franklin Roosevelt—Sierra Club, National Audubon Society, Wilderness Society, National Wildlife Federation—began with a common focus of concern in protecting public lands and wildlife. Groups established since the mid-1960s—Environmental Defense Fund, Friends of the Earth, Natural Resources Defense Council—have as their main focus concern about the threat posed to the environment from various sources of pollution; conservation of the nation's resources; and the contemporary "third stage" issue of biodiversity.

Having said this, it is important to point out that many of the environmental organizations are not necessarily limited to one or two issues but rather are multi-issue groups. For example, although the National Wildlife Federation began as a movement concerned about public lands and wildlife, it has become the largest environmental group engaged in multiple efforts that focus on a vast array of environmental issues, including air and water pollution and biodiversity as well as stratospheric ozone depletion and global warming.

Membership and budgets are important resources for organized interests. As the number of environmental groups has expanded over the years so have the memberships of these groups. For example, Mitchell, Mertig, and Dunlap argue that an upsurge in environmental organizational membership occurred during the decades of the 1960s and 1980s and again in the 1990s. As reported by these researchers, the increase in membership was a result of "more aggressive and outspoken" groups in the 1960s, the "Reagan administration's attacks on environmentalism," in the 1980s, and, in the early 1990s, by the "visibility of ecological problems ranging from . . . beach contamination, the *Exxon Valdez* oil spill, ozone destruction . . . as well as by the substantial mobilization efforts by these organizations made in conjunction with the twentieth Earth Day celebration."[42] During the twenty-year period 1975 to 1995, the membership base of environmental groups had expanded tremendously overall, although it has fluctuated

TABLE 4.6

Characteristics of Environmental Groups (selected)

Group	Date Founded	Membership (1995)	Membership (% change, 1975–1995)	Budget (1995)	Budget (% change, 1985–1995)	Type of Political Activism	Focus*
Sierra Club	1892	550,000	+224	$43 million	+ 96	Conventional	Wild and public lands preservation
National Audubon Society	1905	550,000	+200	43.1 million	+ 80	Conventional	Birds and wildlife preservation
Wilderness Society	1935	275,000	+450	15.2 million	+134	Conventional	Wilderness preservation
National Wildlife Federation	1936	4 million	+ 8	97 million	+111	Conventional	Wildlife and natural resources conservation
Environmental Defense Fund	1967	300,000	+900	25.7 million	+634	Conventional	Pollution, conservation of resources
Friends of the Earth	1969	20,000	+400	2 million	+100	Conventional/ direct act on	Biodiversity
Natural Resources Defense Council	1970	120,000	+243	26.2 million	+303	Conventional	Natural resource conservation

Source: Adapted from Foundation for Public Affairs, *Public Interest Profiles 1996/1997* (Washington, DC: Congressional Quarterly, Inc., 1996), Chapter 6; Rochelle L. Stanfield, "Environmental Lobby's Changing of the Guard Is Part of Movements' Evolution," *National Journal* ˜ 7 (June 8, 1985), 1352.

*Note: For the purpose of classification, we intentionally used a narrow interpretation of the group's primary focus. Because many of the groups address a variety of environmental issues, the reader is encouraged to contact the group directly for more information.

within this time period. Moreover, the increase in numbers was greater for some groups more than others.

Furthermore, revenue increases during these 20 years paralleled the influx of members, which provided greater financial support for environmental organizations to pursue activities geared toward improving the quality of the environment. Environmental groups have a variety of funding sources ranging from individual members to foundation grants. To what extent do these groups receive funds from the membership base—citizens who are individually concerned about environmental quality and are prepared to support environmental groups financially?[43] As we can see, there is wide variation in membership contributions. The Natural Resources Defense Council and the Environmental Defense Fund are much more dependent on membership dues than are the other groups, deriving 61 percent and 59 percent, respectively, of their total financial revenue from members, followed by the Wilderness Society at 49 percent. The National Audubon Society (22 percent), Friends of the Earth (13.7 percent), and the National Wildlife Federation (13 percent) are less dependent on membership contributions. These latter groups obtain considerable financial resources from alternative sources including nature education programs, merchandise sales, and investments, among others, making their activities less vulnerable when membership and membership dues fluctuate.

Although membership and budgets are important resources for environmental organizations, these groups, like other interest groups, require effective leadership. As environmental groups mature, new leaders have pursued strategies that some consider less aggressive but still effective, and at the same time they have broadened their approach in coalition formation with other sectors of society as a way to promote environmentalism.[44] Environmental groups might align with other interests, including business, in order to avoid the kind of conflict that existed in the past. "Green" business is an example of this new orientation. As Michael Kraft has explained:

> Business groups often have been active opponents of environmental protection policy, and pursuit of profit by private corporations and landowners is responsible for the abuse of natural resources in the United States and globally. Many leading business groups continue their efforts to weaken federal environmental laws they believe are too costly. Yet some of the largest and best known U.S. corporations have demonstrated a new willingness to foster sustainable resource use, to support pollution initiatives, and to develop and market green products.[45]

For example, as reported by the Wilderness Society, numerous corporations have established "green" business activities. These include Starkist Seafood Company, which terminated its purchase of tuna not caught in dolphin-safe nets; Patagonia, which donated part of its profits to environmental groups; and Arm and Hammer Baking Soda, which produced a nonphosphate laundry detergent for Earth Day 1970.[46] Nonetheless, the extent to which these efforts will continue (and are indeed altruistic or due instead to consumer and environmental group demands) remains a point of concern for environmentalists. For example, although Exxon Corporation publicized its decision to contribute several million dollars toward the Save the Tiger Fund, the contribution is only a small fraction of the tremendous profits made by the oil company, which uses the tiger as its corporate logo.[47]

In 1982, Friends of the Earth, along with nine other environmental groups including the Sierra Club, National Audubon Society, and Defenders of Wildlife, published a report—rather an indictment—against the Reagan administration.[48] According to this document, the Reagan administration, unlike other presidential administrations, turned its back on the longtime bipartisan support of environmental protection. The indictment was quite comprehensive, ranging from air and water quality to harzardous wastes to public lands to fish and wildlife. In the words of the report:

> President Reagan has broken faith with the American people on environmental protection. . . . he and his appointed officials have simply refused to do the job that the laws require and that Americans expect of their government—to protect the public health from pollution and to use publicly owned resources and lands for the public good. . . . In the name of "getting the government off our backs," they are giving away our natural heritage.[49]

The Reagan administration stood in stark contrast to the Republican Nixon administration, which was identified with the Environmental Protection Agency, National Environmental Policy Act, and Earth Day, among others. Environmental groups had a clearly identifiable enemy they could use to attract members and financial contributions in support of environmental protection, as the Reagan administration could be characterized as launching an assault on the environment. Moreover, public opinion in support of environmentalism was clearly at odds with Reagan's approach to environmental policy. This also bolstered the efforts of environmental groups.

While environmentalists focused on a Republican White House during the 1980s, the congressional elections of 1994 shifted attention to the legislative branch of government when the Republican party captured control of both houses of Congress for the first time in 40 years. While some might argue that this signaled a shift in the public's orientation toward public policy, including the environment, environmental groups supported by public opinion polls argued differently. For example, the president of the National Wildlife Federation, Jay Hair, stated that "Anyone who thought this election was a mandate to undo 25 years of environmental protection had better think again."[50]

Although environmental organizations share a common commitment to environmental quality both at home and globally, the means by which these groups pursue activities toward this common goal differ considerably. Differences exist among the larger national environmental groups and between them and smaller organizations. For example, as reported in a 1995 article in *The Washington Post:*

> Despite its pedigree in the environmental community, the Wilderness Society in recent years has been criticized by more militant environmentalists, who say it is too willing to compromise and too comfortable in Washington's corridor's of power. Such attacks are part of a larger split between activist local and regional conservation groups and larger, wealthier and more moderate organizations such as the Sierra Club and National Wildlife Federation.[51]

Large environmental organizations with mass membership and large budgets have the capacity to engage in multiple activities in their effort to influence government and reach out to the public. As the largest environmental organization in the country, the National Wildlife Federation (NWF) has been active in environmental affairs since its beginning more than six decades ago. While starting out in the mid-1930s at the same time that the first North American Wildlife

Conference was organized during the administration of Franklin D. Roosevelt, the organization has become an influential force in the environmental community. By early 2001 the NWF had been involved in numerous activities including education campaigns, lobbying, broadcasting programs, litigation, and product merchandising, among others.[52]

Although the National Wildlife Federation has been characterized as the most conservative environmental organization, its members have been active players and are committed to protection of the environment. The NWF has been a vigorous participant in promoting air and water quality, toxic waste cleanup, protection of biodiversity and endangered species, and providing solutions to global climatic problems.

The Sierra Club, one of the oldest conservation groups, and the Wilderness Society, founded during the depression of the 1930s, have been engaged in efforts to protect wild and public lands.[53] In the course of doing so they have been challenged by opposition interests including mining, oil, gas, and logging—interests that want to maintain or expand their access to vital and profitable resources. In the effort to set aside public lands as wilderness areas or national parks, conservation efforts have been met by strong opposition by these interests, which felt that resources were being locked up. Nonetheless, these conservation groups cite numerous successes, including the 1964 Wilderness Act, the 1980 Alaska National Interest Lands Conservation Act, the 1994 California Desert Protection Act, and the 1996 Grand Staircase–Escalante National Monument in Utah. Taken together, millions of acres of public lands have been set aside for future generations due, in part, to the activities of these and other environmental groups.

Pollution control and the threat posed by toxic and chemical waste have been at the center of activity for many environmental groups. For example, the Environmental Defense Fund (EDF) was established in 1967 as a result of concerns raised about DDT, first brought to the public's attention by Rachel Carson in her book *Silent Spring*. Although the effort to address the problems posed by DDT began during the Kennedy administration, DDT was not banned nationally until the end of Nixon's first term in office. The EDF stressed the importance of the public and environmental threat posed by DDT and took a novel approach— namely, using the courts to establish environmental law.[54]

INGRID NEWKIRK: SAVING THE ANIMALS

It is difficult to talk about the animal rights organization People for the Ethical Treatment of Animals (PETA) without emphasizing the role played by its cofounder and leader, Ingrid Newkirk. While PETA has engaged in a myriad of activities—some hyperbolic to gain media and public attention and others very serious—the rationale upon which the organization functions reflects the passion for animal welfare held by Ingrid Newkirk. Yet how many people know that Newkirk worked in Washington, DC, with Animal Disease Control for the Commission on Public Health and in law enforcement in Maryland for a quarter century?[1] Newkirk, who was born in England and lived in India, resides in Norfolk, Virginia (the headquarters of PETA), on a small income in a modest apartment. Yet the organization she helped found 20 years ago has grown from a small group to a multimillion-dollar-per-year animal rights political force.

As the head of the largest animal rights organization in the world, Newkirk (as well as her colleagues) practices politics that delight many and bring ridicule from her detractors. PETA's advocacy for animal welfare as well as vegetarianism has attracted many celebrities to its cause, including Pamela Anderson, Alec Baldwin, Ellen De Generes, Courtney Love, Bill Maher, Paul McCartney, Richard Pryor, Steven Segal, William Shatner, Martin Sheen, and Alicia Silverstone, among many others. At the same time, numerous industry spokespersons have articulated their outrage at the tactics employed against their interests. These include circuses as well as the fur, poultry, and milk industries. Moreover, some in the scientific and academic community have spoken out against PETA for its opposition to medical experimentation involving animals.

Under Newkirk's leadership, the goal of PETA is to influence public and corporate policy. Over the years, PETA has been successful in the passage of both federal legislation as well as changes in corporate policy. For example, due to PETA's efforts, the first-ever arrest and conviction for animal experimentation occurred in Maryland in 1981; cosmetic companies including Avon and Revlon agreed to terminate testing on animals; NASA curtailed parts of its monkeys-in-space program; and several leading oil companies including Shell, Texaco, and Mobil agreed to protect birds by capping the tops of exhaust stacks.[2]

In a recent newspaper report investigating the activities of PETA, the organization as well as Newkirk were characterized as going too far in the effort to gain media attention and influence the behavior of large corporations and American consumers.[3] Members of PETA have participated in its "I'd rather go naked than wear fur" campaign, "Cut out dissection" activities where members wear "dissected" frog costumes, and undercover investigations videotaping animal mistreatment. However, Newkirk's group has been accused of insensitivity in its campaign to link milk with cancer when, in billboards, it used a picture of New York City Mayor Rudy Giuliani, who suffers from prostate cancer.[4] And while successful in influencing McDonald's to use more humane practices regarding animal treatment, PETA's effort to show the mistreatment of animals in the meat industry in its "McCruelty to go" campaign received complaints from parents over the graphics on billboards and the packaging and contents of the "McCruelty's Unhappy Meal" lunch box.[5]

In a lengthy letter to the editor, Newkirk responded that PETA is a "community resource" that has a "great team of positive-minded people" who have been subject to "bomb threats, paint thrown against the building, a dead deer dropped on our doorstep and hate mail" all because of its work toward achieving a society that recognizes that animals have rights.[6] According to Newkirk, during the past year alone, for instance,

continued

PETA had engaged in numerous legitimate activities including obtaining a government citation against Georgetown University for its experiments with monkeys; challenging use of animals in tobacco research by enlisting the support of actor Jack Lemmon; bringing charges against a Kansas puppy mill; and having patrons wearing fur being banned from Spa, one of New York's top night spots, among many other actions.[7]

PETA has been characterized as a direct action, radical, extremist group. Yet Newkirk argues that she has never advocated or employed violence. To the contrary, she claims that Peta has engaged in some-times outrageous, sometimes embarrassing activities only to raise public consciousness about a certain aspect of animal welfare. At the same time, Ingrid Newkirk has engaged in numerous legitimate activities, including appearing in guest spots on the *Oprah Winfrey Show, Nightline, 20/20,* and the *Today Show,* as well as writing several books for adults and children.[8] "At any rate," as Newkirk recently stated, "we don't plan to leave anytime soon."

[1]"Earth Day 2000 with Ingrid Newkirk: 'Eat Green,'" at **http://www.ens.lycos.com/ensapr2000/2000L-04-18-01.html.** Retrieved January 4, 2001.

[2]Bill Sizemore, "PETA: Lean and Mean," *The Virginian-Pilot,* December 3, 2000, A1, A12–13; "PETA's History: Compassion in Action," at **http://www.peta-online.org/mc/facts/fsm2.html.** Retrieved January 4, 2001.

[3]See, for example, Sizemore, "PETA: Lean and Mean," A13.

[4]Ibid.

[5]Ibid.

[6]See Ingrid Newkirk, "Letter to the Editor: PETA article's bark is worse than its bite," *The Virginian-Pilot,* December 9, 2000, B8.

[7]See Ingrid Newkirk, "Letters to the Editor," *Port Folio Weekly* 19 (January 2, 2001), 10.

[8]"Earth Day 2000 with Ingrid Newkirk: 'Eat Green.'"

While environmental organizations like the National Wildlife Federation and Sierra Club, for example, have used an array of conventional tactics to further their political agenda, groups like Greenpeace and Earth First! have employed direct action techniques. These "green" groups place greater emphasis on "public education, direct action, and social change."[55] However, where Greenpeace remains within the "legitimate" sphere of organized interests, Earth First! is characterized as a "radical" and/or "violent" group.

Greenpeace has a membership base in the United States (Greenpeace USA) as well as globally (Greenpeace International). The organization has engaged in activities that fit neatly into its media campaigns, which publicize its efforts as well as what it considers threats to the environment and wildlife. Nonviolent, direct action techniques employed by members of Greenpeace include placing themselves in small boats between whales and whaling ships, and hanging large banners from tall buildings.

The political activism of Greenpeace has resulted in tensions between the group and foreign governments. In fact, when Greenpeace sailed a vessel into a French nuclear test zone in the South Pacific in the early 1970s, it was challenged by a French military vessel, damaged, and the nuclear test was completed.[56] Although Greenpeace has gained national as well as international publicity through its direct action campaigns, it has in recent years expanded its activities to include scientific research as well as work with consumer groups and business and industry in order to achieve its goals.[57]

Although Greenpeace engages in direction action protest behavior, its activities are usually within the domain of legal expression. As a counterpoint to Greenpeace among direct action groups is Earth First!, which has been characterized as a "radical" environmental group engaging in political acts that include violent protest behavior. According to Walter Rosenbaum, "radicals often betray an ambivalence, if not a tolerance, about forms of violence . . . condemned from within and without the environmental movement."[58] As a consequence of its philosophical orientation, Earth First! has engaged in "ecotage," which includes, among other things, attempting to block bulldozers from gaining access to forests and posing a direct threat to loggers in the process of cutting down trees with chain saws, by placing metal spikes into trees to prohibit timber companies from harvesting them.[59] According to one political observer of such unconventional politics:

> Unlike the mainstream national environmental organizations, which work within established political and economic frameworks, Earth First! challenges those who embrace environmental compromise and pursue environmental objectives through traditional Madisonian interest group and lobbying processes. Instead members of Earth First! believe that the natural world must be defended through direct action, civil disobedience, and ecosabotage. . . .[60]

As these examples clearly show, the effort to protect the environment is not represented by uniform political practices. To the contrary, environmental groups exhibit a vast array of tactics and strategies in an attempt to secure environmental goals. While the vast majority of members of environmental groups belong to organizations that pursue legitimate political activism, a minority of citizens support directly or indirectly the activities of groups that employ nonviolent, direct action or, at times, violent methods.

Opposition to Environmental Activism: Business and Industry, Sagebrush Rebellion, Wise Use/Property Rights Movement

In addition to the actions of environmental groups, organized interests are also active in pursuing an anti-environmental agenda. Chief among these anti-environmental constituencies are business and industry and citizens involved in the contemporary wise use/property rights movement that is a result, in part, of the Sagebrush Rebellion of the late 1970s. On the one hand, government officials are encouraged by environmental groups to support a pro-environment agenda. On the other hand, "green" opposition is well poised and supported by ample resources to lobby these same governmental officials to be sensitive to what they call the undue burdens imposed on business and industry and property rights.

As far as environmental politics and policy are concerned, anti-environment groups cover a broad range of activism and can be characterized as follows:[61] public relations and corporate sponsored groups, which create a positive image for and work toward reducing the regulatory burden on business and industry; think tanks including the Cato Institute and the Heritage Foundation, which provide counter-arguments to environmentalists' claims regarding threats to the environment; legal foundations, which engage in litigation in opposition to environmental lawsuits by citizens; endowments and charities, which provide financial support for anti-environmental activities; and the wise use/property rights movement, which opposes intrusion of the federal government into environmental affairs at the state and local level. For the purpose of illustration, the following sections focus briefly on three of these cases—namely, business and industry, the Sagebrush Rebellion, and the wise use/property rights movement.

Business and Industry and the Environment

Business and industry have ample resources to use in the effort to promote favorable policies that impact their interests. The business sector has employed traditional political methods including lobbying Congress, working very closely with executive agencies, and participating in the litigation process, and have also used the airwaves, running commercials to "inform" viewers that business is not only concerned about environmental quality but also is doing something about it. Business and industry have also engaged in "greenwashing"—a public relations ploy, according to skeptical environmentalists, whereby companies advertise their "green" business practices.[62]

During the year 2000 presidential primary campaign, the group Republicans for Clean Air, which contributed over $2 million to television ads attacking Republican presidential candidate, Arizona Senator John McCain, was actually Charles and Sam Wyly—two Texas supporters of candidate George W. Bush.[63] Although the campaign contributions were within legal limits, the name of the group was a ruse that misrepresented to the public its purpose as well as its membership. This kind of tactic, however, is not unusual. To the contrary, numerous seemingly pro-environment groups are in reality business and industry groups that have employed a slick means to pursue their interests.

For example, The National Wetlands Coalition is not concerned with protecting the nation's wetlands but rather is committed to reducing the burden of wetlands regulations on real estate and oil and gas interests.[64] Utility companies under the organizational banner The Endangered Species Reform Coalition sought to weaken not strengthen the Endangered Species Act.[65] In an effort to protect their energy interests, the petroleum industry united behind the Marine Preservation Association, which by its name suggested a commitment to the marine and ocean environment.[66]

Why might business and industry engage in this type of activity? During the 1960s and 1970s, numerous landmark pieces of legislation were passed by Congress in support of environmental protection. However, business and industry hold the view that their interests are being sacrificed in the name of environmentalism. According to legal representatives of the business community, the economic sector was caught "in an environmental vice—squeezed by ever-closer scrutiny and harsher penalties, while the complexity and breadth of green laws and regulations make full compliance impossible."[67]

The politics of the 1990 Clean Air Act Amendments illustrate the problems involving environmental groups and business and industry. For 13 years (1977–1990), comprehensive clean air legislation was deadlocked in the Congress and opposed by the Reagan administration. In contrast to his predecessor, George H.W. Bush came into office committed to a clean air bill. Bush used the powerful resources of the presidency to encourage contending interests to support the legislation. After Congress passed the 1990 Clean Air Act, Bush called it "the most significant air pollution legislation in history."[68] Although concerned about effective enforcement of the legislation, environmentalists were delighted with its passage. The bill was called a "cause for celebration and hope," according to the head of the National Clean Air Coalition, and the legislation was described as "a breath of fresh air after a 10 year smog alert" by the Sierra Club president.[69] In contrast to the guarded optimism of environmentalists, the issues of economic development, costs to industry, and threats to jobs were voiced by business and industry.

The Sagebrush Rebellion

Although environmentalists have generally supported federal control over public lands, support for state authority over the public domain is an important issue for interest groups and citizens. The conflict over public land was clearly evident in what became known as the "Sagebrush Rebellion." More than 20 years ago there was a clash of interests between the federal government and sagebrush westerners over the public lands. (The Sagebrush Rebellion was nothing new, however; it had a western antecedent—protests that occurred in the 1920s and again in the 1940s).[70] It has been described as ". . . a conflict over the values that are to govern public land management and use—such as the conflicts between livestock, grazing and wildlife management, extractive resource development and landscape preservation, and hard and soft recreational uses."[71]

According to Sandra Davis and Dale Krane, public policy is the result of the "matrix of reciprocal power relations" across all levels of government which respond in various ways to "private interests."[72] Western public land management can be framed in terms of intergovernmental conflict that reflects the diverse interests of both the governments and the private enterprises involved in the process. As Samuel Hays aptly observed:

> Federal lands inevitably created a contest over the use of federal power. Over the years, conservationists and environmentalists sought to enhance federal authority as friendly to public land interest. Commodity users, on the other hand, had always relied on state authority, on occasion had fostered strategies to transfer federal lands to the states, and had upheld land management in the western states as an appropriate model.[73]

"Sagebrushers" had an ally in Ronald Reagan when he assumed the presidency in 1981. However, their support waned for three reasons. First, Sagebrusher James Watt departed as Secretary of the Interior. Second, Reagan increasingly practiced symbolic rather than substantive support. Third, during the presidential campaign of 1988 George H.W. Bush indicated that he would be an "environmental" president. After his election as president, although Bush appointed Manuel Lujan as

Secretary of the Interior, who was not viewed as an ally by the environmental community, he also appointed William Reilly, former head of the World Wildlife Fund as head of the Environmental Protection Agency. Although the Sagebrush Rebellion of the late 1970s and early 1980s reflected strong opposition by mining, timber, grazing, and other interests to federal intrusion in public land management, federal dominance would, nonetheless, remain in force regarding public lands.

The Wise Use/Property Rights Movement[74]

The Wise Use/Property Rights Movement of the 1990s represents a broad antifederal government/anti-environment philosophy. It is concerned about control over public lands at the state and local level. The issue has become so contentious that there has been renewed demand for "environmental federalism," where political authority over public lands is transferred from the federal government to the states.[75] Moreover, the issue of public land management has taken on a regional context, as members in the West have been concerned about "protecting industrial and agricultural access to public lands and waters at below-market costs, with the primary emphasis on timber, mining, and grazing" while in the eastern part of the country, landowners and developers are concerned about limitations imposed on their activities due to "regulations governing wetlands, endangered species, wild and scenic rivers, and other environmental protections broadly favored by the American public."[76]

An August 1988 conference in Reno, Nevada, attended by individuals, companies, and groups provided a forum for all to express their concerns about what they saw as increasing federal regulatory power in environmental affairs. The conference produced a *Wise Use Agenda*, the result of some 100 papers presented at the conference.[77] The goals of the movement include opposing federal regulatory power that threatens jobs and economic development, support for the multiple use principle to provide access to "locked up" natural resources on public lands, and protection of property rights against the government's power of eminent domain.[78] The conflict over property rights is a controversial issue in the debate over use of public lands. As Cortner and Moote point out:

> Under the ancient concept of eminent domain, government has the right to take private property for public use. However, under the Fifth Amendment of the U.S. Constitution, no property can be taken without just compensation. . . . The question then becomes: when is the burden of governmental regulations of such a magnitude that in effect government has "taken" property and the landowner is deserving of compensation?[79]

The goals of the movements are quite broad, in an effort to counter government regulations that in their view have favored preservation over development. The movement supports, for instance, increased access for drilling, mining, and grazing on public lands (e.g., national parks and forests) and termination of the Endangered Species Act.[80] Although the movement is primarily a contemporary political phenomenon, it has historical antecedents. For example, during the early 1940s, under the rubric of "national security," the timber industry, in an effort to maintain access to public lands and timber, vigorously opposed creation of a new Olympic National Park in the Pacific Northwest.[81] Moreover, in his research about the U.S. national park system, John Miles points out that in the early postwar years of the late 1940s and 1950s, "The powerful drive to log, mine, graze, and develop the American landscape, stimulated by rapid economic expansion, threatened to invade the parks and all wild areas outside the parks."[82] So that, although environmentalists were pleased with congressional legislation in 1950, which joined Jackson Hole National Monument and the Grand Teton National Park, the new national park remained accessible to grazing and hunting interests.[83]

The Wise Use Web site, Center for the Defense of Free Enterprise, provides the rationale for the use of the term "wise use." In contrast to Gifford Pinchot's notion of "wise use," which meant "government control of resources" and "preservation without use," the movement supports "use with preservation" and rejects "government control of resources." Moreover, according to one of the largest wise use groups, People for the West, "Human existence since the beginning has created pollution and changed the environment. The challenge is to determine the acceptable level of tradeoffs involved in different ways of living."[84] Here indeed is the clear contrast with the environmentalist agenda that supports preservation, conservation, and reduction of pollution levels. As environmentalist Aldo Leopold stated years ago:

> Individual landowners and users, especially lumbermen and stockmen, are inclined to wail long and loudly about the extension of government ownership and regulation of land, but (with notable exceptions) they show little disposition to develop the only visible alternative: the voluntary practice of conservation on their own lands.[85]

Conclusion

In American democratic society, there are a variety of ways that citizens are linked to government. Public preferences can be aggregated as input into the political process, for instance, through political parties and organized interests. This analysis of parties and groups has shown that both similarities and differences are evident regarding the role of these institutions as they are involved in environmental politics and policy.

Although environmentalism has been characterized as a bipartisan issue in American politics, party differences remain. Party platforms have increasingly included environmental goals, and most presidents have fulfilled the pledges made by their party. The Reagan administration served as a pivotal point in the evolution of the modern environmental movement in the United States as it embraced a prodevelopment philosophy. As the 2000 presidential campaign illustrated, environmentalists paid close attention to the party platforms of the Democratic and Republican parties, especially since Vice President and Democratic nominee, Al Gore, clearly identified himself as an environmentalist. Gore's publicized personal commitment to environmental quality certainly raised expectations among environmentalists while at the same time affecting business and industry strategies regarding electoral and political mobilization to protect their interests.

Although members of both political parties in Congress and the state legislatures have voted in favor of environmental legislation, Democrats are more closely associated with a "green" voting record. Moreover, given increasing hostility toward the environment by a Republican-controlled Congress since 1994, the election of 2000 took on increasing importance regarding which party would gain or maintain a legislative majority.

During the last century, environmental groups have increased in number and size. In recent years, environmental activism has become an institutionalized part of American politics. Nonetheless, the environmental movement is not unified but rather is diverse in its goals and methods of operation. While some groups are large and multifaceted, others are small and more narrowly focused. The environmental movement has had numerous successes, represented by landmark legislation, presidential action, and courtroom decisions. At the same time, environmentalists have been and will continue to be faced with challenges posed by recalcitrant public officials as well as opposition by business and industry and citizens' groups (e.g., wise use movement) whose values differ with environmentalists or who feel that their interests are threatened by environmental laws and regulations.

Web Sites
Environmental Activism: Political Parties and Interest Groups:

Political Parties

Democratic Party: **www.democrats.org**

Republican Party: **www.rnc.org**

Green Party USA: **www.greenparty.org**

Libertarian Party: **www.lp.org**

Political Index (political parties): **www.politicalindex.com/sect8.htm**

Project Vote-Smart: **www.vote-smart.org**

Organized Interests: Environmental Groups

National Wildlife Federation: **www.nwf.org**

Defenders of Wildlife: **www.defenders.org**

Environmental Defense Fund: **www.edf.org**

Wilderness Society: **www.wilderness.org**

Audubon Society: **www.audubon.org**

Sierra Club: **www.sierraclub.org**

Natural Resources Defense Council: **www.nrdc.org**

Organized Interests: Business, Industry, Property Rights

American Petroleum Institute: **www.api.org**

Northwest Forestry Association: **www.nwforestry.org**

National Association of Manufacturers: **www.nam.org**

Defenders of Property Rights: **www.defendersproprights.org**

Environmental Working Group: (wise use movement) **www.ewg.org**

Endnotes

1   See, for example, Daniel Ogden, "The Future of Environmental Struggle," in Roy Meek and John Straayer, eds. *The Politics of Neglect: The Environmental Crisis* (Boston: Houghton Mifflin, 1971).

2   See, for example, Riley Dunlap and Richard Gale, "Party Membership and Environmental Politics: A Legislative Roll-Call Analysis," *Social Science Quarterly* 55: 670–690.

3   Samuel P. Hays, *Explorations in Environmental History* (Pittsburgh: University of Pittsburgh Press, 1995), 398.

4   Richard Rose, *Do Parties Make a Difference?* Expanded Second ed. (Chatham, NJ: Chatham House Publishers, Inc., 1984), 13.

5   Paul Allen Beck and Frank J. Sorauf, *Party Politics in America*, 7th ed. (New York: HarperCollins Publishers, 1992), 13–14.

6   Gerald M. Pomper and Susan S. Lederman, *Elections in America*, 2nd ed. (New York: Longman, 1980), 173–174.

7   Woodrow Wilson quoted in James W. Davis, *The President as Party Leader* (New York: Greenwood Press, 1992), 10.

8   See, for example, John D. Bradley, "Party Platforms and Party Performance Concerning Social Security," *Polity* 1, 337–358; Ian Budge and Richard I. Hofferbert, "Mandates and Policy Outputs: U.S. Party Platforms and Federal Expenditures," *American Political Science Review* 84, 111–131; Paul T. David, "Party Platforms as National Plans," *Public Administration Review* 31, 303–315.

9   Jeff Fishel, *Presidents and Promise: From Campaign Pledge to Presidential Performance* (Washington, DC: CQ Press, 1985), 187.

10 Stephen J. Wayne, *The Road to the White House 1996* (New York: St. Martin's Press, 1996), 162.

11 See Michael G. Krukones, *Promises and Performance: Presidential Campaigns as Policy Predictors* (Lanham, MD: University Press of America, 1984).

12 Larry J. Sabato, *The Party's Just Begun: Shaping Political Parties for America's Future* (Glenville, IL: Scott, Foresman/Little, Brown College Division, 1988), 56.

13 Seventeen party platforms were formalized at the party conventions during this time period.

14 For example, see Byron W. Daynes and Glen Sussman, *The American Presidency and the Social Agenda* (Upper Saddle River, NJ: Prentice Hall, 2001).

15 See Daynes and Sussman, *The American Presidency and the Social Agenda*.

16 Sabato, *The Party's Just Begun*, 46.

17 Donald R. Matthews and James A. Stimson, *Yeas and Nays: Normal Decision-Making in the U.S. House of Representatives* (New York: John Wiley & Sons, 1975), 2.

18 Barbara Hinckley, *Stability and Change in Congress*, 4th ed. (New York: Harper & Row, Publishers), 210.

19 Ibid., 211.

20 Alan Rosenthal, "On Analyzing States," in Alan Rosenthal and Maureen Moakley, eds. *The Political Life of the American States* (New York: Praeger, 1984), 2. See also Carl E. Van Horn, "The Quiet Revolution," in Carl E. Van Horn, ed. *The State of the States* (Washington, DC: CQ Press, 1989), 8–9.

21 David E. Price, *Bringing Back the Parties* (Washington, DC: CQ Press, 1984), 83–84.

22 The percentage difference index used in Table 4.4 was calculated using the support scores for voting on environmental legislation from Sheldon Kamieniecki, "Political Parties and Environmental Policy," in James P. Lester, ed. *Environmental*

Politics and Policy: Theories and Evidence, 2nd ed. (Durham: Duke Unversity Press, 1995), 159–161. Mean support scores were provided for the 25 states. Because data were apparently missing for some years in different states, we tried to be consistent in presenting the data in Table 4.4 and used the data in appropriate years accordingly for the purpose of comparison.

23 The twenty-five states were placed into the appropriate regional category based upon the Bureau of the Census methodology. See U.S. Bureau of the Census. *Statistical Abstract of the United States: 1999.* (Washington, DC: United States Government Printing Office, 1999).

24 For a good overview of California politics see Charles G. Bell, "California," in Alan Rosenthal and Maureen Moakley, eds. *The Political Life of the American States* (New York: Praeger, 1984), 31–59.

25 "Hope Dries Up for Bill on California Desert," *Congressional Quarterly Weekly Report,* October 1, 1994, 2784.

26 "California Desert Bill Advances," *1993 Congressional Quarterly Almanac* (Washington, DC: CQ Press, 1993), 276.

27 Hanna J. Cortner and Margaret A. Moote, *The Politics of Ecosystem Management* (Washington, DC: Island Press, 1999), 2–3.

28 Steven J. Rosenstone and John Mark Hansen, *Mobilization, Participation, and Democracy in America* (New York: Macmillan Publishing Company, 1993), 101.

29 See, for example, David Truman, *The Governmental Process,* 2nd ed. (New York: Alfred A. Knopf, 1971).

30 Theodore J. Lowi, *The End of Liberalism,* 2nd ed., (New York: W.W. Norton, 1979), 51.

31 Burdett A. Loomis and Allan J. Ciglar, "Introduction: The Changing Nature of Interest Group Politics," in Allan J. Ciglar and Burdett A. Loomis, eds., *Interest Group Politics,* 2nd ed. (Washington, DC: CQ Press, 1986), 24.

32 Terry M. Moe, *The Organization of Interests: Incentives and the Internal Dynamics of Political Interest Groups* (Chicago: The University of Chicago Press, 1980), 167.

33 Ibid., 113.

34 Mancur Olson, *The Logic of Collective Action: Public Goods and the Theory of Groups* (Cambridge, MA: Harvard University Press, 1971), Chapter 3.

35 Loomis and Cigler, "Introduction," 10.

36 Christopher J. Bosso, "After the Movement: Environmental Activism in the 1990s," in Norman J. Vig and Michael E. Kraft, eds. *Environmental Policy in the 1990s: Toward a New Agenda,* 2nd ed. (Washington, DC: CQ Press, 1994), 35.

37 Samuel H. Barnes and Max Kaase, eds. *Political Action: Mass Participation in Five Western Democracies* (Beverly Hills, CA: SAGE Publications, 1979).

38 Charles C. Euchner, *Extraordinary Politics: How Protest and Dissent Are Challenging American Democracy* (Boulder, CO: Westview Press, 1996), 20–21.

39 Thomas C. Beierle, "Public Participation in Environmental Decisions: An Evaluation Framework Using Social Goals," Discussion Paper 99–06 (Washington, DC: Resources for the Future, November, 1998), 2, **http://www.rff.org/disc_papers/PDF_files/9906.pdf.** Retrieved December 15, 1999.

40 Ibid.

41 Jerrell Richer, "Green Giving: An Analysis of Contributions to Major U.S. Environmental Groups," Discussion Paper 95–39. (Washington, DC: Resources for the Future, September 1995), **http://www.rff.org/disc_papers/PDF_files/9539.pdf.** Retrieved December 15, 1999.

42 See Robert Cameron Mitchell, Angela G. Mertig, Riley E. Dunlap, "Twenty Years of Environmental Mobilization," in Riley E. Dunlap and Angela E. Mertig, eds. *American Environmentalism: The U.S. Environmental Movement, 1970–1990* (New York: Taylor & Francis, 1992), 15.

43 Membership data were obtained from Foundation for Public Affairs, *Public Interest Profiles, 1996/1997* (Washington, DC: Congressional Quarterly, Inc., 1996), Chapter 6.

44 See, for example, Rochelle L. Stanfield, "Environmental Lobby's Changing of the Guard is Part of Movement's Evolution," *National Journal*, 17, June 8, 1985.

45 Michael E. Kraft, *Environmental Policy and Politics* (New York: HarperCollins College Publishers, 1996), 201.

46 See the Wilderness Society's Web site at **http://www.wildernesssociety.org.** Retrieved March 9, 2000. See also Tedd Saunders and Loretta McGovern, *The Bottom Line of Green Is Black: Strategies for Creating Profitable and Environmentally Sound Businesses* (New York: Harper San Francisco, 1993).

47 See *The Washington Post*, September 29, 1995, A3.

48 Friends of the Earth, et. al., *Ronald Reagan and the American Environment: An Indictment, Alternate Budget Proposal, and Citizen's Guide to Action* (San Francisco: Brick House Publishing Company, 1982).

49 Ibid., 6

50 Jay Hair quoted in "November 98 Had a Green Tint Wildlife Federation Finds," *The Washington Post*, December 24, 1994, A4.

51 Tom Kenworthy, "Wilderness Society Sold Timber Cut on His Montana Ranch," *The Washington Post*, April 7, 1995, A28.

52 See the National Wildlife Federation's Web site at: **http://www.nwf.org.**

53 See, for example, the Sierra Club's Web site at **http://www.sierraclub.org** and the Wilderness Society's Web site at **http://wilderness.org**

54 See "The Birth of Environmentalism" at **http://www.edf.org/AboutUs/f_birthof. html.** Retrieved March 10, 2000.

55 Michael E. Kraft, *Environmental Policy and Politics: Toward the Twenty-First Century* (New York: HarperCollins College Publishers, 1996), 74.

56 Benjamin Kline, *First Along the River: A Brief History of the U.S. Environmental Movement*, 2nd ed. (San Francisco: Acada Books, 2000), 90.

57 Rogene A. Buchholz, *Principles of Environmental Management: The Greening of Business*, 2nd ed. (Upper Saddle River, NJ: Prentice Hall, 1998), 98.

58 Walter A. Rosenbaum, *Environmental Politics and Policy*, 3rd ed. (Washington, DC: CQ Press, 1995), 26.

59 Zachary A. Smith, *The Environmental Policy Paradox*, 2nd ed. (Englewood Cliffs, NJ: Prentice-Hall, Inc., 1995), 17.

60 Craig A. Rimmerman, *The New Citizenship: Unconventional Politics, Activism, and Service* (Boulder, CO: Westview Press, 1997), 66.

61 The following classification scheme is drawn from a discussion by Carl Deal, *The Greenpeace Guide to Anti-Environmental Organizations* (Berkeley, CA: Odonian Press, 1993), Chapter 2.

62 Switzer, *Green Backlash*, 135–140.

63 Ruth Marcus, "Focus: A Flood of Secret Dollars," *The Virginian-Pilot*, May 22, 2000, A4.

64 See "Recognizing an Anti-Environment Ruse," *National Wildlife*, 30 October/ November 1992, 30.

65 Ibid.

66   Thomas A. Lewis, "You Can't Judge a Group by Its Cover," *National Wildlife*, 30 October/November 1992, 9.

67   Reported in Jacqueline Vaught Switzer, *Green Backlash: The History and Politics of Environmental Opposition in the U.S.* (Boulder, CO: Lynn Reinner, 1997), 105.

68   See "Bush Signs Major Revision of Anti-Pollution Law," *The New York Times*, November 16, 1990, A28.

69   Ibid.

70   See R. McGreggor Cawley, *Federal Land, Western Anger: The Sagebrush Rebellion and Environmental Politics* (Lawrence, KS: University Press of Kansas, 1993), 11–12.

71   John G. Francis and Richard Ganzel, "Conclusion: Public Lands, Natural Resources, and the Shaping of American Federalism," in John G. Francis and Richard Ganzel, eds. *Western Public Lands* (Totowa, NJ: Rowan and Allanheld, 1984), 29.

72   See Sandra K. Davis, "Fighting Over Public Lands: Interest Groups, States, and the Federal Government," in Charles Davis, ed. *Western Public Lands and Environmental Politics* (Boulder, CO: Westview Press, 1997), 11; Dale Krane, "American Federalism, State Governments and Public Policy," *PS: Political Science and Politics*, Vol. 26 (1993), 187.

73   Hays, *Explorations in Environmental History*, 372.

74   Although there are differences between the two movements, there are also common interests shared by them. For the purpose of this brief assessment, we discuss them together.

75   See Terry L. Anderson and Peter J. Hill, eds. *Environmental Federalism* (Lanham, MD: Rowan and Littlefield, 1997).

76   David Helvarg, *The War Against the Greens: The "Wise Use" Movement, the New Right, and Anti-Environmental Violence* (San Francisco, CA: Sierra Club Books, 1994), 11.

77   Thomas A. Lewis, "Cloaked in a Wise Disguise," *National Wildlife* 30 (October/November 1992), 7.

78   See Davis, "Fighting Over Public Lands: Interest Groups, States, and the Federal Government," 22–23.

79   Cortner and Moote, *The Politics of Ecosystem Management*, 115.

80   See, for example, Helvarg, *The War Against the Greens*, 6; Christopher McGrory Klyza, *Who Controls Public Lands? Mining, Forestry, and Grazing Policies, 1870–1990* (Chapel Hill, NC: The University of North Carolina Press, 1996), 147.

81   See John C. Miles, *Guardians of the Parks* (Washington, DC: Taylor & Francis, 1995), 139.

82   Ibid., 166.

83   See William R. Nester, *The War for America's Natural Resources* (New York: St. Martin's Press, 1997), 91.

84   See the People for the USA's Web site at **http://www.pfw.org/pospaper/epeg.html.**

85   Quoted in Cortner and Moote, *The Politics of Ecosystem Management*, 116–117.

5

Congress and Environmental Policy

One of the most distinctive features of constitutional government in the United States is the separation of power between the legislative, executive, and judicial branches of government. This division of authority, with each branch checking and balancing the actions of the other, provides for a creative blending and sharing of responsibility for national policy making. Dividing authority in this way also promotes competition among the branches, each seeking ascendancy, thereby ensuring institutional rivalry, conflict, and inefficiency.[1] The framers deliberately encouraged this interbranch competition because they were anxious to avoid concentrating too much power in any one branch. They also wished to create a government that would be responsive to the diverse interests within the nation.

Congress has an especially important role in making, amending, and rescinding public policy. The policy-making process has been identified as having five stages: problem identification, policy formulation, policy adoption, policy implementation, and policy evaluation.[2] While Congress has a significant part to play in each of these stages, its role is especially important in the policy formulation and adoption stages. It is here that competing proposals for solving public problems are initiated and debated, and coalition building, bargaining, and compromising occur in an effort to build majority consensus around particular initiatives. Congressional appropriations affect agency funding and staffing levels; oversight authority can influence the pace of policy implementation; and hearings and investigations can gather or dispense information to shape agency decisions. Congressional policy making is affected by structural, operational, procedural, and behavioral factors. To understand congressional decision making requires some familiarity with these factors.

The general structure of Congress is familiar to most Americans, especially its bicameral structure composed of a lower house (House of Representatives) with representation based on population and an upper house (U.S. Senate) based on the notion of state equality. The larger House, with its 435 members and two-year terms, was originally thought to be the more popular and responsive of the two bodies. The 100-member Senate, with its six-year terms, was thought to better represent the broader interests of the state and nation and to be a more deliberative body. While the purported advantages of each body might be disputed, it is clear that the operating environments of the two chambers differ considerably. (Table 5.1 shows some of these key differences.) Some have argued, for example, that the larger size of the House, and the power lodged in certain positions (Speaker of the House) and committees (Rules) impedes its effectiveness relative to the Senate in addressing current problems.

The specific institutional characteristics of Congress are less well known, specifically the committee and subcommittee structure, procedural rules, leadership structure, informal behavior patterns, and constitutional authority. These factors help define the institutional context within which policy making occurs, and there is considerable variety from the House to the Senate on many of these matters.

Certain characteristics also distinguish environmental policies from those in other policy domains. David Davis identifies five distinguishing features that set environmental policy apart and make it interesting: high and sustained public interest, issues that elicit emotions or passions, the breadth and scope of environmental effects, the risk to health from inaction or ineffective policies, and the need to understand and manage sophisticated technology.[3]

This chapter examines the role of Congress in environmental policy making, and some of the factors affecting it. It considers the institutional characteristics of Congress, the congressional arenas most relevant to environmental policy making, and the formal and informal decision-making mechanisms, processes, and behaviors that shape environmental policy making. Specific examples are provided to illustrate how these forces influence decisions on environmental matters. Attention is devoted to more recent congressional deliberations on matters of environmental relevance. In recent years, environmental congressional deliberations have resulted in either inaction or minor incremental changes in existing policy rather than the more comprehensive changes sought by environ-

TABLE 5.1

House-Senate Differences: A Summary

House	Senate
435 members serving two-year terms.	100 members serving rotating six-year terms.
House members have only one major committee assignment, thus tend to be policy specialists.	Senators have two or more major committee assignments, tend to be policy generalists.
Speaker's referral of bills to committee is hard to challenge.	Referral decisions are easy to challenge.
Committees almost always consider legislation first before the Senate does.	Committee consideration is easily bypassed.
Scheduling and rules are controlled by majority party.	Scheduling and rules are generally agreed to by majority and minority leaders.
Rules Committee is powerful: controls time of debate, admissibility of amendments.	Rules Committee is weak; few limits on debate or amendments.
Debates are usually limited to one hour.	Unlimited debate unless shortened by unanimous consent or by invoking cloture.
Nongermane amendments may not be introduced from floor.	Nongermane amendments may be introduced from the floor.

Source: James Q. Wilson and John J. Dilulio, Jr. *American Government* (Boston, MA: Houghton-Mifflin, 1998), 343.

mental advocates. The gridlock and stalemate that currently stymies efforts to pass more encompassing environmental policies of the type approved during the environmental heydays of the 1970s is likely to continue to characterize environmental policy in the near term.

How Congress Influences Policy

Structural Factors

Beyond the general structural factors discussed above that distinguish the U.S. Senate from the House of Representatives, there are more specific structural features that characterize congressional decision making and shape environmental policy making. Five such characteristics deserve brief attention. These include fragmentation/dispersion of power, decentralization, multiple checkpoints or avenues of access, parochialism, and short election cycles. Four consequences of these characteristics are important—institutional conflict, incrementalism, gridlock, and the need for integration of policy. Each of these features and its consequences will be considered in turn.

Fragmentation/Dispersion of Power   The environmental policy process in Congress is highly fragmented, with power dispersed widely in several different committees and subcommittees. Nearly two-thirds of the standing committees in the House claim some responsibility for environmental matters. Similar jurisdictional overlap occurs among Senate committees and subcommittees, often leading to rivalry and competition. For example, six different Senate committees and four House committees could claim jurisdiction over bills concerning global warming.[4] Jurisdictional division of labor is sometimes based on subject matter (e.g., Senate Committee on Energy and Natural Resources, House Energy and Commerce Committee) and sometimes on broader concerns that include the environment along with other issues (e.g., Senate Governmental Affairs, House Governmental Operations committees). Often such committees (e.g., the Energy and Mineral Resources Subcommittee of the House Resources Committee) are partial to the interests they purportedly control. For example, in 1996 this particular subcommittee was loaded with representatives from states known for energy production, including Texas and California (each with two representatives), and Tennessee, Wyoming, Louisiana, West Virginia, Idaho, and Colorado (each with one representative); and one representative from Hawaii.[5]

The chairpersons of key legislative committees (e.g., Senate Committee on the Environment and Public Works) and subcommittees (Superfund, Recycling, Solid Waste Management; Toxic Substances, Research, and Development; Clean Air and Nuclear Regulation; and Clean Water, Fisheries and Wildlife) are highly influential in advancing legislation and targeting resources to problems. Woodrow Wilson noted this extraordinary influence several decades ago when he described our form of government as ". . . a government by the chairmen of the Standing Committees of Congress."[6] Power in Congress became more fragmented as a result of reforms adopted in 1970 that reduced the power of committee chairpersons and increased that of subcommittee chairs. Nonetheless, today both committee and subcommittee chairs are able to function as environmental policy entrepreneurs. That is, they can seek ways to bring together a majority on behalf of (or sometimes against) particular environmental issues and proposals. Table 5.2 describes the jurisdiction and lists the chairs of the major committees in both the House and the Senate.

Decentralization   Because of the fragmentation and dispersion of power in Congress, decision making tends to be decentralized. Environmental bills are first crafted and debated in subcommittees, then, if approved, advance to the full committee. Finally, some bills emerge on the floor of the House and Senate for deliberation and vote. Most proposals fail to reach the floor in either chamber. This decentralized decision-making process has been criticized by some; others note its advantages.[7]

On the positive side, the congressional committee structure provides avenues of access for partisans of various stripes which, coupled with access to the courts and state and local government decision-making bodies, offer numerous venues for various advocacy groups to advance their particular environmental agendas. On the downside, transaction costs are high for legislative leaders who are trying to navigate legislative proposals through the labyrinth of committees and subcommittees. They must avoid becoming ensnared in the complex procedures, running afoul of established norms, and getting entangled in the myriad rules of legislative decision making. House and Senate leaders are not without power in this decentralized environment. They have agenda-setting powers, and their preferences can influence chamber priorities. Their personal skills are also important: to be successful, legislative leaders must be adept at bargaining, compromise, and coalition building.

Multiple Checks/Access Points   Decentralized decision making and fragmented power offers both advocates and opponents of environmental policy initiatives numerous access and veto points in the process. Proponents can try to influence the arena in which their proposals are considered, seeking the most congenial environment to enhance prospects for passage of their initiatives. For example, an advocate for change in nuclear energy policy must decide whether to try to have the bill sent for deliberation to the Senate Environmental and Public Works Committee versus the Energy and Natural Resources Committee, or in the House to the Energy and Commerce Committee versus the Interior and Insular Affairs Committee (see Table 5.2). Opponents can fashion strategies to kill ill-advised bills and "at various stages" they are afforded numerous opportunities to defeat them. This was illustrated in recent congressional deliberations over elevation of the Environmental Protection Agency to cabinet-level status (see Chapter 7). Despite approval by subcommittees and committees in both the House and Senate, and a favorable vote on the floor of the Senate, opponents tacked amendments onto the bill in the House Rules Committee. Supporters of the bill resisted these amendments, eventually killing the bill before it reached a floor vote. Passing environmental bills into law is much more difficult than defeating such legislative initiatives.

Table 5.3 (page 130), lists significant environmental legislation that did pass between 1961 and 2000. Some of these are truly landmark laws: the National Environmental Policy Act (1969), the Clean Air Act (1963), the Endangered Species Act (1966), the Comprehensive Environmental Response, Compensation and Liability Act ("Superfund") (1980), and the Clean Air Amendments (1990).[8]

Figure 5.1A (page 131) goes further, showing environmental legislation by category from 1932 through 1998, breaking down the subject matter of laws into six

TABLE 5.2

U.S. Congressional Committees Related to the Environment, 2001

	Senate	
Committee Name	*Chair*	*Description*
Agriculture, Nutrition, and Forestry	Tom Harkin (D), Iowa	Recommends agricultural policy and research; forestry policy; soil conservation; pesticides; food safety; watershed management and flood control, private forest reserves.
Appropriations	Robert Byrd (D), West Virginia	Appropriates funds for all government operations, including Army Corps of Engineers; Bureau of Land Management; Environmental Protection Agency; Food and Drug Administration; Fish and Wildlife Service; Forest Service; international monetary and financial funds; Mineral Management Service, Office of Surface Mining; National Oceanic and Atmospheric Administration; National Park Service; Nuclear Regulatory Commission; Soil Conservation Service, Tennessee Valley Authority.
Commerce, Science, and Transportation	Ernest Hollings (D), South Carolina	Oversees interstate commerce and transportation; hazardous materials transportation; auto fuel efficiency; coastal zone management; inland waterways; marine fisheries; marine mammals; oceans; weather and atmospheric activities; environmental technology research and development; Outer Continental Shelf.
Energy and Natural Resources	Jeff Bingaman (D), New Mexico	Oversees natural energy policy, including international energy affairs; strategic petroleum reserves; Outer Continental Shelf leasing; nuclear waste policy; privatization of federal assets; mining, public lands, forests, and parks; regulation of Trans-Alaska Pipeline System and other oil or gas pipelines transportation systems within Alaska; Natural Petroleum Reserve of Alaska; Alaska National Interest Lands Conservation Act; Antarctica; Arctic research and energy development, scenic rivers, national trails, national recreation areas.
Environment and Public Works	James Jeffords (I), Vermont	Oversees environmental policy, research and development; Clean Water Act; International environmental issues; air, water, noise pollution; highways; fisheries and wildlife; outer continental shelf; flood control; nonmilitary nuclear energy; ocean dumping; public works; solid waste disposal and cleanup; recycling; water resources; toxic substances; indoor air pollution, public works, dams, bridges.

continued

TABLE 5.2

(continued)

Senate		
Committee Name	Chair	Description
Committee on Foreign Relations	Joseph Biden (D), Delaware	Oversees policies on international relations, including economics, trade, oceans, and the environment.
Governmental Affairs	Joseph Lieberman (D), Connecticut	Oversight for all energy, environment, natural resources programs, and agencies, including EPA, Energy, and Interior. Includes agency organization and status.

House		
Committee Name	Chair	Description
Agriculture	Larry Combest (R), Texas	Oversees agricultural policy; forest policy; soil conservation; alternative fuels; pesticides; food safety; plant, soil, and agricultural engineering; protection of birds and animals on agricultural lands.
Appropriations	C.W. Bill Young (R), Florida	Appropriates funds for all government operations, including Army Corps of Engineers; Bureau of Land Management; Environmental Protection Agency; Food and Drug Administration; Fish and Wildlife Service; Forest Service; Department of Interior; International monetary and financial funds; Mineral Management Service, Office of Surface Mining, National Oceanic and Atmospheric Administration; National Park Service; Nuclear Regulatory Commission; Soil Conservation Service; Tennessee Valley Authority.
Committee on the Budget	John R. Kasich (R), Ohio	Recommends spending and revenue targets for the rest of Congress, including those committees with jurisdiction over environmental legislation.
Commerce	Tom J. Bliley, Jr. (R), Virginia	Oversees national energy policy and regulation; energy resources; energy conservation; power generation and marketing; solar energy; renewable energy; synthetic fuels; nuclear energy; interstate energy compacts; health and the environment; public health and quarantine; transportation of hazardous materials; solid and hazardous waste; Superfund; clean air and acid rain; groundwater; pesticides; safe drinking water; environmental labeling and toxic substances.
Government Reform and Oversight	Dan Burton (R), Indiana	Oversight for all energy, environmental, natural resources programs and agencies, including EPA, Energy, and Interior. Includes agency organization and status.

Resources	Don Young (R), Alaska	Authorizes budget and programs for national parks, national wildlife refuges, wild and scenic rivers, national trails, national recreation areas, National Wilderness Preservation System, Land and Water Conservation Fund; Native American Lands and Affairs; water rights and resources, fisheries; federal lands; parks and natural resources; interstate water compacts; minerals, mines, and mining; irrigation and reclamation; groundwater; nuclear energy and waste regulation.
Science	F. James Sensenbrenner, Jr. (R), Wisconsin	Oversees National Science Foundation, exploration of outer space, scientific research and development, climate and atmospheric research, biotechnology policy, Office of Science and Technology Policy; energy research and development; agricultural research; National Weather Service; National Oceanic and Atmospheric Administration; nuclear energy; facilities.
Transportation and Infrastructure	Bud Shuster (R), Pennsylvania	Authorizes flood control; pollution of navigable waters; bridges and dams; highways; Superfund; groundwater; hazardous materials, and transportation; wetlands; water power; inland waterways; railroads; transportation.

Source: Adapted and updated from "Environmental Turf in the New Congress," *The Environmental Forum* (March/April, 1995), 38–43; and "Congress 1995: An Environmental Scorecard," *Audubon* (March/April, 1995), 26–27.

categories: forestry, water conservation, land management, wildlife, natural resources, and air. Certain laws contained policy changes in more than one of these categories. The bar chart shows the variations in substantive legislative topics over time. For example, legislation regarding water conservation has been passed in each of the six decades shown, but laws regarding air pollution are concentrated in the past three decades. Legislation related to forestry shows more of a U-shaped distribution, with a flourish of activity in the 1930s, relative inactivity in the next several decades, and greater activity in the post-1984 period. The distribution of legislation in land management, natural resources, and wildlife is more even or uniform across the six-decade period. With data arrayed by decade, Figure 5.1B (page 132) plots the extent of legislative activity related to the environment from the 1930s onward, with the average for the 1970s, 1980s, and 1990s exceeding the average of any of the preceding four decades. One cautionary note: More environmental legislation does not necessarily mean more pro-environmental laws. For example, some of the legislation passed in the 1980s and 1990s actually weakened environmental protection. Also, Figure 5.1C (page 132) shows that the average amount of legislation passed on these topics in presidential election years is considerably higher than the average in nonpresidential election years.

Parochialism Electoral imperatives requiring legislators to provide particularized benefits to their constituents mean that local and regional concerns often trump

TABLE 5.3

Significant Pro-Environmental Legislation 1961–2000

Legislation	Public Law Number	Year	Senate D/R	House D/R
Clean Air Act	88-206	1963	67/33	258/177
Wilderness Act	88-577	1964	67/33	258/177
Land and Water Conservation Fund Act	88-578	1964	67/33	258/177
Water Quality Act	89-234	1965	68/32	295/140
Highway Beautification Act	89-285	1965	68/32	295/140
Endangered Species Conservation Act	89-669	1966	68-32	295/140
Air Quality Act	90-148	1967	64/36	247/187
National Wild and Scenic Rivers Act	90-542	1968	64/36	247/187
National Trail System	90-543	1968	64/36	247/187
Endangered Species Act Amendments	91-135	1969	57/43	243/192
National Environmental Policy Act	91-190	1970	57/43	243/192
Water Quality Improvement Act	91-224	1970	57/43	243/192
Resource Recovery Act	91-512	1970	57/43	243/192
Environment Education Act	91-516	1970	57/43	243/192
Clean Air Act Amendments	91-604	1970	57/43	243/192
Alaska Native Claims Settlement Act	92-203	1971	54/44	254/180
Water Pollution Control Act	92-500	1972	54/44	254/180
Environmental Pesticides Control Act	92-516	1972	54/44	254/180
Marine Mammal Protection Act	92-522	1972	54/44	254/180
Marine Protection, Research, and Sanctuaries Act	92-532	1972	54/44	254/180
Noise Control Act	92-574	1972	54/44	254/180
Coastal Zone Management Act	92-583	1972	54/44	254/180
Endangered Species Act Amendments	93-205	1973	56/42	239/192
Safe Drinking Water Act	93-523	1974	56/42	239/192
Toxic Substances Control Act	94-469	1976	60/37	291/144
Federal Land Policy Management Act	94-579	1976	60/37	291/144
Resource Conservation and Recovery Act	94-580	1976	60/37	291/144
National Forest Management Act	94-588	1976	60/37	291/144
Surface Mining Control and Reclamation Act	95-87	1977	61/38	292/143
Clean Air Act Amendments	95-95	1977	61/38	292/143
Clean Water Act Amendments	95-217	1977	61/38	292/143
Superfund	96-150	1980	58/41	277/157
Alaska National Interest Lands Conservation Act	96-487	1980	58/41	277/157
Nuclear Waste Policy Act	97-425	1983	46/54	269/166
Resource Conservation and Recovery Amendments	98-616	1984	46/54	269/166
Safe Drinking Water Amendments	99-339	1986	47/53	253/182
Superfund Amendments and Reauthorization	99-499	1986	47/53	253/182
Clean Water Act Amendments	100-4	1987	54/46	257/178
Nuclear Waste Policy Amendments	100-203	1987	54/46	257/178
FIFRA Amendments	100-532	1988	54/46	257/178
Ocean Dumping Act	100-688	1988	54/46	257/178
Clean Air Act Amendments	101-549	1990	55/45	260/173
Energy Policy Act	102-486	1992	57/43	267/167
California Desert Protection Act	103-433	1994	57/43	258/175
Safe Drinking Water Act Amendments	104-182	1996	48/52	204/230
Food Quality Protection Act	104-170	1996	48/52	204/230
Transportation Equity Act	105-178	1998	45/55	207/227

Source: Adapted and updated from Dennis L. Soden and Brent S. Steel, "Evaluating the Environmental Presidency," in Dennis L. Soden, ed. *The Environmental Presidency* (Albany NY: SUNY Press, 1999), 315–317; Jacqueline V. Switzer, *Environmental Politics: Domestic and Global Dimensions* (Boston: Bedford/St Martin's, 2001), Appendix A, 311–314; and Norman J. Vig and Michael E. Kraft, eds. *Environmental Policy* (Washington, DC: CQ Press, 2000), Appendix 1, 389–395.

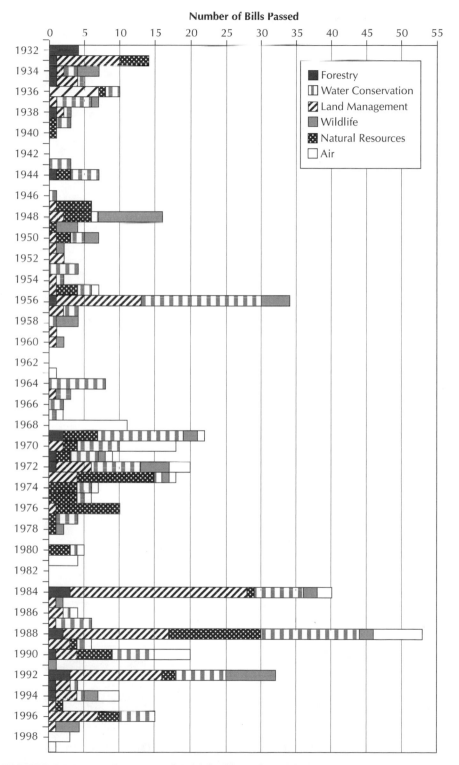

FIGURE 5.1A *Environmental Legislation 1932–1999*

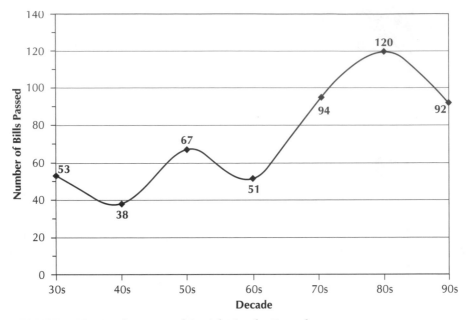

FIGURE 5.1B   *Environmental Legislation by Decade*

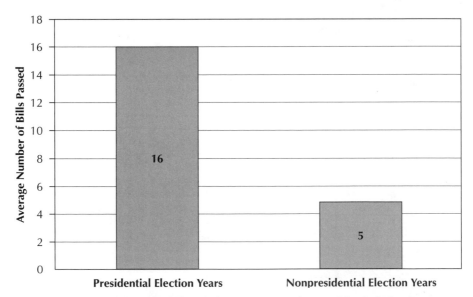

FIGURE 5.1C   *Environmental Legislation Average by Presidential Election Years*

national policy considerations. Most environmental policies are of two types: regulatory or distributive.[9] Regulatory policies restrict or extend the options that citizens or business might pursue to achieve their objectives, often through use of sanctions or incentives. Distributive policies confer "particularized benefits" or subsidies upon individuals, groups, or institutions. As Michael Kraft points out, environmental protection policies are usually regulatory, while natural resource and conservation policies are typically distributive.[10] Members of Congress stand to gain political points with their constituents from distributive policies that offer tangible benefits to "the folks back home." Such pork barrel projects provide a powerful motivation for vote-hungry legislators. In the quest for such parochial benefits, legislators often resort to vote trading, or logrolling, offering support for a fellow legislator's priority project in return for the promise of reciprocal support on a project benefiting one's own constituents. For example, in the energy and water area, Senator A might offer support to Senator B for a water project in B's district in return for B's support of a riverfront park in A's district.

Regional politics can come into play as well. For example, the issue of acid rain was addressed in the Clean Air Act of 1990, which required power plants to either install expensive scrubbers to remove sulfur dioxide from smokestacks or to switch to low-sulfur coal. Stanfield notes the differential regional effects of such a policy:

> The benefits of reducing acid rain would accrue primarily to the Northeast, while the billions of dollars in costs would land on the Midwest—from the loss of high-sulfur coal jobs and the considerable financial investment in pollution control. The West is somewhat sympathetic to control, which would benefit its low-sulfur coal industry, but not to a national subsidy program that would spread the cost burden beyond the Midwest.[11]

Policy debates of this type reinforce former Speaker of the House Tip O'Neill's well-known observation that "all politics is local."

Short Election Cycles   Members of Congress must keep their eyes on the electoral calendar, particularly those in the House of Representatives, who face voters every two years, and the one-third of the Senate that is elected every two years. Elected officials are forced by condensed election cycles to consider policy proposals from a short-term time perspective. Legislators must be in tune with public opinion; they favor proposals that bring substantial or quick benefits and those with low or deferred costs. Policy proposals are assessed in part based on whether they threaten or enhance the electoral fortunes of legislators. This leads to what Walter Rosenbaum calls "the tyranny of the immediate," where pressing problems with immediate consequences are given priority over longer-term concerns.[12] The compressed time perspective and preoccupation with reelection, not surprisingly, might lead legislators to defer action on longer-range problems such as global warming and act more quickly on localized problems such as hazardous waste.[13]

Incrementalism   The structural fragmentation within Congress, together with that resulting from federalism, separation of powers, and bureaucratic fiefdoms, makes integrated policy difficult and incrementalism all but inevitable. Incrementalism is policy making by small steps—policy change often results in minor modifications or adjustments in the status quo, infrequently in rapid, comprehensive, or radical change.[14] Congressional policy making, in the environmental policy area and others as well, often involves carving up policies into manageable pieces and attacking them piece by piece with little attention to the interrelationships among the parts. In the past few decades there has been reliance on command-and-control regulation and technology-specific standards, as well as programmatic emphasis on various environmental areas (e.g., air and water). Experimentation with other approaches (e.g., market incentives, pollution prevention) has been infrequent, episodic, and primarily at the margins of public policy.[15]

Gridlock   Policy gridlock is often the result of divided government, partisan bickering, constitutional divisions of power, and interest group maneuvering.[16] Gridlock occurs when different institutions are unable to resolve conflicts, with each blocking the other, preventing the development and enforcement of policy. When Congress is unable to resolve conflicts, its inability to act means public problems are not addressed. Divided government and environmental policy gridlock prevailed in the 1980s and 1990s. As a consequence, consensus has been difficult or impossible to achieve on major new environmental initiatives, renewal of existing programs has been problematic, and where policy change has occurred it has typically involved minor modification of past policy. Presidential proposals have been ignored or defeated in Congress, and the president has vetoed congressionally approved initiatives. Kraft attributes this policy stalemate to five factors in addition to divided authority and conflicting institutional and political incentives: intractable environmental problems, lack of public consensus on environmental policy, powerful special interests, high-cost solutions, and absence of effective political leadership.[17]

Institutional Conflict   The framers of the Constitution did not seek to avoid institutional conflict in the interest of promoting efficient decision making; they sought instead to ensure conflict and some inefficiency by establishing federalism and the separation of powers in three branches of government. Institutional conflict was also built into the constitutional relationship between the two chambers of Congress and among the committees and subcommittees in each chamber. It is not surprising that legislative turf battles are commonplace.

Fragmented authority has evolved among diverse agencies in the executive branch as well; adding to the conflict is that, once passed, policies must be implemented. Further, competition between the political parties and between the White House and Congress, particularly in the recent years of fierce partisanship, exacerbates conflict and adds to the obstacles facing those hoping to fashion rational, comprehensive environmental policies.

Examples of such discord abound: President Clinton and the post-1994 Republican Congress were at loggerheads over such issues as wetlands protection, endangered species protection, federal agency enforcement of environmental statutes, and regulation of air and water pollution.[18] Frequently conflict includes disagreement about both the ends (purposes) and the means (strategies) of environmental policy, but in recent years further conflict has resulted because Congress has had the edge over the president in initiating new policies. As noted by Sussman and Kelso:

... Congress, which has overshadowed the president in environmental initiatives, has sought to influence environmental policy via its control over the legislative process and oversight function, especially the authority vested in the powerful committee system.[19]

This congressional "edge" is especially evident when congressional partisanship is strong and when the party commanding a majority in both houses of Congress is a different party from the president's, as occurred in the 104th, 105th, and 106th Congresses.[20]

Need for Integrated Policy   Institutional fragmentation in Congress and other governmental institutions makes it difficult to forge consensus on what to do and how to do it, complicating the task of achieving integrated environmental policy.[21] The overlapping legislative committee jurisdictions and semiautonomous subcommittee activities involve numerous policymakers, each with their own agenda, resources, and prerogatives and operating with little or no coordinating effort. Congressional deliberations are also influenced by iron-triangle or issue-network relationships with administrative agencies and environmental interest groups (see Chapter 7). These subgovernments angle for approval or defeat of legislative policies that promote or do not impede their organizational interests.[22] Such networks improve prospects for communication, bargaining, and consensus building among diverse interests; however, each participant has a vested interest and jurisdictional turf to protect and may resist proposals for change that threaten their interest, turf, or primacy in the policy process.

Operational Characteristics

While these structural features and their consequences are important in understanding the institutional context of congressional decision making, certain operating mechanisms are also significant—specifically, the role of authorizing statutes, appropriations processes, and oversight activities. The success or failure of policy formulation and implementation often depends on legislative actions in these areas.

Authorizing Statutes   Enabling legislation not only sets broad goals and standards for environmental policies, it also specifies how those goals are to be implemented, sometimes in considerable detail. For example, such statutes might specify that risk-based approaches be used or that technology-based strategies be undertaken. The extent to which costs must figure into the decision differs from statute to statute. National policy goals are sometimes articulated in enabling legislation; other times, goal setting might be reserved for state action. Fiorino discusses this variation in the content of authorizing statutes indicating that some laws specify the medium to be used in reducing pollution, others the sector (public versus private) responsible for funding, and still others the impact of pollution (e.g., acid rain).[23] Congress clearly sets the direction of environmental policy by crafting authorizing statutes.

Appropriations   An alternate stream in the policy process involves the allocation of resources to carry out environmental policies. An important distinction is the role of congressional authorization and appropriation committees. Authorizing committees give agencies the legal authority to operate and specify the funding levels; appropriations committees give agencies the authority to spend money on environmental problems. Authorizing committees (i.e., standing committees) have close ties to the agencies they oversee. For example, the Senate Energy and Natural Resources Committee and the House Interior and Insular Affairs Committee authorize funds for the Park Service in the Department of Interior, just as congressional agriculture committees authorize funds for the Department of Agriculture. Authorized funding levels often exceed appropriations.[24]

Influential appropriations committee and subcommittee chairs and ranking members can channel funds to projects and locales that coincide with their priorities. Riders to appropriation bills can fund studies or earmark funds to pet projects. Environmental interest group leaders and their counterparts from business and industry know that it is important to stay on the good side of influential appropriations committee members; astute administrative agency leaders are aware of this requirement as well, especially if they want agency monies targeted to specific problems.[25] During the 104th and 105th Congress, Republican strategists relied heavily on the budget and appropriations process via funding cuts and riders as "backdoor" approaches to reform policy and constrain agencies, in lieu of enacting new statutes.[26]

Oversight   We have mentioned the important congressional committees that engage in oversight in both the House and Senate (see Table 5.2). In Chapter 2, oversight was also considered as one of the regulatory "sticks" that the federal government uses in its relations with states and localities. While oversight can and sometimes does lead to extensive control (critics refer to this as micromanagement), it can also be loose and ad hoc, depending on the preferences of those on the congressional committees and subcommittees. Oversight can facilitate or impede administrative change. Committee chairs often determine the scope and intensity of oversight activity. They can also influence which departments and agencies are responsible for particular programs.

For example, Representative Morris Udall was chair of the Interior Committee and chief sponsor of the Surface Mining Act creating the Office of Surface Mining. This office reasonably could have been placed in the Environmental Protection Agency, but Representative Udall wanted it put in the Department of the Interior because his committee had oversight responsibility for the Department of the Interior, but not the EPA. Davis uses this example to show how government procedures can influence environmental policy, and how members of Congress seek to keep new agencies within their jurisdiction.[27]

In some instances a broad range of oversight tools might be used—requests for agency testimony, congressional letters of inquiry, investigations, audits, reports, political pressure on agency personnel, and the like.[28] Agencies often object to intrusive congressional oversight, viewing it as disruptive and threatening to their autonomy. In response, they may attempt to manage Congress by developing close ties with the committee and subcommittee chairs and staff and cultivating a favorable view of agency purposes and programs. Sometimes agency heads and committee or subcommittee chairs jointly criticize agency performance. For example, shortly after her appointments as EPA head, Carol Browner complained at a House subcommittee hearing that she was "appalled" by her agency's "total lack of management, accountability, and discipline." The chair of the subcommittee agreed, citing the EPA as "one of the worst cesspools" of which he was aware.[29] In other instances, congressional oversight is routine, narrow, and nonintrusive. Certain committees are more likely than others to assume a significant oversight role—specifically, the Senate Committee on Environment and Public Works and the House Energy and Commerce Committee. The General Accounting Office is an auxiliary unit of Congress that conducts audits and evaluations of various publicly funded programs, and issues reports of its findings. Figure 5.2 presents the views of critics and defenders of Congress's oversight role.

Processes and Behavioral Characteristics

The structural characteristics and operational mechanisms in the legislative branch create and shape the environment in which public policy is made and carried out. A more specific examination of the policy process, especially as it influences environmental policy, involves examination of the modes of decision making and behavioral dynamics found in the legislative arena. Here the focus is on the nature of decision processes (detailed policy guidance, micromanagement) and links to relevant constituencies (partisanship, group pressures). Also considered is the political maneuvering (credit claiming), symbolic and self-serving politics (symbolism/policy layering, pork barreling, nongermane riders), and additional features tied to environmental policy making (reactive decision making, science

FIGURE 5.2   *A Summary of Views from Critics and Defenders of Congress's Oversight Role*

Critics

- Congresspersons (via committees and subcommittees) micromanage policy, ignoring the big picture.

- Congresspersons misuse positions of authority (e.g., committee chairs) to advance their own agendas and highlight their own issues.

- Congresspersons dramatize problems, seek bureaucratic solutions, impose rigid and unrealistic requirements on agencies, and then criticize the agencies for ineffectiveness.

- Congresspersons inadequately assess what is required to address problems, fail to allocate sufficient resources, and do not provide adequate support to implement programs.

- Congresspersons are anxious to gain the political benefits of attacking problems, but less prone to bear the costs of solutions.

Defenders

- Administrative agencies have had problems in issuing rules and achieving congressionally approved goals.

- Administrative agencies in the past have been reluctant to set firm standards and enforce legal mandates.

- Congress and environmental groups have often offset the White House's reluctance to act more aggressively on environmental problems.

- Congress has acted as a "conscience" for environmental resources—asserting public concern and holding agencies accountable for responding to it.

Source: Adapted with permission from Daniel J. Fiorino, *Making Environmental Policy* (Berkeley, CA: University of California Press, 1995), 68–69.

and politics, competing values, and public interest). These processes and behavioral characteristics, together with the structural features and operating mechanisms previously considered, provide additional insight into the legislative process and the environmental policies that emerge.

Detailed Policy Guidance As noted in Chapter 7, administrative agencies derive considerable power when they are given substantial discretionary authority. In recent years, Congress has reduced administrative discretion by specifying in considerable detail the standards, deadlines, and regulatory mandates. This leaves little "wiggle room" for administrators, who are expected to toe the line in conformance with congressional directives. In part, this move away from delegation to more controlling policy guidance is a reflection of the growing distrust between Congress and the White House regarding environmental policy—another consequence of divided government. Republican control of the White House in the 1980s led to environmentally hostile administrative actions that in turn resulted in a reassertion of congressional control, in the form of specific statutory guidance on environmental matters. The use of inflexible language and detailed prescriptive regulations, while a consequence of administrative foot-dragging or inaction, increases the costs of environmental regulation. It does, however, preserve congressional prerogatives to establish environmental policy, reduce the likelihood of poor administration, and enable aggrieved parties to bring legal action when agency administrators do not meet their responsibilities.[30] The flip side sometimes occurs as well: Congress may approve statutory language that is ambiguous, vague, and subject to multiple interpretations, resulting in part from legislators' inability to achieve consensus. In such instances it is left to the administrative agencies and courts to resolve the ambiguities through bargaining or litigation.[31]

Micromanagement In an effort to curb administrative discretion, particularly at the Environmental Protection Agency, Congress has tightened its legislative controls. Ironically such controls have been encouraged by both pro-industry congresspersons and by pro-environmental legislators—each seeking to influence EPA implementation and enforcement activities—one side seeking implementation delays and enforcement that is relaxed or sympathetic to business concerns, and the other side seeking to carry out legislatively mandated regulations in a timely and aggressive manner. These conflicting perspectives have led to battles over legislative language and resource allocation. As legislative guidance becomes more specific and controls tighten, administrative flexibility and discretion decrease, sometimes resulting in implementation failures or delays, reduced agency credibility, and increased litigation.[32] Those who view this trend favorably argue that tightened congressional control strengthens the hand of agency administrators by providing a counterweight to other influential agencies like the Office of Management and Budget; those with less favorable views question the extent of helpful guidance or support received by agencies from such close oversight.[33]

Partisanship Environmental policy issues often arouse partisan passions among legislators. While legislators in both parties like to be viewed as pro-environment, the votes on key issues indicate clear differences among Democrats and Republicans (see Chapter 4). The bipartisan League of Conservation Voters (LCV) and the Sierra Club (SC) issue national environmental scorecards rating legislators each year. Table 5.4 reports LCV and SC scorecard results for 1999 for the leadership of environmental committees. In the Senate, the Republican chairs have an average LCV score of 9 and an average SC score of 0, compared to the ranking Democrat's scores of 62 and 73, respectively. In both cases the chair and ranking minority party's scores are below the average for their respective parties. The average for Republican chairs is below the average for the Senate as a whole on both ratings; conversely, the average score for ranking Democrats is above the average for the Senate on both measures. A similar pattern is evident in the House, where the Republican chair's average LCV score is 1 and the average SC score is 0, while the ranking Democrat's score LCV score is 69 and the average SC score is 72; in each case these scores are below the average for the respective party. The Democrats' LCV and SC scores, and those of their ranking members, are well above that of the corresponding Senate and House average scores, and the Republicans' LCV and SC scores and leadership ratings are considerably below that of the average in each chamber.

Partisanship does make a difference in legislative voting behavior on environmental issues. Clearly the Democrats have a more pro-environment voting record on these issues than their Republican counterparts.[34] Other national legislative scorecards reinforce this point. For example, the Competitive Enterprise Foundation (CEF) issued a 1994-voting scorecard. The CEF advocates the principles of free enterprise and limited government. It is based on the belief that free markets and competition best serve the public interest. The CEF ratings cover issues that the organization considers to be key votes dealing with environmental issues. The CEF scores for Republican Senate and House chairs are 70 and 84, and for ranking Democrats are 28 and 28 respectively (see Table 5.4). In this instance, the chairs and ranking members in both legislative chambers are more supportive than member legislators of their respective parties on CEF issues. The Republican CEF scores and those of their committee chairs are well above the corresponding Senate and House average scores, and the Democrats' CEF scores and leadership ratings are considerably below the average in each chamber. The Republicans are clearly more in sync with CEF purposes than the Democrats on these key pro-business environmental votes.

Ideological and stylistic differences exist between Republicans and Democrats on environmental matters as well. Democrats are more likely to favor activist government, support intervention in business, and favor command-and-control regulation to achieve environmental objectives. Republicans rely more heavily on market-based approaches and seek alternatives to traditional command-and-control strategies. Figure 5.3 provides a continuum on the role of government regarding environmental policy.[35] In general, Republicans would prefer steps 1, 2, or 3 on the continuum—heavy reliance on the market and some controls, especially at the state and local level—while Democrats likely prefer 3, 4, and 5—government controls developed and implemented at all levels of government.

It should be noted that there is also an ideological continuum within political parties regarding environmental issues. For example, in a 1995 journalistic

TABLE 5.4

Rating the Leadership of Environmental Committees: National Environmental Scorecard, 1999

		Senate						
		Scores*			Ranking	Scores		
Committee	Chairman	LCV	SC	CEF	Democrat	LCV	SC	CEF
Agriculture	Lugar (IN)	33	0	22	Harkin (IA)	89	100	50
Appropriations	Stevens (AK)	0	0	75	Byrd (WV)	22	17	33
Commerce, Science, and Transportation	McCain (AZ)	11	0	78	Hollings (SC)	56	83	25
Energy and Natural Resources	Murkowski (AK)	0	0	88	Bingaman (NM)	67	83	22
Environment and Public Works	Smith (NH)	0	0	89	Baucus (MT)	78	83	11

Committee Leaders Compared to Party Average

Senate Committee Chair Average	Chairmen	9	0	70	Ranking Democrat	62	73	28
Senate Party Average	Republican Average	13	9	61	Democrat Average	76	86	17

Senate Average: LCV=41; SC=47; CEF=41

		House						
		Scores			Ranking	Scores		
Committee	Chairman	LCV	SC	CEF	Democrat	LCV	SC	CEF
Agriculture	Combest (TX-19)	0	0	92	Stenholm (TX-17)	0	13	88
Appropriations	Young, B. (FL-10)	0	0	56	Obey (WI-7)	94	88	14
Commerce	Bliley (VA-7)	0	0	92	Dingell (MI-16)	81	86	22
Resources	Young, D. (AK-AL)	6	0	96	Miller,G (CA-7)	94	100	8
Transportation & Infrastructure	Shuster (PA-9)	0	0	-	Oberstar (MN)	75	75	8

Committee Leaders Compared to Party Average

House Committee Average	Chairmen	1	0	84	Ranking Democrat	69	72	28
House Party Average	Republican Average	16	19	77	Democrat Average	78	83	18

House Average: LCV=46; SC=50; CEF=47

Source: Adapted from: **http://congress.scorecardlcu.org/leadership.htm http://www.vote-smart. org/index.phtml**

*LCV= League of Conservation Voters; SC= Sierra Club; CEF= Competitive Enterprise Foundation

1. _____2. _____3. _____4. _____5.

1. Free market
2. Use of market forces with some government controls
3. Government controls on the state and local level (which may or may not utilize market or market-like mechanisms)
4. Government controls developed on the national level and implemented on the state or local level
5. Controls developed and implemented on the national level (total national control)

Source: Zachary A. Smith, *The Environmental Paradox* (Englewood Cliffs, NJ: Prentice Hall, 1992), 30.

FIGURE 5.3   *Continuum on the Role of Government in Environmental Policy*

profile of conservative House Majority Whip Tom DeLay, R-TX, he was asked whether there is any regulation he would like to see retained. He replied, "I can't think of one," later comparing the EPA to the Gestapo. More moderate legislators like the late John Chafee, R-RI, former chair of the Senate Environment and Public Works Committee, attempted to balance two seemingly irreconcilable objectives: being a good Republican and a good environmentalist, a tricky balancing act.[36] Similarly, ranking Democrats on environmentally relevant committees vary from conservative Senator Robert Byrd (WV, Appropriations—LCV score=22, SC score=17) to liberal Tom Harkin (IA, Agriculture—LCV score=89; SC score=100) and from conservative Representative Charles Stenholm (TX, Agriculture—LCV score=0, SC score=13) to liberal George Miller (CA, Resources—LCV score=94, SC score=100).

SENATOR JOHN CHAFEE: ENVIRONMENTAL DEFENDER[1]

Senator John Chafee of Rhode Island, a moderate Republican who championed environmental issues in Congress for more than 20 years, died in 1999, in his fourth U.S. Senate term. Chafee was the only Republican to be elected to the Senate from Rhode Island in the past 68 years, a testament to his ability to cross party lines. The remainder of the state's congressional delegation is Democratic. "When you think of the term 'bipartisan,' you immediately think of John Chafee, known throughout his beloved Rhode Island simply as 'the man you can trust,'" said President Bill Clinton following the Senator's death. "I am particularly grateful for his . . . concern for the environment . . ."

As chairman of the Senate Environment and Public Works Committee, Chafee played a key role in drafting major environmental regulation, including the Clean Air Act, Clean Water Act and Safe Drinking Water Act. He also created the National Estuary Program to protect coastal resources, and helped steer the bill to enactment over a veto attempt by

continued

President Ronald Reagan in 1987. The senator was an early proponent of steps to study the problem of global climate change caused by the emission of carbon dioxide and other greenhouse gases. He helped bring about a more aggressive national strategy to address the problem, winning Senate approval of the UN climate change treaty, an agreement to limit greenhouse gas emissions signed in 1997 by the United States and 142 other nations at the Rio Earth Summit.

Chafee authored the Superfund program, created in 1980 to direct and fund the cleanup of hazardous waste dump sites and leaking underground storage tanks across America. The program has made millions of dollars available for the cleanup of sites nationwide. The senator also wrote the 1993 law establishing the nation's first indoor air hazard research and response program. Included in the legislation were provisions to expand "sick building" assessments and develop state indoor air plans to reduce exposure to such hazards as radon, asbestos, and tobacco smoke.

The Oil Pollution Act of 1990, which requires spillers to pay for oil cleanup and to compensate injured parties, was crafted in part by Chafee. To further preserve fragile coastal regions, Chafee sponsored the Coastal Barrier Resources Act of 1982, updated in 1990, which established a system of shoreline areas to be protected from development. The senator worked aggressively for wetlands conservation, helping to expand the National Wildlife Refuge System and reforming tax policy to encourage the preservation of open space. He sponsored the North American Wetlands Conservation Act to preserve the wetlands habitat of migratory birds, and authored the successful law to reverse the decline of the striped bass. Further, Chafee sought to create a link between U.S. environmental goals and transportation policy. Beginning with legislation approved in 1991 and strengthened in 2000, states can use highway funds for public transit improvements, mitigation of traffic congestion, auto vehicle inspection and maintenance, bicycle and pedestrian projects, and historic preservation activities.

Chafee received the League of Conservation Voters 1999 Lifetime Achievement Award. At a press briefing held by the Republicans for Environmental Protection (REP), Republican senators and representatives in attendance acknowledged that they looked to Chafee for leadership on environmental issues. On learning of Chafee's death, REP director Sam Booher remarked, "That is a loss, that's a loss both to the Republican party and to those of us in the Republican party that care about the environment." "His leadership steered our nation on a course of environmental conservation and protection," said Sierra Club executive director Carl Pope, "Like the lands he fought to protect, Senator Chafee is widely admired and completely irreplaceable."

---

[1]Excerpted and adapted with permission from **http://ens.lycos.com/ens/oct99/1999L-10-25-06.html**.

Nonetheless, Davis points out that when times change and their electoral prospects require it, parties and politicians can change their colors quickly: President Nixon recognized that supporting clean air and water policies could garner votes, while President Reagan pursued an anti-environment agenda in the 1980s. Republican members of Congress elected in 1994 took actions hostile to the environment, only to reverse course (or moderate their hostility) in the mid-1990s to conform more closely to favorable public opinion on pollution control issues.[37]

CASE STUDY: THE EVERGLADES RESTORATION ACT

The issue of Everglades restoration was examined in Chapter 2 in the context of the sugar tax fight in Florida. Everglades restoration emerged on the national policy agenda as well. Indeed, the 106th Congress passed and President Bill Clinton signed an Everglades rescue bill that U.S. Senator Bob Graham, D-FL, and U.S. Representative Clay Shaw, R-FL, have described as "[t]he largest environmental restoration project in the history of the world."[1]

With all of the obstacles to congressional passage of major environmental legislation, and the rancor among the political parties in recent years, what accounts for successful passage of this bipartisan legislation? Votes in the House (394–14) and the Senate (85–1) indicate broad consensus behind the $7.8 billion plan to restore health to the threatened Everglades.[2] Strong support from the Clinton White House, the EPA, both political parties, both presidential nominees in the 2000 election, environmentalists, Florida political leaders, and agricultural interests, including the sugar industry, together with detailed proposals from the Army Corps of Engineers, help explain the successful passage of this legislation.[3] The pivotal role of Florida in the presidential race was not inconsequential.

The Everglades restoration project is expected to take three decades to complete. It will entail a massive federal effort to restore water flow through the 300-mile Everglades "river of grass." The Everglades' natural water flow was disrupted by several years of flood-control efforts, resulting in the disappearance of about half of the ecosystem. Human encroachment and sugar farm pollution have threatened and endangered diverse species in the region. With half the funds coming from Washington and the other half from Florida, the legislation (the Water Resources Development Act or WRDA) authorizes an initial $1.4 billion for 10 construction projects and 6 pilot projects, and program authority facilitating speedier implementation of smaller projects.[4] The remainder of the comprehensive plan will be included in subsequent WRDA initiatives starting in 2002. Token opposition to the bill came from fiscal conservatives who objected to pork-related "pet projects" attached to the bill and the open-ended funding provisions.

continued

There are six intended benefits from the Everglades restoration plan:

- Restore the health of more than 2.4 million acres of south Florida's ecosystem, including the Everglades National Park
- Improve Lake Okeechobee's health
- Virtually eliminate damage resulting from releasing fresh water to the estuaries
- Enhance water deliveries to area bays (Florida and Biscayne)
- Upgrade water quality
- Provide flood protection and improve water supply[5]

The plan for "replumbing" the Everglades ecosystem, originally submitted by the U.S. Army Corps of Engineers, involves scrapping 240 miles of levees and canals and constructing new reservoirs, aquifers, and pumping stations. This would allow for water to be captured and redistributed in a manner similar to that existing prior to the ecosystem's degradation. It would also ensure that sufficient water supply would exist to support continued population growth in south Florida and the needs of the area's agricultural interests.[6]

This case serves as an example of a success story in environmental policy making. It illustrates that bipartisanship in Congress is possible, however rare, and that gridlock is not inevitable. However, achieving this consensus did not come easily or quickly. It required years of planning, educating, cajoling, and negotiating for this policy to be approved. Indeed, it is the only major environmental bill to receive approval in the 106th Congress.[7]

[1]"Senate Approves Everglades Restoration Project," at **http://www.cnn.com/2000/US/09/25/everglades.ap/**; "Everglades Restoration Project Nears Completion in Congress," at **http://europe.cnn.com/10/20/congress.everglades.ap/**

[2]"Everglades Restoration Project Nears Completion in Congress."

[3]Ibid.; "U.S. Senate Backs Massive Everglades Restoration," at **http://www.envirolink.org/environews/2000/9/25**; "Senate Approves Restoration Project."

[4]**http://www.evergladesplan.org/the_plan.p1.htm**.

[5]Ibid.

[6]Ibid.; "Plans for the Everglades: Proposal to Restore 'River of Grass,'" at **http://www.abcnews.go.com/everglades990407.html**.

[7]"Senate Approves Everglades Restoration Project."

Group Pressures Pressures from environmental advocacy groups and industry interests often exacerbate conflict and hamper achieving consensus in Congress.[38] For example, reformers point to the need for more integrated environmental policy and management, but Rosenbaum points out that privileged interests represented in environmental subgovernments have undermined or resisted such efforts.[39] Just as organized groups resist change, they can also promote it. Environmental groups are often strategically poised to capitalize on dramatic events or "crisis" situations, to press for policy changes that address the problem in question. For example, massive oil spills and rivers catching fire prompted advocacy groups to call for legislative solutions. Absent such drama, environmental groups will seek other ways to move lower-salience issues (such as the dangers of radon exposure) to greater visibility and salience by effective use of media, lobbying, and public relations. However, some observers have questioned whether environmental groups have the political resources necessary to exert significant influence in the legislative process.[40]

Probusiness groups are equally or more adept at drawing attention to their concerns as they seek support for initiatives like regulatory reform in an effort to reduce the compliance costs they view as burdensome. With the multiple avenues for access discussed previously, there are ample opportunities for resource-rich groups to articulate their preferences to members of Congress. For example, prodevelopment forces underwritten by resource-extraction industries, and pro-preservation interests who want protection whatever the costs, compete to have their voices heard and heeded in the legislative arena. Iron triangles and issue networks facilitate this communication for those who are included in these "subgovernments" (see Chapter 7). Also, groups with money to give legislators to aid in their reelection efforts are well positioned to have their policy preferences considered. For example, one analysis of Federal Election Commission records indicates that industries spent more than $57 million in campaign contributions between 1989 and the elections in 1994, on lobbying to weaken the Clean Water Act.[41] Similar connections have been noted between campaign contributions and congressional votes to weaken other environmental laws, including restrictions on pesticides and protections for endangered species and wetlands.[42]

AIR POLLUTION: THE DIRTY DOZEN AND AIR QUALITY[1]

The League of Conservation Voters has identified a Congressional "Dirty Dozen" that they targeted for defeat in the 2000 election. Seven members of this group were defeated; five were elected. LCV spent approximately $3,391,000 to defeat these candidates (see table). The LCV scorecard on these dozen members of Congress ranged from 0 to 33 percent during the 106th Congress. By contrast, the league identified six "Environmental Champions" and spent nearly $700,000 to elect these candidates. The LCV scores for these six candidates, where available, were much higher. Election-related expenditures by the league included television, radio, and newspaper advertisements; hiring full-time campaign staff; grassroots campaigns; direct mail, door-to-door canvassing; utilizing phone banks; and election-eve polling. Key to all of these efforts was focusing public attention on the anti- and pro-environmental records of the candidates.

The candidates' record on environmental matters generally, and air pollution specifically, was an important consideration for voters. The latter was especially true in the campaigns of several members of the Dirty

continued

Dozen. For example, polling in James Rogan's campaign showed that his vote to weaken the California Clear Air Act and his anti–clean air record were significant factors for those voting against him, especially for independent voters. Also, LCV polls indicated that clean air was a very important determinant of voting decisions in the Norfolk area during the Virginia Senate race involving George Allen and Chuck Robb, and among Washington voters in the Senate contest involving Slade Gorton and Maria Cantwell. The league's polling also showed that voters gave strong support to Representative Jim Maloney of Connecticut, in large measure because of his votes against efforts to weaken the Clean Air Act.

U.S. Representative Christopher Shays is identified by LCV as an environmental champion because of his aggressive support for environmental issues and his fight for clean air. His lifetime LCV average score is 95 percent, scoring 100 percent on 8 of the last 11 scorecards. His tireless advocacy of more stringent clean air standards is especially important for his home state because nitrogen oxide emissions from the region's coal-fired power plants pollute Connecticut's air. Shays voted repeatedly (1995, 1998) to bolster the Environmental Protection Agency's regulatory authority over air quality. His cosponsorship of H.R. 2900 (Clean Smokestacks Act) requiring all power plants to comply with emission standards of the Clean Air Act is further evidence of his environmental leadership.

The Dirty Dozen and Environmental Champions[2]

Dirty Dozen	LCV Score 1995 %	LCV Score 1996 %	LCV Score 1997 %	LCV Score 1998 %	LCV Score 1999 %	LCV Score 2000 %	LCV Score 106th Congress %	LCV Spending on Campaign to Defeat Candidate
Defeated Candidates 2000								
Abraham (MI)	7	0	14	13	0	0	0	$705,000
Grams (MN)	0	8	0	0	11	0	6	N/A
McCollum (FL)	8	15	19	15	13	7	10	$ 26,000
Rogan (CA-27)	N/A	N/A	38	15	6	7	7	$275,000
Kuykendall (CA-36)	N/A	N/A	N/A	N/A	25	43	33	$235,000
Runbeck (MN-4)	N/A	N/A	N/A	N/A	N/A	N/A	N/A	$182,000
Gorton (WA)	0	8	0	0	11	0	6	$440,000
Victorious Candidates 2000								
Burns (MT)	0	0	0	0	0	0	0	$292,000
Allen (VA)	N/A	N/A	N/A	N/A	N/A	N/A	N/A	$520,000
Northup (KY-3)	N/A	N/A	19	8	0	14	7	$373,000

Dirty Dozen	LCV Score 1995 %	LCV Score 1996 %	LCV Score 1997 %	LCV Score 1998 %	LCV Score 1999 %	LCV Score 2000 %	LCV Score 106th Congress %	LCV Spending on Campaign to Defeat Candidate
Traficant (OH-17)	15	15	6	15	19	14	17	$ 52,000
Rogers (MI-8)	N/A	N/A	N/A	N/A	N/A	N/A	N/A	$291,000

Environmental Champions 2000	LCV Score 1995 %	LCV Score 1996 %	LCV Score 1997 %	LCV Score 1998 %	LCV Score 1999 %	LCV Score 2000 %	LCV Spending on Campaign to Elect Candidate
Chafee (RI)	N/A	N/A	N/A	N/A	100	100	$249,000
Hoeffel (PA-13)	N/A	N/A	N/A	N/A	94	92	$136,000
Saxton (NJ-3)	38	62	63	69	63	64	$120,000
Maloney (CT-5)	N/A	N/A	88	77	81	92	$186,000
Inslee (WA-1)	N/A	N/A	N/A	N/A	100	100	$ 5,000
Shays (CT-4)	100	100	100	100	100	92	N/A

[1]Adapted from **http://www.lcv.org/**. Last update November 21, 2000.

[2]Ibid.

Credit Claiming and Pork Barreling Members of Congress have a continuing interest in their reelection prospects. Research on congressional self-interest notes the connection between a congressperson's pursuit of legislative policy goals and his or her overriding desire to win reelection.[43] An important avenue to reelection is showing voters what you have done to make their lives better. "Credit claiming" is a way for a legislator to convince voters that he or she, as an elected representative, is doing something to improve the constituents' life. Such improvements may include pork barreling—providing projects, grants, and contracts that benefit the home constituents. Mayhew points out that providing specific, tangible, localized benefits and making clear the representative's active role in securing these benefits provides a possible electoral payoff for the legislator.[44] In the environmental protection domain, Lyons notes that there are numerous potential particularized benefits that legislators can distribute, such as federal water projects, sewage waste treatment construction grants, and designation of new parks.[45] Credit claiming can also occur as legislators work to safeguard constituent interests by protecting jobs or preserving health. Elected officials are eager to provide such environmental pork barreling to their constituents and to claim credit for their efforts. As Lyons observes, "The U.S. political system offers to politicians abundant incentive to provide tangible and specific policy benefits, yet relatively little incentive to provide benefits that are diffuse or intangible."[46]

Riders In recent years, efforts to reauthorize major environmental legislation such as the Endangered Species Act and the Superfund law have been unsuccessful. This has led some to question whether Congress has either the will or capacity to engage in environmental lawmaking of the type approved in earlier decades.[47] The recent inability to pass major environmental legislation has led to the use of stealth strategies by some. A popular tactic used by anti-environmental legislators in the past few years has been to attach riders to appropriation bills. A rider is like a "hitchhiker on a freight train," an amendment to a bill that is not germane to the bill's purpose and may be used to restrict, redefine, substantially modify, or cease operations of a federal program. Some of these riders are in excess of 100 pages. This tactic was widely used in 1995 when a partial cause for the government shutdown was the close-to 60 controversial riders that were attached to appropriation bills.[48] In that same year the EPA appropriations bill included 17 riders stipulating key programmatic activities that would not receive funding.[49]

One egregious example is the timber rider appended to the 1995 recessions bill. It allowed renewed logging in the ancient forests of the Pacific Northwest, stating that such logging need not comply with several existing environmental laws, including the Clean Water Act, the National Environmental Policy Act, the National Forest Management Act, and other laws.[50] The use of such anti-environment riders was especially pronounced during the 104th and 105th Congresses; however, such tactics continued to bedevil environmental activists by 1999.[51] Riders are often a ploy used by Congress to gain leverage over White House reservations about a policy. When Congress attaches riders to funding bills, for example, it becomes necessary for the president, lacking an item veto, to veto the entire spending bill or approve it with the unpalatable amendments.[52]

Some observers have predicted that instead of comprehensive reform legislation, the future is likely to see increased use of stealth strategies by those seeking to weaken environmental requirements. Piecemeal change through appropriations riders or other forms of nongermane legislation may be used to circumvent debate and minimize accountability for decisions. However, those preferring more straightforward legislative strategies suggest that this "stealth" trend is unlikely to succeed indefinitely. Cannon argues that governmental agencies and environmental advocates are alert to the dangers of piecemeal approaches and likely to respond aggressively when they are tried, and that fundamental policy issues are too visible and environmentalists too vigilant to be continually compromised by stealth strategies.[53]

Symbolism, Policy Layering, and Blame Avoidance   One way that members of Congress can show their interest in environmental policy is to engage in policy symbolism. Policy symbolism takes two forms—namely, congressional resolutions that lack legal force but express legislative concern about a problem or issue, and legislative actions that clarify policy goals and have potential impacts, but which are intended to fall short of goal accomplishment.[54] Legislators might try to claim credit and avoid responsibility for policy failure by taking symbolic actions. For example, they could specify the goals or aspirations for a policy and then either fail to allocate the necessary resources for it to succeed, or deliberately complicate enforcement or implementation, attributing subsequent problems to bureaucratic inaction.[55]

Lyons alludes to policy layering as another form of symbolism whereby contradictions exist between new and existing policy goals. He notes examples of instances where layering of new policy objectives on top of existing ones renders the accomplishments of initial objectives impossible; specifically he cites the example of the Endangered Species Act of 1973 "which has forced the Fish and Wildlife Service to contend with countless government programs destructive of endangered wildlife habitat, and which Congress has underfunded so seriously that recovery plans have been implemented for only a handful of species."[56] Policy symbolism and layering may, in some instances, placate environmental interest groups seeking reassurance and support. Blame avoidance is a strategy used by legislators to mask their actions and put the blame on others (e.g., declining to impose regulations but instead delegating that task to administrative agencies).[57]

Reactive Decision Making   Congressional decision making on environmental matters is often in response to a dramatic event or perceived crisis. Reacting to fluctuations in public opinion, legislators often display what Rosenbaum refers to as "'pollutant of the year' mentality." For example, problems like Love Canal and the chemical explosion in Bhopal, India, provided impetus for passage of Superfund legislation and its amendments; the *Exxon Valdez* oil spill spurred Congress to pass the Oil Pollution Prevention Act of 1990.[58] As Rosenbaum observes, "reactive policy making assures an environmental agenda in which place and priority among programs depend less on scientific logic than on political circumstance. Often the losers are scientifically compelling environmental problems unblessed with political appeal."[59] Reactive decision making also leads to policy implementation difficulties because often agencies are given new programmatic responsibilities, one on top of the other, with little advance notice and with insufficient resources to effectively carry out their new tasks.[60] For example, in 1980 Congress passed Superfund legislation. Superfund used revenue from a tax imposed on industry, along with federal funds, for locating and cleaning up existing hazardous waste sites. Subsequent amendments added significant new duties and responsibilities to the EPA regarding hazardous wastes without a proportionate increase in agency staff and budget.[61]

Science and Politics   Scientific and technical issues require a level of sophistication that is often lacking among "scientific amateurs" in Congress, many of whom typically come from a legal or business background. This is certainly true on such environmentally complex matters as ozone depletion, nuclear energy, and pesticides. Congresspersons often have neither the time nor the expertise to tackle such difficult and intricate problems, preferring instead to shift such matters to staff, professionals, or interest group experts. However, a distrustful Congress may be reluctant to grant administrative agencies the flexibility they need on scientific matters to effectively provide environmental protection.[62] Also, they may be skeptical about scientific claims.

For example, a dispute arose in the House Committee on Science of the 104th Congress regarding the quality of evidence supporting environmental policy legislation. The Republican majority was receptive to the arguments of critics who maintained that costly environmental policies were passed without sufficient scientific evidence of the targeted environmental problems. They contended that those who stood to gain from federal research funding had politicized science and that policy proposals were fashioned to address environmental problems whose severity had been overstated. Those taking that position regarding "distorted science" referred to such examples as the evidence supporting the

1992 decision to ban chlorofluorocarbons (CFCs) to protect the ozone layer, proposals to reduce greenhouse gases to curb global warming, and initiatives to regulate dioxin-containing chemicals.[63] They used such arguments and examples as a rationale for reducing funding for environmental research. Democrats disputed these arguments. George E. Brown, Jr., ranking minority member of the House Committee on Science, captured the essence of the dispute:

> Someone who places the highest value on protecting the environment is more likely to be willing to act not to prevent harm and take the chance that such actions will later turn out to be unnecessary. To ensure that harm is avoided, such a person is willing to risk incurring the costs of unnecessary action and does not require a high level of scientific certainty to justify his or her policy position. Someone who places a higher value on economic issues, on the other hand, is more likely to postpone action and bet that harm will not occur. Such a person believes that it is more important to avoid the costs of unnecessary action than to prevent an uncertain harm and thus requires a high level of scientific certainty to justify the economic costs of a policy action.[64]

In the end, Brown notes the hearings did not substantiate claims of scientific wrongdoing.

Competing Values   As noted above, debates concerning environmental policy often involve discussion of competing values such as environmental protection, economic concerns, and equity considerations (depicted in Figure 5.4).[65] Environmental advocates are often on the opposite side of issues from business and industry interests. Not surprisingly, probusiness concerns often revolve around economic preoccupation with the costs of complying with "burdensome" government regulations and the desire to ensure that benefits exceed the

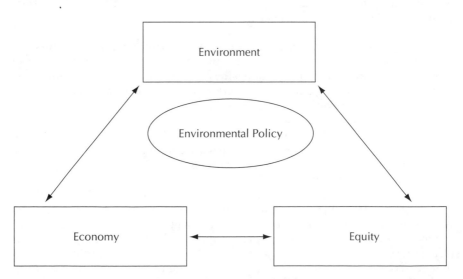

FIGURE 5.4   *A Perspective on Environmental Policy*
Source: Jaap Vos, "Teaching Environmental Planning and Policy by Linking Theory and Praxis," *Journal of Public Affairs Education* 6 (2), 2000, 108.

costs before such regulations are imposed on business. Environmentalists are much more inclined to identify the benefits derived from environmental protection measures and to understate or discount the importance of the cost side of the equation. Government interests must also examine legislative proposals with an eye on equity considerations, seeking to craft legislation that will take into account fairness issues (e.g., environmental justice policy) together with environmental protection and economic concerns. This juggling act of trying to balance trade-offs among competing values is another of the complexities involved in achieving consensus on goals and means among the diverse players in the environmental policy process. Much of the political conflict surrounding environmental policy revolves around how to strike a balance among these competing values.

Because this juggling act is difficult, policies addressing such values are often inconsistent. For example, some laws may authorize agencies to issue and enforce environmental standards, with no mention of cost considerations. Others mandate action regardless of cost. Still others require considerations of cost without requiring similar attention to benefits, or mandate assessment of both costs and benefits.[66] When agencies do conduct cost-benefit analyses, some have criticized the validity and reliability of their economic assessments and suggested that Congress should form an independent office to replicate regulatory analyses.[67] Sometimes the conflicting values are hard to put a dollar value on, such as saving species from extinction and protecting private property rights.[68] Recently equity considerations have received increased attention by legislators as well. For example, "environmental racism" concerns connect environmental regulation with civil rights, seeking to address circumstances where environmental problems (toxic waste sites, pollution dumping industries) adversely and disproportionately affect minority communities.[69] This has led to policies seeking to ensure environmental justice.

Public Interest   Given the structural characteristics, the operating environment, and the process/behavioral patterns cited above, it is a wonder that congresspersons do approve environmental policies that advance broader public interest concerns. James Q. Wilson uses a four-part framework to examine public policy, focusing on the distribution of costs and benefits. His typology includes majoritarian politics (widely distributed costs and benefits), interest group politics (narrowly concentrated costs and benefits), entrepreneurial politics (narrowly concentrated costs, widely distributed benefits), and client politics (widely distributed costs, narrowly concentrated benefits).[70] Figure 5.5 provides examples of environmental policies falling into each cell of this typology.[71] There are some instances in which a relatively unorganized public wins a policy fight against organized interests. Using Wilson's typology this occurs in entrepreneurial politics where the benefits accrue to a broad public constituency and the costs are imposed on a narrow organized interest. Research by Wilson and by Arnold suggests that prevailing in such battles requires congresspersons who are skilled and dedicated, issues that capture the attention of the public at large, and incentives in the form of electoral payoffs as inducements for the congressional "policy champion" or entrepreneur.[72] Examples of such entrepreneurship include Senator Edmund Muskie's championing of air pollution legislation in the 1970s and Senator George Mitchell's leadership for air pollution policies in 1990.

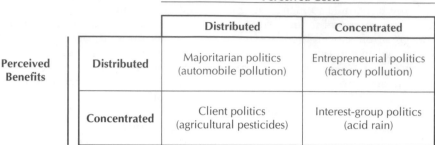

	Perceived Costs	
	Distributed	**Concentrated**
Perceived Benefits **Distributed**	Majoritarian politics (automobile pollution)	Entrepreneurial politics (factory pollution)
Concentrated	Client politics (agricultural pesticides)	Interest-group politics (acid rain)

FIGURE 5.5   *Classifying and Explaining the Politics of Different Policy Issues*
Source: Adapted from James Q. Wilson and John J. Dilulio, Jr., *American Government* (Boston: Hougton Mifflin, 1998), 479, 653–662.

Representatives John Dingell and Henry Waxman have provided similar entrepreneurial leadership on environmental policy in the House.

It is clear that members of Congress vary in their motivation to serve the public interest. As Andrews has observed, "Members of Congress may be statesmen seeking the long-term good of the society, decent but parochial representatives of their constituents, or merely self-interested incumbents selling themselves to interest groups to finance their own reelections."[73] Getting the statesmen, the home-style legislators, and the self-promoting careerists to agree on environmental policy is a major challenge and requires discovery of common ground that simultaneously serves a combination of public and private interest objectives.

Conclusion

The flurry of legislative activity in the environmental decade of the 1970s created the foundation for the more incremental modifications in policy that followed in the 1980s and 1990s. It is unlikely that in today's political environment there will be comprehensive environmental initiatives initiated by Congress and approved by the president. With the election of George W. Bush and close to parity between the parties in Congress, it is more likely that environmental policy in the near term will be incremental rather than reflecting new policy initiatives.

What is the prognosis for future legislative action on environmental policy? The preceding analysis of structural factors, operational characteristics, and behavioral/process features provides some clues. The structural factors are intractable and the consequences are predictable. The institutions of government were designed to disperse power; this fragmentation is evident in Congress, with its two chambers and decentralized decision centers providing access to numerous competing interests. Short election cycles and the parochial focus on reelection will continue to influence legislative deliberations regardless of future partisan electoral outcomes. These structural factors guarantee institutional conflict and tilt the system toward incrementalism and short-term thinking, and away from integrated approaches to policy problems. Electoral outcomes may well determine the extent to which policy gridlock continues to accurately describe congressional decision making. Like structural characteristics, operating mechanisms are unlikely to change in substantial ways. Congress will continue to make policy by authorizing statutes, appropriating funds, and overseeing agency implementation. The number and type of statutes approved, the size of appropriations, and the extent of oversight might change based on future election outcomes, but the mechanisms will still operate in much the same way before and after the votes are counted.

It is in the behavioral/process area where changes are most likely to occur. Detailed policy guidance and micromanagement result in part from breakdown in trust and from policy differences between various participants in the policy process, most notably the White House and executive agencies on the one hand and Congress on the other. Were the same political party to control both the White House and the two chambers of Congress, the trust gap and policy differences would likely shrink, along with many of the incentives for detailed policy guidance and micromanagement. Competing perspectives on environmental policy will continue to divide Democrats and Republicans as well as environmental advocates and business/industry partisans. Those favoring a legal/regulatory approach emphasizing absolute standards and de-emphasizing compliance costs will continue to be pitted against those preferring an economic strategy emphasizing market mechanisms and de-emphasizing political interference. These cleavages make environmental policy conflict inevitable, but do not preclude the possibility of bipartisan cooperation. The reelection imperatives of members of Congress make credit claiming, riders, and pork barreling indispensable, and there is no reason to believe that symbolism, policy layering, and blame avoidance will take on less importance in the future. Similarly, legislators are likely to continue to engage in reactive decision making, but opportunities do exist for more proactive policy entrepreneurs to strike out in new directions to advance pro-environment agendas.

Future congressional deliberations on environmental matters will undoubtedly involve questions about the quality of the scientific evidence supporting specific policy proposals, the extent of the risk for action or inaction, and the likelihood that the proposed solutions would actually ameliorate the targeted problems. Those pushing an environmental agenda will need to marshal facts to support claims about environmental "threats" and to make the case that limited resources should be spent on environmental protection rather than on other competing problems. Value conflicts will persist as legislators seek to maintain a balance among a trio of environmental, economic, and equity concerns. Congressional deliberations will continue to reflect the mixed motives of legislators themselves: public interest, self-interest, and parochial representation interests will simultaneously be weighed and traded off against each other. Amidst these competing scientific claims, conflicting values, and mixed motives, there is some consensus that environmental policies require greater flexibility and that more attention must be given to weighing the costs and benefits of policy alternatives.

Environmental protection and cost-effective policies are not mutually exclusive. Wasteful spending can be avoided without rolling back environmental protection. While environmental policy debates in the past have been "confrontational in style and polarizing in practice,"[74] this does not have to be the case in the future. Politically savvy and skilled legislative leadership, an aroused and active public, and an attractive set of policy proposals with appeal to the electorate are needed to build on this consensus and to take constructive action. Such conditions are necessary if comprehensive new environmental initiatives are going to successfully weave their way through the labyrinthine legislative obstacle course.

> **Web Sites**
> **Congress and Environmental Policy:**
>
> Search bills of the 107th Congress: **http://thomas.loc.gov/home/c106/hot-subj.html**
>
> Search major legislation by topic, title, bill type, and number:
> **http://thomas.loc.gov/bss/d107/hot-subj.html**
> **http://thomas.loc.gov/bss/d107/hot-titl.html**
> **http://thomas.loc.gov/bss/d107/hot-bill.html**
>
> Congressional Record of the 107th Congress:
> **http://thomas.loc.gov/j107/j107index1/.html**
>
> Committees of the U.S. Senate: **www.senate.gov/committees/index.cfm**
>
> Committees of the U.S. House of Representatives: **www.house.gov/ CommitteeWWW.html**
>
> Hearings of Congressional Committees:
> **www.senate.gov/legislative/legis_legis_committees.html**
>
> Congressional Hearings on the Web: **henry.ugl.lib.umich.edu/ libhome/Documents.center/comm.html**
>
> General Accounting Office: **www.gao.gov**
>
> Project Vote Smart: **www.vote-smart.org/congresstrack/status.phtml**
>
> Library of Congress: **www.loc.gov**
>
> *Source:* Adapted from Project Vote Smart, Vote Smart Web (Yellow Pages), 2000 edition, 18–28.

Endnotes

[1] Joy A. Clay, "Congressional Government," in Jay M. Shafritz, *International Encyclopedia of Public Policy and Administration,* Vol. 1 (Boulder, CO: Westview, 1999), 497–498.

[2] See John E. Anderson, *Public Policymaking,* 3rd ed. (Boston: Houghton Mifflin, 1997); Thomas R. Dye, *Understanding Public Policy,* 9th ed. (Upper Saddle River, NJ: Prentice Hall, 1998); B. Guy Peters, *American Public Policy: Promise and Performance,* 5th ed. (NY: Chatham House, 1999).

[3] David H. Davis, *American Environmental Politics* (Chicago, IL: Nelson-Hall, 1998), 23.

[4] Jacqueline Vaughn Switzer, *Environmental Politics: Domestic and Global Dimensions,* 3rd ed. (Boston: Bedford/St. Martin's, 2001), 76–77.

[5] B. Guy Peters, *American Public Policy: Promise and Performance,* 31.

[6] Woodrow Wilson, *Congressional Government* (Houghton, Mifflin & Co., 1885; reprint Johns Hopkins University Press, 1981), 82.

[7] Michael E. Kraft, *Environmental Policy and Politics* (NY: HarperCollins, 1996), 65.

8 See Glen Sussman and Mark A. Kelso, "Environmental Priorities and the President as Legislative Leader," in Dennis L. Soden, ed. *The Environmental Presidency* (Albany, NY: SUNY Press, 1999), 113.
9 See Theodore Lowi, *The End of Liberalism*, 2nd ed. (New York: W.W. Norton, 1979); Randall P. Ripley and Grace A. Franklin, *Congress, the Bureaucracy, and Public Policy*, 5th ed. (Pacific Grove, CA: Brooks Cole, 1991).
10 Michael E. Kraft, *Environmental Policy and Politics*, 12.
11 Rochelle Stanfield, "The Acid Rainmakers," *National Journal*, June 14, 1986, 1500–1503.
12 Walter A. Rosenbaum, *Environmental Politics and Policy*, 4th ed. (Washington, DC: CQ Press, 1998), 106.
13 Mary Cooper, "Environmental Priorities: The Issues," *CQ Outlook*, June 5, 1999, 9.
14 See Charles Lindblom, "The Science of 'Muddling Through,'" *Public Administration Review* 19, 1959, 79–88; Thomas R. Dye, *Understanding Public Policy*, 27–29; B. Guy Peters, *American Public Policy*, 145–148.
15 See Michael Lyons, "Political Self-Interest and U.S. Environmental Policy," *Natural Resources Journal* 39, Spring 1999, 271–294; and Daniel J. Fiorino, *Making Environmental Policy* (Berkely, CA: University of Calaifornia, 1995).
15 David L. Feldman, Jean H. Peretz, and Barbara D. Jendrucko, "Policy Gridlock in Waste Management: Balancing Federal and State Concerns," *Policy Studies Journal* 22 (4), 1994, 589–605.
17 Michael E. Kraft, "Environmental Policy in Congress: From Consensus to Gridlock," in Norman J. Vig and Michael E. Kraft, eds. *Environmental Policy* (Washington, DC: CQ Press, 2000), 124–125.
18 Glen Sussman and Mark A. Kelso, "Environmental Priorities and the President as Legislative Leader," 118.
19 Ibid.
20 Dennis Soden, "Presidential Roles and Environmental Policy," in D. L. Soden, ed. *The Environmental Presidency* (Albany, NY: SUNY Press, 1999), 7.
21 See Henry M. Jackson, "Environmental Policy and the Congress," *Public Administration Review* 28 (4), 305; Jacqueline Vaughn Switzer, *Environmental Politics: Domestic and Global Dimensions*; Walter A. Rosenbaum, *Environmental Politics and Policy*.
22 Michael E. Kraft, *Environmental Policy and Politics*, 61–63.
23 Daniel J. Fiorino, *Making Environmental Policy*, 63–64.
24 Stephen W. Schmidt, Mack C. Shelley, and Barbara A. Bardes, *American Government and Politics Today* (Belmont, CA: West/Wadsworth, 1999), 299.
25 Daniel J. Fiorino, *Making Environmental Policy*, 67–68.
26 Michael E. Kraft, "Environmental Policy in Congress: From Consensus to Gridlock," 133.
27 David H. Davis, *American Environmental Politics*, 19.
28 Elise S. Jones and Will Callaway, "Neutral Bystander, Intrusive Micromanager, or Useful Catalyst? The Role of Congress in Effecting Change Within the Forest Service," *Policy Studies Review* 23 (2), 1995, 337–350.
29 Example cited in Susan Welch, John Gruhl, John Comer, Susan M. Rigdon, and Michael Steinman, *American Government*, 7th ed. (Belmont, CA: West/Wadsworth, 1999), 575.
30 R. Shep Melnick, "Pollution Deadlines and Coalition for Failure," in Michael S. Greve and Fred L. Smith, Jr., eds. *Environmental Politics: Public Costs, Private Rewards* (NY: Praeger, 1992).

[31]   Walter A. Rosenbaum, *Environmental Politics and Policy*.

[32]   Walter A. Rosenbaum, *Environmental Politics and Policy*, 103; Elise S. Jones and Will Callaway, "Neutral Bystander, Intrusive Micromanager, or Useful Catalyst? The Role of Congress in Effecting Change Within the Forest Service," 337–350.

[33]   D. Fiorino, *Making Environmental Policy*, 63.

[34]   See **http://congress.scorecardlcu.org/leadership.htm** and **http://www.vote-smart. org/index.phtml**.

[35]   Zachary A. Smith, *The Environmental Policy Paradox* (Englewood Cliffs, NJ: Prentice Hall, 1992), 30.

[36]   Allan Freedman, "Prospects in Senate Brighten for Rewrite of Species Law," *Congressional Quarterly Weekly Report*, 55 (20), 1997, 1125.

[37]   David H. Davis, *American Environmental Politics*, 18; Brad Knickerbocker, "'Careful Balance' May Save Endangered Species Act," *Christian Science Monitor* 89 (207), September 19, 1997, 4.

[38]   See Arthur Bentley, *The Process of Government* (Chicago: University of Chicago Press, 1908); David Truman, *The Governmental Process* (NY: Knopf, 1951); Robert A. Dahl, *Who Governs?* (New Haven, CT: Yale University Press, 1961).

[39]   Walter A. Rosenbaum, *Environmental Politics and Policy*, 106.

[40]   Zachary A. Smith, *The Environmental Policy Paradox*, 43.

[41]   Vicki Monks, "Capital Games," *National Wildlife* 34 (3), 1996, 25.

[42]   Ibid., 26; see also "Looking Ahead to the 105th," *The Environmental Forum* (January/February, 1996), 33.

[43]   See David R. Mayhew, *Congress: The Electoral Connection* (New Haven, CT: Yale University Press, 1974), 32–61; Michael Lyons, "Political Self-Interest and U.S. Environmental Policy," 284.

[44]   David R. Mayhew, *Congress: The Electoral Connection*, 14–18.

[45]   Michael Lyons, "Political Self-Interest and U.S. Environmental Policy," 285.

[46]   Ibid, 275.

[47]   Karin Sheldon, "Where are the Leaders of Yesteryear?," *The Environmental Forum* 15 (3), 1998, 42.

[48]   Sharon Buccino, "Public Demand Will Spur Congress," *The Environmental Forum* 15 (3), 1998, 38.

[49]   Michael E. Kraft, "Environmental Policy in Congress: From Consensus to Gridlock," 133.

[50]   Patricia Byrnes, "Congressional Year-End Report Card No Good," *Wilderness* 59 (211), 1995, 4–7.

[51]   See Margaret Kriz, "Hazards for Environmentalists," *National Journal* 31 (38), September 18, 1999, 2630; and League of Conservation Voters, "1996 House Vote Descriptions," **http://www.lev.org/lcv96/files/hvotes.html**.

[52]   Vicki Monks, "Capitol Games," 22–30.

[53]   Jonathan Z. Cannon, "If Not In This Congress, Then a Future One," *The Environmental Forum* 15 (3), 1998, 39.

[54]   See David R. Mayhew, *Congress: The Electoral Connection*, 132; Michael Lyons, "Political Self-Interest and U.S. Environmental Policy," 287.

[55]   See David R. Mayhew, *Congress: The Electoral Connection*; Morris P. Fiorina, *Congress: Keystone of the Washington Establishment* (New Haven, CT: Yale University Press, 1977); Michael E. Kraft, *Environmental Policy and Politics*, 11.

[56]   Michael Lyons, "Political Self-Interest and U.S. Environmental Policy," 289; see also Walter A. Rosenbaum, *Environmental Politics and Policy*.

57   See Morris P. Fiorina and Paul E. Peterson, *The New American Democracy* (Needham Heights, MA: Allyn and Bacon, 1998), 604; Murray Edelman, *Symbolic Uses of Politics* (Urbana, IL: University of Illinois Press, 1964).

58   See Walter A. Rosenbaum, *Environmental Politics and Policy*, 99; Michael E. Kraft, *Environmental Policies and Politics*, 58.

59   Walter A. Rosenbaum, *Environmental Politics and Policy*, 100.

60   Ibid.

61   Steven W. Schmidt, et. al., *American Government and Politics*, 573–574.

62   Richard A. Merrill, "Congress as Scientists," *The Environmental Forum*, 11 (1), 1994, 20.

63   George E. Brown, Jr., "Environmental Science Under Siege in the U.S. Congress," *Environment* 39 (2), 1997, 12–20.

64   Ibid, 17.

65   See Jaap Vos, "Teaching Environmental Planning and Policy by Linking Theory and Praxis," *Journal of Public Affairs Education* 6 (2), 2000, 108; John S. Dryzek, *The Politics of the Earth: Environmental Discourses* (NY: Oxford University Press, 1997), Chapter 3; David V. Edwards and Alessandra Lippucci, *Practicing American Politics* (NY: Worth, 1998), 493.

66   Daniel J. Fiorino, *Making Environmental Policy*, 35.

67   Randall Lutter, "The Role of Economic Analysis in Regulatory Reform," *Regulation* 22 (2), 1999, 38.

68   Brad Knickerbocker, "'Careful Balance' May Save Endangered Species Act," 4.

69   Benjamin Ginsberg, Theodore J. Lowi, and Margaret Weir, *We the People: An Introduction to American Politics* (NY: W.W. Norton, 1999), 637.

70   James Q. Wilson, *American Government*, 5th ed. (Houghton-Mifflin, 1997), 433–437.

71   See James Q. Wilson and John J. Dilulio, Jr., *American Government*, 7th ed. (Boston, MA: Houghton-Mifflin, 1998), Chapter 22.

72   See James Q. Wilson, *American Government*; R. Douglas Arnold, *The Logic of Congressional Action* (New Haven, CT: Yale University Press, 1990); Michael E. Kraft, *Environmental Policy and Politics*, 58–59; Jacqueline Vaughn Switzer, *Environmental Politics: Domestic and Global Dimensions*, 3rd ed.; Michael Lyons, "Political Self-Interest and U.S. Environmental Policy," 271–294.

73   Richard N.L. Andrews, *Managing the Environment, Managing Ourselves* (New Haven: Yale University Press, 1999), 6–7.

74   Marian R. Chertow and Daniel C. Esty, "Environmental Policy: The Next Generation," *Issues in Science and Technology* 14 (1), 1997, 77.

The Environmental Presidency

In order to assess how presidents have responded to the environment, we will focus our attention on the *modern presidency* beginning with Franklin D. Roosevelt. As the first modern president, Roosevelt was also the first chief executive to pay considerable attention to the environment and, in particular, to enhance and develop public land conservation. FDR was even accorded the honor by some environmentalists as having introduced the "Golden Age of Conservation" to America.[1] Much of his effort on behalf of the environment focused on his first term in office (1932–1936) and was, not surprisingly, tied to the critical concerns of the Depression.

Looking at the years since Franklin Roosevelt, the period from 1945 through 1974 was probably the most productive period as far as protecting the environment and natural resources.[2] During these years, securing the coastal zones, preserving sea mammals, as well as restricting ocean dumping, combating water pollution, and limiting pesticides became priorities for a number of presidents and congresspersons.

While protecting the environment has been quite a popular issue with the public, it has never fared particularly well as an election issue. Its popularity can be seen in Table 6.1, which indicates that when a Gallup poll asked in 1998 which statement comes closer to what people were thinking at the time, 68 percent selected "protection of the environment should be given priority, even at the risk of curbing economic growth," whereas only 24 percent agreed with the statement that "economic growth should be given priority, even if the environment suffers to some extent."[3] Its difficulty as an election issue can be seen in how people have failed to consider it as critical when compared with other more pressing concerns. This is shown in a second 1998 Gallup poll that asked 1,028 adults the following question: "What do you think is the most important problem facing this country today?" The "environment" got only 1 percent support from those surveyed, whereas "the economy in general" received 12 percent support. Other noneconomic issues in that survey that received support included ethics/moral/family decline (15%), dissatisfaction with government (14%), education (13%), crime/violence (10%), and drugs (9%), among others.[4] Furthermore,

TABLE 6.1

Public Preference for Environmental Protection or Economic Growth, 1995–1998

	Environmental Protection	Economic Growth	No Opinion
April 17–19, 1998	68%	24%	8%
July 25–27, 1997	66%	27%	7%
April 17–19, 1995	62%	32%	6%

Source: Based on "Short Subjects," *The Gallup Poll Monthly,* No. 391 (April 1998), 43

The *question asked* of the public was:

Q. 43. "Switching subjects again, here are two statements which people sometimes make when discussing the environment and economic growth. Which of these statements comes closer to your own point of view—Protection of the environment should be given priority, even at the risk of curbing economic growth, *or,* economic growth should be given priority, even if the environment suffers to some extent?

the response in 1998 showed a wider gap between those who sided with the economy and those who supported the environment than when the survey was previously conducted in 1997. In that year, 6 percent selected the "economy in general" compared to 2 percent who selected the "environment."[5]

Roles of the Modern President

In considering how presidents have dealt with this issue of the environment, we will analyze the modern presidency by examining a president's five major roles. The theoretical framework we will adopt revolves around the *role* approach first developed by Raymond Tatalovich and Byron W. Daynes in *Presidential Power in the United States.*[6] A *role* is defined here as a "set of expectations by political elites and the citizenry that define(s) the scope of presidential responsibilities within a given policy area."[7] The role concept is important in helping to explain why a president succeeds or fails in a particular situation and at a specific task, and whether a president is free to negotiate with a coalition of interests. A role can also help explain why a president appears assertive or passive in response to such an issue as the environment.

The five presidential roles are *commander-in-chief*—the only presidential role specifically listed in Article II of the Constitution, and a role that refers to the president as the nation's highest military leader; *chief diplomat*—a role that defines the president's position as spokesperson to and negotiator with other nations. Since both of these roles allow a president to deal with foreign affairs, we will combine them when looking at how the president deals with the environment in an international setting.

The third role we will consider is that of *chief executive*—a role associated with governing and that involves the president with the bureaucracy, administrative staff,[8] cabinet, and domestic policy making. The president's fourth role is that of *legislative leader*—concerned with the president's important relationship to Congress. Finally, we will take account of the president as *opinion/party leader*—a combined role linking the president to the public through the political party and public opinion.

The strength of each of these roles depends on formal authority and such political resources as 1) the ability of a president to make decisions; 2) the public's potential to disapprove of presidential actions; 3) a president's individual expertise in exercising the role; and 4) conditions of crisis that may enhance and enlarge the power of the president in a particular role.

Based on these variables and the political resources normally attending these roles, the five presidential roles can be distributed along a *power continuum* (Figure 6.1) from the two strongest roles—*commander-in-chief* and *chief diplomat*—to the weaker two roles—*legislative leader* and *opinion/party leader*—with the *chief executive* role falling in the middle.[9] While there are exceptions to this distribution, namely, when a president like Lyndon Johnson is able to strengthen a typically weak role like that of legislative leader, or when a Franklin D. Roosevelt or a Ronald Reagan mesmerizes the public in the role of opinion/party leader, one can normally expect these roles to distribute themselves along the continuum as described. The above-mentioned exceptions are due to the individual skills of a particular president, but remain exceptions that cannot be routinized or passed on to succeeding presidents.

The Diverse Environment and Presidential Response

Environmental issues have over the years become quite diverse. Whereas environmental concerns from the 1930s through the 1970s tended to focus our attention on clean air and water, forest conservation, preservation of natural resources, and public land use, today the environmental issues that concern a president may include safe drinking water, overpopulation, preserving certain species while preventing the spread of species alien to particular ecosystems, as well as limiting toxic waste and the chemical pollution of agricultural lands. In addition, the scope and reach of environmental policy has broadened over time as we have increased both our technological capabilities and our contact with other nations. Today an issue such as polluted air can become critical at a local level at the same time that it is an acute multinational concern.

Given the environment's diversity and expansive reach, then, presidents are going to become involved—to one extent or another—with the subject. Whether that involvement is extensive or modest, whether it is supportive of or limiting

Most Powerful				Least Powerful
Commander-in-Chief	Chief Diplomat	Chief Executive	Legislative Leader	Opinion/Party Leader

FIGURE 6.1   *Role Power Continuum*
Source: Based on Byron W. Daynes, Raymond Tatalovich and Dennis L. Soden, *To Govern a Nation: Presidential Power and Politics* (New York: St. Martin's, 1998), Chapter 1, "Presidential Roles, Power, and Policy," 1–11.

to the environment, will depend on how important the issue is to a president's social agenda.

Most contemporary presidents, with few exceptions, have acted favorably toward the environment, reflecting the predominant attitude of the American electorate. For six decades, in fact, Democratic and Republican presidents have publically endorsed and worked for pollution control and have supported conservation of resources. Where presidents from the two parties have differed, of course, has been in the selection of the specific environmental issue of focus; in the intensity of their reaction to that issue; and in the level of government they have preferred to work through to respond to that issue.

The President as Opinion/Party Leader

The Role

The president as opinion/party leader attempts to mobilize public support for policies and programs of the administration as well as for the party. This role, compared to the other presidential roles, is the weakest of the five, lacking a formal authoritative base. Nonetheless, presidents have employed a variety of techniques as opinion/party leader, in the effort to influence public opinion through such outlets as news conferences, major and minor policy speeches, and appearances before partisan and nonpartisan groups.

The framers of the U.S. Constitution were wary of "direct" democracy and political parties, which is one reason why this role is not alluded to in the Constitution. This does not suggest, however, that for certain presidents this role has become unimportant in influencing policy. James Davis has suggested that "[a]mong the many hats that the president wears, none is more important to his long-term success than that of party leader."[10] Because there are so few resources associated with the role, however, to be a successful opinion/party leader, a president must rely on personal influence, political skills, and mastery of the "bully pulpit."

But this particular role has a dual focus: a president finds himself acting as a voice for both the people and his party. Further complicating a president's efforts in this role are the constraints put on the president through separation of powers and a decentralized Congress. Despite these limitations, however, if a president's party maintains majority control in both houses of Congress, this role can help in advancing a president's policy priorities.

Opinion/Party Leader and the Environment

Those presidents who have considered the environment a primary priority have often reserved a portion of their most formal and most visible constitutionally sanctioned address—the State of the Union message—for expressing their views on the environment. While the State of the Union message serves as the president's opening address to Congress, the president's speech is fully covered by the national media, allowing the president to focus attention on those issues he feels most keenly about, hoping to convince policymakers in attendance, as well as the public, about these priorities. On several occasions, Presidents Franklin Roosevelt, Harry Truman, and Dwight Eisenhower used their State of the Union messages to emphasize their concern about natural resources and the environment, stressing the "wise use" of them. While Truman emphasized both conservation and economic development, Eisenhower added a caveat to his support for the environment. He insisted that conservation could best be handled under the control of state and local authority rather than under federal authority.

Eisenhower's position on delegating authority to the state and local levels was probably the more typical Republican position than that advocated by Richard Nixon, who became the leading Republican activist on the environment. Early in Nixon's presidency, for example, he declared the 1970s the "decade of the environment." To show how serious he was about this, he reserved a portion of his 1970 State of the Union address to frame its importance, suggesting that "restoring nature to its natural state is a cause beyond party and beyond factions."[11]

During his first term in office, Nixon determined that his focus on the environment would be both diverse and all-encompassing. It was to include a focus on clean water, on the constraints of air pollution, and on new ways to increase the number of national parks and to expand open space.[12] The public seemed in support of the president, with more than half (53%) of the American public indicating that environmental quality was the most important problem facing the nation—in a national poll, crime was the only issue that outranked it.[13] This sort of public approval, in fact, was in all likelihood the main reason that the president became initially involved with the environment as an agenda issue.[14] Stanley I. Kutler, in his 1990 book, *The Wars of Watergate: The Last Crisis of Richard Nixon*, argued persuasively that early in Nixon's first term, he noted that he had never really been interested in environmental issues. In a recorded conversation, Nixon indicated to John Ehrlichman, one of his closest aides, how he thought environmentalists were "Overrated," and that they served only the "privileged." Their issue, Nixon continued, "was just 'crap,' and for 'clowns,' and 'the rich and [Supreme Court Justice William O.] Douglas.'"[15]

Having said this, however, Nixon was a consummate enough politician to recognize a popular issue when he saw it. Indeed, his speeches and actions in support for the environment tended to follow public opinion quite closely, and, in Dennis L. Soden and Brent S. Steel's words, "ebb and flow" with public opinion.[16] Yet Nixon also recognized how widespread demands were from the leaders in both parties to support a cleaner environment. Thus it was in his 1970 State of the Union message that the president devoted more than a third of his time to environmental issues, even proclaiming in particular that now he was fully involved with this issue: "[t]he program I propose to Congress will be the most comprehensive and costly program in this field in America's history."[17] Despite what appeared to be Nixon's all-out support for the environment in this address, two years later the president continued to doubt the public's real devotion to the issue, suggesting in a 1972 taped conversation that the people still "don't give a shit about the environment."[18]

Although Nixon had his doubts about the public's authentic concern for the environment, Ronald Reagan's overall record on this issue was quite different. Reagan, as opinion/party leader, tended to thumb his nose at public support for the environment. This was an unusual attitude for a president to have, in light of the American public's rather stable support of environmental initiatives. In fact, almost 7 out of 10 Americans supported environmental protection that risked threatening economic growth.[19] While Reagan entered the White House proclaiming in speeches his support for environmental protection, at the same time he supported development and regulatory relief for business, an action that tended to undermine environmental protection.

President Reagan also urged Congress to change its orientation on environmental issues and cut back on federal funding for the environment, in an effort to shift more responsibility to the states. In his July 14, 1984, radio address, he asked Congress for additional money for the environment so that the federal government could purchase additional national park land and in the process allow the states to take more responsibility for environmental issues.[20]

Reagan was consistent in his demands of Congress on environmental policy, requesting that private enterprise become more involved with environmental concerns.

This attitude did cause him to face some public opposition from those in Congress supportive of the environment. While there was some environmental legislation passed and initiatives taken during his presidency, few of these could be attributed to Reagan's efforts as opinion/party leader.

George Bush, by contrast, wanted to be an "environmental president" and used the election campaign to identify himself as such. While there was little mention of the environment in his major speeches, one could see his interest in and support for environmental issues in his press conferences and minor speeches. Thus, Bush entered the White House as a self-proclaimed "environmental president." Many environmentalists, however, were not convinced by his rhetoric, believing that he had reversed his own position too often on environmental issues as vice president to now be believed as the "environmental" president. In 1992, President Bill Clinton expressed his reservations about Bush's sincerity as an "environmentalist" when he commented on Bush's use of symbolism over substance, telling the public that now that he was in office "the days of photo-op environmentalism are over."[21]

It was Bill Clinton who initially was seen by environmentalists as the "great green hope" after environmentalists had endured 12 years of Reagan and Bush. Based on the 30 promised proposals the Clinton-Gore team indicated they would focus on,[22] it was strange that Clinton, as opinion/party leader, actually emphasized the environment in fewer speeches than any of his Democratic and Republican counterparts. In his last State of the Union address, Clinton did make clear that the environment had been and would continue to be an important issue during his presidency; but he felt compelled to defend his approach to the environment by suggesting that a president could be supportive of both the environment and economic development. As he stated: "I am grateful for the opportunities the vice president and I have had to work hard to protect the environment and finally to put to rest the notion that you can't expand the economy while protecting the environment." Clinton then recalled what his record on both had been, suggesting that "As our economy has grown, we have rid more than 500 neighborhoods of toxic waste and ensured cleaner air and water for millions of families. In the past three months alone, we have acted to preserve more than 40 million acres of roadless lands in our national forests and created three new national monuments." He then proposed quite an ambitious program for the coming year that would extend beyond his own presidency. His proposal consisted of creating a permanent conservation fund to "restore wildlife, protect coastlines, and save natural treasures from California redwoods to the Everglades. This Lands Legacy endowment represents by far the most enduring investment in land preservation ever proposed."[23]

Typically, Clinton reserved his "major" environmental proposals not for his State of the Union addresses but for his Earth Day speeches given in April of each year. In his 1994 Earth Day speech, for example, Clinton made his public and party commitment to environmental protection quite clear by citing the words of President John Kennedy, who had indicated that "It is our task in our time and in our generation to hand down, undiminished to those who come after us, as was handed down to us by those who came before, the natural wealth and beauty which is ours."[24]

Major/Minor Speeches of Modern Presidents

So how have presidents as opinion/party leaders in general responded to the public's support of the environment? If we look first at social policy issues covered in the presidents' major speeches[25] (Table 6.2), the environment was the most frequently cited issue referred to by presidents Franklin D. Roosevelt through Clinton—27 of the 58 major social agenda speeches (nearly half of them) delivered by these 11 presidents dealt with the environment. In the presidents' minor speeches (Table 6.3), it should be noted that it was Richard Nixon and George Bush who spoke more about

TABLE 6.2

Major Speeches of the Eleven Modern Presidents Focused on Social Issues, 1932–1996

The Issue	Percent of the Total
Homosexuality	0.0%
Pornography	5.2
Abortion	6.9
Gun Control	10.3
Affirmative Action	31.0
Environment	46.6
Total	100.0% (n = 58)

Source: Adapted from Byron W. Daynes and Glen Sussman, *The American Presidency and the Social Agenda* (Prentice Hall, 2001), 46.

TABLE 6.3

Minor Speeches of the Eleven Modern Presidents Dealing with the Environment,* 1932–1996

Presidents	Number of speeches
F. Roosevelt	21
H. Truman	36
D. Eisenhower	16
J. Kennedy	22
L. Johnson	59
R. Nixon	87
G. Ford	28
J. Carter	49
R. Reagan	39
G. Bush	83
B. Clinton	26
Total	466

*Note: Minor speeches include presidential news conferences, press releases, reporter interviews, speeches to interest groups, and speeches before town meetings.

the environment than did any of their Democratic and Republican counterparts. These two presidents were followed by Democrats Johnson and Carter who most frequently mentioned the environment. Other presidents focused on the environment in their minor speeches much less frequently, with Eisenhower ranking lowest, mentioning the environment in only 16 of his speeches in the two terms he served.

Summary

As we made clear, this particular role is a president's weakest. As we suggested elsewhere in this chapter, several of the other presidential roles are secured either in the Constitution, in statutory law, or in tradition and provide a more secure basis for presidential power than is this role. As opinion/party leader, the president lacks many of the resources inherent in the other roles and must therefore rely solely on personal skills.

While the environment has not been a major issue in the agendas of most presidents when acting as opinion/party leader, some have paid particular attention to the issue in their speeches. One might say, then, that the opinion/party leader role is *important*, but *weak*. It is important because a president can influence environmental policy in this role, and can persuade public sentiment for or against the issue. It is weak, however, because the opinion/party leader faces a number of constraints including a divided political system, lacking the authority and resources of other roles to easily compensate for this.[26]

The President as an Environmental Legislative Leader

The Role

For most presidents, the legislative leader role provides access to moderate political resources. It is a role in which Congress has the substantial advantage if not dominant influence.[27] Congress can either support presidential action, shape a president's agenda, or come out in direct opposition to the president's efforts. Yet success as a legislative leader is important to the president because the overall accomplishments in office are quite often determined by achievements in this role.

A successful legislative leader must often rely on external political resources, creativity, and political persuasion to facilitate an administration's environmental focus. A president must assertively use individual skills as a negotiator and persuader, since there is little real authority attending this role.

Tools Available to the Legislative Leader to Facilitate Environmental Legislation

Veto A president's Article II veto power gives greatest leverage in the legislative process since so few regular vetoes are ever overridden by a two-thirds vote in both houses of Congress.[28] Yet early presidents rarely used the veto, and when they did it was only to determine constitutionality. Beginning with Andrew Jackson, presidents began to use the veto to shape public policy and advance their agendas.

Modern presidents, having a focus on the environment have relied on the veto primarily to protect environmental gains they have secured as legislative leaders. Through his veto of an amendment to the Federal Water Pollution Control Act in

1960, for instance, Dwight Eisenhower was able both to protect clean water as well as to ensure that the federal government did not accumulate excessive power at the expense of the states.[29] On October 17, 1972, Richard Nixon vetoed the Federal Water Pollution Act Amendments of 1972 because they were too expensive. He stated "I am compelled to withhold my approval from S 2770 . . . a bill whose laudable intent is outweighed by its unconscionable $24 billion price tag."[30] Congress clearly felt otherwise and the next day it overrode his veto by a vote of 247–23 in the House and 52–12 in the Senate.[31]

For the first two years of Clinton's presidency he did not make use of the veto power. In 1995, however, Bill Clinton cast his first 11 vetoes, as Table 6.4 indicates, one of which was used as a defensive strategy to ward off unwanted Republican attacks against what he considered the environmental advances his administration had made during his first years in office. Clinton's veto was used specifically to shield the national park system from severe financial cuts Republicans in Congress had threatened to make had they been able to pass HR 1977—Department of Interior and Related Agencies Appropriations Act 1996—a bill that would have greatly restricted public activities in park preserves.[32] Despite the fact that these had been the first vetoes in three years, congressional Republicans still disparagingly labeled President Clinton "Veto Bill."

By 1999 Clinton was still having to rely on the veto to protect the environment. On October 22, 1999, the president vetoed an Interior budget bill passed by Congress because it did not fully fund his environmental program, which included his Lands Legacy program, climate change program, clean water effort, and assistance to Native Americans.[33]

The Budget   A successful environmental program requires funding. One could tell how important the environment was to Franklin Roosevelt's administration by examining the budgetary allotments he set aside for the environment. In 1935 he devoted as much as 20.8 percent of his budget to environmental projects; even his lowest environmental budget outlays reached 11.2 percent in 1936.[34]

Other presidents have also shown how crucial money is in supporting environmental policy. Richard Nixon asked congressional leaders in his Annual Budget Message for Fiscal Year 1972 for $2.4 billion more than Congress was willing to provide for environmental proposals.[35] Despite Congress's refusal, Nixon the next year changed his strategy and asked Congress for $5 billion for the environment, but this time requested that the money be allotted to the states to assist them in their environmental programs.[36] Not surprisingly, this was approved.

Ronald Reagan found he could just as easily use budgetary funds to starve environmental legislation as to support it. In 1985 Reagan cut funding of a Soil and Water Conservation bill in order to "avoid the specter of higher interest rates, choked-off investment, renewed recession, and rising unemployment."[37] Some of Reagan's efforts at budget cutting were frustrated, however, by the Democratically controlled Congress, which refused to support the president's efforts to cut funding from the Environmental Protection Agency.[38]

Bill Clinton was quite aware that he needed additional money to build a strong environmental agenda. He was particularly bothered by what he perceived as monetary constraints that were threatening his plan to restore the Florida Everglades in the Water Resources Development Act of 1996. While the federal government was to pay 35 percent of the total, Clinton wanted it to pay at least

TABLE 6.4

President Bill Clinton's Vetoes, 1993–1999

Year	Number	Subject Matter	Date
1993	0		
1994	0		
1995	11	FY 1995 Rescissions/Supplemental	June 7
		Lift Bosnia arms embargo	Aug. 11
		1996 Legislative branch appropriations	Oct. 3
		Temporarily increase public debt limit	Nov. 13
		FY 1996 Continuing appropriations	Nov. 13
		FY 1996 Budget reconciliation	Dec. 6
		FY 1996 *Interior appropriations*	Dec. 18
		FY 1996 VA-HUD appropriations	Dec. 18
		FY 1996 Commerce-Justice-State appropriations	Dec. 19
		Shareholder lawsuits	Dec. 19
		FY 1996 Defense authorization	Dec. 28
1996	6	Welfare overhaul	Jan. 9
		Late-term abortion ban	April 10
		State Department authorization	April 12
		Product liability lawsuits	May 2
		Labor-management teams	July 30
		Land acquisition in wildlife refuge	Oct. 2
1997[1]	3	Disaster relief emergency spending	June 9
		Second/third trimester abortion ban	Oct. 10
		Restoration of 38 projects struck from military construction spending law	Nov. 13
1998	5	Expand tax benefits of education savings accounts	July 21
		Create school vouchers in D.C.	May 20
		Punish countries offering assistance to Iran's missile program	June 23
		Limited appropriations for agriculture/nutrition	Oct. 7
		Reauthorization and reorganization of State Department	Oct. 21
1999	5	Tax cuts	Sept. 23
		D.C. appropriations	Sept. 28
		Commerce-Justice-State appropriations	Oct. 25
		Foreign operations appropriations	Oct. 28
		Labor-HHS appropriations	Nov. 3

Source: The following Table for 1993–1998 was constructed from veto information from *Congressional Quarterly Almanacs* for the appropriate years; The information on the 1999 vetoes was taken from *Congressional Quarterly Weekly Reports* for the indicated months

[1]Clinton vetoed only three bills in 1997, but he used his line-item veto authority to take certain items from 11 other bills.

50 percent, since he was concerned that state money would run out before the total restoration project was completed.[39]

Clinton was ever aware of congressional power over the budget and on May 29, 1999, he pleaded with Congress to reject the proposed budget bills that would have anti-environmental riders on them. He was most concerned that if Congress passed such measures they would threaten public health as well as the environment.[40] Again in September 1999, Clinton became quite impatient with Congress for its opposition to global warming and to other environmental concerns. As Clinton charged, "Finally, I call on Congress to withdraw all appropriations 'riders' aimed at strangling programs that save energy, save consumers and business money, and reduce global warming pollution."[41]

Bill Signing   Certain presidents have found that their environmental priorities attract greater visibility through bill signing ceremonies. George Bush, for example, indicated a number of times that clean air was a high priority of his, particularly the quality of air in polluted urban areas. In signing the Clean Air Act of 1990, he issued a mission statement suggesting that passage of this law had been the culmination of a year-long crusade on his administration's part to fashion this legislation. As he pointed out, "it is my mission to guarantee it for this generation and for the generations to come. . . . Mission defined, mission accomplished."[42]

When it appeared the public needed another reminder that Bush had labeled himself an "environmental president," the president responded by using a September 18, 1991, ceremony at the Grand Canyon to sign an Environmental Agreement bill. He praised the agreement as a major landmark since it had been passed as a result of bringing together a heterogeneous group of supporters.[43] Despite this signing, not everyone believed that Bush was really a committed environmentalist. He therefore found it necessary the next year to repeat his commitment to the environment as he signed the Los Padres Condor Range and River Protection Act in June 1992, but this time the bill signing took place in Washington, DC, and not on the rim of the Grand Canyon.[44]

Presidents have on occasion also used these signing opportunities to criticize Congress for not responding the way they felt it should. President Clinton, when he signed the Safe Drinking Water Act Amendments of 1996, accused Congress of being too slow to react to environmental problems at hand. Because of this, he conjectured, some of the funds that might have been provided for safe drinking were no longer available.[45]

Individual Legislative Leaders

In 1932 to 1933 Franklin Roosevelt established himself as an effective legislative leader in the now classic first "100 days," during which the president encouraged the passage of 14 major pieces of legislation including establishment of the Civilian Conservation Corps and the Tennessee Valley Authority.[46] FDR also showed that the environment would be a focus of his by using every State of the Union address (except in 1936) to talk about the environment.[47] Roosevelt's legislative agenda focused on a select but manageable number of domestic environmental issues that showed his primary interest in forestry and national parks. The other issues that received some attention during Roosevelt's first term included water conservation, land management, wildlife, and natural resources.[48]

Truman and Eisenhower contributed little as legislative leaders, with the exception of the Federal Water Pollution Control Act in 1948 that Truman signed and the four pieces of legislation attributed to Eisenhower, including the Air Pollution Control Act of 1955, the Federal Water Pollution Control Act of 1956, the Water Facilities Act of 1958, and the Federal Hazardous Substances Labeling Act of 1960.[49]

FDR AND THE "GOLDEN AGE"

When we think *Roosevelt* and the *environment* we are likely to think of Teddy Roosevelt, Franklin's fifth cousin. While "TR" has many environmental successes attached to his name, among modern presidents, few can rival Franklin Roosevelt's accomplishments. Indeed, it was Franklin Roosevelt who has been applauded for introducing the "Golden Age of Conservation."[1]

Franklin Roosevelt, unlike others, was able to take his passion for forestry and the out-of-doors and use it to confront the disastrous unemployment and depressed economy. This president skillfully devised a program to benefit both the environment and the economy, establishing the Civilian Conservation Corps (CCC) to employ millions of citizens desperate for employment to work in the national parks and forests, building roads and trails and planting trees to help prevent flood and soil erosion. For him, conservation was closely tied to America's values. As he stated, "There is nothing so American as our national parks. The scenery and wildlife are native. The fundamental idea behind the parks is native. The parks stand as an outward symbol of this great human principle."[2]

In looking at various aspects of the Roosevelt presidency, we can tell the seriousness of his efforts for and on behalf of the environment by looking, first, at those who were in his administration. The most important of those sympathetic to the environment included Henry Wallace, FDR's Secretary of Agriculture and later vice president, and Harold Le Clair Ickes, Roosevelt's Secretary of the Interior from 1933 until 1946. These men were probably FDR's most important and closest advisers.

Equally important, of course, was the growth in government focus on resolving some of the environmental concerns. These new agencies and bureaucracies included not only the CCC, but also the Soil Conservation Service, the Soil Erosion Service, the National Resources Board, the Works Progress Administration, and the Division of Grazing.

Beyond the appearance of this administration, Roosevelt's skill as legislative leader in Congress allowed him to become an effective negotiator and organizer of coalition support. In addition, Roosevelt devised a healthy budget for the environment, at 20.8 percent of the general budget in 1935.[3]

FDR showed great strength in the weakest of presidential roles, viz., opinion/party leader. Roosevelt knew how to communicate with the public and sell his environmental program to Congress. It helped Roosevelt, as well, having a strong party base in Congress.

continued

> Overall, FDR was a strong environmental leader, an effective "environmental president." He tended to maximize his own personal resources and skills in making the environment important as a White House value.
>
> ---
>
> [1]Richard Lowitt, "Conservation, Policy On," in *Encyclopedia of the American Presidency*, Leonard W. Levy and Louis Fisher, eds., 4 vols. (New York: Simon and Schuster, 1994), 1: 289.
>
> [2] "Radio Address Delivered at Two Medicine Chalet" (August 5, 1934) in *Public Papers and Addresses of Franklin D. Roosevelt: The People Approve*, compiled by Samuel I. Rosenman, 5 vols. (New York: Random House, 1938), 3: 359.
>
> [3]Byron W. Daynes, William D. Pederson, and Michael P. Riccards, *The New Deal and Public Policy* (New York: St. Martin's, 1998), 116.

John Kennedy did not spend much time as a legislative leader worrying about the environment. Only two major pieces of legislation could be attributed to his legislative leadership—one of which included amendments to that same Water Pollution Control Act that was passed during the Truman years. The second bill of importance was the 1963 Clean Air Act.

Unlike these previous presidents, Lyndon Johnson encouraged passage of several important pieces of legislation focusing on water resources, the wilderness, land and water conservation, water quality, solid waste, highway beautification, natural gas, noise abatement, rivers, and trails.[50] In fact, 18 major bills were passed during the Johnson years, most of which were signed by the president during his first term in office.[51]

Richard Nixon assured that the 1970s would be the decade for environmental awareness, used the legislative leader role to support passage of the National Environmental Protection Act, used the executive order to create the Environmental Protection Agency, and encouraged passage of more pieces of environmental legislation than were passed in any other modern-day Congress.[52] Of the 25 pieces of environmental legislation that became law under Nixon, all but four were passed during his first term.[53] The Nixon legislation was broad and diversified, beginning with the National Environmental Policy Act—an act that for the first time required "environmental impact statements," and allowed public input before projects were undertaken. Other acts passed during this period treated such subject matter as endangered species, coal mine safety, water quality, clean air, hazardous materials, occupational safety and health, ocean dumping, pesticides, oil spills, and noise.[54] The characteristic that most typified the Nixon years was the intensity of congressional activity focused on the environment —somewhat reminiscent of the Roosevelt years in Congress. In reflecting on Nixon's legislative leadership, Soden and Steel lamented, "[s]ince that time, the environmental legislative record is less rambunctious and less fast-paced, and has come to address amendments and reauthorizations more than new legislation."[55]

Gerald Ford's presidency was somewhat vulnerable, given general opposition to his presidency as a result of the Watergate scandal. In addition, the economy received primary attention throughout the Ford years. Thus Gerald Ford did not enjoy the sort of "environmental" presidency that Richard Nixon had experienced. In fact, of the five public laws that were passed during his time in office, Ford opposed two of them—the Safe Drinking Water Act (PL 93-523) and the Toxic Substances Control Act (PS 94-469). The other three 1976 legislative acts involved a Resource Conservation and Recovery Act (PS 94-580), a Federal Land Policy Management Act (PL 94-579), and a National Forest Management Act (PS 94-588).

The Carter presidency was also a troubled presidency, but for very different reasons. Environmentalism, and the energy crisis in particular, took much of Carter's attention domestically. Despite the fact that Carter had some difficulty working with other Democrats in Congress, he was instrumental in getting Congress to pass some important energy acts including the Public Utilities Regulatory Policy Act, as well as appointing a Task Force on National Energy Policy.[56] He was also able to use the powers of his office to promote passage of a Clean Air Act and amendments to the Clean Water Act. In addition, he encouraged congresspersons to increase the Superfund resources and to pass the Surface Mining Control and Reclamation Act in 1977.

Of the Carter environmental bills that were most important during these years, the Alaska National Interest Lands Conservation Act of 1980 (PS 96-487) would probably head the list. It was also Carter's most controversial effort, if for no other reason than the vast expanses of land that were to be set aside by Congress and the president—it involved some 103 million acres and caused a great deal of concern on the part of the Alaska delegation in Congress. As Cecil Andrus and Joel Connelly put it, "Carter managed to leave behind a legacy of volcanic craters, alpine lakes, ancient forests and tundra, and federal land managers who weren't devoted only to drilling, digging up and cutting down the great resources of America's forty-ninth state."[57]

Ronald Reagan posed somewhat of a puzzle for students of the presidency and environment. He came into office with the desire to cut back on the environmental advances that had been made over the years. While there were some environmental bills that were passed during his presidency—including the Safe Drinking Water Amendments (PL 99-339) of 1986 and the Ocean Dumping Act of 1988 (PL 100-688)—the Hazardous and Solid Waste Amendment of 1984 became the most important environmental bill that year. Environmental activists in Congress probably deserve most of the credit for passage of these bills, however, since Reagan vetoed more environmental legislation than he supported. For example, he opposed the Superfund Amendments and Reauthorization Act of 1986 (PL 99-499), the Nuclear Waste Policy Amendments of 1987 (PL 100-203), as well as the Clean Water Act Amendments of 1989 (PL 100-203).[58]

George Bush pledged in 1988 to be a "Republican president in the Teddy Roosevelt tradition. A conservationist. An *environmentalist*."[59] Bush's support of the Clean Air Act Amendments (PL 101-549) served as a way to prove that his own claim to be an "environmental" president was accurate. This support also acted as a way for him to distance himself from Ronald Reagan and from the negative feelings that environmentalists had about the Reagan record. Unfortunately, Bush did not keep this focus toward the end of his presidency, as he, too, began to lash out at "environmental extremists."[60]

AIR POLLUTION: TO AIR IS BUSH—THE 1990 CLEAN AIR ACT

During the campaign and early in his presidency, George H.W. Bush labeled himself America's "environmental president," even "a Republican in the Teddy Roosevelt tradition."[1] Supporting and encouraging passage in 1990 of comprehensive amendments to the Clean Air Act became key to ensuring that the president was willing to protect America's environment. Yet the Clean Air Act that President Bush supported would become a legislative act tailored to the president's particular concerns and interests. These interests included supportive members of Congress and industrial interests that requested protection from having to pay excessive costs to clean up the environment. Even market incentives were built into the act, allowing purchase of licenses to pollute, or as it has been referred to, purchasing "effluent rights."[2] The act was to restrict automobile exhaust and reduce urban smog, control toxic pollutants from chemical plants, and monitor the discharge from electric power plants in order to stem acid rain.[3]

The act, however, attracted its share of opponents from both parties inside and outside Congress. One of those opponents, Democrat John Dingell of Michigan, was also chair of the House Commerce Committee, responsible for jurisdiction of the act. He was particularly concerned that the act did not exert too harsh a penalty against Detroit's automobile industry. Supporting the Dingell position to weaken the act were a number of Midwest congresspersons opposed to it because they saw that the utility companies and the coal industry in their constituencies would end up having to pay excessive costs for cleanup. In addition, John Sununu, Bush's chief of staff, attempted to weaken the act in October 1990, advocating that fewer restrictions should be leveled against the Midwest utility companies.[4]

As a result, President Bush came out firmly against the concerns of the Midwest utility companies, but refused to pressure the automobile industry in like manner. This uneven advocacy against air pollution by the president tended to weaken his position among environmentalists as an "environmental president."

Despite the fact that the Clean Air Act of 1990 was far from what environmentalists had hoped for, and cost between $25 and $30 billion a year,[5] it became one of the few domestic accomplishments during Bush's years in office.

[1]See George P. Brockway, "*The Dismal Science*: Pollution—Going Once, Going Twice...," *The New Leader*, October 30, 1989, 14.

[2]George P. Brockway, "*The Dismal Science*," October 30, 1989, 14.

[3]Paul Quirk, "Domestic Policy: Divided Government and Cooperative Presidential Leadership," in Colin Campbell and Bert A. Rockman, *The Bush Presidency: First Appraisals* (Chatham, NJ: Chatham House, 1991), 86.

[4]Colin Campbell, S.J., "The White House and Presidency under the 'Let's Deal' President," in Colin Campbell and Bert A. Rockman, *The Bush Presidency: First Appraisals* (Chatham, NJ: Chatham House, 1991), 212.

[5]Michael Duffy and Dan Goodgame, *Marching in Place: The Status Quo Presidency of George Bush* (New York: Simon & Schuster, 1992), 281, Endnote 63.

Bill Clinton's record is mixed as well. He was quite successful in reaching both Democrats and Republicans in the first year of the 103rd Congress and encouraging them to support his environmental priorities. This resulted in Congress supporting the procurement of land in Colorado, Montana, and Idaho, creation of a New Mexico recreational area, and protection of fishing rights along the Atlantic coast.[61]

Clinton could not strike a consensus with Republicans in the 104th Congress, however, once House Republicans became the majority party under Newt Gingrich. The Republicans' ideological guidepost, the Contract with America, also posed threats to environmental legislation. Risk assessment, cost-benefit analysis, and doing away with unfunded mandates that were incorporated in the contract served to delay implementation of environmental legislation.[62] Moreover, efforts on the part of the Republicans to reduce health protections, public safety, and environmental regulations were also frequent during this period. According to Carol Browner, Environmental Protection Agency head, this Congress would "undermine virtually every public-health and environmental protection that Americans have come to depend on."[63] House Republicans also reduced Fish and Wildlife Service programs by $2 billion, making it impossible to list additional endangered animals in the protected category. In addition, congressional Republicans took $1.3 billion from a fund set aside to ensure safe drinking water.[64] Also, budgeting for the national park system was reduced by 36 percent, risking closure of more than 200 national parks.[65]

In reflecting on the Republican control of the new Congress, environmentalist Michael W. Robbins, editor of *Audubon* magazine, stated that "[w]hat's alarming is the ignorance and radical anti-government view. . . held by some congressmen now chairing key House committees. In their 'hurl-out-the-baby-with-the-bath water' zeal to reduce the federal government, these ideologues assault the very idea of the commonwealth."[66] In the view of the League of Conservation Voters, the 104th Congress had perhaps "the worst environmental voting record of any Congress in the past 25 years."[67]

While Clinton's environmental focus had been more broadly oriented than that of most earlier presidents, his programs also ran into stiffer opposition. This occurred when he supported increasing fees for public mining as well as increasing grazing fees and restricting certain activities on public lands. He also defended the Clean Water Act and the Endangered Species Act, and tried to encourage strengthening of the Superfund to clean up the environment. Clinton confronted the ire of Republican-controlled Utah when he set aside 1.8 million acres of land in that state as the Grand Staircase–Escalante National Monument without first notifying any of Utah's policymakers.[68] The president then turned to the California desert, which became a focus of attention in his effort to strengthen his environmental legacy. Unlike his approach toward Utah residents, in establishing the Grand Staircase–Escalante National Monument, Clinton solicited support from the California congressional delegation and California citizens, and received it in abundance by the passing of the California Desert Protection Act in 1994.[69]

CASE STUDY: UP THE GRAND STAIRCASE—CLINTON AND THOSE UTAH REPUBLICANS

Bill Clinton visited Utah only a few times as president. He probably would never have come had his daughter Chelsea not wanted a college break and skiing trip in the powdered snows of Park City. One reason for his reluctance in visiting the state was, no doubt, based on the fact that Utah for years has been considered the most rigidly Republican state of all, just recently losing this title in the 2000 presidential election, to Utah's sister states Idaho and Wyoming.[1] Utah, in fact, had been so inhospitable to Clinton in 1992 that he had come in *third* in total votes for president, behind Republican George Bush and Independent Ross Perot.

Just prior to the 1996 election, Bill Clinton saw that because of his rather shaky environmental record, he needed to secure his base among environmentalists if he was going to win election. Utah seemed to be the natural state for his focus on regaining flagging environmental interest—he decided to create a new monument in a state where 64.2 percent of public lands were already owned by the federal government.

And so it was that on September 18, 1996, Bill Clinton, from his vantage point on the North Rim of the Grand Canyon, Arizona, announced that 1.7 million acres in southeastern Utah would now be known as the Grand Staircase–Escalante National Monument.

Within the state, reaction was fierce. Southern Utah ranchers saw this as a way to destroy their lifestyle by inviting unwanted tourism into the area. Utah's Republicans saw it as an act of cowardice coming from a Democratic president who feared even coming into this Republican state to make his announcement. The monument was also seen by a large number of Utah's anti-Washington, antigovernment, state rightists as a classic example of an all-powerful and meddlesome federal government invading an ideologically conservative state and stripping it from benefiting from 1.7 million acres of mineral-rich public land.

Voters in Utah's Third Congressional District—the district most affected by the monument—took out their ire on then-Democratic Representative Bill Orton, the only Democrat in the Utah delegation. Voters suspected that he knew about this action and should have stopped it. Actually, Orton did not know, nor could he have stopped the determined President Clinton. As a result, Orton lost his seat to Republican

Chris Cannon, who later became one of the House Managers in Clinton's impeachment hearing.

So what came of the Clinton effort? Well, environmentalists were resecured in the Democratic camp for 1996; but more important, Secretary of the Interior Bruce Babbitt, feeling somewhat guilty for having ignored Utah interests, and Utah Republican Governor Mike Leavitt brought political civility back into the confrontation, devising a "new partnership" between federal and state governments that has, since 1997, become a model for working through similar differences in environmental policy.

[1]See Jim Woolf, "*We're No. 3:* Utah Bumped as Top GOP Stronghold," *Salt Lake Tribune,* November 14, 2000, A1.

Environmentalists did question Clinton's support of the 1995 Emergency Salvage Timber Logging Sale program, which was attached as a rider to the 1995 Budget Rescission Act and which environmentalists saw as a threat to forests.[70] Environmentalists would also have liked to have seen President Clinton be more aggressive in his support of environmental causes. They thought him too passive, for example, in his efforts in California. Passage of the Desert Protection Act, environmentalists felt, was due more to the assertiveness of California policymakers and the public than from Clinton's own activity. Overall, environmentalists remained somewhat frustrated with Clinton's legislative efforts.[71]

Summary

There has been significant environmental legislation, as Glen Sussman and Mark Kelso argue, that every president since Kennedy has at least signed, if not advocated. Those most active in encouraging the pro-environmental legislation that added important ingredients to the environmental movement included Franklin Roosevelt, Lyndon Johnson, Richard Nixon, and Jimmy Carter.[72]

Richard Nixon and George Bush as legislative leaders—and Bill Clinton, to a limited extent—also employed creative techniques to lead Congress to becoming a positive part of the environmental movement. These presidents were all quite actively involved in protecting the environment.

The President as an Environmental Chief Executive

Chief executive may seem quite a powerful role for the president, since the framers of the Constitution determined that a chief executive should not share power with any advisory body. Yet the president in this role is often frustrated because the Constitution places fragmented power across the bureaucracy, often making it difficult for the president to exercise control over the executive branch.

When it comes to influencing policy, however, the president as chief executive does have at least two effective means to effect control. Namely, in the creation of *office structures* and in the *staffing* of government.

The Office Structures

Federal agencies have been established or have undergone alteration in their focus as a result of presidential *reorganizations*, which has had both a positive and a negative effect in facilitating environmental policy.

Franklin Roosevelt took full advantage of this, letting both his passion for the environment and his desire to put people back into the work force prevail, when he created the Civilian Conservation Corps (CCC). The CCC must be considered his most important contribution toward improving the quality of the environment. It was the first New Deal agency approved in 1933 by the Congress, and it not only put people back to work during the Great Depression, but it put them to work in national parks and forests. This resulted in the building of roads, visitor pathways, and other improvements benefiting public areas.[73] Roosevelt also created a number of other agencies with an environmental or conservation thrust, including the Office for Soil Erosion, the National Park Service, the Rural Electrification Administration, the Forest Service, the Bureau of Reclamation, and the Bureau of Fisheries.

The most ambitious reorganization plan of any president belonged to Richard Nixon, who planned to weaken the clientele-related departments of Agriculture, Commerce, Labor, and Transportation in order to allocate their functions to four new "super" departments—one of which would be called Natural Resources. This "super" department would focus on environmental affairs. In this reorganization—which never came about because of Nixon's resignation—the new Cabinet would have been limited to 8 departments rather than the 11 under previous presidents. Congress refused to approve the plan, however, even though it was sympathetic to the need for overall government reorganization.

While the "super" Cabinet reorganization failed, Nixon's creation of three other environmental agencies did not. These include the Environmental Protection Agency, the Environmental Quality Council, and the Citizens' Advisory Committee on the Environment.

The Environmental Protection Agency   The most successful of these agencies has been the Environmental Protection Agency (EPA), created in 1970.[74] It was established as an independent executive agency to protect and safeguard both the public health as well as the environment and, in 1998, had an annual budget of approximately $6.44 billion with a staff of 18,045 persons.[75]

Bill Clinton tried to elevate the Environmental Protection Agency (EPA) to Cabinet status.[76] Unfortunately for environmental policy, this proposal did not attract sufficient support among members of Congress, and even ran into serious opposition from at least one congressperson, Representative Billy Tauzin (D-LA), who insisted on a congressional investigation of the EPA to examine it for any "illegal" involvement in the environment.[77]

Federal Emergency Management Agency   Another important agency that has helped to shape environmental policy is the Federal Emergency Management Agency (FEMA) that was established during Jimmy Carter's administration in 1979 in order to protect property from national emergencies and disasters of all sorts. FEMA was staffed in 1998 with 4,888 persons, with a budget of $3.698 billion.[78]

A number of presidents, on using FEMA, have been criticized for not responding quickly enough to disasters, or for responding too quickly to them. Although FEMA has been helpful to presidents, it does suffer certain important weaknesses. As has been suggested, FEMA has little "regulatory authority, very limited mandating ability, relatively small budget and grant-issuance power, weak research capacity, professional and occupational conflicts (especially at the local level), inadequate agency self-evaluation, weak clientele support, [and] vacillating governor and state legislative support for emergency management. . . ."[79]

Other Reorganizations   On other occasions Congress has proven to be quite uncooperative with presidential plans for reorganization. In the 1960s, Lyndon Johnson unsuccessfully encouraged Congress to create a Department of Natural Resources in the executive branch. Congress was not so enthusiastic about this proposal and LBJ did not gain the support he had hoped for.

In 1977, Jimmy Carter attempted to obtain Congress's approval to create a Department of Energy. He received support for his efforts, but for this support he had to submit to major modifications of his proposal, even having to strip the department's authority to control energy prices.

An interesting addition to the Executive Office of the President under President Bush was Vice President Dan Quayle's Council on Competitiveness. This controversial advisory council was created as part of the plea that President Bush made in his January 28, 1991 State of the Union address, demanding of his Cabinet that they issue no new federal regulations for 90 days until an extensive review could be conducted of all regulations. The main purpose of Quayle's council was to oversee Cabinet activity and remove any regulation that might interfere with business competitiveness.[80] As was suggested by one critic, the council left neither "fingerprints" nor a "paper trail" that might justify its decisions.[81] Environmentalists were most unhappy with this council because it always favored business interests over the environment.[82]

The Council on Competitiveness came to an abrupt and unceremonious end under Bill Clinton, however, as he quickly abolished it through executive order in his first full day in office.[83] Clinton established, instead, a scaled-down version of it that was more accessible to the public. It became more of a review process that proposed that all written and oral communication between the White House and outside interests be written into the public record.

The Clinton-Gore "reinventing" of government allowed the Clinton administration to reorganize and reduce the size of federal government, making government less expensive and more efficient.[84] In so doing it was seen to give some support to the environment as one of Clinton's priorities, since it would "protect people, not bureaucracy; promote results, not rules; get action, not rhetoric."[85] Yet another result of the "reinvention," which was not greeted warmly by environmentalists, was the 12 percent reduction in the federal work force that affected some of the very agencies that dealt directly with environmental policy. These included the Department of Energy (reduced by 53 persons), the Environmental Protection Agency (reduced by 38 persons), the Department of the Interior (reduced by 29 persons), and the Federal Emergency Management Agency (reduced by 22 persons).[86]

Clinton did make a number of other structural changes in the executive branch that were designed to facilitate environmental policy, including creation of the National Biological Service, the White House Office on Environmental Policy, and the Council on Sustainable Development, which was specifically established to "integrate economic and environmental policies."[87] As Norman J. Vig and Michael E. Kraft argue, "the Clinton administration must be given credit for raising environmental considerations to a higher level of attention in the White House. The Office of Environmental Policy was in contact with the vice president's office, Cabinet secretaries, and other White House staffs on a daily basis."[88]

To introduce bio-based technology, Clinton organized an Interagency Council on Bio-based Products and Bio-energy.[89] The council prepares strategic plans for the president, outlining how the development of bio-based products and bio-energy will come about. Those products that the council is responsible for include commercial and industrial chemicals, pharmaceuticals, and products with large carbon sequestering capacity.[90]

Another new council recently introduced was based on Clinton's concern for "invasive species"—those species whose introduction might encourage environmental or economic harm to citizens. The new Federal Invasive Species Council will provide information and give advice to the president on preventing the introduction of invasive species.[91]

The D.C. Model   Like some presidents before him, Bill Clinton has used the federal government to showcase the potential for energy saving and protection for the environment. In his 1993 Earth Day speech, Clinton first announced that he was going to use the White House as an example of how to improve energy efficiency and environmental proficiency. In December 1999 he was able to report that the White House had actually saved $300,000 a year, which included $138,000 saved from installing more efficient lighting, $37,000 saved as a result of installation of a new heating and air conditioner system, and $15,000 saved from new timers and sprinklers that had been put to use. Other federal agencies were urged to follow this example, with the president hoping that the future occupant of the White House would see similar savings in all areas of the federal government by the year 2010.[92]

Presidential Appointments

While it is very important for a chief executive to have the structural capability to meet administrative needs, if a president has selected the right person for the position, he or she can often compensate for a lack of structure.

The Cabinet is the oldest advisory body associated with the president, but as a collective whole it has never been very important in strengthening the president's social agenda. Individual secretaries, however, have been excellent in doing just that.

Franklin Roosevelt combined the creation of new offices with the appointment of activist environmentalists and conservationists during his first term in office. His most important appointments included Harold Ickes, his Secretary of the Interior, and Henry Wallace, his Secretary of Agriculture, both of whom were FDR's closest and, at times, most impassioned advisers on conservation and the environment. Other important FDR environmental appointments included Rexford Tugwell, a staff aide; Hugh Bennett of the Soil Erosion Service; Arno Camerer of the

National Park Service; Morris L. Cooke of the Rural Electrification Administration; F.S. Silcox of the Forest Service; Elwood Mead of the Bureau of Reclamation; and Frank T. Bell of the Bureau of Fisheries.[93] Many of those named served in Roosevelt's environmental "kitchen Cabinet."

One of the reasons that Lyndon Johnson had a secure hold on environmental policy was the work of his Secretary of the Interior, Stewart Udall, a Kennedy holdover appointee. Udall was strongly supported by environmentalists. He was an enthusiastic supporter of conservation and the national park expansion, and worked to improve the quality of people's experience of the park system. Through Udall's leadership at Interior, as well as the enthusiastic public support of the Johnson program, LBJ enjoyed a successful environmental presidency.

One could immediately see the change in direction taken when Ronald Reagan came into office. Reagan slowed progress on the environment in the appointments he made. As Richard Nathan described it, Reagan's "administrative presidency" worked toward reversing years of bipartisan support for the environment in Congress.[94] Michael Kraft also observed, "Virtually all environmental policies were to be reevaluated [by Reagan], and reversed or weakened, as part of the president's larger political agenda."[95]

Reagan's campaign against federal law and the environment led him to appoint Ann Burford as the head of the Environmental Protection Agency. He encouraged her to limit environmental funding, deregulate, and restrict enforcement of federal environmental rules. Reagan used his authority to encourage the EPA to be more supportive of business interests. Norman J. Vig and Michael E. Kraft point out that this appointment was part of an attempt to control policy from within the bureaucracy. Reagan further showed his antagonism toward federal involvement with the environment with his appointment of James Watt, his first Secretary of the Interior; he encouraged Watt to limit funding and cut back on enforcement of federal rules.[96] Indeed, in appointing Ann Burford to the EPA and James Watt as Secretary of the Interior, a not-too-subtle message was sent to Americans that Ronald Reagan was not a close friend of the environment. These appointments also reflected Reagan's efforts to perpetuate his conservative philosophy throughout his bureaucracy.

George H.W. Bush surprised many by appointing some active environmentalists to his administration.[97] William Reilly, his selection to head the EPA, was a former president of the World Wildlife Fund and Conservation Foundation. Michael Deland, who had previously served as New England director of the Environmental Protection Agency, was made chair of the Council on Environmental Quality.[98] On the other hand, Bush also made appointments that convinced environmentalists that there would be little change from the difficult years of Ronald Reagan. Secretary of the Interior Manuel Lujan, Jr., was one example. He had previously made it quite clear as a Republican congressperson from New Mexico that as far as public lands were concerned there would be "no major departures" from the days of Ronald Reagan.[99]

Bill Clinton's environmental appointees were quite impressive. Mark Dowie estimated that Clinton hired about "two dozen environmentalists,"[100] placing them throughout government agencies and departments, with some holding down newly created positions inside such unlikely departments and agencies as the State Department,[101] National Security Council, and the Office of Management and Budget.[102]

The most important administrative pro-environmental appointments Clinton made, of course, were Vice President Al Gore and Secretary of the Interior Bruce Babbitt—both of whom had proven reputations among environmentalists prior to their appointment to the administration. Vice President Al Gore, for example, was one of the most visible of the vice presidents and took much of the responsibility in the administration for the advancement of environmental policy.

Other environmental activists included Carol Browner, director of the Environmental Protection Agency; Mollie Beattie, head of the Fish and Wildlife Service; Jack Ward Thomas, head of the Forest Service; Kathy McGinty, manager of the newly created White House Office on Environmental Policy; and Roger Kennedy, superintendent of the National Park Service.[103]

Clinton's selection of Gore, Babbitt, and Browner was a positive signal to the environmental community that this president felt the environment was a worthwhile issue on which to focus and that he would attempt to stay close to environmentalists' needs.

Techniques Used by the Chief Executive to Advance Environmental Priorities

Proclamations   A president may use the powers of chief executive to recognize a specific interest group, segment of industry, or activity taken on by individuals or groups by designating a particular week or special days on their behalf. The environment has benefitted from this option, such as in 1999 when Clinton declared April 19 through April 25 "National Park Week."[104] In setting this week apart Clinton hoped the public would remember those who work to preserve the national parks, which now include 378 sites that are regularly visited by 285 million persons a year.[105] Clinton did the same thing on October 15, 1999, when he declared the week of October 17 through 23 "National Forest Products Week, 1999." Again, the purpose in the designation was to get people to remember the importance of forests and their contribution to the welfare of the nation.[106]

Executive Orders   Many presidents have seized the advantage of executive orders to introduce change. In relying on this power, a president is not held captive to a Congress that might wish to oppose the president's programs. Franklin Roosevelt saw the wisdom in this as he used executive orders to advance conservation and environmental concerns in 1934 and to strengthen his hold over the environment by withdrawing public lands for conservation purposes.[107] Richard Nixon also introduced several important environmental policy changes by executive order, including the attempt to eliminate all air and water pollution in federal buildings.[108] Ronald Reagan used executive orders to better regulate and control environmental policy, such as with Executive Order 12291, which enabled the Office of Management and Budget to review new regulatory proposals.

Bill Clinton also introduced several new environmental programs through use of executive orders including his 1993 policies dealing with clean air and his 1999 Clean Water Action Plan.[109] His policies for cleaner air involved his Clean Car Initiative system.[110] A potentially more controversial environmental program introduced by executive oder in 1999 involved Clinton's energy program, which focused attention on bio-based technologies. The administration argued this program would both enhance the economy and help overcome global warming. The executive order was designed to coordinate all federal efforts concerning biomass fuels and material to hasten their development during the twenty-first century.[111]

Summary

The chief executive role offers the president a moderately strong platform from which to operate to strengthen environmental policy. Important progress can be made in facilitating an environmental agenda through both creation of new federal agencies and in reorganization of existing agencies. As important as structure, presidents have found, has been the staffing of those agencies when that staffing selects individuals sympathetic to the environment.

The President as an Environmental Commander-in-Chief/Chief Diplomat

The two roles that focus a president's attention on foreign affairs are *commander-in-chief* and *chief diplomat*. These are a president's strongest roles in terms of authority and resources. While the commander-in-chief role was originally but a military title, it has become a role far broader than this, a role that former Associate Supreme Court Justice Robert Jackson described as "the most dangerous one to free government in the whole catalogue of powers."[112]

The strength of the commander-in-chief is impressive, since decision making tends to be centralized and major decisions may involve only the president and a select number of key advisers. Another strength to the president operating as commander-in-chief is the natural well of public support for the presidency. A further advantage the president enjoys comes from access to exclusive information and the ability to monopolize it.

The president as chief diplomat is in almost as powerful a role. Constitutionally, the powers of foreign affairs are shared with Congress, but custom, judicial decisions, and statutory law have favored executive dominance. In addition, further leverage to the president in the area of foreign affairs has come from Supreme Court decisions such as the opinion of John Marshall in 1800 stating: "The President is the sole organ of the nation in its external relations, and its sole representative with foreign nations."[113]

Despite the fact that these two roles are the president's most powerful ones, they are also the roles that in the past have seldom been used by an environmental president. Yet policy issues of the environment are increasingly becoming more susceptible to international pressure as the world has been drawn closer together. For these issues, which do have international consequences, constitutional authority in this combined role puts the president in a very strong decision-making position. Russell Train argued that during Nixon's years in office, for instance, "internationally the United States was recognized and accepted as the world leader in environmental protection programs."[114]

Although environmentalism has not always been a part of every president's agenda, it will be more difficult in the future to ignore the international consequences of, say, conservation of natural resources and protection of air and water in the global arena. For example, we can assess the proportion of international environmental agreements reached by American presidents in relation to the total number of all international agreements (Table 6.5). A cursory examination of interna-

TABLE 6.5

Number of International Agreements (by President) Dealing with the Environment as a Percentage of All Agreements, 1949–1996

President	International Environmental Agreements[1] (N)	Percent of All Agreements[2] (%)
Truman	96	11.3
Eisenhower	275	14.3
Kennedy	117	14.1
Johnson	247	22.2
Nixon	248	19.1
Ford	165	21.3
Carter	312	26.7
Reagan	350	28.0
Bush	186	18.4
Clinton	252	25.2

Source: This Table is adapted from material in Lyn Ragsdale, *Vital Statistics on the Presidency: Washington to Clinton* (Washington, DC: Congressional Quarterly, 1996), 318–321. The more current data on Bill Clinton came from Lyn Ragsdale, *Vital Statistics on the Presidency*, revised ed. (Washington, DC: Congressional Quarterly, 1998), 329.

[1]Environmental agreements include agreements that focus on energy, communications, weather and navigation stations, land transfers, transportation, space and aeronautics, and the environment in general. See the categories adopted by Lyn Ragsdale, *Vital Statistics on the Presidency: Washington to Clinton* (Washington, DC: Congressional Quarterly, 1996), 321.

[2]Agreements include treaties, executive agreements, conventions and protocols. See Lyn Ragsdale, *Vital Statistics on the Presidency: Washington to Clinton* (Washington, DC: Congressional Quarterly, 1996), 321.

tional environmental agreements suggests that they constitute a rather small proportion of all agreements, ranging from a high of 28 percent to a low of 11.3 percent.

All presidents from Franklin Roosevelt through Bill Clinton have negotiated environmental agreements either on a bilateral or multilateral basis. Franklin Roosevelt, for example, used agreements in support of conservation. During a campaign stop in West Virginia during the 1936 presidential campaign, FDR considered it important to outline for the voters his administration's accomplishments in wildlife conservation. These included the Migratory Bird Treaty concluded with Mexico, which complemented a similar treaty concluded earlier with Canada.[115]

With few exceptions, as Table 6.5 points out, the number of environmental agreements over the years has increased with each succeeding administration. By the time Richard Nixon assumed the presidency, global concerns were endangered species and oil spills that threatened to pollute the world's oceans. It was suggested, in fact, by R. Michael M'Gonigle and Mark W. Zacher that "[v]irtually all recent advances in international regulations for oil pollution control have resulted from American pressure"[116] and, we might add, from Nixon's efforts. As Nixon stated in California in 1969, "This country can no longer afford to squander valuable time before developing answers to pollution and oil slicks from wells, tankers, or any other source. Every method in existing technology must be developed to control and remove oil pollution."[117] By the 1980s and 1990s, new global issues had emerged including stratospheric ozone depletion, acid rain, biodiversity, and global warming.

During the past two decades, the president has played an important role regarding several significant international agreements covering "new" global environmental threats. Scientific concern about the hole in the ozone and its consequences arose in 1974. Even though several countries, including the United States, imposed a ban on "nonessential chlorofluorocarbons" (CFCs), and the Vienna Convention for the Protection of the Ozone Layer of 1985 called on nations to take "appropriate measures to protect the ozone layer," substantive international action did not result until 1987.[118] That action came in the form of the Montreal Protocol of 1987, an agreement that required those who signed it to agree to work toward substantive reductions in production of CFCs. This agreement also created a few surprises for environmentalists when Ronald Reagan— whose domestic environmental agenda had been loudly criticized by environmentalists—signed it. As Reagan explained, "The Montreal Protocol is a model of cooperation. It is a product of the recognition and international consensus that ozone depletion is a global problem."[119] It was further strengthened by Bill Clinton who persuaded the Senate to fund the agreement.[120]

Cleanup of the air between Canada and the United States failed to achieve resolution until George H.W. Bush assumed the presidency and signed an air quality agreement with Canada in 1991, as an important step in an effort to resolve the acid rain problem.[121] This worked to dispel the anger expressed by Canada's prime minister, who had charged the Reagan administration with coming up with an "unacceptable" policy for resolving the problems created by acid rain. The prime minister legitimately argued that "the United States would be pretty upset with me if I were dumping my garbage in your backyard. That's exactly what is happening, except this garbage is coming from above."[122]

While George H.W. Bush used presidential power to ensure passage of the Clean Air Act Amendments in 1990, that same year Bush failed to sign a carbon dioxide emissions reduction agreement, along with most of the other industrialized countries at the United Nations World Climate Conference, submitting instead to political and business pressures.[123]

In 1992 at an Earth Summit in Rio, environmentalists were again disappointed with President Bush because he signed the global warming treaty only after it had been significantly weakened. The treaty required those countries that signed it to share the technologies and costs of maintaining the environment. He would agree only to persuade delegates to support his plan on global warming gases, but that plan excluded all binding timetables for reducing emissions or specific levels of emissions.[124] Although President Bush had campaigned that he would be the "environmental" president, his behavior at the summit indicated quite clearly a reversal in his commitment to environmental priorities. Moreover, Bush stood alone in the international forum by his refusal to sign the Biodiversity Treaty. His refusal to sign left the United States isolated among the host of international delegates.[125]

After winning the presidency in 1992, Bill Clinton signed the Biodiversity Treaty; however, that international agreement was held up in the United States Senate, since the Senate refused to bring it up for ratification. Clinton also signed the 1997 Kyoto Protocol that did much the same thing that the Biodiversity Treaty did in terms of trying to cooperatively maintain the environment. But the Senate has yet to pass this Protocol as well.[126]

George H.W. Bush also did the groundwork for Clinton on the North American Free Trade Agreement (NAFTA) in 1991. In addition to citing the economic benefits of free trade between the United States and Mexico, Bush highlighted his position that "prosperity offers the surest road to worker safety, public health, and indeed, environmental quality."[127] Bill Clinton eventually signed the NAFTA agreement for the United States in 1993, arguing that the legislation would provide both regional economic development and environmental protection. This was a position not shared by all environmentalists. In fact, with the signing of NAFTA, along with the General Agreement on Tariffs and Trade (GATT), Clinton managed to do damage to his relationship with many environmentalists such as those belonging to the Sierra Club, Friends of the Earth, and other groups. Environmentalists were convinced that the agreements lacked essential guarantees for environmental protection.[128]

Summary

The environment has been increasingly important in foreign affairs because the president has been engaged in both environmental diplomacy and national security issues related to the environment. Nearly every president, beginning with FDR and through Clinton, has signed important bilateral or multilateral agreements that have affected the environment.

The president not only represents an important position in American politics but also is a central figure in the international community, as Woodrow Wilson recognized long ago. As such, the president recognizes that the activities of individual nations have environmental consequences of a regional and international scale. The problem of acid rain during the Reagan administration is a good example of how the actions of one nation (i.e., United States) impinge on the quality of life in another country (Canada). The debates over stratospheric ozone depletion and global warming show the interconnections between countries. Disappearance of the ocean's fish resources has involved many nations' well-being. The prospect of war over access to resources such as water or oil always remains a dangerous prospect, and may constitute a new challenge for the president as chief diplomat and commander-in-chief, as global environmental issues quite possibly dominate the twenty-first century.

Conclusion

Not all presidents have responded the same way toward the environment. Some have actively supported environmental issues, while others have been aggressively opposed to them, with yet others symbolically responding to the challenges posed by the issue but doing nothing of substance (Table 6.6). Among the early modern presidents, FDR enthusiastically supported environmental issues. As opinion/party leader, he included environmental priorities in his State of the Union messages. As legislative leader, he included environmental funding in his budgets. As chief executive, he created several offices that fostered environmental protection.

Among the later modern presidents, Richard Nixon proved to be the most successful in promoting environmental priorities. It is unclear, however, what his

TABLE 6.6

Presidential Types Based on Their Approach to Environmental Policy

Activist	Symbolic
F. Roosevelt	H. Truman
L. Johnson	D. Eisenhower
R. Nixon	J. Kennedy
J. Carter	G. Ford
R. Reagan[1]	
G. Bush	
B. Clinton[2]	

[1] Ronald Reagan was an "activist" in opposition to environmental policy.

[2] Bill Clinton had a mixed record that fits between the activist and symbolic.

motives were. Nevertheless, one cannot deny his success. As chief executive, chief legislator, and opinion/party leader he became the modern "environmental" president. His impressive legislative record, along with his establishment of important executive agencies and declaration of the 1970s as the decade of the environment, was fully supported by the climate of the times, including public opinion and the impact of the first Earth Day. Nixon relied on each of the five major presidential roles to advance environmental interests.

All presidents have shaped the environment in one way or another. Nixon's successors—Carter, Reagan, Bush, and Clinton to a more limited degree—also used their power to shape environmental policy. In addition to his effort in energy conservation, Jimmy Carter signed into law the Superfund Act and also supported preserving public land in Alaska. As legislative leader, George Bush assisted Congress in passing the 1990 Clean Air Act but then began to reverse himself on other environmental priorities after feeling pressure from business and fellow Republicans in Congress. As chief executive, Bill Clinton appointed several environmentalists to important positions, including head of the EPA and the Department of the Interior, as well as set aside the 1.8 million acres of Utah land as a new national monument. But as legislative leader, Clinton's record was disappointing to environmentalists. The only major piece of legislation passed during his first term dealt with public lands in California. Yet, as chief executive he set aside a considerable amount of public lands near the end of his administration.

Ronald Reagan was an activist, but used his power as chief executive to reverse environmental progress, choosing economic development instead of environmental preservation. In the words of Vig and Kraft, "The 'environmental decade' came to an abrupt halt with Reagan's landslide victory in 1980. Although the environment was not a major issue in the election, Reagan was the first president to come to office with an avowedly anti-environmental agenda."[129] Considering the Reagan presidency as a whole, Carolyn Long, Michael Cabral, and Brooks Vandivort conclude that Reagan was quite an enemy of the environment. They argued:

> President Reagan used power resources to develop environmental policy to dismantle environmental protections. He made controversial political appointments to positions that had power over the environment, proposed drastic cuts to the budgets of environmental agencies, and used deregulation and executive

agreements to undercut much of the progress toward environmental protection that had been made under previous administrations.[130]

Much of what Reagan did to undercut the environment, as these researchers suggested, necessitated bypassing Congress and relying instead on his role as chief executive to frustrate environmental advancement through the use of staffing and appointment of such anti-environmental figures as Ann Burford, head of the Environmental Protection Agency, and James Watt, Secretary of the Interior. As well, Reagan severely reduced the budgets and personnel of environmental agencies.[131]

Sometimes it is not always clear where the president's true feelings lie. Even those presidents who would be considered supportive of the environment may not

---

Web Sites
The Environmental Presidency:

President and Vice President: **www.whitehouse.gov/WH/Welcome.html**

Presidential Research: **www.metalab.unc.edu/lia/president/President-directory.html**
www.pub.whitehouse.gov/search/everything.html

Executive Office: **www.whitehouse.gov/WH/EOP/html/EOP_org.html**

Cabinet: **www.whitehouse.gov/WH/Cabinet/html/cabinet_links.html**

Departments:

Justice: **www.usdoj.gov**

State: **www.state.gov**

Treasury: **www.treas.gov**

Defense: **www.defenselink.mil**

Presidential Libraries:

Franklin D. Roosevelt: **www.academic.marist.edu/fdr**

Harry S Truman: **www.trumanlibrary.org**

Dwight D. Eisenhower: **redbud.lbjlib.utexas.edu/eisenhower/ddehp.htm**

John F. Kennedy: **www.cs.umb.edu/jfklibrary/index.htm**

Lyndon Johnson: **www.lbjlib.utexas.edu**

Richard Nixon: **www.nixonfoundation.org**

Gerald Ford: **www.ford.utexas.edu**

Jimmy Carter: **carterlibrary.galileo.peachnet.edu**

Ronald Reagan: **www.reagan.utexas.edu**

George H.W. Bush: **www.csdl.tamu.edu/bushlib**

Bill Clinton: **www.Clintonpresidentialcenter.com/lib_index.html**

have strengthened it in all aspects. Comparing prosecution rates of individuals caught violating pollution laws, for example, one finds a mixed record. According to court records kept by the Public Employees for Environmental Responsibility (PEER), prosecutions of environmental violations actually fell under the Clinton administration during the 1996–1998 period, from what they were under George Bush during the years 1989–1991. The report found a 27 percent decrease in prosecutions and a 10 percent decline in conviction rates during these comparative years. As Executive Director Jeff Ruch of PEER suggested, "The criminal environmental enforcement record of the previous incumbent was clearly better by virtually every measure of prosecutorial effort."[132]

While we have focused primarily on those presidents among the 11 who were most active in responding to the environment, there were several presidents who could only be said to offer "symbolic" responses, if not to be said to ignore the environment altogether. Those who fit into this category include Truman, Eisenhower, Kennedy, and Ford (again see Table 6.6).

While environmental concerns are never going to dominate the agenda of all presidents, as countries become more interlinked, environmental considerations will continue to be shared, will become interlinked with other issues of consequence such as national security, and the president's place in the international community will become even more important in shaping the environment.

Endnotes

1 See Richard Lowitt, "Conservation, Policy On," in *Encyclopedia of the American Presidency*, Leonard W. Levy and Louis Fisher, eds., 4 Vols. (New York: Simon & Schuster, 1994), 1: 289.

2 See Michael E. Kraft, *Environmental Policy and Politics* (New York: HarperCollins, 1996), 71.

3 Fourteen years prior to the time this question was asked, the public responded in nearly the same way, with 61 percent supporting the idea that "Protection of the environment should be given priority even at the risk of curbing economic growth," and 28 percent supporting the statement that "Economic growth should be given priority, even if the environment suffers to some extent." See "Short Subjects," *The Gallup Poll Monthly*, no. 391 (April 1998), 43.

4 The larger, more encompassing category of "Economic problems"—which included the economy in general, taxes, unemployment/jobs, federal budget deficit, stock market, high cost of living/inflation, recession, and other specific economic problems—received 27 percent support in this Gallup poll question. See "Short Subjects," *The Gallup Poll Monthly*, no. 396 (September 1998), 34.

5 See "Short Subjects," *The Gallup Poll Monthly*, no. 396 (September 1998), 34.

6 Discussion of the theoretical framework has been taken from Raymond Tatalovich and Byron W. Daynes, *Presidential Power in the United States* (Monterey, CA: Brooks/Cole, 1984).

7 Byron W. Daynes, Raymond Tatalovich, and Dennis L. Soden, *To Govern a Nation: Presidential Power and Politics* (New York: St. Martin's Press, 1998), 2.

8 Because all of our presidents up through 2000 have been men, the masculine pronoun is used in this chapter. In addition, references to the presidency and presidents in general also use the masculine pronoun. Let us be quite clear, however: this usage in no way excludes the possibility or anticipation that in the future women may well occupy this position. In fact, popular candidate Elizabeth Dole

had as good a chance as anyone in securing the Republican party nomination for president in the year 2000, had she been well funded.

9   This role distribution first appeared in Raymond Tatalovich and Byron W. Daynes, *Presidential Power in the United States* (Monterey, CA: Brooks/Cole, 1984), 16. We also included this continuum in Byron W. Daynes, Raymond Tatalovich, and Dennis L. Soden, *To Govern a Nation: Presidential Power and Politics* (New York: St. Martin's Press, 1998), 2.

10   James W. Davis, *The President as Party Leader* (New York: Greenwood Press, 1992), 1.

11   Congressional Quarterly, *Nixon: The First Year of His Presidency* (Washington, DC: Congressional Quarterly Press, 1970), 2.

12   Congressional Quarterly, *Nixon: The First Year of His Presidency* (Washington, DC: Congressional Quarterly Press, 1970), 3.

13   Mary Etta Cook and Roger H. Davidson, "Deferral Politics: Congressional Decision Making on Environmental Issues in the 1980s," in Helen M. Ingram and R. Kenneth Godwin, eds. *Public Policy and the Natural Environment* (Greenwich, CT: JAI Press Inc., 1985), 48.

14   A number of scholars support the notion that Richard Nixon's interest in the environment was a politically motivated response to public interest. These include Walter Rosenbaum, *Environmental Politics and Policy*, 3rd ed. (Washington, DC: CQ Press, 1995), 79–80; Jacqueline Vaughn Switzer, *Environmental Politics: Domestic and Global Dimensions* (New York: St. Martin's, 1994), 16; Mark K. Landy, Marc J. Roberts, and Stephen R. Thomas, *The Environmental Protection Agency: Asking the Wrong Questions* (New York: Oxford University Press, 1990), 30–33; and Richard E. Cohen, *Washington at Work: Back Rooms and Clean Air* (New York: Macmillan, 1992), 15–16.

15   Stanley I. Kutler, *The Wars of Watergate: the Last Crisis of Richard Nixon* (New York: Alfred A. Knopf, 1990), 78.

16   See Dennis L. Soden and Brent S. Steel, "Evaluating the Environmental Presidency," in Dennis L. Soden, ed., *The Environmental Presidency* (Albany, NY: State University of New York Press, 1999), 330.

17   Richard Nixon, "Annual Message to the Congress on the State of the Union, January 22, 1970," *Public Papers of the Presidents of the United States: Richard Nixon* (Washington, DC: U.S. Government Printing Office, 1971), 13.

18   Taped conversation, April 19, 1972, tape 39, 23–46, NP quoted in Melvin Small, *The Politics of Richard Nixon* (Lawrence, KS: University Press of Kansas, 1999), 197.

19   Lydia Saad, "Poll Releases, April 22, 1999: Environmental Concern Wanes In 1999 Earth Day Poll," **http://www.gallup.com/poll/releases/pr990422.asp**. Retreived July 7, 1999; George Gallup, Jr., *The Gallup Poll: Public Opinion 1991* (Wilmington, DE: Scholarly Resources, Inc., 1992), 189.

20   See U.S. President, radio address to the nation on environmental issues—July 14, 1984. *Public Papers of the Presidents of the United States* (Washington, DC: Office of the Federal Register, National Archives and Records Service, 1986), Ronald Reagan, 1984, 1045–1046.

21   See Bill Clinton, "Remarks Announcing a New Environmental Policy," *Weekly Compilation of Presidential Documents*, 29, no. 6 (1993), 42.

22   This figure of 30 promised proposals comes from a compilation from Bill Clinton and Al Gore from their book, *Putting People First: How We Can All Change America* (New York: Times Books, 1992). The compilation was constructed by Charles O. Jones and appeared in table form in his book *Clinton and Congress 1993–1996* (Norman, OK: University of Oklahoma, 1999), 66.

23 "The Text of President Clinton's State of the Union Address to Congress," *New York Times*, January 28, 2000, A17.

24 Bill Clinton, "Remarks on the Observance of Earth Day, April 21, 1994," *Public Papers of the Presidents of the United States: William J. Clinton* (Washington, DC: U.S. Government Printing Office, 1995).

25 When speaking of *major speeches* we have references to such speeches as the State of the Union messages, addresses to Congress, the Inaugural Address, and speeches to the nation. *Minor speeches* refer to such events as news conferences, press releases, interviews with reporters, speeches to interest groups, and town meetings. Professor Daynes and Sussman use this breakdown of speeches in their recent book, *The American Presidency and the Social Agenda*, (Prentice Hall, 2001). For a speech to qualify as a speech dealing with the environment, a three-line rule was used when counting the speeches, wherein at least three lines of the speech had to relate to the environment before it was counted as an environmental speech.

26 Raymond Tatalovich and Byron W. Daynes, eds., *Social Regulatory Policy: Moral Controversies in American Politics* (Boulder, CO: Westview, 1988), 122.

27 Two early studies that support this idea area are Lawrence H. Chamberlain, *The President, Congress and Legislation* (New York: Columbia University Press, 1946) and Ronald C. Moe and Steven C. Teal, "Congress as Policy-Maker: A Necessary Reappraisal," *Political Science Quarterly*, September 1970, 443–470.

28 See the following sources: *Congressional Quarterly's Guide to the Presidency* (Washington, DC: Congressional Quarterly, 1989), 451; *Congressional Quarterly Weekly Report*, December 19, 1992, 3925–3926; and *Weekly Compilation of Presidential Documents* 1995–1996 (Washington, DC: U.S. Government Printing Office).

29 U.S. President, "Veto of Bill to Amend the Federal Water Pollution Control Act, February 23, 1960," *Public Papers of the Presidents of the United States* (Washington, DC: Office of the Federal Register, National Archives and Records Service, 1961), Dwight D. Eisenhower, 208–210.

30 U.S. President, "Veto of the Federal Water Pollution Control Act Amendments of 1972—October 17, 1972," *Public Papers of the Presidents of the United States* (Washington, DC: Office of the Federal Register, National Archives and Records, 1972), Richard Nixon, 991.

31 U.S. President, *Public Papers of the Presidents of the United States* (Washington, DC: Office of the Federal Register, National Archives and Records Service, 1975), Richard Nixon, 1974, 990–993.

32 "Message to the House of Representatives Returning Without Approval the Department of the Interior and Related Agencies Appropriations Act, 1996," *Weekly Compilation of Presidential Documents* 31, no. 51 (December 18, 1995), 2198.

33 Office of the Press Secretary, "Statement by the Press Secretary," The White House **Publications-Admin@Pub.Pub.WhiteHouse.Gov**, October 22, 1999. Retrieved October 22, 1999.

34 While Clinton's percentages were much lower, Clinton's overall budget, of course, was much higher. In 1994 Clinton devoted 1.3 percent to the environment, whereas in 1995 he designated 1.4 percent of the budget for environmental pursuits. For Roosevelt, the first-term budget figures were based on funding for the Departments of Agriculture and Interior and the Federal Power Commission, whereas the Clinton figures came from environmental funds granted to the Departments of Energy, Interior, and Agriculture.

35 See U.S. President, Annual Budget Message to Congress, Fiscal Year 1972—January 29, 1971, *Public Papers of the Presidents of the United States* (Washington,

DC: Office of the Federal Register, National Archives and Records Service, 1972), Richard Nixon, 1971, 46–68.

36   See U.S. President, Annual Budget Message to Congress, Fiscal Year 1974—January 29, 1993, *Public Papers of the Presidents of the United States* (Washington, DC: Office of the Federal Register, National Archives and Records Service, 1975), Richard Nixon, 1973, 32–48.

37   U.S. President, "Letter to the Speaker of the House of Representatives and the President of the Senate on Soil and Water Conservation—March 22, 1985," *Public Papers of the Presidents of the United States* (Washington, DC: Office of the Federal Register, National Archives and Records Service, 1986), Ronald Reagan, 1985, 426.

38   See examination of budget outlays for the EPA, Defense Department, Interior and Energy Departments in Dennis Soden and Brent S. Steel, "Evaluating the Environmental Presidency," in Dennis Soden, ed., *The Environmental Presidency* (Albany, NY: State University of New York Press, 1999), 319–320.

39   U.S. President, "Statement on Signing the Water Resources Development Act of 1996—October 12, 1996," *Public Papers of the Presidents of the United States* (Washington, DC: Office of the Federal Register, National Archives and Records Service, 1998), William J. Clinton, 1996, 1830–1831.

40   Office of the Press Secretary, "Protecting Our Water and Our Environment," The White House **Publications-Admin@Pub.Pub.WhiteHouse.Gov**, May 29, 1999. Retrieved May 29, 1999.

41   Office of the Press Secretary, "Statement by the President," The White House **Publications-Admin@Pub.Pub.WhiteHouse.Gov**, September 27, 1999. Retrieved September 27, 1999.

42   "Remarks on Signing the Bill Amending the Clean Air Act," November 15, 1990, *The Presidential Papers Infobase*, CDdex Information Group. E-mail **cdex@autosim.com**. Lindon, UT.

43   See U.S. President, Remarks at an environmental agreement signing ceremony at the Grand Canyon—September 18, 1991, *Public Papers of the Presidents of the United States* (Washington, DC: Office of the Federal Register, National Archives and Records Service, 1992), George Bush, 1991, 1173–1176.

44   See U.S. President, Statement of signing the Los Padres Condor Range and River Protection Act—June 19, 1992, *Public Papers of the Presidents of the United States* (Washington, DC: Office of the Federal Register, National Archives and Records Service, 1993), William J. Clinton, 1992, 985–986.

45   See U.S. President, Remarks on signing the Safe Drinking Water Act Amendments of 1996—August 6, 1996, *Public Papers of the Presidents of the United States* (Washington, DC: Office of the Federal Register, National Archives and Records Service, 1998), William J. Clinton, 1996, 1262–1263.

46   Roger Biles, *A New Deal for the American People* (DeKalb, IL: Northern Illinois University Press, 1991), 34–45.

47   See Byron W. Daynes, "Two Democrats, One Environment: First-Term Efforts of Franklin Roosevelt and Bill Clinton to Shape the Environment," in Byron W. Daynes, William D. Pederson, and Michael P. Riccards, *The New Deal and Public Policy* (New York: St. Martin's, 1998), 115.

48   See Byron W. Daynes, "Two Democrats, One Environment" Ibid., 116.

49   A listing of these major legislative acts comes from Dennis L. Soden and Brent S. Steel, "Evaluating the Environmental Presidency," in Soden, ed., *The Environmental Presidency* (Albany, NY: State University of New York, 1999), 315–317.

50 Ibid.
51 Russell Train, "The Environmental Record of the Nixon Administration," *Presidential Studies Quarterly*, Vol. 26, no. 1 (Winter 1996), 185–196.
52 Michael E. Kraft, *Environmental Policy and Politics* (New York: HarperCollins College Publishers, 1996), 71–74.
53 See Dennis L. Soden and Brent S. Steel, "Evaluating the Environmental Presidency," in Soden, ed., *The Environmental Presidency* (Albany, NY: State University of New York, 1999), 315–316.
54 Ibid. Also see Raymond Tatalovich and Mark J. Wattier, "Opinion Leadership: Elections, Campaigns, Agenda Setting, and Environmentalism," in Dennis L. Soden, ed., *The Environmental Presidency* (Albany, NY: State University of New York, 1999), 166–168, for a detailed look at the most important legislation that came out during Nixon's years.
55 See Dennis L. Soden and Brent S. Steel, "Evaluating the Environmental Presidency," in Soden, ed., *The Environmental Presidency* (Albany, NY: State University of New York, 1999), 318.
56 When announcing this Task Force, Carter also suggested that some persons in his own administration might serve on the Task Force including Secretary of the Treasury W. Michael Blumenthal, Secretary of Energy James R. Schlesinger, Secretary of Commerce, Juanita M. Kreps, and two of the president's chief advisers, Stuart Eizenstat and Charles Schultze. See "Energy and Inflation Task Forces," *Public Papers of the Presidents of the United States* (Washington, DC: Office of the Federal Register, National Archives and Records Service, 1980), Jimmy Carter, 1979, Vol. 2, 1216–1217.
57 Cecil Andrus and Joel Connelly, "Lessons of the Land: How Carter's Interior Secretary Won a Compromise in the Great Alaska Lands Debate," @ **http://www.adn.com/weak/wearkive/we981108.htm**. Retrieved November 8, 1999.
58 The basic Nuclear Waste Policy Act (PL 97-425) of 1983 did pass Congress, but its amendments did not.
59 See John Holusha, "Bush Pledges Aid for Environment," *New York Times* (September 1, 1988), 9.
60 Michael E. Kraft, *Environmental Policy and Politics*, op. cit., 81.
61 See *Congressional Quarterly Almanac, 103rd Congress, 2nd Session, 1993* (Washington, DC: Congressional Quarterly, 1994), 49: 278–285; and *Congressional Quarterly Almanac, 103rd Congress, 2nd Session, 1994*, op.cit., 50: 254–267.
62 See Ed Gillespie and Bob Schellhas, eds., *Contract with America* (Random House: Times Books, 1994), 125–141.
63 "Gingrich Flashes His 'Green' Card, but Is Color Faded?" *Salt Lake Tribune*, February 17, 1995, A1.
64 Bob Benenson, "Environmental Laws Take a Hit," *Congressional Quarterly Weekly Report* (March 18, 1995), 797.
65 Public opposition to these cuts forced the House to cut its requests back to 10 percent. See "The President's Radio Address," *Weekly Compilation of Presidential Documents* 31, no. 35 (August 26, 1995), 1457; see also "Clinton to Take a Swing at 'Anti-Green' GOP," *Salt Lake Tribune*, August 18, 1995, A1.
66 Michael W. Robbins, "Earth Day and Clear Days," *Audubon* 97, no. 2 (March–April 1995), 6.
67 Paul Rauber, "Elephant Graveyard," *Sierra* 81, no. 3 (May/June 1996), 24.
68 Martin A. Nie, "'It's the Environment, Stupid!' Clinton and the Environment," *Presidential Studies Quarter* 27, no. 1 (Winter 1997), 44.

[69] See Norman J. Vig, "Presidential Leadership and the Environment: From Reagan and Bush to Clinton," in Norman J. Vig and Michael E. Kraft, eds., *Environmental Policy in the 1990s* (Washington, DC: CQ Press, 1994), 89–90.

[70] Ibid.

[71] See Walter Rosenbaum, *Environmental Politics and Policy*, 3rd ed. (Washington, DC: Congressional Quarterly, 1995), 325.

[72] See a splendid listing of significant legislation in Glen Sussman and Mark Andrew Kelso, "Environmental Priorities and the President as Legislative Leader," in Dennis Soden, ed., *The Environmental Presidency* (Albany, NY: State University of New York Press, 1999), 134–135.

[73] U.S. President; "Three Essentials for Unemployment Relief (CCC, FERA, PWA), March 21, 1933;" *Public Papers and Addresses of Franklin D. Roosevelt* (New York: Macmillan Company, 1938), Franklin D. Roosevelt, 1933, 80–84.

[74] U.S. President, "Special Message to the Congress About Reorganization Plans to Establish the Environmental Protection Agency and the National Oceanic and Atmospheric Administration, July 9, 1970," *Public Papers of the Presidents of the United States* (Washington, DC: Office of the Federal Register, National Archives and Records Service, 1971), Richard Nixon, 1970, 578–586.

[75] Department of Commerce, Economics and Statistics Administration, Bureau of the Census, *Statistical Abstract of the United States: 1998*, 118th ed. (Washington, DC: Department of Commerce, 1998), 353.

[76] U.S. President, "Remarks on Earth Day, April 21, 1993," *Public Papers of the Presidents of the United States* (Washington, DC: Office of the Federal Register, National Archives and Records Service, 1994), William J. Clinton, 1993, 468–472.

[77] "Call for an Investigation Into Activities of the Environmental Protection Agency," *Congressional Record—House*, 104th Congress, 1st Session, May 9, 1995, H4609–H4616.

[78] Department of Commerce, Economics and Statistics Administration, Bureau of the Census, *Statistical Abstract of the United States: 1998*, 118th ed. (Washington, DC: Department of Commerce, 1998), 353, 339.

[79] Richard T. Sylves, "Ferment at FEMA: Reforming Emergency Management,"*Public Administration Review*, 54 (3)(1993), 307.

[80] See Elizabeth A. Palmer, "White House War on Red Tape: Success Hard to Gauge," *Congressional Quarterly Weekly Report*, May 2, 1992, 1155.

In its short history it became a major deregulatory voice of the administration, involved in environmental issues including clean air policies, industrial safety laws, automobile emission laws, and food and drug regulations. As its last political and ideological battle before the Clinton administration took over, the Quayle council attempted to tackle one more environmental issue by again redefining the meaning of "wetlands" in response to pressures by farmers and developers who wanted wetlands reduced in size. Had the council succeeded in its efforts, it would have preceded a congressionally sanctioned study by the National Academy of Sciences, ordered to settle the scientific dispute over wetlands. See John H. Cushman, Jr., "Quayle, in Last Push for Landowners, Seeks to Relax Wetland Protections," *New York Times*, November 12, 1992, A8.

[81] See Cornelius Kerwin, *Rulemaking: How Government Agencies Write Law and Make Policy* (Washington, DC: CQ Press, 1994), 85; and Michael E. Kraft, *Environmental Politics and Policy in the 1990s* (NY: HarperCollins, 1995), 19.

[82] Cornelius M. Kerwin, *Rulemaking: How Government Agencies Write Law and Make Policy* (Washington, DC: Congressional Quarterly, 1994), 184.

83 Bill Clinton was instrumental in 1993 in strengthening the Environmental Protection Agency in both its enforcement program and bringing greater focus to the program. This enabled the agency to ensure greater compliance with environmental laws by having additional authority to punish polluters. See Press Release, "A Look at EPA Accomplishments: 25 Years of Protecting Public Health and the Environment," December 1, 1995 @ **www.epa.gov/history/topics/epa/25b.htm**. Retieved April 19, 2001.

84 See Donald F. Kettl, "Did Gore Reinvent Government? A Progress Report," *New York Times*, September 6, 1994, A19.

85 Al Gore, *The Best Kept Secrets* (Washington, DC: U. S. Government Printing Office, 1996), 90.

86 Ibid., 17.

87 President's Council on Sustainable Development. See **http://www.whitehouse.gov/PCSD**. Retrieved December 11, 1999.

88 Norman J. Vig and Michael E. Kraft, eds., *Environmental Policy: New Directions for the Twenty-First Century*, 4th ed. (Washington, DC: Congressional Quarterly Press, 2000), 111.

89 Office of Press Secretary, "President Clinton and Vice President Gore: Growing Clean Energy for the 21st Century," **Publications-Admin@Pub.Pub.WhiteHouse.Gov**, August 12, 1999. Retrieved August 12, 1999.

90 Office of the Press Secretary, "Executive Order: Developing and Promoting Biobased Products and Bioenergy," **Publications-Distribution@pub.pub.whitehouse.gov**, Executive Order on Developing Biobased Products, August 12, 1999. Retrieved August 12, 1999.

91 Office of the Press Secretary, "Executive Order: Invasive Species," **Publications-Distribution@pub.pub.whitehouse.gov**, February 3, 1999. Retrieved February 3, 1999.

92 Office of the Press Secretary, "The Greening of the White House: Saving Energy, Saving Money and Protecting our Environment," The White House **Publications-Admin@Pub.Pub.WhiteHouse.Gov**, December 2, 1999. Retrieved August 2, 1999.

93 Jay Darling, originally appointed to head the Bureau of Biological Survey, became disillusioned with FDR's approach to the environment and became one of his chief critics on the administration's wildlife conservation program.

94 Richard Nathan, *The Administrative Presidency* (New York: Wiley, 1983).

95 Ibid., 79.

96 Karen O'Connor and Lee Epstein, "Rebalancing the Scales of Justice," *Harvard Journal of Law and Public Policy*, Fall 1984, 483–506.

97 See Philip Shabecoff, "Bush Lends an Ear to Environmentalists," *New York Times*, December 1, 1988, 13.

98 See Norman J. Vig and Michael E. Kraft, eds., *Environmental Policy: New Directions for the Twenty-First Century*, 4th ed. (Washington, DC: Congressional Quarterly Press, 2000), 105.

99 Ibid.

100 See Mark Dowie, "Friends of Earth—or Bill? The Selling (Out) of the Greens," *The Nation*, April 18, 1994, 514.

101 U.S. President, "Nomination for Posts at the Department of State, May 6, 1993," *Public Papers of the Presidents of the United States* (Washington, DC: Office of the Federal Register, National Archives and Records Service, 1994), William J. Clinton, 1993, 468–472.

102 On July 20, 1995, for example, President Clinton announced his intention to appoint Eileen B. Claussen as Assistant Secretary for Oceans, Environment, and International Scientific Affairs for the State Department. "President Names Eileen Claussen to Serve as Assistant Secretary of State for Oceans, Environment, and International Scientific Affairs," Office of the Press Secretary, The White House, July 20, 1995, Almanac Information Server, 19.

103 Jim Baca, Clinton's first Bureau of Land Management chair, was another activist who later quit the administration, disillusioned with Clinton's decision-making style.

104 Office of the Press Secretary, "National Park Week, 1999," The White House, **Publications-Admin@Pub.Pub.WhiteHouse.Gov**, April 16, 1999. Retrieved April 16, 1999.

105 Ibid.

106 Office of the Press Secretary, "National Forest Products Week, 1999," **Publications-Admin@pub.pub.whitehouse.gov**, October 15, 1999. Retrieved October 15, 1999.

107 U.S. President, "A Typical Executive Order (No. 6910) on Withdrawal of Public Lands to be Used for Conservation and Development of Natural Resources, November 26, 1934," *Public Papers and Addresses of Franklin D. Roosevelt* (New York: Macmillan Company, 1938), Franklin D. Roosevelt, 1934, 477–479.

108 U.S. President, "Statement on Signing an Executive Order for the Control of Air and Water Pollution at Federal Facilities, February 4, 1970," *Public Papers of the Presidents of the United States* (Washington, DC: Office of the Federal Register, National Archives and Records Service, 1971), Richard Nixon, 1970, 78.

109 Office of the President, "Memorandum on Clean Water Protection," May 29, 1999, *Public Papers of the President of the United States*, Vol. I (Washington, DC: Office of the Federal Register, National Archives and Records Service, 2000), William J. Clinton, 1999, 857.

110 U.S. President, "Remarks on the Federal Fleet Conversion to Alternative Fuel Vehicles, December 9, 1993," *Public Papers of the Presidents of the United States* (Washington, DC: Office of the Federal Register, National Archives and Records Service, 1994), William J. Clinton, 1993, 2145–2146.

111 Office of the Press Secretary, "Developing and Promoting Biobased Products and Bioenergy," The White House **Publications-Admn@Pub.Pub.WhiteHouse.Gov**, August 12, 1999. Retrieved August 14, 1999.

112 See Warren W. Hassler, Jr., *The President as Commander in Chief* (Menlo Park, CA: Addison-Wesley, 1971), 11.

113 Justice Sutherland quoting John Marshall in *U.S. v. Curtiss-Wright Export Corp.*, 299 U.S. 304 (1936).

114 Russell Train, "The Environmental Record of the Nixon Administration," *Presidential Studies Quarterly* 26, no. 1 (Winter 1966), 195.

115 "Campaign Address at the Mountain States Forest Festival, Elkins, West Virginia, October 1, 1936," *The Public Papers and Addresses of Franklin D. Roosevelt*, Vol. 2 (New York: Random House, 1938), 396–400.

116 R. Michael M'Gonigle and Mark W. Zacher, *Pollution, Politics, and International Law: Tankers at Sea* (Berkeley: University of California Press, 1979), 289.

117 "Statement on Coastal Oil Pollution at Santa Barbara, California, February 11, 1969," *Public Papers of the Presidents: Richard Nixon, 1969* (Washington, DC: Government Printing Office, 1970), 93.

118 Marvin S. Soroos, "From Stockholm to Rio and Beyond: The Evolution of Global Environmental Governance," in Norman J. Vig and Michael E. Kraft, eds. *Environmental Policy in the 1990s*, 3rd ed. (Washington, DC: CQ Inc., 1997).

119   "Statement on Signing the Montreal Protocol on Ozone-Depleting Substances, April 5, 1988," *Public Papers of the Presidents of the United States: Ronald Reagan* (Washington, DC: U.S. Government Printing Office, 1990), 420–421.

120   Office of the Press Secretary, "President Clinton and Vice President Gore Protecting Our Ozone Layer, September 16, 1999," The White House, **Publications-Admin @pub.pub.whitehouse.gov**. Retrieved September 16, 1999; Amendment No. 1795 restored to the Montreal Protocol Fund in the amount of $1,897,000,000. "Amendment No. 1795," *Congressional Record—Senate*, 106th Congress, First Session, vol. 145, September 24, 1999, S11406.

121   "Remarks by the President and Prime Minister Brian Mulroney of Canada at the Air Quality Signing Ceremony in Ottawa, March 13, 1991," *Public Papers of the Presidents of the United States: George Bush* (Washington, DC: U.S. Government Printing Office, 1991), 254–257.

122   Quoted in *New York Times*, April 25, 1988, A10.

123   Marvin S. Soroos, "From Stockholm to Rio: The Evaluation of Global Environmental Governance," in Norman J. Vig and Michael E. Kraft, eds. *Environmental Policy in the 1990s*, 2nd ed. (Washington, DC: Congressional Quarterly Inc., 1994), 313–314.

124   Ibid., 295.

125   Rudy Abramson, Norman Kempster, and James G. Zang, "Bush Will Not Sign Wildlife, Habitat Treaty," *Los Angeles Times*, May 30, 1992; Russell Mittermeier and Peter Seligmann, "U.S. Should Take a Stand on Biodiversity," *Christian Science Monitor*, July 17, 1992.

126   "Issue Forum" *Washington Post*, October 25, 1999, S1.

127   "Remarks at a Meeting with Hispanic Business Leaders in Houston, Texas, April 8, 1991," *Public Papers of the Presidents of the United States: George Bush* (Washington, DC: U.S. Government Printing Office, 1991), 345–348.

128   It was the Sierra Club, Friends of the Earth, and Public Citizen that unsuccessfully challenged NAFTA in federal court, demanding that there first be an Environmental Impact Statement required before it could be passed. See Martin A. Nie, "'It's the Environment, Stupid!' Clinton and the Environment," *Presidential Studies Quarterly* 27, no. 1 (Winter 1997), 43.

129   Norman J. Vig and Michael E. Kraft, eds., *Environmental Policy: New Directions for the Twenty-First Century*, 4th ed. (Washington, DC: Congressional Quarterly Press, 2000), 101.

130   Carolyn Long, Michael Cabral, and Brooks Vandivort, "The Chief Environmental Diplomat: An Evolving Arena of Foreign Policy," in Soden, ed., *The Environmental Presidency* (Albany, NY: State University of New York, 1999), 210.

131   Carolyn Long, Michael Cabral, and Brooks Vandivort, "The Chief Environmental Diplomat: An Evolving Arena of Foreign Policy," in Soden, ed., *The Environmental Presidency* (Albany, NY: State University of New York, 1999), 211.

132   Russell Mokhiber and Robert Weissman, "Prosecution of Environmental Crimes Has Fallen During Clinton Administration," *Liberal Opinion Week*, December 6, 1999, 2.

CHAPTER 7

Executive Agencies and Environmental Policy

The Constitution created three major branches of government. These are the legislative to create laws, the executive to enforce laws, and the judicial to interpret laws. Yet few of us are familiar with what many call the fourth branch of government, the array of administrative and regulatory agencies. While the Constitution makes no mention of this fourth branch, there are currently more than 100 federal agencies in operation, employing some 1.8 million federal employees. At the state and local level far more administrative agencies and public employees carry out the work of government. To help you understand environmental politics and policy, this chapter concentrates on the roles and functions of these administrative agencies.

The fourth branch of government is sometimes referred to as the bureaucracy. While the popular use of that term is often negative, focusing on such unfavorable characteristics as impersonality, sluggishness, and rigidity, more positive characterizations include predictability, neutrality, deliberateness, and ability to mobilize to complete tasks.[1] Actually, dividing the word into two parts—*bureau* (or "office" in French) and *cracy* (or "form of rule" in Greek)—helps us appreciate the meaning of the term. Classic writings spell out the crucial elements of bureaucracy's inner structure, beyond the notion of "government by offices and desks."[2] Six characteristics stand out: division of labor (fixed jurisdictional areas), hierarchy (clear superior-subordinate relations), written documentation (as opposed to oral understandings), specialized expertise, a duty ethic characterizing officials, and a predictable set of general rules.[3] Typically bureaucrats are contractually obligated to the organization, work full-time under its control, and identify their career with it, although recent studies of U.S. public service suggest that these traditional descriptions are changing.[4] Nonetheless, the above characteristics of bureaucratic structures help us understand the nature of administrative agencies and their operations.

Federal administrative agencies derive their power from Congress and the president and, ultimately, the people, who delegate tasks to them to be sure the business of government is carried out. Agencies are most often created through enabling statutes that delegate powers to them so they may advance the public interest. In addition to creating administrative agencies, enabling legislation often specifies the agency's location, resources, longevity, authority, and the means of exercising its delegated powers. The president has reorganization powers to shift, merge, or close down agencies, subject to certain limitations.[5] While administrative agencies may be referred to as a fourth branch of government, this is not accurate because they lack the independence of traditional branches, remaining under the control of the three Constitutional branches. Nonetheless, it is estimated that "over 90 percent of the laws that regulate our lives, whether at work or at play, are now made by our public administrators, not by our legislators or our traditional lawmakers."[6]

In completing delegated tasks, bureaucrats, or public servants, exercise considerable administrative discretion. The need to control bureaucratic discretion to avoid threats to representative government was recognized by Alexander Hamilton and James Madison, among others.[7] These and other early Americans expressed concern that delegating too much power to appointed officials, who are not subject to electoral control, is a potential threat to democracy. In response, Congress decided to require certain administrative decision-making processes to remain open to public participation.

Additional constraints on agency and bureaucratic discretion include limits set by legislators and the courts; incorporated in civil servants' political or ideological outlook to serve the interests of citizens; and linked to professional administrative standards, with public servants desiring to behave ethically when making public decisions.[8] These various limits, together with other bureaucratic characteristics (e.g., written documentation or "red tape") help keep appointed bureaucrats accountable to the people, albeit indirectly and not always successfully.

Those working in administrative agencies are part of the "doing" side of government; that is, they implement the objectives of the organization. They translate general laws into more specific rules, regulations, and bureaucratic routines. In doing so they engage in two other important functions: rule making and administrative adjudication. Rule making, sometimes referred to as secondary legislation, involves establishing standards that can be applied to a class of individuals or an industry. Administrative adjudication, or "order making," involves the application of rules to specific individuals or firms to resolve disputes with regulated parties. Both functions are significant because in each case civil servants are often required to both interpret and implement the law, in which case they are essentially engaging in lawmaking.[9] Thus administrative agencies have legislative powers (rule making), judicial powers (adjudication), and also executive powers (investigating misconduct). Consequently, they are crucial participants in the policy-making process.

Environmental Agencies and Public Policy Making

Several federal administrative agencies deal with the environment in one way or another, including 11 Cabinet-level departments.[10] Five agencies in particular, two Cabinet-level departments and three others, are especially important in considering the institutional context of environmental policy implementation: the

Environmental Protection Agency (EPA), the Department of the Interior (DOI), the Department of Energy (DOE), the Nuclear Regulatory Commission (NRC), and the Council on Environmental Quality (CEQ). EPA is the most important agency affecting environmental matters. EPA works with its state counterpart agencies to implement and enforce environmental protection laws. If states fail to meet their responsibilities, EPA will intervene.

Before briefly considering these agencies, some preliminary distinctions about agency types are in order. Agencies can be classified as executive, independent, or hybrid. *Executive agencies* are those headed by an administrator who is appointed by the president, with advice and consent of the Senate. They are typically located in one of the 14 Cabinet-level departments (e.g., the Occupational Health and Safety Administration is within the Department of Labor). *Independent agencies* are not part of a Cabinet department, and they are headed by commissioners appointed by the president with advice and consent of the Senate, but serve for fixed terms of office and can only be removed for cause (e.g., Nuclear Regulatory Commission). *Hybrid agencies*, sometimes referred to as independent executive agencies, are not located within an executive branch department (e.g., the Environmental Protection Agency, the Federal Emergency Management Agency). A single administrator appointed by the president heads them and they report directly to the president rather than to a department-level secretary. Keeping these distinctions in mind, let's briefly introduce four important environmental agencies.

The Department of the Interior (DOI), a Cabinet-level executive department, was created in 1845. Its responsibilities are to restore and maintain the health of public lands, natural resources, and waters under federal management so that they are used and developed in ways that are environmentally appropriate. It seeks to achieve a balance between natural resource preservation and economic growth—a formidable task given the competing interests of those who prefer expanded use of natural resources (e.g., timber, mining, recreation interests) and those seeking to preserve natural resources. It also has responsibilities for preservation of plant and animal species and habitats.

STEWART L. UDALL: CHAMPION OF ENVIRONMENTAL VALUES[1]

Stewart L. Udall was Secretary of the Interior during both John F. Kennedy's and Lyndon B. Johnson's administrations. He is credited with transforming Interior from a narrowly focused unit oriented primarily to the western states to a truly national department. During his tenure in the Cabinet (1961–1969) he became the administration's foremost spokesperson for environmental and conservation matters.

Udall was born on January 31, 1920, outside St. John's, Arizona. He served in the U.S. Army Air Corps in World War II as a tail gunner. He received his bachelor's and law degrees from the University of Arizona, subsequently practicing law in Tucson and serving as school district trustee and as Pima County Attorney in the early 1950s. He was active in

Democratic politics, managing three losing gubernatorial candidates in 1948, 1950, and 1952. Udall ran successfully for U.S. Congress (1955–1961) and served on the Education and Labor Committee as well as the Interior and Insular Affairs Committee. He co-founded the Democratic Study Group in 1959. Udall lent support to Adlai Stevenson's unsuccessful presidential bid in 1956, and worked hard for John F. Kennedy's successful campaign four years later. He was rewarded with the post of Secretary of the Interior.

Udall was one of the youngest secretaries in a relatively youthful Cabinet and the only Secretary of the group to have previously served in Congress. His approach to executive leadership was to forge partnerships and foster bipartisan support for environmental initiatives. He developed a close working relationship with Orville Freeman, Secretary of Agriculture, and together they actively pursued innovative environmental policies. His ability to reach across party lines to promote environmental measures was aided by his prior experience as a member of Congress and the relationships he cultivated there. He had close relationships with such Republicans as U.S. Representatives John Finley Baldwin, Jr., John Rhodes, and John Baldwin, U.S. Senator Orrin Hatch, and future Secretary of the Interior in the Nixon administration, Rogers C.B. Morton. Later, in the Reagan years, this bipartisan spirit on environmental matters dissipated.

Three talents very much in evidence during Udall's stewardship of the Department of the Interior were his ability to recruit outstanding talent, his commitment to acquiring the necessary knowledge to make sound decisions, and his long-term view of environmental policy. Recruiting Roger Revelle as science advisor and the seminal research he conducted helped increase public awareness and inform policy decisions on world hunger and global warming. Similarly, recruitment of George Hartzog as Director of National Parks paid tremendous dividends attributable to his lengthy tenure as a noted exemplar of effective public service.

Udall's long-term perspective is apparent in his support for environmental initiatives while both in and out of office, including the establishment of national seashores as well as land and water conservation fund legislation; support for Rachel Carson (author of *Silent Spring*) during her congressional hearings on the use of pesticides; authorship of numerous articles on environmental matters; and promotion of projects to improve the Appalachian trail and to create the Sonoran Desert National Park. While his record as Secretary of the Interior was not unblemished (e.g., approval of oil leases that ultimately resulted in the infamous Santa Barbara oil spills, unsubstantiated conflict of interest charges promoted by his immediate Nixon administration successor Secretary Walter J. Hickel), his persistent and steadfast commitment to environmental protection is his most notable legacy.

[1]Adapted with permission from Henry B. Sirgo, "The Ethical Leadership of Secretary of the Interior Stewart L. Udall," unpublished paper presented at the annual meeting of the Southern Political Science Association, Atlanta, Georgia, November 8–11, 2000.

A Cabinet secretary heads the DOI. Presidential appointments to this position have seldom encountered Senate opposition. Indeed, there have been only four instances where significant opposition occurred on conformation votes for the Secretary of the DOI: votes on Walter Hickel (1969), Stanley Hathaway (1975), James Watt (1981), and William Clark (1983).[11]

The DOI's 1999 annual budget was $7.8 billion, with a staff of 71,872. Included as subunits within the DOI, among other units, are the Bureau of Land Management, the National Park Service, the Bureau of Reclamation, the Bureau of Indian Affairs, and the U.S. Fish and Wildlife Service, all vitally important to environmental protection efforts. The Bureau of Land Management administers 264 million acres of public lands, mostly in a dozen western states. It works to sustain the health and diversity of these lands for public use and enjoyment. The National Park Service promotes and regulates the use of national parks. Its purpose is to conserve natural and historic objects, scenery, and wildlife within the parks. The Bureau of Reclamation manages, develops and protects water and related resources. It seeks to protect local economies and preserve natural resources through effective use of water. The Bureau of Indian Affairs is concerned with promoting economic opportunity and protecting trust assets of American Indians and their tribes. The U.S. Fish and Wildlife Service is primarily responsible for fish, wildlife, and plant preservation, including migratory birds, endangered species, and marine mammals.

The Department of Energy (DOE) was created as a Cabinet-level executive department in 1913. In 1999 it had a budget of $16 billion and a staff of 15,937 federal employees and 102,683 contractor employees. DOE takes the lead in promoting diverse energy sources, efficient energy use, and improved environmental quality, among other things. It has an important role in promoting science and technology and in national security, but for our purposes its role in energy and environmental matters is the chief focus. DOE encourages energy efficiency by exploring new energy-related technologies, increasing customer choice of energy sources, and ensuring adequate and clean energy supplies. It also aims to minimize U.S. vulnerability to events that could reduce energy supplies. DOE seeks to improve environmental quality by controlling risks and threats (e.g., safety, health, environmental) from agency actions, cleaning up contaminated areas, and developing new technologies for ameliorating environmental problems.

The Nuclear Regulatory Commission, an independent agency, was created in 1974. Its budget in 1999 was $470 million. The NRC's mission is to ensure the public health and safety and protection of the environment in the use of nuclear materials. Its broad responsibilities include regulating nuclear power reactors; transport, storage, and disposal of nuclear materials and waste; and the uses of nuclear materials (e.g., medical, academic, industrial). It issues licenses to construct and operate nuclear facilities and matters relating to nuclear materials (possessing, transporting, using, handling, and disposing of them). Five commissioners head the NRC, each appointed by the president and confirmed by the Senate, for 5-year terms. One of them is appointed chairperson by the president.

The Council on Environmental Quality, an advisory unit to the president, was created by the National Environmental Policy Act (NEPA) of 1970. In 1999 its budget was $2.68 million. The CEQ gathers and analyzes data, keeps the president informed about progress toward the goal of a cleaner environment, recommends environment-related legislation, and issues a public report annually on the state of environmental quality. It also aids federal agencies in meeting their responsibilities to complete Environmental Impact Statements. After severe budget and staff cuts under Republican presidents in the 1980s, and an initial proposal by President Clinton to abolish the CEQ in the early 1990s, its fortunes rose in 1995 when the Clinton administration merged the newly formed Office of Environmental Quality into the CEQ.[12]

Budget outlays for these four agencies, together with that of the EPA, are shown in Table 7.1 for the period 1970 to 2000.

This descriptive information about particular environmental agencies shows the differences that exist among such federal agencies, including structure, mission, resources, and independence. Even more important is the role that administrative agencies play in the public policy-making process. We will examine four concepts or processes that help to explain their role: rule making, adjudication, iron triangles, and issue networks.

One way that administrative agencies make public policy, as stated previously, is to develop, change, and eliminate government rules. In doing so they

TABLE 7.1

Outlay by Department or Agency (Dollars in Millions)

	Department of the Interior	Department of Energy	Environmental Protection Agency	Nuclear Regulatory Commission	Council on Environmental Quality
1980	4,472	7,261	5,603	399	3.13
1981	4,456	11,757	5,242	441	2.54
1982	3,944	11,657	5,081	466	0.94
1983	4,547	10,590	4,312	465	0.93
1984	4,943	10,991	4,076	466	0.70
1985	4,820	10,587	4,490	444	0.88
1986	4,785	11,026	4,867	400	0.67
1987	5,046	10,693	4,904	401	0.81
1988	5,143	11,166	4,871	439	0.83
1989	5,207	11,387	4,906	420	0.85
1990	5,825	12,084	5,108	439	1.47
1991	6,090	12,479	5,769	465	1.87
1992	6,541	15,523	5,950	513	2.56
1993	6,881	16,942	5,930	540	2.56
1994	7,071	17,839	5,855	535	0.68
1995	7,486	17,617	6,351	524	1.78
1996	6,785	16,203	6,046	473	2.15
1997	6,770	14,467	6,164	477	2.44
1998	7,274	14,438	6,284	477	2.50
1999	7,815	16,048	6,750	470	2.68
2000 est.	8,397	15,269	7,040	470	2.82
2001 est.	8,496	16,365	7,453	488	3.02
2002 est.	8,726	16,779	7,517	N/A	N/A
2003 est.	9,105	16,952	7,486	N/A	N/A
2004 est.	9,312	17,116	7,525	N/A	N/A

Source: **http://w3.access.gpo.gov/usbudget/fy2001/hist.html#h4**. Plus additional information compiled by the authors from information provided by the Nuclear Regulatory Commission and the Council on Environmental Quality.

follow procedures outlined in the Administrative Procedure Act (APA) of 1946. Congress, the president, and the judiciary have acted to ensure that rule making occurs in ways that are consistent with their priorities and values. The APA requires that agencies inform the public by a notice in the *Federal Register* of their intent to develop a rule, inviting public comment. Subsequently, agencies assemble the required data, including comments from the public and other interested parties, to formulate a proposed rule or regulation and, again, publish a notice in the *Federal Register* inviting public comment. Draft rules are also submitted to the White House Office of Management and Budget (OMB) for its review and approval. This duty to inform serves two purposes: it notifies the public of the rationale, purpose, and implications of the rule thereby enabling them to better participate in the process, and it offers a way for Congress, the president, and the judiciary to hold agencies accountable.

Public participation involves the submission of written comments on proposed rules. The APA seeks to prevent preferential access to the rule-making process and allows for other opportunities for public involvement (e.g., public hearings, consensual rule development, cross-examination of agency rule makers). The exact nature of the participation depends on the formality of the rule-making process.[13] Accountability is maintained under APA by judicial review of both the substance and process of rule making, by congressional oversight of the rule-making process (e.g., budget, investigation, appointments), and by presidential oversight of the process (e.g., submissions of regulatory agendas, OMB review of proposed and final rules). Once the agency has received and considered public comments and other related materials submitted to it by interested parties, the final rule is published in the *Federal Register* together with the agency's response to important issues raised in connection with the review. (A somewhat similar process is found when states' agencies engage in rule making.)[14]

Another way administrative agencies make public policy, in addition to rule making, is administrative adjudication of specific cases. Adjudication is conducted under provisions of the APA. When it makes its judgment, a public agency determines the winner and loser and issues an order to one of the parties in the dispute. Orders resulting from administrative adjudication are directed to the disputants in conflict, the general public is excluded from participation, and adjudicative facts, not legislative facts, are the basis for deliberation. Administrative orders are designed to address past disputes, not to give general policy guidance for the future; nonetheless, orders do set precedents. What occurs is a case-by-case approach to creating regulatory policies.

While APA legislation spells out the procedures to be followed for both rule making and adjudication, the requirements for each differ. Adjudication involves dispute resolution of past behavior and results in policies directed at specific named parties in a dispute. By contrast, rule making aims to control future conduct regulating parties in general.[15] In reality, these conceptual distinctions are not as neat as they may appear, and often there is confusion about which form of discretionary authority administrative agencies should exercise.

Yet another way to analyze the role of administrative agencies in the policy process is to consider the avenues of access available to those wishing to influence the formulation and adoption of policies. Access refers to the actual inclusion of various interests in the decision-making process. Access and its influence in policy making can be explained by considering the function of "iron triangles" and "issue networks." Iron triangles or subgovernments refer to the cooperative, stable relationships that exist among participants in the policy process, specifically an administrative agency, a congressional committee, and related interest groups. Years ago Douglas Cater described iron triangles in this way:

> In one important area of policy after another, substantial efforts to exercise power are waged by alliances cutting across the [executive and congressional] branches of government and including key operatives from outside. In effect, they constitute subgovernments of Washington comprising the expert, the interested, and the engaged.[16]

Each of these participants represents a point on the triangle and together this triad helps shape policy in a particular domain. For example, in the nuclear energy policy domain during the 1950s and 1960s the iron triangle consisted of the Atomic Energy Commission (an independent agency in the executive branch), the Joint Committee on Atomic Energy (in Congress), and key interest groups from the nuclear power industry (e.g., General Electric, Westinghouse, Combustion Engineering, Babcock & Wilcox).[17] Together this triad of participants influenced the development of nuclear energy policy during this period. Similarly, the current subgovernment for energy policy might include administrative agencies (DOI, DOE, NRC), congressional committees (Senate Energy and Natural Resources, Environment and Public Works; House Commerce, Resources, and Science Committees) and particular interest groups (e.g., American Public Power Association, National Coal Council, Environmental Defense Fund, Sierra Club).[18] To depict the environmental protection subgovernment is even more complex (See Figure 7.1).[19]

Issue networks are composed of those concerned with the particular policy area and share common interests or stakes in decisions. These include elected and appointed officials, consultants, policy experts, activists, and interest groups. Given the proliferation of interest groups, activists, and policy experts in recent years, especially surrounding highly technical matters like nuclear energy, issue networks provide a better description of the current policy participants. Figure 7.2 is a visual depiction of both the earlier iron triangle configuration and the more recent (1970s to 1990s) issue network for the nuclear energy domain.[20] The issue network consists of the four key environmental agencies at the core—EPA, DOI, DOE, and NRC—with four standing committees in the Senate and House, and 10 or 11 other more loosely related groups having access, involvement, and influence in the policy process. The salience of the nuclear energy issue increased as a result of the accident at the Three Mile Island reactor in 1979, leading to heightened pressures to tighten government regulations and intensified turf battles in Congress regarding nuclear reactors.[21]

It should be noted that turf battles are not unique to Congress, and such conflicts are clearly present in the interactions among environmental agencies as well. These are partially a result of overlapping jurisdictions, competing agency interests, and disagreement about goals. One consequence of such conflicts is that integration of environmental management is often lacking.[22]

Having briefly considered the missions and key functions of four federal environmental agencies, the rule making and adjudication processes, the role of iron triangles and issue networks, and the potential for conflict among agencies, our attention turns to the most important federal agency, the EPA. We begin by

Executive Departments and Agencies

Environmental Protection Agency
Agriculture Department
Energy Department
Department of the Interior
Department of Transportation
National Oceanic and Atmospheric Administration

Key Congressional Committees

Senate
Appropriations
Energy and Natural Resources
Environment and Public Works
Finance
Commerce, Science, and
  Transportation

House of Representatives
Agriculture
Appropriations
Resources
Science

Selected Interest Groups

Environmental Groups
Sierra Club
National Audubon Society
Friends of the Earth
Environmental Defense Fund
National Wildlife Federation
National Parks and Conservation Association
Izaak Walton League of America
Natural Resources Defense Council
Environmental Action Foundation
Greenpeace
Consumer Energy Council
Electricity Consumers Resource Council
Americans for the Environment
Renew America
Union of Concerned Scientists
Clean Water Action Act
Conservation International

Industry Groups
American Petroleum Institute
Chemical Manufacturers Association
National Association of Chemical Distributors
Mineralogy Society of America
National Coal Council
National Environmental Development
  Association
Petroleum Marketers Association of America
American Gas Association
Independent Petroleum Association of America
American Public Power Association
National Rural Electric Cooperative Association
National Petroleum Refiners Association
Natural Gas Supply Association
Compressed Gas Association

FIGURE 7.1 *The Environment Subgovernment*
Source: Adapted from Stephen J. Wayne, G. Calvin Mackenzie, David M. O'Brien, and
Richard L. Cole, *The Politics of American Government* (St. Martin's/Worth, 1999), 679.

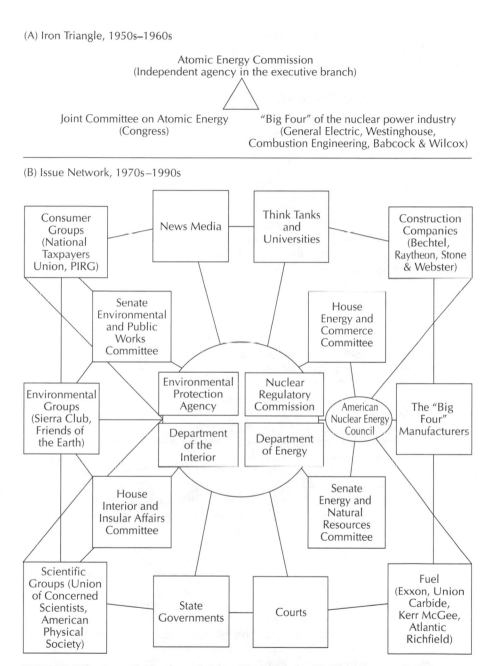

(A) Iron Triangle, 1950s–1960s

Atomic Energy Commission
(Independent agency in the executive branch)

Joint Committee on Atomic Energy   "Big Four" of the nuclear power industry
(Congress)   (General Electric, Westinghouse,
                         Combustion Engineering, Babcock & Wilcox)

(B) Issue Network, 1970s–1990s

Consumer Groups (National Taxpayers Union, PIRG)

News Media

Think Tanks and Universities

Construction Companies (Bechtel, Raytheon, Stone & Webster)

Senate Environmental and Public Works Committee

House Energy and Commerce Committee

Environmental Groups (Sierra Club, Friends of the Earth)

Environmental Protection Agency

Nuclear Regulatory Commission

American Nuclear Energy Council

The "Big Four" Manufacturers

Department of the Interior

Department of Energy

House Interior and Insular Affairs Committee

Senate Energy and Natural Resources Committee

Scientific Groups (Union of Concerned Scientists, American Physical Society)

State Governments

Courts

Fuel (Exxon, Union Carbide, Kerr McGee, Atlantic Richfield)

FIGURE 7.2   *Iron Triangle and Issue Network for Nuclear Energy Policy*
Source: Morris P. Forina and Paul E. Peterson, *The New American Democracy* (Needham Heights, MA: Allyn and Bacon, 1998), 470.

briefly describing the internal organization of the EPA, and follow with more extended analysis of the external political environment of the agency using "stakeholder theory" as a framework.

The Environmental Protection Agency: A Brief Profile

The EPA was created by President Nixon's executive order in 1970. The agency brought together various preexisting forms of pollution control into one federal regulatory unit. It has a broad and ever-expanding mission to protect, safeguard, and improve public health and the natural environment, in the areas of air, water, and land. Solid waste, pesticides, radiation, and toxic-substance control fall under the jurisdiction of EPA as well. Indeed, former EPA head William Ruckelshaus drew an analogy between EPA's mission and efforts to give someone an appendectomy while the person is running the 100-yard dash.[23] New pollutants or responsibilities are continually added to EPA's tasks, creating a moving target and making it difficult for the agency to complete one task before taking on another.

CASE STUDY: GENETICALLY ENGINEERED CORN

The issue of genetically engineered (GE) corn recently ignited debate over environmental safety when an academic study reported that monarch butterflies died as a result of ingesting toxic Bt corn (*Bacillus thuringiensis*) pollen.[1] Environmentalists called on the EPA to reduce the adverse effects of Bt corn pollen by restricting the planting of genetically engineered Bt corn. GE corn is disallowed in foods because of human allergy concerns. The issue took on new importance when a form of GE corn was discovered in Taco Bell taco shells sold in grocery stores.[2] The FDA is responsible for protecting the public from GE plant pesticides, including this type of corn, which is not approved by the EPA.

Genetically modified corn received EPA approval in 1995 for producing insect poisons.[3] This was necessary because crops had been infested by the European corn borer, leading to more than a billion dollars annually in crop destruction in the United States. It is estimated that the presence of the natural insecticide Bt in organic farming cuts insect feeding by about 90 percent.[4] The agency subsequently registered more than a dozen different Bt pesticides for use in corn.

Unfortunately, treasured species like the monarch butterfly, and some endangered species such as the Karner Blue butterfly, were poisoned along with the pests. This occurred because Bt corn coats the leaves of plants adjacent to cornfields with toxic pollen, and the butterflies then feed on these leaves.

Loss of biodiversity and beneficial insects has propelled this issue onto the agenda of environmental interest groups and government regulatory agencies. Environmental advocacy groups sought EPA regulations or contracts with Bt corn growers, requiring that Bt corn fields be encircled by 660-foot-wide borders of non-Bt corn. It was thought that these "buffer zone" borders would restrict the toxic pollen that was jeopardizing butterfly habitats. Concern about other endangered or threatened butterflies or moths that might be adversely affected by the poison Bt corn pollen led an environmental group—Environmental Defense Fund—to request that EPA coordinate its efforts with other federal agencies. Greenpeace, an international environmental group, is another vocal opponent of "agrotechnology" such as GE corn. Environmentalists and consumer groups, especially those in Europe, have strongly objected to GE foods and have expressed concern about the need to label GE ingredients in animal feed.[5]

Discovery of the GE corn in taco shells sold under the Taco Bell brand heightened concern that a product that was registered for animal feed was illegally present in foods that people eat. An EPA scientific advisory panel was inconclusive on the issue of whether a variety of genetically engineered corn (Cry9C) caused allergic reactions.[6] Because GE corn is unapproved for human consumption, producers must ensure that GE corn is distinguishable from grain that has obtained approval for food use; not doing so would be a violation of EPA restrictions that could result in the loss of a producer's license.

The dynamics of the grain industry have been disrupted because new sorting, segregating, and distribution techniques are required when testing for the Cry9C protein. This has led processors to call on EPA to allow a tiny portion of Cry9C to be accepted in food. Friends of the Earth, an environmental group, along with a coalition of health, consumer, and environmental groups (Genetically Engineered Food Alert), called on the Food and Drug Administration to recall and test all GE corn products.[7]

Administrative agencies like the EPA and FDA are created to protect the public and the environment. They are embroiled in controversial issues like biotech corn on a regular basis.

---

[1]"EPA Asked to Limit Genetically Engineered Corn to Protect Butterflies," **http://www.edf.org/pubs/NewsReleases/1999/Jul/c_butterflies.html**;
David Barboza, "Gene-Altered Corn Changes Dynamics of Grain Industry." *New York Times* (December 11, 2000), A-1, A-20.

[2]Biotech Critics Cite Unapproved Corn in Taco Shells," **http://www.thecampaign.org/newsupdates/sept00e.htm.**

[3]Eric Colvin, "Genetically Engineered Corn Sparks Debate Over Environmental Safety," **http://www.richmond.edu/~journalm/outlook/colvin.html.**

[4]"EPA Asked to Limit Genetically Engineered Corn to Protect Butterflies."

[5]Eric Colvin, "Genetically Engineered Corn Sparks Debate Over Environmental Safety."

[6]"Government Probes Biotech Corn Allegation," **http://www.thecampaign.org/newsupdates/sept00f.htm.**

[7]"Contaminant Found in Taco Bell Taco Shells, Food Safety Coalition Demands Recall by Taco Bell, Philip Morris," **http://www.thecampaign.org/newsupdates/sept00f.htm.**

The EPA promotes its mission by implementing and enforcing federal environmental laws, integrating its efforts with those of other governmental units, and using the best available scientific information to reduce environmental risks. However, its budget rarely keeps pace with its responsibilities, making implementation and enforcement problematic.[24] Some observers note that its issue-specific organizational structure and other impediments make integration of its internal and external activities difficult.[25] Further, its ability to do high-quality scientific work has been hampered by understaffing and declining capacity to conduct long-range environmental research.[26] The EPA does seek to inform major stakeholders about environmental and health threats and to engage them in a partnership to prevent or reduce such threats.

Figure 7.3 shows EPA's organizational structure. The agency's administrator reports directly to the president. It has issue-specific programs in air and water, radiation, solid waste and emergency response, and pesticides and toxic substances. Separate units exist for research and development, environmental information, enforcement and compliance, administration and resources, and international activities, allowing for some integration of activities. Some scholars have called for a new direction in environmental management that would require changes in agency structures, including that of the EPA. For example, Schilling and Schulz call for a transition toward more integrated "ecosystem management" that involves moving "from managing single species or components of ecosystems to managing whole ecosystems."[27] They argue that the historical evolution of agencies like the EPA has been an incremental process consisting of "multitudes of different components, each dedicated to purposes prominent at the time of their founding."[28] They argue that resulting structures make these agencies ill equipped to pursue more integrated approaches to environmental management.[29]

Some EPA functions are centralized in Washington, D.C., while others are decentralized. EPA staff in Washington is responsible for rule making, but much of the environmental policy implementation occurs in the 10 regional offices, where two-thirds of the agency staff is employed, and in state, tribal, and local governments. EPA staff has increased substantially from its first full year of operation (in 1971 with 7,000 staff) to the recent 18,743 staff. Similar increases can be seen in its budget (in 1971, $3.3 billion; to a current, $6.75 billion).[30] Budgets were severely cut in the Reagan years, but increased in the Bush-Clinton period.

Currently the EPA is composed of technical experts committed to environmental protection, but in recent years the agency has been criticized for being reactive (responding to public concerns) rather than proactive (generating new policy alternatives).[31] A variety of proposals to reform the agency have been put forward by the Scientific Advisory Board, the General Accounting Office, the National Academy of Sciences, the National Academy of Public Administration, the Partnership for Reinventing Government, the Office of Inspector General, and others.[32] Probably the best single source of information on EPA's current goals and performance targets is found in the EPA Draft 5-Year Strategic Plan (required by the 1993 Government Performance and Results Act, completed June 2000). It summarizes the agency's top 10 strategic goals and longer-term objectives as well as specific accomplishments the agency intends to achieve over the next several years. In addition, it specifies the means and strategies EPA will em-

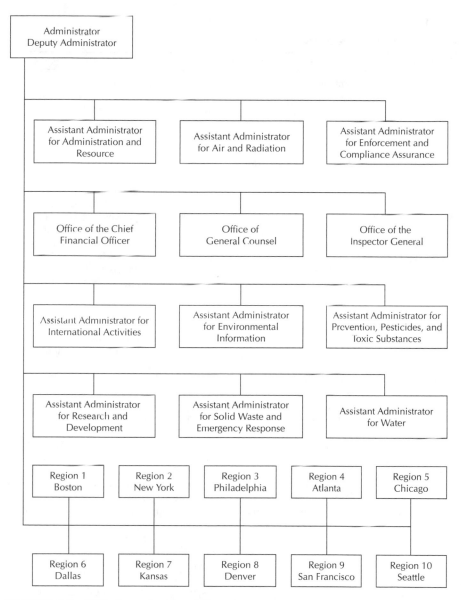

FIGURE 7.3   *EPA Organizational Structure*
Source: **http://www.epa.gov/epahome/organization.htm**, updated July 2000.

ploy to accomplish its goals, and the external factors that may affect its ability to achieve its objectives. It also considers high-priority programs that cut across EPA strategic goals and the ways that EPA measures and assesses its progress. The plan indicates that EPA is using new tools and approaches to become more performance-based, flexible, informative, and inclusive, although its new reforms have been the subject of some criticism (Table 7.2).[33]

TABLE 7.2

EPA Innovative Strategies and Programs

EPA Core Programs	Innovative Tools and Approaches	Activities and Results
Market-Based Solutions	Emissions "cap and trade" program	Expanded use of economic incentives by placing a cap on sulpher dioxide emissions from electric utilities, then allocating the utilities "allowances" for their emissions that can be banked or traded.
Superfund	Administrative reforms	Allowed for reduced time and cost of cleanup, resulting in more than three times as many Superfund cleanups being completed between 1993 and 1999 as occurred in the previous 12-year period.
Projecty XL (eXcellence and Leadership)	Alternative regulatory approaches	A partnership program between EPA and its stakeholders that encourages the use of new tools and approaches.
Compliance	Audit policy	Promotes flexibility and offers incentives as EPA waives or reduces penalties for companies that evaluate their environmental management and that take actions to disclose and correct violations. Some 700 companies disclosed violations at over 2,700 facilities. EPA cut total penalties by 90%.
Partnerships	Encourage voluntary action by stakeholders; National Environmental Performance Partnership System (NEPPS)	Worked with the chemical industry on a voluntary information collection initiative; reduced greenhouse gas emissions based on voluntary actions (35 million metric tons a year); forms NEPPS performance partnership agreements with states.
Innovations in Science	Integrated approach to environmental management	Integrated data collected by satellites, with data collected in streams, soils, marshlands, and beaches in mid-Atlantic and western states.
Information and Public Involvement	Use of new information technologies	Two EPA Internet sites—Envirofacts Data Warehouse and EnviroMapper—provide direct access to information about environmental activities and enable users to view and query information about EPA-regulated facilities.
Sector-Based Approach	Common Sense Initiative (CSI)	CSI was a 1994–98 pilot program for six large and small industry sectors testing approaches to environmental regulation.
Environmental Justice	Protect all Americans from significant environmental risks	Collaboration with the Interagency Work Group on Environmental Justice and the National Environmental Justice Advisory Council to address concerns of high-risk communities.

Source: Adapted from U.S. Environmental Protection Agency, Draft 2000 Strategic Plan, Washington, DC: EPA, 2000. Retrieved on July 24, 2000.

Other innovative environmental and managerial initiatives are encouraged by the National Partnership for Reinventing Government (NPRG). The EPA has responded to "reinvention fever" in various ways.[34] One indication of their response is the recognition given to the EPA for receipt of numerous Hammer Awards. NPRG recognized innovative efforts by giving out Hammer Awards, named after purchasing reforms that replaced $600 hammers with $6 versions. The awards recognize government agencies, including the EPA, for programs that contrast with past examples of government inefficiency. They recognize teams of federal employees and their partners whose work results in a government that "works better and costs less." Over 1,200 such awards were given between 1994 (when the program began) and July 2000. Hammer Awards single out significant contributions in support of "reinventing government" principles (see Table 7.3, p. 214).

In the next section we shift attention from the internal purpose, structure, resources, and initiatives of the EPA to its relations with those in its external environment.

Stakeholder Analysis and the Environmental Protection Agency

Stakeholder theory can be applied to public organizations such as the EPA to show the existing network of relationships with other institutions and groups that affect the agency. A *stakeholder* is an individual, group, or institution having a "stake," or interest in an organization.[35] A common definition of stakeholder is "any group or individual who can affect or is affected by the achievement of an organization's purpose."[36] Primary stakeholders are those without whose continuing support the agency cannot survive, while secondary stakeholders are those that are not directly engaged in the agency's activities but can affect or are affected by it.[37] Stakeholders can influence the agency's mission, its strategy, and its operations. Stakeholders may differ in their perceptions about the agency's role and performance. An assumption of stakeholder management is that the continued operation and prosperity of an agency depends on the extent to which it meets the needs of relevant stakeholders, and that an agency's success hinges on satisfying major stakeholders.

AIR POLLUTION: COLLABORATIVE GAMES— REFORMULATED GASOLINE

Executive agencies possess delegated authority from Congress to develop rules and regulations for administering legislative program mandates. Once Congress passes legislation and the president signs it, rule making begins. This can be done in two ways: traditional rule making or regulatory negotiation (reg-neg). Traditional rule making typically involves seven steps: agencies propose regulations; interested parties comment; proposed regulations are published; administrative hearings are held; hearings and comments are reviewed by the agency; final regulations are adopted and published in the Code of Federal Regulations;

continued

and administrators implement programs.[1] Under reg-neg the process is different: a group of affected stakeholders collaborate on the rule's content, sharing information and seeking consensus for rules that all sides can endorse.[2] Publication in the *Federal Register* and public comments remain part of the process.

In 1990 Congress passed the Clean Air Act, mandating that parts of the country experiencing major ozone smog problems use reformulated gasoline (RFG). RFG treats conventional gasoline with oxegenate additives originating from ethanol and methanol. EPA opted for reg-neg rather than traditional rule making in the case of RFG, enabling direct negotiations among stakeholders in the period between the initial notice and final comments. Key stakeholders were the auto and oil industries, environmental advocates, government agencies (DOE, EPA, state regulators), and producers.[3] EPA was responsible for developing regulations. Once trust developed, these stakeholders focused on the crucial issue of how to implement pollution standards rather than on the content of the standards themselves.[4]

The relative success of reg-neg can be attributed to several factors, including EPA's commitment to and experience with stakeholder collaboration; the leadership of EPA's assistant administrator, Bill Rosenberg; binding agreements preventing executive branch interference or circumvention of the reg-neg process; and dissatisfaction with traditional rule making and litigation as alternative strategies.[5]

Despite the presence of these factors, the process was not without its glitches. Keeping the 35 reg-neg participants on track without splintering the coalition was a major challenge; indeed, at one point the ethanol lobby temporarily defected from the coalition when other reg-neg stakeholders responded unfavorably to their request for a lower standard.[6] Eventually some win-win agreements were struck; notably, between environmentalists and state regulators, on the one hand, and the alternative fuel and oil industries, on the other, regarding a stringent baseline to use as a starting point for assessing progress in emissions reductions and concerning ways to achieve compliance by monitoring and enforcement. These industry concessions were offset by industry gains in more flexible rule implementation mechanisms, new compliance measures based on "averaging" fuel emissions within a geographic area rather than on a gallon-by-gallon basis, and other cost-saving initiatives.[7]

The RFG case has been cited as an example of "the importance of pluralism by the rules."[8] An alternative interpretation suggests that the energy industry might be engaging in symbolic politics to soothe public concern about the environment, extracting concessions unlikely to be achieved under traditional rule making, and avoiding meaningful actions to protect the environment.[9] While each of these explanations is plausible, for our purposes the case is significant because it highlights the crucial role of an executive agency like the EPA in environmental regulation, the importance of leadership, and stakeholder management by a competent public servant—as well as the alternative formats that can characterize the administrative rule making process.

---

[1] Bernard H. Ross, Cornelius Kerwin, and A. Lee Fritschler, *How Washington Works: The Executive's Guide to Government* (Sun Lakes, AZ: Thomas Horton & Daughters), 1996.

[2] Edward P. Weber. *Pluralism by the Rules: Conflict and Cooperation in Environmental Regulation* (Washington, DC: Georgetown University Press, 1998), 126.

[3] Ibid., 123–124.

[4] Ibid., 128.

[5] Ibid., 129–130, 137.

[6] Ibid., 135–136.

[7] Ibid., 131–135.

[8] Ibid., 137.

[9] George A. Gonzalez, Review of *Pluralism by the Rules* in the *American Political Science Review* 93, 2 (1999), 461.

Agencies like the EPA must try to maintain a workable balance among multiple and competing interests, rather than being unduly influenced by a single stakeholder. Figure 7.4 is a stakeholder map putting the EPA in the center and its various stakeholders around it. While this simplifies the EPA's highly political environment, it provides a framework for considering the extent to which the agency is in sync with stakeholder interests. The five primary stakeholders, identified in bold

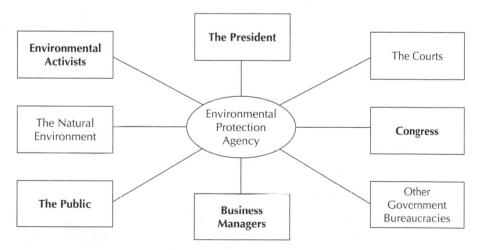

FIGURE 7.4 *Environmental Protection Agency Stakeholders*

TABLE 7.3

Selected Hammer Awards Given for Environmental Excellence

Agency	Program	Description
Environmental Protection Agency	Enforcement and Compliance	EPA's Office of Enforcement and Compliance Assurance, recognized for establishing small business compliance, centers in partnership with industry. This shift away from traditional enforcement creates simple explanations of regulations and offers guides to cost-effective compliance technologies. Internet and toll-free access to information is provided.
Environmental Protection Agency	Chemical Exposure Information	A joint program between the EPA and several industry trade associations that is designed to collect chemical exposure information and unify emergency planning. Establishes a voluntary system for manufacturers to give EPA firm information for agency use to evaluate risks associated with chemicals and facilities.
Environmental Protection Agency	33/50 Program	A program that challenged U.S. industries to reduce voluntary emissions of 17 toxic chemicals 33 percent by 1992 and 50 percent by 1995. It shows how government and business can work as partners without additional regulations.
Environmental Protection Agency	Small System Peer Review Team	This initiative brings together the EPA, state and local agencies, and water system owner-operators in a cooperative effort to improve drinking water quality in areas where compliance has typically been low.
Interior Department and Environmental Protection Agency	Appalachian Clean Streams Team	A team of 16 Office of Surface Mining employees and three EPA workers was recognized for this team effort to combine federal, state, and local resources to help reclaim some 7,000 miles of eastern waterways fouled by acid drainage from abandoned coal mines.
Nuclear Regulatory Commission	Multi-Agency Radiation Survey	Five Nuclear Regulatory Commission employees functioned as part of a multi-agency team that made significant contributions via a radiation survey and site investigation manual, which is a guide for decontamination.
Interior Department	Office of Surface Mining Oversight Team	OSM's 10-member oversight team revamped the way OSM oversees state coal reclamation programs by putting more emphasis on "on-the-ground reclamation" and less on record keeping and writing violations.
Environmental Protection Agency	Managing Risks of Chemical Technology	Union Carbide Association and EPA recognized for joint efforts in managing risks of a new chemical technology, Triton SP splittable surfactants, without burdensome regulatory controls.

Source: Adapted from Peter Farley, "EPA Gets Hammer," *Chemical Week* (November 6, 1996), 49; Peter Farley, "EPA Hammered Again," *Chemical Week* (November 27, 1996), 39; Tom Meersman, "Hammering Away at Government Waste," *Star Tribune (Minneapolis, MN),* June 19, 1996, 1D; "EPA's Team Effort Pays Off," *Managing Today's Federal Employees,* 1, (March 22, 2000); "OSM's Appalachian Clean Streams Team Won a Hammer Award," *Inside Energy/with Federal Lands* (October 28, 1996), 15; "Kudos," *Nuclear New* (June, 1999), 74; "OSM Oversight Gets Hammer Award," *Mine Regulation Reporter* 10 (July 28, 1997); "Carbide Surfactant Lauded by US," *Chemical Market Reporter* 252 (December 22, 1997), 18.

type, are the ones we will focus on in this brief discussion: namely, the president, environmental activists, the public, business managers, and Congress.

The President: View of the EPA from the White House

Presidents are primary stakeholders of administrative agencies because they have various tools at their disposal that can influence agency behavior. These tools include appointment power, issuing of executive orders, power of the Office of Management and Budget for screening proposed agency rules and recommending agency budgets, and removal and reorganization powers.[38]

Presidents from Nixon to Clinton have had definite ideas about the role of the EPA and the importance of environmental protection relative to other concerns. Presidential actions clearly influence the operation of executive agencies like the EPA. In addition to use of the tools noted above, presidents may influence agencies when they pursue particular policy initiatives. As noted above, the EPA is but one of several executive agencies with an environmental purpose, but its role as the premier federal agency for environmental regulation warrants special attention. The following view of the EPA from the White House relies heavily on the research of Landy, Roberts, and Thomas regarding the history of the EPA,[39] and is supplemented by research from other sources.

President Richard Nixon established the EPA by Executive Order in 1970 to put pollution control programs in a separate umbrella agency, directly accountable to the president. From the outset there was disagreement about the agency's mission, and differing expectations among stakeholders. The president saw the EPA as a "balancer and integrator" that would protect the environment without hindering industrial growth and resource development. Others in Congress and the environmental community viewed the agency as a quasi-independent unit and the champion of environmental values against countervailing pressures from less environmentally friendly stakeholders.[40] President Nixon was committed to conflicting objectives—empower environmental regulators, but restrict their power and scope. William Ruckelshaus, a State Assistant Attorney General from Indiana, was appointed as the first EPA administrator (see Table 7.4). Ruckelshaus organized the EPA into five divisions, some by function (Planning and Management, Enforcement and General Counsel, Research and Monitoring), others by program (Air and Water, Pesticides, Radiation and Solid Waste). His top priority for action, contrary to President Nixon's preference, was enforcement, thereby downplaying other functions (e.g., research and development, comprehensive environmental management). His enforcement actions helped to establish the EPA's credibility. He was also committed to implementing the recently amended 1970 Clean Air Act and controlling regulatory costs.

A year after the EPA was formed, the Office of Management and Budget (OMB) began conducting "Quality of Life Reviews," subjecting proposed EPA regulations to scrutiny by other federal units under the guidance of the OMB. This review process was designed to give fiscal and economic development concerns their due when drafting regulations; however, environmentalists thought the EPA administrator should have the last word on the content of environmental regulations. Most EPA staff efforts during the Ruckelshaus era concentrated on air and water pollution, and he helped to emphasize global environmental concerns.[41] When Ruckelshaus left the EPA, his replacement was Russell Train, a career public servant. Train was successful in cultivating congressional support

TABLE 7.4

Biographical Information on EPA Administrators, 1970–2001

Administrator	Start	End	Biographical Information
Christie Todd Whitman	1/31/01		Whitman served as Governor of New Jersey from 1993 to 2001. As Governor her environmental efforts focused primarily on seeking cleaner air, water, and land. She helped to gain voter approval of a plan to dredge the state's ports and to preserve open space and farmland. She helped establish a watershed management program. Under her governance in New Jersey environment budgets, regulations, staffs and fines for polluters were reduced.
Carol M. Browner	01/21/93	1/20/01	Browner knew environmental regulation from both a Washington and a state perspective. Previous to being appointed as head of the EPA, Browner was Secretary of Florida's Department of Environmental Regulation from 1991 to 1993. From 1986 to 1988, she worked in Washington for then-Senator Lawton Chiles. She also served as Legislative Director for then-Senator Al Gore. In addition, Browner served as General Counsel for the Florida House of Representatives' Government Operations Committee during 1980 and worked for Citizen Action, a grassroots consumer group in Washington, D.C.
William K. Reilly	02/06/89	01/20/93	Reilly had both vast legal and environmental experience. During the past 20 years, he held five environment-related positions. The most recent were President of both the World Wildlife Fund—U.S. and the Conservation Foundation. An Alumnus of Yale University, Reilly holds a law degree from Harvard University and a master's degree in Urban Planning from Columbia University.
Lee M. Thomas	01/04/85	01/20/89	Thomas first joined the EPA in 1983 as Acting Assistant Administrator for Solid Waste and Emergency Responses. That same year he was designated Acting Deputy Administrator until a permanent deputy could be confirmed. Prior to joining the EPA, Thomas served as Executive Deputy Director and Associate Director for State and Local Programs and Support of the Federal Emergency Management Agency (FEMA).
William D. Ruckelshaus	05/18/83	01/04/85	Ruckelshaus returned for a second time as EPA administrator, having served initially from 1970 to 1973 as the head of the agency.

Administrator	Start	End	Biographical Information
Anne M. (Gorsuch) Burford	05/20/81	03/09/83	Served as EPA Administrator from 1981 to 1983. Burford had both legal and legislative experience. Her legal experience included service as the Deputy District Attorney of Denver, 1971 to 1973, and as Hearing Officer for the Real Estate Commission and State Boards of Cosmetology, Optometric Examiners, Professional Nursing, and Veterinarian Medicine, 1974 to 1975. Burford also served as lawyer for the Mountain Bell Corporate Law Department from 1975 to 1981. Her legislative experience included service as a member of the Colorado State House of Representatives, 1976 to 1980, and as a member of then President-elect Reagan's transition team, serving on the Advisory Committee in Intergovernmental Relations.
Douglas M. Costle	03/07/77	01/20/81	Costle was a lawyer with vast experience in both federal and state environmental matters. From 1969 to 1970 he was Senior Staff Associate, Environmental and Natural Resources, for the President's Advisory Council on Executive Organization, where he headed the study that recommended creation of the EPA. From 1975 to 1977 Costle served as Assistant Director for Natural Resources and Commerce at the U.S. Congressional Budget Office, and prior to his EPA nomination he was on President Carter's transition team for government organization.
Russell E. Train	09/13/73	01/20/77	Served as EPA Administrator from 1973 to 1977. Previously, during 1970 to 1973, Train served as the first Chairman of the White House's Council on Environmental Quality (CEQ). In 1970 he testified to the Ash Council regarding the need for an agency to serve as the cutting edge of environmental policy in government. He had also served as Undersecretary of the Interior from 1969 to 1970 and as President of the Conservation Foundation from 1965 to 1969.
William D. Ruckelshaus	12/04/70	04/30/73	Before becoming the Administrator for the EPA in 1970, Ruckelshaus served as Deputy Attorney General in Indiana and as Chief Counsel for the Office of the Attorney General. Ruckelshaus has also served as Minority Attorney in the Indiana Senate and as member and Majority Leader of the Indiana House of Representatives.

Source: Biographical profiles retrieved from the Internet (July, 2000).

for the EPA, which helped in resisting hostile moves from some in the Nixon White House.

President Gerald Ford retained Russell Train as the EPA administrator, but Train's close ties to congressional supporters served to limit White House influence over EPA activities and to solidify its role as environmental advocate during Ford's presidency. "Inflation impact statements" were required by President Ford for all significant regulatory proposals and reviewed by the Council on Wage and Price Stability. Environmental programs received less attention under Ford because the salience of the energy issue took priority over environmental matters, there was growing concern about increased regulatory compliance costs, and the push for new environmental initiatives receded. As Switzer and Bryner note, "The environmental slate for Gerald Ford is a clean, albeit empty, one."[42]

President Jimmy Carter appointed Douglas Costle as EPA administrator. He was involved earlier in efforts to create the EPA and had achieved success as an administrator in Connecticut. He had a solid financial management background, having worked at both the Office of Management and Budget and the Congressional Budget Office. Costle's management team incorporated appointees with strong ties to "outside constituencies"—the White House, Congress, and the environmental community. President Carter's administrative reform agenda was taken seriously by Costle, who implemented zero-based budgeting, civil service reform, and other initiatives identified with the administration. Public support for environmentalism was tempered by concern about the cost of regulatory compliance, and Costle worked to persuade the public of EPA's value, stressing its important public health mission as well as the role it played in pollution abatement. Reflective of this shift in emphasis from ecological balance to public health, Costle highlighted the problems associated with environmental toxins, pesticides, and hazardous materials as well as the agency's more aggressive stance toward environmental disease. The EPA budget grew during Carter's administration despite concerns about expenditure reductions.

President Ronald Reagan appointed three different EPA administrators—Anne (Gorsuch) Burford, William Ruckelshaus, and Lee Thomas—all committed to varying degrees to advancing Reagan's agenda of less government and to ensuring that benefits from EPA's regulations justify the costs. This differs from Carter administration EPA officials, who maintained that regulatory costs should not be considered in setting certain environmental standards.[43] Responding to his electoral base, President Reagan's approach to environmental regulation had a decidedly probusiness and conservationist flavor, promoting the economy by relaxing regulations protecting clean air, clean water, and toxic waste. Relying on the tools of the "administrative presidency" and executive discretion rather than statutory revisions, regulatory relief was provided by appointing ideologically compatible loyalists to EPA posts, lax enforcement of environmental statutes, reorganization, regulatory oversight, budget cuts, and staffing reductions.[44] The White House retained substantial control by appointing mostly EPA outsiders and political allies to top positions in the agency. Under Burford, divisions were abolished, promotions were political, staff morale declined, and many career senior executives and professionals left government service.

From 1980 to 1989, the EPA staff had increased very little, but its responsibilities expanded. During the same period, overall federal expenditures on environmental protection and natural resources, with inflation adjusted, dropped by some 10 percent.[45] Executive Order 12291 curtailed EPA independence by requiring that the Office of Management and Budget review all proposed agency rules and regulatory rules under the guidance of the White House Task Force on Regulatory Relief chaired by Vice President Bush. This and a subsequent Reagan executive order (E.O. 12498) required that major proposed agency rules undergo cost-benefit analysis, or regulatory impact analysis, and that agencies submit an annual regulatory agenda to the OMB to ensure consistency with the president's priorities.

Aligned with President Reagan's priority of providing "regulatory relief" and "getting government off the back of business," the EPA delegated authority to the states wherever possible. Severe budget cuts and staff reductions were especially pronounced between 1980 and 1983, hindering enforcement of existing environmental laws and administrative regulations. The EPA survived the hostile efforts of the Reagan administration to undercut its authority and diminish its role. Eventually Burford resigned under pressure, having responded more to the president and business interests than to Congress and other key stakeholders, and was replaced by EPA's first director, William Ruckelshaus, who restored the agency's credibility through seasoned leadership and judicious appointments despite a tight budget. EPA's most significant actions during the Ruckelshaus years were to recruit a competent leadership team, improve relations with Congress and the media, tighten the agency's enforcement effort, educate the public about environmental risks, and advocate (without success) a new policy initiative to cut sulphur dioxide emissions and reduce the amount of acid rain.[46] Once Reagan was reelected, Ruckelshaus resigned and Lee Thomas, a public adminstration careerist, took his place. Thomas emphasized ecology concerns, both local and global, especially the areas of hazardous waste, ozone depletion and global warming. He placed renewed emphasis on strong enforcement. Ruckelshaus and Thomas both received high marks for honesty, managerial talent, and hard work.

President George H.W. Bush entered office after conducting a pro-environment campaign, more in sync with public preferences on this issue than his predecessor. His appointment of moderate conservationist William Reilly, a past president of both the Conservation Foundation and the World Wildlife Fund—U.S., as EPA administrator was consistent with this modestly pro-environment theme. However, as one senator noted during Reilly's confirmation hearing, the new administrator "inherits an atmosphere that has been polluted with ill will."[47] Other members of the senior management team included former Justice and Energy Department officials, an academic, and an insider who rose through the EPA ranks. EPA's enforcement efforts under Reilly resulted in an increase in the number of felony indictments from prior years. Also, President Bush helped secure an international agreement on CFCs and created the President's Commission on Environmental Quality to press for pollution prevention and conservation through public/private partnerships. EPA staff morale and budget improved during the Bush years, but relative to its expanding tasks the agency remained understaffed and underbudgeted.

Congress influenced the EPA during this period by micromanaging the agency and imposing specific legislative mandates with deadlines and timetables. While Bush was generally supportive of Reilly and the EPA, hostility toward the agency was evident from other administration officials including the vice president, the first White House chief of staff, and the head of OMB. Vice President Dan Quayle chaired the Competitiveness Council, which was criticized by environmentalists as being too accommodating to business interests, insensitive to environmental concerns, and an impediment against implementation of environmental legislation.[48] The council blocked agencies from issuing regulations mandated by environmental laws. Bush also was criticized for his failure to support the Earth Summit and failure to sign the biodiversity treaty. Caught in the middle between anti-environmental forces in the administration and pro-environmental interests outside, Reilly faced a difficult balancing act in carrying out the agency's mission as environmental advocate, especially toward the end of the Bush administration.

President Bill Clinton's election campaign was pro-environment, and his appointments to the EPA were drawn disproportionately from the environmental community. Carol Browner, the EPA administrator, and Kathleen McGinty, the White House Office of Environmental Policy (OEP) head, were both former legislative aides to Vice President Al Gore. Environmentalists filled appointments to such key EPA posts as Assistant Administrators for Policy Planning and Evaluation, Assistant Administrator for Air, and General Counsel, signaling that environmental advocacy would characterize the EPA's role in the Clinton administration. Near the start of the Clinton administration the EPA was involved in a power struggle with the State Department over control of international environmental policy, with the White House OEP over domestic environmental matters, and with the Congress over the possible Cabinet-level status of the EPA.[49] The newly-created White House OEP merged with the existing Council on Environmental Quality, to coordinate federal environmental policy and work with the security, economics, and domestic policy councils together with related federal agencies to address global environmental problems and promote pro-environmental technologies.[50] Also, the White House was slow in filling several top EPA positions, and early on Browner expressed concern about agency mismanagement, thereby distancing herself from the previous administration and from long-serving senior managers in the agency. President Clinton eliminated the Council on Competitiveness, which his two predecessors had used to thwart EPA regulations, and revoked Reagan's two executive orders, 12291 and 12498, but he retained a form of White House regulatory review. Also, between 1990 and 1994, the EPA beefed up enforcement efforts, posting record high numbers of prosecutions and fines for environmental violations.

Despite the pro-environment appointments of the EPA's senior managers, reform of the regulatory review process, and increased enforcement, the conservative political climate in the Congress impeded an aggressive regulatory approach by the agency.[51] The Republican-controlled Congress did not repeal major environmental laws, but, as one observer noted, their efforts to curb regulatory activity were "the equivalent of a neutron bomb: a tactical weapon that leaves the legal edifice of environmental laws standing but kills all the bureaucrats."[52] As a result of these and other reform efforts, EPA staff reductions and increased reliance on external as opposed to in-house research occurred during Clinton's first term. While the Clinton administration was committed to market-based environmentalism that rewarded conservation and "green business practices," it also supported the idea that the best way to ensure environmental protection was to charge polluters for degrading the Earth.[53] Pollution prevention and reduction was also emphasized along with collaborative approaches such as regulatory negotiation ("reg-neg"), alternative dispute resolution (ADR), and environmental dispute resolution (EDR).[54] The administration fought off attempts by congressional lawmakers to approve major regulatory reform and to curtail environmental regulatory activities through the budget process. In fact, President Clinton established the President's Council on Sustainable Development to better integrate environmental and economic policy. The EPA during the Clinton administration also did more than prior administrations to emphasize "environmental justice," an issue that resonated with the president's electoral base. During his second administration, President Clinton's "reinventing government" initiative sought to reform the EPA together with other departments and agencies of the federal government.

The first four months of the George W. Bush administration sent important signals about the redirection of environmental policy and of EPA efforts. Ostensibly justified by a desire to avoid an economic recession, the new administration sought to soften environmental regulations. A series of decisions alarmed environmentalists and portended a changed climate in Washington. These started with a reversal of Mr. Bush's campaign pledge to impose mandatory limits on carbon dioxide. Withdrawal of the Clinton administration's rule to cut the amount of arsenic in the nation's drinking water, suspension of other regulations requiring mining companies to finance cleanups, and backpedaling on authorizing a federal agency to prohibit mines that inflict irreparable harm on the environment were among the early actions by the new administration. The Bush budget proposals included a 6.4 percent cut in EPA's budget. These decisions together with withdrawal from the Kyoto Protocol on climate change, permission for road building in previously-protected areas of the national forests, and budget proposals that will undercut lawsuits to require the listing of specific plants and animals as endangered species added to an outcry from environmentalists, some of whom called for EPA head Whitman's resignation. The EPA did decide not to change a Clinton administration rule enlarging protection of the nation's wetlands. Whitman, wishing to avoid being portrayed as an anti-environment director of the EPA, encouraged environmental advocates to adopt a "wait and see attitude" regarding administration proposals.

Clearly, presidents can influence environmental policy by effectively managing the rule-making process. This is evident from the above summary of presidential actions: Nixon and Ford tried to anticipate the impact of proposed regulations by subjecting them to "quality of life reviews" and requiring "inflation impact statements"; Carter used an executive order to establish the Regulatory Analysis Review Group (RARG) to enlarge administrative review and comment on pending regulations; Reagan also issued an executive order placing a regulatory moratorium on new rules and requiring cost-benefit analysis; Bush established the Council on Competitiveness to assess the impact of proposed rules on the economy; Clinton-Gore introduced reinventing government initiatives to reduce red tape and improve governmental performance; and first hints from the George W. Bush administration indicate a relaxation of environmental rules in favor of economic development priorities. These efforts over seven different presidential administrations illustrate the importance of the president as a stakeholder to administrative agencies like the EPA.[55] This brief review also highlights the differing perspectives of various presidents regarding the role, mission, and operation of the EPA. EPA administrators ignore presidential preferences at their peril, but they do have the potential of relying on other influential stakeholders (e.g., Congress, environmental activists) as a counterweight when actions by the president are at variance with agency mandates or priorities. This is illustrated by the agency's ability over time to resist President Reagan's efforts to retreat from environmental protection efforts. Actions by President Reagan's appointees to both the EPA and the Office of Management and Budget, as well as President Bush and Vice President Quayle's enhanced role for the Competitiveness Council, however, show that the president is a formidable stakeholder who can substantially impact the EPA's operations. Other stakeholders also affect the fluctuating fortunes of the EPA, as we will see below.

Environmental Activists, Business Managers, and the Public: Perceptions of EPA Performance

Three key groups that affect and are affected by the EPA are environmental activists, business regulatory officers, and the general public. The Pew Research Center recently surveyed these three key stakeholders to solicit their views of the agency's performance and their support for the agency's mission (Table 7.5A).[56] All three stakeholder groups—the general public, business regulatory officers, and environmental advocates—gave the EPA better marks than the government as a whole. However, there are sharp differences in how the three groups evaluate overall performance of the EPA, especially between environmen-

TABLE 7.5A

Stakeholders' Ratings of the Environmental Protection Agency

Assessment of the EPA	General Public %	Business Regulatory Officers %	Environmental Advocates %
Favorability Scores			
EPA	68	53	84
Federal Government	48	35	68
EPA Agency Performance			
Excellent/Good	47	41	68
Feelings About Agency			
Angry	3	8	0
Frustrated	39	50	42
Content	54	39	56
EPA Speed of Transaction			
Doesn't Work Too Slowly	24	24	14
Forms/Rules			
Not Overly Complex	20	12	30
Employees Courteous	56	61	80
Suspicion and Faith			
Equal Treatment for All	20	24	36
Never Certify Unsafe	65	70	70
Support for Agency Mission			
Percent Support	62	44	88

Source: Adapted from the Pew Research Center for the People & the Press, "Performance and Purpose: Constituents Rate Government Agencies," (April 2000), **http://www.people-press.org/npr00mor.htm**. Retrieved June 30, 2000.

tal advocates (68% excellent/good) and regulatory officers (41% excellent/good). One caveat noted in the study is whether respondents were really able to distinguish between the performance of the EPA in meeting its responsibilities and the performance of subnational environmental agencies. All three constituent groups were critical of the EPA for working too slowly and making their rules and forms too complex. However, criticisms of the bureaucratic process do not extend to criticisms of the EPA's employees: majorities in each stakeholder group indicate that the agency's employees are courteous and professional.

Disparities among the three respondent groups were evident regarding assessments of the EPA's technical capability and its policy decisions. It is not a surprise that environmental advocates were much more supportive than those from business. The views of the agency's fairness and honesty are low, with most general public and business officer respondents saying that the agency gives preferential treatment to some groups. Environmental advocates have divided opinions on this issue. However, majorities in all three groups show greater confidence in the EPA's handling of safety issues. Predictably, those who give EPA high performance marks also view it more positively than do those who think the agency performs poorly (Table 7.5B). Respondents are more critical about the means (cumbersome bureaucratic processes) than the ends (policy priorities) in question. Regarding mission support, it is not surprising that respondents differ: two-thirds of the general public and 8 in 10 environmental advocates support the EPA's mission; only 4 in 10 business officers agree. As expected, mission support is correlated with favorability assessments. The report notes, "Support for the purpose of the agency even affects attitudes of environmental officers at manufacturing firms, who express reservations about the EPA in general. More than 80% of environmental officers who agree that strict environmental laws are worth the cost view the EPA favorably; only one-quarter of those who disagree with this trade-off hold a similar view."[57]

TABLE 7.5B
Links to EPA Favorability Ratings

	EPA Performance Rating	
EPA Favorability Rating	High %	Low %
Favorable	86	25
Unfavorable	12	73
Don't Know/Refused	2	2
	Percent Favorable	
Stakeholder Group	Support Mission %	Reject Mission %
General Public	77	55
Business Regulatory Officers	82	25
Environmental Advocates	84	_*

*Numbers have been omitted due to small sample size.

Source: Adapted from the Pew Research Center for the People & the Press, "Performance and Purpose: Constituents Rate Government Agencies," (April 2000), **http://www.people-press.org/npr00mor.htm**. Retrieved June 30, 2000.

It is clear that these three stakeholder groups are important to the EPA's success. They can affect the agency's operations, but their interests often differ—and they vary in their judgments about the agency's performance. Administrative agencies like the EPA need to identify the interests of such stakeholders, to consider how and when to act toward them, and adjust their agency's priorities to take into account stakeholder preferences. Sometimes agencies succeed at this task, other times they fail. If stakeholders are supportive rather than antagonistic, it can greatly influence the ability of the agency to advance its initiatives. However, it is not always easy to respond to competing and sometimes contradictory claims and to tailor strategies in order to address the interests of multiple constituencies. This balancing act in satisfying diverse claimants is a test of the effectiveness of agencies that serve "multiple constituencies." Satisfying these diverse interests is especially complicated when attempting to respond to the conflicting interests and agendas found in the U.S. Congress.

The public is an especially important stakeholder for government agencies like the EPA to consider because we expect policymakers to respond to fluctuations in public sentiments.[58] Survey data collected by the National Science Foundation provides insights regarding the public's level of self-assessed knowledge and its level of interest in selected policy issues.[59] Table 7.6 reports findings from these surveys for 11 policy issues over five separate time periods in the 1990s. Two policy areas are of special relevance—environmental pollution and use of nuclear energy. While one issue (new medical discoveries) has had consistently high index scores (in the 80s using a 0–100 scale) measuring the level of interest, environmental pollution scores have hovered in the 70s (with 51% "very interested" in 1999) and have subsided somewhat in the 1990s. Nonetheless, environmental pollution is tied with local school issues for second place among the 11 issues in terms of public interest. Public interest in the use of nuclear energy to generate electricity is lower and dropped from 64 in 1990 to 54 in 1995, but there was minimal change in the level of interest in the late 1990s. When asked how well-informed Americans think they are about these matters, index scores for environmental pollution fell from 60 in 1990 to 48 in 1999 and for nuclear energy dropped from 37 in 1990 to 29 in 1999. As EPA stakeholders, the public interest in environmental pollution and nuclear power exceeds their knowledge about these issues, and their knowledge of pollution is greater than that of nuclear power. However, pollution continues to be among the more salient of the scientific and technological issues to the American public.

It is clear that most Americans do not fully understand the nuances involved in environmental pollution policy and even fewer understand nuclear energy policy. Such high-tech issues serve to limit public participation in a democracy. As Edwards and his colleagues note, it is a continuing challenge during policy debates for government agencies like EPA to maintain a balance between technological expertise and public participation.[60] Agencies like the EPA are a repository of scientific expertise, but they must be mindful of the public's desire for input on even highly complex technological issues.

The Congress: Whether to Increase the EPA's Power

Congress is an influential stakeholder of administrative agencies because it can expand or limit their authority. This can be done through its oversight role, investigating power, authority to kill an agency or amend its enabling statute (not

TABLE 7.6

Level of Public Interest and Knowledge Regarding Selected Policy Issues, 1990–1999

Issue	Level of public interest in policy issues					How well-informed Americans think they are about policy issues				
	1990	1992	1995	1997	1999	1990	1992	1995	1997	1999
Local school issues	67	71	72	73	71	55	55	59	61	58
New medical discoveries	83	82	83	83	82	53	51	52	56	53
Economic issues and business conditions	70	74	68	68	65	53	56	52	51	50
Issues about new scientific discoveries	63	61	67	70	67	42	39	42	48	44
Environmental pollution	80	77	74	72	71	60	57	52	51	48
Military defense policy	73	68	60	59	64	51	49	40	39	44
The use of new inventions and technologies	64	64	66	69	65	38	38	40	44	43
International and foreign policy issues	68	62	48	47	53	51	46	36	36	40
Space exploration	50	47	50	55	51	37	33	33	41	37
Agricultural and farm issues	48	–	47	49	47	36	–	35	38	33
The use of nuclear energy to generate electricity	64	57	54	54	55	37	32	29	31	29
Sample size	2,033	2,001	2,006	2,000	1,882	2,033	2,001	2,006	2,000	1,882

Source: Adapted from National Science Foundation, NSF Survey of Public Attitudes Toward and Understanding of Science and Technology (Washington, DC: NSF Division of Science Resource Studies), 1999.

applicable in the case of the EPA), budget authority, power to pass guidance legislation, and power to advise on and consent to appointments.[61] The legislative branch clearly shapes policy during the implementation stage. For example, Congress and the EPA sometimes go back and forth when making or implementing public policies, as Rochelle Stanfield observed:

> "In air pollution control, solid waste disposal, and other environmental protection programs, Congress passes laws, EPA implements them in ways displeasing to Congress, Congress passes more specific laws, EPA again carries them out to the dissatisfaction of Congress, and Congress threatens to enact even more specific laws."[62]

The consideration of Congress as a stakeholder of EPA will now be examined in greater detail and in the context of a specific decision—whether to elevate EPA to Cabinet-level status. Presidents from both parties have sought congressional endorsement of a stronger role for the Environmental Protection Agency by elevating it to Cabinet-level status. However, efforts by the Clinton administration to make EPA the 15th cabinet agency generated substantial opposition and the proposal ultimately failed in the 103rd Congress. The debate and action on this initiative is instructive as an example of how Congress, as a stakeholder of the EPA, can influence its ability to meet its environmental protection responsibilities. It further illustrates a broader issue: the difficulties presidents face in flexing political muscle in an era when Congress is intent on denying the president any major or even symbolic legislative victory.[63] It also highlights the different agendas in Congress that can obscure the aims of administrative reform and the legislative maneuvering that can block passage of initiatives designed to enhance implementation and enforcement of environmental protection laws.

In 1990 the House approved an EPA Cabinet bill, but it died due to disagreements between the president and Congress over how much power the agency should possess.[64] A year later a bill to give Cabinet status to the EPA, supported by President Bush, passed the Senate, but the House failed to act on the measure.[65] More recently, the Clinton administration made this issue a top legislative agenda item, viewing the bill as a way to place environmental concerns front and center among pending policy decisions. Proponents hoped Cabinet status would increase compliance with environmental laws and strengthen the hand of federal environmental regulators. Opponents objected to enlarging the government and adding new command-and-control environmental regulations.

The specific debate involved more than elevating the EPA to Cabinet status. The Senate version would have changed EPA programs by abolishing the White House Council on Environmental Quality (CEQ) and transferring its data collecting responsibilities to an EPA bureau. CEQ had responsibilities for reviewing federal compliance with environmental laws, including agency completion of environmental impact studies and preparing annual reports on environmental trends. The proposed Department of the Environment would absorb these functions, and a pared down White House Office of Environmental Policy would be the staff arm of the president on environmental matters. Several leading environmental groups opposed shifting CEQ's responsibilities to the new department, fearing that it would lead to more lax enforcement of environmental regulations.[66] Despite these concerns, the Senate Governmental Affairs Committee approved the Senate version by voice vote and, subsequently, the Senate Environment and

Public Works Committee approved the provisions under its jurisdiction by voice vote as well.

On the floor of the Senate there appeared to be bipartisan support for increasing EPA clout, primarily in international negotiations, and growing concern about the fragmentation of authority for environmental regulation. Some lawmakers worried that the bill would take away powers from other departments (e.g., Interior), and others thought that it would increase bureaucracy. Four amendments were proposed that resulted in recorded votes; three were defeated and one passed. A pared-down version of the legislation was tabled on a 54–42 vote because it was deemed insufficient to address needed reforms in EPA management and organization. An amendment was also easily defeated (70–26) that would have mandated the new department to offset any reasonably expected costs of regulations. A third amendment was tabled on a close 50–48 vote that would require additional reports documenting monies spent (more than $100,000) and jobs lost (more than 10,000) resulting from all congressional statutes or federal regulations. An amendment passed to create an environmental justice office that would collect data and report on problems in poor neighborhoods that might be disproportionately and adversely affected by environmental hazards.[67] A proposed amendment requiring governmental compensation to private property owners who lost land due to new land-use regulations was sidestepped due to limitations on debate, and a weakened amendment to streamline the wetlands designation process was approved by a voice vote.[68] Senate approval of the final bill was secured by a vote of 79–15 (Table 7.7). Democrats supported the measure with only one defection (Senator Bob Kerrey), while Republicans supported the measure by a 2 to1 margin.

In the House the debate was more contentious, and multiple agendas and legislative maneuvering were more evident. Democrats had ambitious interest in a bill with broad coverage. They also had an interest in beefing up the agency's civil rights protections, ensuring that it compiled accurate environmental data, and

TABLE 7.7

Party Support for the Creation of the EPA

Senate	Yeas	Nays	No Votes
Republican	28	14	3
Democratic	51	1	3
Independent			
Total	79	15	6
House			
Republican	5	167	4
Democratic	185	60	12
Independent	1		
Total	191	227	16

Sources: **http://www.senate.gov/activities/103-1/vote_00114.html** and **http://143.231.123.93/ cgi-bin/vote.exe?year+1994=rollnumber=4**.

Note: Senate= S.171 (May 4, 1993), Department of Environmental Protection Act
House= H.R. 3425 (February 2, 1994), Department of Environmental Protection Act

improving its management structure. And they were also interested in promoting environmental justice, avoiding requirements for environmental health risk assessments, and curbing abuses of contractors. Republicans, by contrast, preferred a spare bill that would simply designate the EPA as a Cabinet-level department.

Committee deliberations in the House were concentrated in the House Government Operations Committee and the House Rules Committee. The Government Operations Committee voted 31–11 to approve the bill designating the EPA as a Cabinet-level department and addressing some managerial issues.[69] Additions to the bill included provisions reforming contracting provisions, creating subagencies (Bureau of Environmental Statistics and Office of Environmental Justice), requiring performance targets for the new agency, and creating an advisory committee dealing with environmental health risks.[70] While Democrats had planned to use the bill to significantly enhance the clout of the EPA and comprehensively rewrite environmental policy, Republicans had their own plans that reflected the financial concerns of subnational governments, which had to implement costly federal environmental mandates.

By voice vote, a Republican sponsored amendment was approved to create an Office of Environmental Risk to advise the new secretary. Simpler substitute bills to merely elevate the EPA to Cabinet status were rejected, as were proposals to delay creation of the new agency for one year—both by voice vote. An agreement was forged to delay action on the abolition of the CEQ and to transfer its responsibility to the new department.

Prior to voting on the substance of the bill, those opposing the bill blocked it from coming to the floor on a procedural vote. The House was considering whether to adopt the rule prepared by the House Rules Committee regarding the procedure for proposing amendments and debating the proposal. The proposed rule would limit amendments to those concerning the new department's administrative structure or rules. It would bar policy amendments such as those that might reduce the department's ability to develop policies for protecting public health and the environment.[71] Legislators voted 191–227 to defeat a resolution (YEA, is the pro-environment vote) that would have established rules for floor debate on the bill (see Table 7.7). Sixty Democrats broke party ranks, joining a nearly unanimous group of Republicans to defeat the rule.[72]

The rule was rejected to avoid consideration of a pivotal amendment that would require the new department to conduct risk assessment studies on the cost of all proposed regulations. Risk assessment and cost-benefit analysis—both hot-button issues—were salient agenda items for those lawmakers concerned about heavy-handed federal environmental regulation and costs imposed on subnational governments and businesses. Opponents to this amendment feared that it would place economic concerns ahead of public health and environmental matters. They also believed that the EPA was already doing cost-benefit analysis and risk assessment, making the requirement superfluous as well as costly and time-consuming.[73] Rejection of the rule was a defeat for those seeking to enhance the clout of federal environmental regulation. They withdrew the legislation, realizing that approval of the proposed amendments was likely and that such approval would undercut and paralyze the new department. A subsequent effort to graft the Senate's EPA bill onto an unrelated bill (the reauthorization of the 1974 Safe Water Drinking Act) failed when that bill died without approval.[74]

Without making too much out of a single case, especially one that generated modest attention from the public and lawmakers, some insights about environmental policy making can be gleaned from the case. Legislative stalemate in this instance affected the capability of the premier federal environmental agency to more effectively implement environmental protection measures. It reflects the cleavages existing among lawmakers. Some would like to raise the priority of environmental matters and enhance the federal regulatory role. Others are equally committed to reducing costs of environmental regulations, assessing risks, and diminishing the burdens on those affected by environmental mandates (businesses, citizens, state and local governments). Still others share both sets of concerns.

The case illustrates how opponents of legislative initiatives can use amendments, procedures, and delaying tactics to scuttle a bill once thought to be a cinch for passage. It also highlights the difficult task confronting Democratic congressional leaders and the White House when they try to patch together coalitions to support controversial environmental proposals. The absence of interest group support for parts of the proposal along with their refusal to seek compromise on other parts was also evident, as was the breakdown in party discipline among legislators. While there was rhetorical consensus among lawmakers behind the idea of giving the environment a stronger voice in government, "extra baggage" attached to the bill became the lightning rod leading to defections from the initial consensus and resulting in the measure's demise. Agreement was impossible, in part, because of the inability, or unwillingness, of proponents to engage the opposition, to provide a forum where concerns could be voiced, and to seek common ground.

It is clear from the above examples that stakeholders differ in terms of their perceptions, power, and policy preferences regarding the EPA's efforts to regulate the environment. The political climate is continually changing as partisan control of the executive and legislative branches of government shifts from one party to the other, and the views of the public, business managers, and environmental activists are often at variance when it comes to actions taken by the EPA. This creates a complex political environment for EPA administrators, who must try to understand and predict stakeholder activity and gauge the legitimacy, urgency, and power of various claimants or constituency groups on specific issues. The above discussion of stakeholders does not consider the role of the courts, other administrative agencies, state and local officials, scientists, academics, pollution control professionals, political parties, the media, or other influencer groups.[75] It does highlight the political challenge facing agency administrators, who must manage their stakeholder relationships in a way that achieves the purposes of the agency. This challenge is not unique to the EPA, but is also encountered by managers of the Interior and Energy Departments, the Nuclear Regulatory Commission, and, to a lesser extent, the Council on Environmental Quality.

Conclusion

This chapter highlighted the role of administrative agencies, the sources and limits of their power, the processes by which they make decisions, and the institutional context in which they operate. While there are a number of other agencies that formulate, implement, and enforce environmental policies beyond those considered here, we emphasized the important functions played by five key agencies, especially the Environmental Protection Agency. We indicated how administrative rule making and adjudication result in environmental policy, and how iron triangles and issue networks operate. Both the internal operating environment and selected external stakeholders of the EPA were examined. We showed how Congress and the president can influence the actions of administrative agencies, and how the public, regulated businesses, and environmental activists view the agency and the issue of environmental protection.

The mini-case study of the president's proposal to elevate the EPA to Cabinet-level status illustrated the gridlock that prevails in Washington on environmental matters. Despite support by a Republican and Democratic president, apparent consensus on the basic proposal, and approval by various congressional committees, the measure failed because of controversial amendments, procedural maneuvering, and conflicting agendas in Congress. The Democrats saw the measure as a way to make more comprehensive changes in environmental policy and heighten the power and visibility of the agency while Republicans viewed it as an opportunity to introduce risk assessment requirements and to reduce the burdens on those complying with costly environmental regulations.

The Environmental Protection Agency, like other administrative units, is actively pursuing alternatives to the costly and cumbersome command-and-control regulatory system. While top-down command-and-control regulations continue to be necessary, the EPA is simultaneously experimenting with a variety of approaches. It is also simultaneously working on both pollution control and pollution prevention; however, progress on the prevention side has been slow to materialize. The EPA is also actively involved in reinventing itself, in response to the Clinton-Gore reform proposals, thus far with mixed success. It is too early to tell whether these "reinventing" initiatives will continue under the

---

Web Sites
Executive Agencies and Environmental Policy:

Department of Agriculture (USDA): **www.usda.gov**

Department of Energy (DOE): **www.doe.gov**

Department of the Interior (DOI): **www.doi.gov**

Environmental Protection Agency (EPA): **www.epa.gov**

Federal Emergency Management Agency (FEMA): **www.fema.gov**

Food and Drug Administration (FDA): **www.fda.gov**

Nuclear Regulatory Commission (NRC): **www.nrc.gov**

U.S. Federal Government Agencies: **www.lib.lsu.edu/gov/fedgov.html**

U.S. Government Information Sources: **www.nttc.edu/gov_res.html**

U.S. Forest Service: **www.fs.fed.us**

Source: Adapted from Project Vote Smart, Vote Smart Web (Yellow Pages), 2000 Edition, 2–9.

George W. Bush administration. As policy making becomes more complex, and iron triangles give way to issue networks, the EPA has responded with more emphasis on partnerships and strategies for dealing with external stakeholders. In response to the 1993 Government Performance and Results Act, the EPA has developed its five-year strategic plan, which includes many of these initiatives. Given the political climate in Congress, it is unlikely that major new environmental initiatives are going to be approved legislatively in the near term. Administrative agencies have the potential to revitalize environmental protection efforts, but to do so, agencies like the EPA will need to continue to be responsive to current trends, to work with other agencies toward a system of integrated ecosystem management, and to reinvigorate their efforts through more aggressive, proactive actions.

Endnotes

1. Ralph P. Hummel, "Bureaucracy," in Jay M. Shafritz, ed., *International Encyclopedia of Public Policy and Administration*, Vol. 1 (Boulder, CO: Westview, 1998), 307–309.
2. Benjamin Ginsberg, Theodore J. Lowi, and Margaret Weir, *We the People: An Introduction to American Government* (NY: Norton, 1999), 541.
3. Hummel, "Bureaucracy," 309; see also Max Weber, *Economy and Society: An Outline of Interpretive Sociology*, in Guenther Roth and Claus Wittich, eds.; translation Ephraim Fischoff, et al. (New York: Bedminster Press, 1968).
4. Paul C. Light, *The New Public Service* (Washington, DC: Brookings Institution, 1999).
5. The president lacks the authority to alter the jurisdiction or structure of Cabinet-level departments or independent regulatory commissions, but he is authorized under the Reorganization Act to submit a reorganization plan to Congress, transferring functions among agencies. Congress, in turn, must approve the plan within 90 days for it to become effective. Within the Executive Office of the President, the president is authorized to reorganize the staff agencies.
6. Kenneth F. Warren, "Adjudication," in Jay M. Shafritz, ed., *The International Encyclopedia of Public Policy and Administration*, vol. 1 (Boulder, CO: Westview, 1999), 24–25.
7. Raymond W. Cox III, "Administrative Discretion," in Shafritz, ed., *International Encyclopedia of Public Policy and Administration*, 37–40. See *Federalist* #10 and Weber, *Economy and Society: An Outline of Interpretive Sociology*.
8. Ibid, 38–39.
9. Ginsberg, et al., *We the People*, 542.
10. Michael E. Kraft, *Environmental Policy and Politics* (New York: HarperCollins, 1996), 63.
11. Mark Kelso, "Presidents and Environmental Policy: Republican 'Demons' and Democratic 'Angels'?," unpublished paper delivered at the annual meeting of the Western Political Science Association, San Francisco, March 1996, 15.
12. Nancy K. Kubasek and Gary S. Silverman, *Environmental Law* (Upper Saddle River: Prentice Hall, 2000), 130–132.
13. Participation varies depending on whether rule making is formal or informal. See Kubasek and Silverman, 82–86, for explanation of the distinction. See also B. Guy Peters, *American Public Policy: Promise and Performance*, 5th ed. (New York: Chatham House, 1999), Chapter 4.

14   Cornelius M. Kerwin, "Rulemaking," in Jay M. Shafritz, ed., *International Ency-clopedia of Public Policy and Administration*, vol. 4 (Boulder, CO: Westview, 1999), 2006–2010; Kraft, *Environmental Policy and Politics*, 111; Steven J. Cann, *Administrative Law*, 2nd ed. (Thousand Oaks, CA: Sage, 1998), Chapter 7; Cornelius Kerwin, *Rulemaking: How Government Agencies Write Law and Make Policy* (Washington, DC: CQ Press, 1994).

15   Warren, "Adjudication," 26.

16   See Douglas Cater, *Power in Washington* (New York: Random House, 1964), 17.

17   Morris P. Fiorina and Paul E. Peterson, *The New American Democracy* (Needham Heights, MA: Allyn and Bacon, 1998), 470; see also Frank R. Baumbartner and Bryan D. Jones, "Agency Dynamics and Policy Subsystems," *Journal of Politics* 53 (November, 1991), 1044–1074; and Seong-Ho Lim, "Changing Jurisdictional Boundaries in Congressional Oversight of Nuclear Energy Regulation: Impact of Public Salience" (Paper presented at the annual meeting of the American Political Science Association, 1992).

18   See Stephen J. Wayne, G. Calvin Mackenzie, David M. O'Brien, and Richard L. Cole, *The Politics of American Government* (New York: St. Martin's/Worth, 1999), 636.

19   Ibid., 679.

20   Fiorina and Peterson, *The New American Democracy*, 470.

21   Ibid., 471. See also Hugh Heclo, "Issue Networks and the Executive Establishment," in Anthony King, ed., *The New American Political System* (Washington, DC: American Enterprise Institute, 1978), 87–124.

22   D.S. Slocombe, "Implementing Ecosystem-Based Management: Development of Theory, Practice and Research for Planning and Managing a Region," *BioScience* 42 (9), 612–648; also Melissa A. Schilling and Martin Schultz, "Improving the Organization of the Environmental Management: Ecosystem Management, External Interdependencies, and Agency Structures," *Public Productivity Review* 21 (3), 1998, 296, 297.

23   Quoted in David Bollier and Joan Claybrook, *Freedom from Harm* (Washington, DC: Public Citizen and Democracy Project, 1986), 95.

24   See Kraft, *Environmental Policy and Politics*, 80; and Kubasek and Silverman, *Environmental Law*, 124; see also Susan Welch, John Gruhl, John Comer, Susan M. Rigdon, and Michael Steinman, *American Government* (Belmont, CA: Wadsworth, 1999), 577.

25   Kubasek and Silverman, *Environmental Law*, 103.

26   Kraft, *Environmental Policy and Politics*, 103.

27   Schilling and Schultz, "Improving the Organization of the Environmental Management: Ecosystem Management, External Interdependencies, and Agency Structures," *Public Productivity Review* 21 (3), 1998, 296, 297.

28   Ibid, 296, 297.

29   Melissa A. Schilling and Martin Schultz, "Improving the Organization of the Environmental Management: Ecosystem Management, External Interdependencies, and Agency Structures," 296, 297; see also Marian R. Chertow and Daniel C. Esty, "Environmental Policy: the Next Generation," *Issues in Science and Technology* 14 (1), 1997, 73–81; and Walter A. Rosenbaum, *Environmental Politics and Policy* (Washington, DC: CQ Press, 1998), 108–110.

30   Kraft, *Environmental Policy and Politics*, 102; "Civilian Employment of the Federal Government," Statistical Analysis and Services Division, U.S. Office of Personnel Management (May 1999), *World Almanac 2000*, 148.

31 Kraft, *Environmental Policy and Politics,* 103; Carnegie Commission, *Environmental Research and Development: Strengthening the Federal Infrastructure* (New York: Carnegie Commission on Science, Technology, and Government December,1992); Carnegie Commission, *Risk and the Environment: Improving Regulatory Decision Making* (New York: Carnegie Commission on Science, Technology, and Government, 1993; Kubasek and Silverman, *Environmental Law,* 99.

32 See U.S. Environmental Protection Agency Draft 2000 Strategic Plan, Office of the Financial Officer (June 2000), Chapter 4; see also Walter A. Rosenbaum, "The EPA at Risk: Conflicts over Institutional Reform," in Norman J. Vig and Michael E. Kraft, *Environmental Policy in the 1990s* (Washington, DC: CQ Press, 1997), 143–167; Richard N.L. Andrews, *Managing the Environment, Managing Ourselves* (New Haven, CT: Yale University Press, 1999), 250–252.

33 Alison Maxwell, "Does EPA Lack Common Sense," *Government Executive,* 29 (9) (September 1997), 50; Anonymous, "EPA Reinvention Rapped," *Government Executive* 28 (11) (November 1996), 6; John L. Dobra and Jeanne Wendel, "Pursuing Environmental Goals: Regulations vs. Markets," in Dennis L. Soden and Brent S. Steel, eds., *Handbook of Global Environmental Policy and Administration* (New York: Marcel Dekker, 1999).

34 See Gerald Zeitz, "Employee Attitudes Toward Total Quality Management in an EPA Regional Office, *Administration and Society* 28 (1), 1996, 120–143; Al Gore, *The Best Kept Secrets in Government* (Washington, DC: U.S. Government Printing Office, 1996); Kubasek and Silverman, *Environmental Law,* 101, 102; and Scott R. Furlong, "Reinventing Regulatory Development at the Environmental Protection Agency," *Policy Studies Journal* 23 (3), 1995, 466–481.

35 Jonathan P. West, "Stakeholder," in Jay Shafritz, *International Encyclopedia of Public Policy and Administration* (Boulder, CO: Westview, 1998), 2119–2121.

36 R. Edward Freeman, *Strategic Management: A Stakeholder Approach* (Boston, MA: Pitman, 1984.

37 See Max B.E. Clarkson, "A Stakeholder Framework for Analyzing and Evaluating Corporate Social Performance," *Academy of Management Review* 20 (1), 92–117; Donna J. Wood, *Business and Society* (New York: HarperCollins, 1994); Steven L. Wartick and Donna J. Wood, *International Business and Society* (Malden, MA: Blackwell Business, 1998), Chapter 5.

38 Kubasek and Silverman, *Environmental Law,* 94; Cann, *Administrative Law,* 27; Phillip J. Cooper, *Public Law and Public Administration* (Itasca, IL: Peacock, 2000), 375.

39 Marc Landy, Marc J. Roberts, and Stephen R. Thomas, *The Environmental Protection Agency: Asking the Wrong Questions From Nixon to Clinton* (New York: Oxford University Press, 1994), Chapter 2; see also Dennis L. Soden and Brent S. Steel, "Evaluating the Environmental Presidency," in Dennis L. Soden, ed., *The Environmental Presidency* (Albany, NY: SUNY Press, 1999), 313-354.

40 Ibid., 33.

41 Jacqueline V. Switzer with Gary Bryner, *Environmental Politics: Domestic and Global Dimensions* (New York: St. Martin's, 1998), 49–50. See also Alfred A. Marcus, *Promise and Performance: Choosing and Implementing an Environmental Policy* (Westport, CT: Greenwood Press, 1980), Chapter 3.

42 Ibid., 51.

43 Lawrence Mosher, "EPA Reversing Course," *The National Journal* 13 (17), 1981, 743.

44 Lawrence Mosher, "Reagan's Environmental Federalism—Are the States Up to the Challenge?" *The National Journal,* 14 (5), 1982, 184–186.; Switzer with

Bryner, *Environmental Politics*, 53; Norman J. Vig, "Presidential Leadership and the Environment: From Reagan to Clinton," in Norman J. Vig and Michael E. Kraft, *Environmental Policy* (Wasington, DC: CQ Press, 2000), 102. See also Richard A. Harris and Sydney M. Milkis, *The Politics of Regulatory Change* (New York: Oxford University Press, 1989). Susan J. Tolchin and Martin Tolchin, *Dismantling America* (Boston: Houghton-Mifflin, 1983); Glen Sussman and Mark A. Kelso, "Environmental Priorities and the President as Legislative Leader," in Dennis L. Soden, ed., *The Environmental Presidency* (Albany, NY: SUNY Press, 1999), 113–146; and Carolyn Long, Michael Cabral, and Brooks Vandivort, "The Chief Environmental Diplomat: An Evolving Arena of Foreign Policy," in Dennis L. Soden, ed., *The Environmental Presidency* (Albany, NY: SUNY Press, 1999).

45 Kraft, *Environmental Policy and Politics*, 89.

46 Landy, *The Environmental Protection Agency*, 35, 36.

47 Marshall Yates, "The EPA Under Bush: A New Direction," *Public Utilities Fortnightly* 123 (5), 1989, 34.

48 Kraft, *Environmental Policy and Politics*, 115.

49 Margaret Kriz, "Shaky Times," *The National Journal* 25 (25), 1993, 1566.

50 Ronald Begley, "Clinton Creates Environment Post," *Chemical Week* (February 17, 1993), 19; Switzer with Bryner, *Environmental Politics*, 57.

51 Landy, *The Environmental Protection Agency*, 306–309.

52 John H. Cushman, Jr., "Republicans Clear-Cut Regulatory Timberland," *New York Times* (March 5, 2995), E-16.

53 Ronald Begley, "Candidates Face Off on Environment," *Chemical Week* (September 23, 1992), 30.

54 Edward P. Weber, "The Theory and Practice of Collaborative Policy and Dispute Resolution Mechanisms: The Case of Environmental Policy," in Dennis L. Soden and Brent S. Steel, eds., *Handbook of Global Environmental Policy and Administration* (New York: Marcel Dekker, 1999), 124.

55 Cornelius Kerwin, *Rulemaking: How Government Agencies Write Law and Make Policy* (Washington, DC: CQ Press, 1994); and Jonathan P. West and Glen Sussman, "Implementation of Environmental Policy: The Chief Executive," in Dennis L. Soden, ed., *The Environmental Presidency* (Albany, NY: SUNY Press, 1999), 77–111.

56 The Pew Research Center for the People and the Press, *Performance and Purpose: Constituents Rate Government Agencies* (April 2000), **http://www.people-press.org/npr00mor.htm**.

57 Ibid., 7, 8.

58 David Vogel, *Fluctuating Fortunes: The Political Power of Business in America* (New York: Basic Books, 1988).

59 National Science Board, *Science and Engineering Indicators 2000* (Arlington, VA: National Science Foundation, 2000), 8-4-8-6.

60 George C. Edwards, Martin P. Wattenberg, and Robert L. Lineberry, *Government in America: People, Politics and Policy*, 7th ed. (New York: Longman, 1996), 499.

61 Cann, *Administrative Law*, Chapter 3; Kubasek and Silverman, *Environmental Law*, 95; and Cooper, *Public Law and Public Administration*, Chapter 10.

62 Rochelle L. Stanfield, "Stewing Over Superfund," *National Journal* (August 8, 1987), 2031.

63 Marc Lacey, "Blocked by Congress, Clinton Wields a Pen," *New York Times* (July 5, 2000), A13.

64 See "Action Delayed on Elevating EPA's Status," *CQ Almanac* (1993), 266.

65 Ibid., 266.

66 Ibid., 266.

67 Ibid., 267.

68 Ibid., 268.

69 Ibid., 268.

70 "EPA Remains Outside Cabinet," *CQ Almanac* (1994), 244.

71 Ibid., 244.

72 Richard E. Cohen, "An Ominous Rumbling in the Ranks," *The National Journal* 26 (February 12, 1994), 379; see also League of Conservation Voters, "1994 National Environmental Scorecard," **http://www.lcv.org/lcv94/House-issues.html**.

73 "EPA Remains Outside Cabinet," 244.

74 Ibid., 244.

75 The courts are an especially important stakeholder because it is estimated that industrial corporations challenge EPA rulings about 85 percent of the time. See William Grieder, *Who Will Tell the People* (New York: Simon & Schuster, 1992), 110.

CHAPTER 8

The Environmental Court

In describing the functions of the Supreme Court, one initially must acknowledge that it is the highest court in the federal system, possessing authority to hear and process cases. Yet, the Supreme Court is distinct in that not only does it interpret statutes, but also it can choose the cases it hears.[1] However, this may not be the Court's most important role as it relates to the environment. It may be the Court's influence as a powerful *policymaker* that is its most important characteristic. The Court is a political institution similar to other federal institutions, but unmistakably distinct in other ways. It is a political body, and as such, Lawrence Baum argues, "makes important decisions on major issues."[2] Elaborating further, Stephen Wasby explains that:

> People react to the Court not only in terms of its procedures but also in terms of its results. They treat it not only as a legal institution deciding specific cases but also as another agency of government, making policy by its decisions just as legislators and executive agencies make policy. As it makes policy, the Court interacts with these other branches of government, and public reaction to the Court's decisions (its policy statements) forces the Court to become an actor in the policy system. . . .[3]

The Court is a policymaker because it is a "participant in social conflict" serving both "system stability and responsible government through conflict management."[4] When a social issue like the environment is involved, however, the Court can become more than a mere participant in social conflict; it can, in fact, become the "primary decision maker"[5] to influence and shape the social agenda and, in some cases, such as abortion—and *Roe v. Wade* in particular—become the primary cause for the social conflict.

Court Involvement with Environmental Issues

To enhance our understanding of the Court's treatment of the environment we need to ask *why* the court saw fit to become involved with environmental issues and *when* this took place. On the one hand this involvement seems unreasonable since Supreme Court justices are often ill-prepared to sit in judgment on such perplexing questions as environmental concerns. This feeling of distance from environmental issues has been a factor since the early 1900s, when the Court first reluctantly agreed to make a multistate judgment on pollution, which illustrated the complexity of environmental issues. The justices found these decisions not to their liking.[6] This is one reason why some critics feel judges are ill-equipped to handle environmental questions; others who are concerned about judicial decisions on environmental matters suggest that judges are "unsuited to make policy decisions in technical areas such as pollution control because they must respond to individual demands for justice."[7]

The elaborate nature of the environment and its diversity is a major problem for judges. Reflecting on this, Robert V. Percival explains that because of environmental complexity, judges will often respond to environmental cases much as they do to tax cases, namely, tending to "shy away from or defer to the views of specialists in the area."[8] Percival illustrates this by recalling a conference in 1976 in which justices gathered to discuss the merits of the *Union Electric Co. v. U. S. Environmental Protection Agency* case.[9] Then Associate Justice William Rehnquist commented that the Clean Air Act was a "harsh and draconian statute," while Chief Justice Burger, equally frustrated by the case, suggested that its problems could be attributed to "letting a lot of little boys on Congressional staffs write legislation in noble prose that often takes little account of realities."[10]

This standoffish attitude by some members of the Court has encouraged a deference to administrative decisions. A good example of this is the Court's decision in *Vermont Yankee Nuclear Power Corporation v. NRDC* (1978),[11] wherein the Court supported the agency rule-making procedure over judicial decision making.[12]

Reasons for the Court's Involvement

One answer as to *why* the Court is involved with the environment was given years ago by one astute observer and critic of the American system, Alexis de Tocqueville. He, on examining the operation of the American political system, noted that "[t]here is hardly a political question in the United States which does not sooner or later turn into a judicial one."[13] This could certainly be said of environmental issues as well as all social issues; moreover, this would suggest the added political importance of the Court in American government and politics, where few important policy issues avoid Court consideration.

One other reason for the Court's involvement may rest with the concerns for the "technical expert" and the sort of judgments that he or she might make regarding environmental questions. Not everyone supports the expert's judgment—many are more concerned with potential damage to the environment that might result from their involvement. These people see judges as the necessary counterbalance to this sort of technocracy.[14]

The Evolution of Court Involvement in Environmental Affairs

Attention paid by the Court to the environment is relatively recent. It has been only since the 1970s that environmentalists have turned to the Court for assistance. Lettie Wenner argues that this was at the same time that "considerable skepticism had grown up around the ability of administrative agencies to carry out the goals of Congress." Thus the Courts were used, as Wenner maintains, "to force the Environmental Protection Agency and other governmental organizations to carry out the policies articulated in the laws."[15]

In the 1930s and 1940s environmental and conservation questions brought to the Court were infrequent. Environmental issues were few in number then, and were limited to fewer categories than one sees today. Furthermore, remedies relied on by the Court in resolving environmental conflicts were the remedies of trespass, personal injury, and damage liability.[16]

It was not until the 1970s that the *"judicialization"* of environmental policy making occurred—a period that saw a sizable number of court decisions involving the environment.[17] One thing that could have encouraged people to approach the Court at this time was the increasing interest in *public health,* which focused attention on the negative consequences of *bad air, polluted water,* and *hazardous waste* as causes for ill health.[18] These issues have remained some of the most enduring environmental issues of concern. Other environmental staples that have been around since the early 1970s can be found in Table 8.1.

Some of the cases of consequence that were decided involving air, water, and hazardous waste included the *water pollution* case of *Train v. City of New York* (1975)—a case brought by New York City against the administrator of the Environmental Protection Agency. This class action suit concerned an allotment of funds that had been authorized by the 1972 Amendments of the Federal Water Pollution Control Act. Agreeing with lower court decisions, the Supreme Court ruled that the EPA had to allot all funds that had been authorized.[19]

A second water pollution case, *EPA v. California ex rel. State Water Resources Control Board* (1976), was decided the next year. This case involved the administrator of the Environmental Protection Agency, who claimed a federal exemption from complying with state permit programs established under the Federal Water Pollution Control Act Amendments of 1972. The states of California and Washington filed petitions to review the EPA's decision by the

TABLE 8.1

The Supreme Court and Environmental Issues

Issues	Year of First Court Attention
Parks	1971
Lands	1972
Noise pollution	1973
Dams	1978
Fishing	1981
Mining	1981
Waste disposal	1981
Water	1982
Air pollution	1984
Private property	1986
Trade rights	1986
Whaling	1986
Timber	1988
Resource conservation	1989
Habitat modification	1995

Note: Derived from Table 8.2.

administrator. The Supreme Court ruled that federal installations that discharged water pollutants were under the same obligation to comply with restrictions listed in the Federal Water Pollution Control Act Amendments of 1972 as nonfederal facilities.[20]

A final water pollution case of importance in the 1970s was the *E. I. duPont de Nemours & Co. v. Train*, 430 U.S. 112 (1977), which involved companies producing inorganic chemicals that asked for review of the EPA's various regulations enacted under the Federal Water Pollution Control Act Amendments of 1972. Specifically, these companies looked for special exemption from federal regulations for their plants. The Supreme Court, however, refused to hear variances from those standards of performance.[21]

As far as the *clean air* decisions were concerned, in 1975 the Court decided, in the case of *Train v. Natural Resources Defense Council* (1975), that nonprofit organizations and individuals could seek changes in the EPA clean air standards as long as the changes did not compromise the basic mandate of the Clean Air Amendments.[22]

In *Hancock v. Train* (1976), the attorney general of Kentucky required federal installations to first obtain a state permit before operating air contaminant sources. The Supreme Court ruled that although the Clean Air Act obligates federal facilities discharging air pollutants to comply with state requirements, they are not required to obtain permits.[23]

The hazardous waste cases that made their way onto the Court's agenda in the 1980s and 1990s included *Ohio v. Kovacs*, 469 U.S. 274 (1985), in which the state of Ohio filed a complaint in Bankruptcy Court seeking a declaration that debtors' obligations to clean up a waste disposal site should not be forgiven due to bankruptcy. The Supreme Court ruled against the state claiming that a state court injunction requiring it to clean up the site was a "debt" or "liability on a claim" subject to discharge under the Bankruptcy Code and as such the debtor is not required to clean up the hazardous waste site.[24]

Following passage of an Alabama state statute imposing an additional fee on all hazardous waste not generated in the state but disposed of in state facilities, an operator of a commercial hazardous waste facility sought for relief, challenging the constitutionality of the statute. The Supreme Court, in the 1992 case of *Chemical Waste Management, Inc. v. Hunt*, 504 U.S. 334, held that the additional disposal fee discriminated against interstate commerce in violation of the commerce clause. As such, the Court ruled in favor of the hazardous waste operator.[25]

Contemporary Environmental Issues

Air, water, and hazardous waste cases still make it onto the agenda of the Court on a regular basis, which allows new generations of people to focus their attention on these staple environmental issues. But there are also other environmental issues the Court may need to respond to in the future. A number of those issues were featured in Vice President Al Gore's 1992 book, *Earth in the Balance*.[26] Gore makes a case for politics responding to these "new" issues, which he identifies as *global warming*, *overpopulation*, and *stratospheric ozone depletion*. These issues are distinct compared to "older" pollution issues (see Chapter 1). As Huber has suggested, however, "there is politically important space" that opens up for newly elected President George W. Bush to become a protector of the more traditional conservation issues such as "wilderness areas," "national parks," and "national forests," despite Bush's rather dismal environmental record as governor in Texas.[27]

Consequences of Court Involvement in Environmental Affairs

A number of the environmental cases decided since the 1970s have divided the Supreme Court in various ways (Table 8.2 page 243). Many of these cases were decided as a result of close votes among Court members, including those dealing with lands, noise, emissions control, property, whaling, trade rights, and timber. Still other cases were decided by majority votes of Court members. These cases dealt with parks, environmental impact, air and water pollution, fishing, resource conservation, construction, mining, and waste disposal. In his examination of those environmental cases decided between the 1970 and 1991, Percival found similar results suggesting that "more than a third of the environmental cases. . . were decided unanimously; more than 30 percent generated only one or two dissents while slightly less than one-third were decided over three or four dissents." He attributed this unusual decision-making pattern to the complexity of environmental law. He added further that "[i]n some cases the Justices struggle during the process of drafting a majority opinion to find a consistent rationale for reaching a particular result."[28]

An Eco-Friendly Court?

During the period 1970–1999 there have been more Court case decisions supportive of the environment than opposed to it. Does this mean that the Supreme Court is a reliable *eco-friendly institution*? Do those decisions supporting the environment suggest that the Court has made a firm commitment to the environment?

Consistency of Response

Much of the answer, it would appear, depends on Court *membership* and *leadership*. It is safe to say that there has been little consistency of opinion among justices as to their understanding and sensitivity to the environment over time. For example, the Burger Court assumed a nonactivist role in the case of *Sierra Club v. Morton* (1972) in refusing to recognize public interest plaintiffs. The Court chose a narrow statutory interpretation of Section 10 of the Administrative Procedure Act (APA) even though a broader interpretation was possible. While the Court followed an established legal tradition, one can question the adaptability of its response to environmental problems.[29] One senses a rather weak commitment to the environment, in this instance, on the part of the Burger Court.

In his study of individual justices' votes in the environmental cases from 1970 through 1991, Percival discovered that those justices who were most sympathetic to environmental interests included[30] William O. Douglas, supporting the environment 68.8% of the time in 16 cases; Thurgood Marshall, supporting the environment 60.0 % of the time in 85 cases; Harry Blackmun, supporting the environment 54.7% of the time in 86 cases; William J. Brennan, Jr., supporting the environment 54.2% in 83 cases; and John Paul Stevens, supporting the environment 52.2% in 69 cases.[31]

WILLIAM O. DOUGLAS: THE "GREENEST" OF THEM ALL

William O. Douglas's life covered the period from 1898 through 1980—some 82 years—which allowed this Connecticut-born Associate Justice of the Supreme Court to witness remarkable change. He was appointed to the Supreme Court in 1939 by Franklin Roosevelt as the 82nd justice of that Court, serving until 1975. While there, he wrote some 800 Supreme Court decisions,[1] as well as a number of books, articles, and speeches. In his writings, the most popular topics he focused on included civil liberties, foreign policy, conservation, and the wilderness.[2]

Douglas's understanding of the environment came largely from his early personal experiences with the wilderness while growing up in Yakima, Washington. These experiences enhanced his love for the outdoors. James Duram maintained that Douglas wrote of nature's role as a "teacher, friend, enemy, emotional catharsis, mystery, and above all, something that can help man regain perspective on his place in the earth's environment."[3]

Douglas felt that preserving the wilderness was essential to the virtues of American character. In his book, *A Wilderness Bill of Rights*,[4] he pointed to technology and excessive population growth as the greatest threats to the wilderness areas.

Douglas's personal attitude toward the environment did, as one might expect, affect his outlook on the Court. In the case of *Air Pollution Variance Board of Colorado v. Western Alfalfa Corp.* in 1974,[5] for example, he supported a Colorado Health inspector's efforts to visually test emissions from smokestacks, assuring him that it was a legitimate way to ensure air quality and that he could do it without violating the Fourth Amendment's law against unreasonable searches.

Douglas also tried to expand access to the Court for environmentalists by assuring legal standing for environmental groups. An example of this could be seen in the 1972 case of *Sierra Club v. Morton*,[6] in which he even encouraged "standing" before the Court for inanimate natural areas such as "valleys, alpine meadows, rivers, lakes, estuaries, beaches, ridges, groves of trees, swampland, or even air that feels the destructive pressures of modern technology and modern life."[7]

Finally, Douglas defended sanctuary in the urban environment in a 1974 decision, *Village of Beel Terre v. Boraas*.[8] Douglas was willing to defend a residential ordinance protecting "family values, youth values, and the blessings of quiet seclusion and clean air making the area a sanctuary for people."[9]

Thus one can see how this Justice who gained so much enjoyment from the environment, for 36 years willingly defended it by expanding opportunities for others.

---

[1] James C. Duram, *Justice William O. Douglas* (Boston: Twayne Publishers, 1981), 56.

[2] Ibid.

[3]Ibid.

[4]William O. Douglas, *A Wilderness Bill of Rights* (Boston: Little, Brown and Co., 1965).

[5]*Air Pollution Variance Board of Colorado v. Western Alfalfa Corp.*, 416 U.S. 861 (1974)

[6]*Sierra Club v. Morton*, 405 U.S. 727 (1972).

[7]405 U.S. 727, 743

[8]*Village of Belle Terre v. Boraas*, 416 U.S. 1 (1974)

[9]Ibid.

While William O. Douglas did not participate in many environmental cases before he left the court, he was the primary defender of the environment. This was revealed in several of the dissents he wrote, including those in the 1973 cases of *Salyer Land Co. v. Tulare Lake Basin Storage District*, 410 U.S. 719 (1973) and *Associated Enterprises v. Toltec Watershed Improvement District*, 410 U.S. 743. In the *Avery* and *Hadley* dissent, he stated quite pointedly:

> It is also inconceivable that a body with the power to destroy a river by damming it and so deprive a watershed of one of its most salient environmental assets does not have 'sufficient impact' on the interests of people generally to invoke the principles of *Avery [v. Midland County]* and *Hadley [v. Junior College Distict]*.[32]

One could argue that Douglas's interest in the environment—he wrote several books including *Of Men and Mountains* in 1950 and *A Wilderness Bill of Rights* in 1965—did affect the way he voted in behalf of environmental policy making.[33]

Justice Stevens also has quite a sophisticated interest and understanding of the environment, demonstrated by his dissenting opinion in the case of *Dolan v. City of Tigard*, 512 U.S. 374 (1994):

> In our changing world one thing is certain: uncertainty will characterize predictions about the impact of new urban developments on the risks of floods, earthquakes, traffic congestion, or environmental harms. When there is doubt concerning the magnitude of those impacts, the public interest in averting them must outweigh the private interest of the commercial entrepreneur.[34]

Considering the favorable environmental votes of Justices Douglas, Powell, and Kennedy, and their attitudes toward the environment—Douglas's love of the outdoors, Powell's passion for the forests and historic preservation, Kennedy's experience with selecting developing property in California—Lazarus concludes that one can best tell a justice's position on the environment from his or her personal experiences with the natural environment. As he states:

> A Justice's affinity for the natural environment, in turn, influences his or her conceptualization of the legal issues presented in an environmental protection setting. For many, moreover, an appreciation of environmental law's objectives and the legitimacy and strength of the evolutionary demands that they place on competing legal doctrines and on lawmaking institutions originates in personal experience. It is apparently unlikely to be the exclusive product of abstract, dispassionate thinking wholly removed from the natural environment that serves as environmental law's core inspiration.[35]

TABLE 8.2

Major Environmental Court Cases, 1935–2000 by Environmental Orientation

Year	Case Name	Cite	Pro/Anti Env.	Description	Majority	Dissent	Concur	Pres.
1935	U.S. v. Oregon	195 US 1	pro	Bird Reservation	9-0 Hg, VD, Mr, Br, Su, Bt, St, R, C			FDR
1942	Tulee v. State of Washington	315 US 681	anti	Fish Conservation	9-0 St, Rb, Bk, Rd, F, D, Mp, Bn, J			FDR
1968	Puyallup Tribe v. Dept. of Game of Washington	391 US 392	pro	Fish Conservation	9-0 Wn, Bk, D, H, Bn, Sw, W, Ft, M			RMN
1970	Hickel v. Oil Shale Corp.	400 US 480	pro	Oil Shale Mining	4-2 D, Bl, Bk, Bn; H, W, M not participating	Sw, Bg		RMN
1971	Citizens to Preserve Overton Park v. Volpe	401 US 402	pro	Public Parks	6-2 M, H, Bg, W, Sw, Bl; D not participating	Bk, Bn	Bl	RMN
1971	Ohio v. Wyandotte Chemicals Corp	401 US 493	anti	Mercury Pollution	8-1 H, M, Bn, Bg, W, Sw, Bl, Bk	D		RMN
1971	U.S. v. International Minerals & Chemical Corp.	402 US 558	pro	Corrosive Liquid	6-3 D, Bg, Bl, M, W, Bk	Sw, H, Bn		RMN

continued

TABLE 8.2
(continued)

Year	Case Name	Cite	Pro/Anti Env.	Description	Majority	Dissent	Concur	Pres.
1972	Sierra Club v. Morton	405 US 727	pro	Public Lands	4-3 Sw, M, W, Bg; R, P not participating	D, Bn, Bl		RMN
1973	EPA v. Mink	410 US 73	anti	Nuclear Testing	6-3 W, P, Bg, Bl, Sw; R not participating	D, Bn, M (in part)	W	RMN
1973	Sayler Land Co. v. Tulare Lake Basin Water Shortage Dist.	410 US 719	anti	District General Elections	6-3 R, Bl, P, Sw, W, Bg	D, Bn, M		RMN
1973	Assoc. Enterprises v. Toltec Watershed Improve. Dist.	410 US 743	anti	Water District Voting	6-3 Per Curiam Opinion reflecting views of R, Bl, P, Sw, W, Bg	D, Bn, M		RMN
1973	Askew v. American Waterways Operators, Inc.	411 US 325	pro	Oil Spill	9-0 D, W, P, Bg, Bl, R, Bn, Sw, M			RMN
1973	U.S. v. Penn. Industrial Chemical Corp.	411 US 655	pro	Refuse Discharge	4-5 Bn, D, W, M	Bg, Sw, P, Bl, R		RMN
1973	U.S. v. Students Challenging Regulatory Agency Procedures (SCRAP)	412 US 669	anti	Recycling Surcharge	8-0 Sw, Bn, Bl (joined all), D, M (in part), Bg, W, R (in part) P not participating	D (in part) W, Bg, R (in part) M (in part)		RMN
1974	Air Pollution Variance Board v. Western Alfalfa Corp.	416 US 861	pro	Air Pollution	9-0 D, Bg, Sw, W, Bl, P, R, Bn, M			RMN

continued

Year	Case Name	Cite	Pro/Anti Env.	Description	Majority	Dissent	Concur	Pres.
1975	Train v. City of New York	420 US 35	pro	Federal Environment Allotment	9-0 W, Bg, Bn, Sw, M, Bl, P, R	D-concurred in the result		Ford
1975	Train v. Campaign Clean Water	420 US 60	pro	Federal Environment Allotment	9-0 Per Curiam opinion reflecting the views of W, Bg, Bn, Sw, M, Bl, P, R	D concurred in the result		Ford
1975	Train v. Natural Resources Defense Council	421 US 60	pro	Air Quality Standards	7-1 R, Bg, Bn, Sw, W, M, Bl P not particpating	D		Ford
1975	Alyeska Pipeline Service v. Wilderness Society	421 US 240	anti	Attorney's Fee for Environ. litigation	5-2 W, Bg, Sw, Bl, R D, P not participating	Bn, M		Ford
1975	Aberdeen & Rockfish Railroad Co. v. SCRAP	422 US 289	pro	Environ. Impact of Recyclables	7-1 W, Bg, Bn, Sw, M, Bl, R P not participating	D (in part)		Ford
1976	Train v. Colorado Public Interest Research Group	426 US 1	anti	EPA Jurisdiction	8-0 M, Bg, Sw, P, R, Bl, W, Bn Sv not participating			Ford
1976	Cappaert v. US	426 US 128	pro	Fish Preservation	9-0 Bg, W, Bn, M, Bl, P, Sv, Sw, R			Ford
1976	Hancock v. Train	426 US 167	pro	Air Pollution	7-2 W, Bg, Bn, M, Bl, P, Sv	Sw, R		Ford
1976	EPA v. California rel. State Water Resources Control Board	426 US 200	pro	Federal Exemption	7-2 W, Bg, Bn, M, Bl, P, Sv	Sw, R		Ford

TABLE 8.2
(continued)

Year	Case Name	Cite	Pro/Anti Env.	Description	Majority	Dissent	Concur	Pres.
1976	Kleepe v. New Mexico	426 US 529	pro	Roaming Horses	9-0 M, Bg, Bn, Sw, P, R, W, Bl, Sv			Ford
1976	Union Electric Co. v. EPA	427 US 246	pro	Air Quality Standards	9-0 M, R, Bl, Bn, Sv, Sw, W, P, Bg		P, Bg	Ford
1976	Kleepe v. Sierra Club	427 US 390	anti	Impact Statement	7-2 P, Bg, Sw, W, Bl, R, Sv	M, Bn (in part)	M, Bn (in part)	Ford
1977	E.I. duPont de Nemours & Co. v. Train	430 US 112	pro	EPA Jurisdiction	8-0 Sv, R, Bg, Sw, Bn, M, W, Bl; P not participating			JEC
1977	EPA v. Brown	431 US 99	pro	Vehicle Air Pollution	8-1 Per curiam opinion reflecting the views of R, Bg, Sw, Bl, Bn, W, M, P	Sv		JEC
1978	Adamo Wrecking Co. v. U.S.	434 US 275	anti	Emission Standards	5-4 R, Bg, W, M, P	Sw, Bn, Bl, Sv	P	JEC
1978	Vermont Yankee Nuclear Power Corp. v. Natural Resources Defense Council	435 US 519	anti	Nuclear Power Plant Licensing	7-0 R, Bg, Sw, W, M, Sv, Bn Bl, P not participating			JEC
1978	Baldwin v. Montana Fish & Game Commission	436 US 371	pro	Elk Hunting	6-3 Bl, Bg, Sw, P, R, Sv	Bn, W, M	Bg	JEC
1978	Tennessee Valley Authority v. Hill	437 US 153	pro	Endangered Species—Snail Darter	6-3 Bg, Bn, Sw, W, M, Sv	P, Bl, R		JEC
1978	City of Philadelphia v. New Jersey	437 US 617	anti	Waste Disposal	7-2 Sw, Bn, W, M, Bl, P, Sv	R, Bg		JEC
1978	U.S. v. New Mexico	438 US 696	anti	Water Rights	5-4 R, Bg, Sw, Bl, Sv	P, Bn, W, M		JEC

Year	Case Name	Cite	Pro/Anti Env.	Description	Majority	Dissent	Concur	Pres.
1979	Andrus v. Sierra Club	442 US 347	anti	Budget Decrease	9-0 Bn, Bg, R, Sw, Sv, M, W, Bl, P			JEC
1979	Andrus v. Allard	444 US 51	pro	Bird Preservation	9-0 Bn, R, Bl, M, W, Sw, P, Sv		Bg (decision only)	JEC
1979	Kaiser Aetna v. U.S.	444 US 164	anti	Developed Pond	6-3 R, Bg, W, Sw, Sv, P	Bl, Bn, M		JEC
1980	Strycker's Bay Neighbor. Council v. Karlen	444 US 223	anti	Housing Development	8-1 Per Curiam opinion reflecting views of Bn, Sw, Sv, Bg, R, P, W, Bl	M		JEC
1980	Andrus v. Shell Oil Company	446 US 657	anti	Shale Deposits	6-3 Bg, Bl, Sv, R, W, P	Sw, Bn, M		JEC
1980	U.S. v. Ward	448 US 242	pro	Oil Spill	8-1 R, Bg, Bn, Sw, P, W	Sv	Bl, M	JEC
1980	EPA v. National Crushed Stone Assn.	449 US 64	pro	Pollution Discharge	8-0 W, Bg, Bn, Bl, R, M, Sw, Sv; P not participating			JEC
1980	Minnesota v. Clover Leaf Creamery	449 US 456	pro	Waste Disposal	7-1 Bn, Bg, Sw, W, M, Bl R not participating	S, P (in part)	P (in part)	JEC
1981	San Diego Gas & Electric Co. v. City of San Diego	450 US 621	pro	Power Plant Rezoning	5-4 Bl, Bg, W, R. Sv	Bn, Sw, M, P	R	RWR
1981	California v. Sierra Club	451 US 287	anti	Water Diversion Facilities	9-0 W, Bn, M, Bl, Sv		R, Bg, Sw, P (decision only) Sv	RWR
1981	Hodel v. Virginia Surface Mining & Reclamation Assn.	452 US 264	pro	Mining Regulations	9-0 M, Bn, Bg, Sw, W, Bl, P, Sv		R, Bg, P	RWR

continued

TABLE 8.2
(continued)

Year	Case Name	Cite	Pro/Anti Env.	Description	Majority	Dissent	Concur	Pres.
1981	*Hodel v. Indiana*	452 US 314	pro	Mining Regulations	9-0 M, Bg, Bn, Sw, W, Bl, P, Sv		R (in the decision), Bg	RWR
1981	*Middlesex County Sewerage Authority v. National Sea Clammers Assn.*	453 US 1	anti	Sewage Discharge	9-0 P, Bg, Bn, Sw, W, M, R		Sv, Bl (in part and in the decision)	RWR
1981	*Commonwealth Edison Co. v. Montana*	453 US 609	pro	Coal Production Taxation	6-3 M, Bg, Bn, Sw, W, R	Bl, P, Sw	W	RWR
1981	*Weinberger v. Catholic Action of Hawaii Peace Education Project*	454 US 139	anti	Nuclear Weapon Storage	9-0 R, Bg, W, M, P, Sv, OC		Bl, Bn	RWR
1982	*Weinberger v. Romero-Barcelo*	456 US 305	anti	Water Pollution Discharge	8-1 W, Bg, Bn, M, Bl, P, R, OC	Sv	P	RWR
1982	*Sporhase v. Nebraska ex re. Douglas*	458 US 941	pro	Water Rights	8-2 S, Bg, Bn, W, M, R, Bl, P	R, OC		RWR
1983	*North Dakota v. U.S.*	460 US 300	pro	Wetland Acquisition	7-2 Bl, Bg, Bn, W, M, P, Sv	OC, R (in part)		RWR
1983	*Metropolit. Edison Co. v. People Against Nuclear Energy*	460 US 766	pro	Nuclear Power Plant Operation	9-0 R, Bn, Bg, Bl, W, M, Sv, OC, P			RWR
1983	*Pacific Gas & Electric Co. v. State Energy Resources Conser. & Develop. Commission*	461 US 190	anti	Nuclear Power Plants	9-0 W, Bg, Bn, M, P, R, OC		Bl, Sv (decision only)	RWR

Year	Case Name	Cite	Pro/Anti Env.	Description	Majority	Dissent	Concur	Pres.
1983	Baltimore Gas & Electric Co. v. Natural Resources Defense Council	462 US 87	anti	Waste Storage	8-0 OC, Bg, Bn, Sv, R, M, W, Bl; P not participating			RWR
1984	Silkwood v. Kerr-McGee Corp.	464 US 238	pro	Plutonium Leak-age Retribution	5-4 W, Bn, R, Sv, OC	Bl, M, P, Bg,		RWR
1984	Secretary of the Interior v. California	464 US 312	anti	Offshore Oil and Gas Licenses	5-4 OC, Bg, W, P, R	Sv, Bn, M, Bl		RWR
1984	Summa Corp. v. California ex rel. State Lands Commission	466 US 198	anti	Public Trust Easement	8-0 R, Bn, Bl, Bg, OC, P, W, Sv; M not participating			RWR
1984	Escondido Mutual Water Co. v. La Jolla Band of Mission Indians	466 US 765	pro	Hydroelectric Licenses	9-0 W, Bn, Bl, P, OC, Sv, R, M, Bg			RWR
1984	Chevron USA v. Natural Resources Defense Council	470 US 837	pro	Air Pollution	6-0 Sv, Bg, Bn, W, Bl, P / M, R, OC not participating			RWR
1985	Ohio v. Kovacs	469 US 274	anti	Waste Cleanup	9-0 W, OC, R, Sv, P, Bg, M, Bn, Bl		OC	RWR
1985	Chemical Mfrs. Ass'n. v. Natural Resources Defense Council	470 US 116	anti	Toxic Pollutants	5-4 W, Bg, Bn, P, R	M, Bl, Sv, OC (in part)		RWR
1985	U.S. v. Riverside Bayview Homes	474 US 121	pro	Water Rights	9-0 W, Bl, Bn, Bg, P, OC, R, M, Sv			RWR

continued

TABLE 8.2
(continued)

Year	Case Name	Cite	Pro/Anti Env.	Description	Majority	Dissent	Concur	Pres.
1986	Midlantic National Bank v. New Jersey Dept. of Environ. Protection	474 US 494	pro	Toxic Waste Cleanup	5-4 P, Bl, Bn, M, Sv	R, Bg, W, OC		RWR
1986	Exxon Corp. v. Hunt	475 US 355	pro	Cleanup Tax	7-1 M, Bg, Bn, W, Bl, R, OC P not participating	Sv		RWR
1986	Dow Chemical Co. v. U.S.	476 US 227	pro	EPA Investigation	7-2 Bg, W, R, Sv, OC Bl P (in part)	P, Bn, M, Bl, (in part)	P (in part)	RWR
1986	Japan Whaling Ass'n. v. American Cetacean Society	478 US 221	anti	Whaling Regulations	5-4 W, P, Bg, Sv, OC	M, Bn, Bl, R		RWR
1986	Penn. v. Delaware Valley Citizens Council for Clean Air	478 US 546	pro	Environ. Activists Compens.	6-3 W, Sv, OC, P, R, Bg	Bl, M, Bn (in part)	Bl, M, Bn (in part)	RWR
1987	International Paper v. Ouelette	479 US 481	anti	Water Pollution	5-4 P, R, W, OC, Sc	Bl, M, Bn (in part) Sv, Bl (in part)	Bn, M, Bl (in part) Sv (in part)	RWR
1987	Keystone Bituminous Coal v. De Benedictis	480 US 470	pro	Coal Mining	5-4 Sv, Bn, W, M, Bl	R, P, OC, Sc		RWR
1987	Amoco Production v. Village of Gambell	480 US 531	anti	Oil Exploration	9-0 W, R, Bn, M, Bl, P, OC, Sv, Sc (Sv, Sc in part)	Sv, Sc (in part and in the decision)		RWR
1987	California Coastal Comm. v. Granite Rock Co.	480 US 572	pro	National Forest	5-4 OC, R, Bn, M, Bl	P, Sv (in part) Sc, W	P, Sv (in part)	RWR

Year	Case Name	Cite	Pro/Anti Env.	Description	Majority	Dissent	Concur	Pres.
1987	First English Evangelical Lutheran Church v. County of Los Angeles	482 US 304	anti	Flood Protection	6-3 R, Bn, W, M, P, Sc	Sv, (Bl, OC in part)		RWR
1987	Penn. v. Delaware Valley Citizens Council for Clean Air	483 US 711	anti	Vehicle Emission	5-4 W, R, P, Sc, OC	Bl, Bn, M, Sv	OC (in a narrower opinion, concurred in part)	RWR
1987	Nollan v. California Coastal Comm.	483 US 825	anti	Beach Access	5-4 Sc, R, W, OC, P	Sv, Bl, Bn, M,		RWR
1987	Gwaltney of Smithfield Ltd. v. Chesapeake Bay Foundation	484 US 49	anti	Clean Water	8-0 M, R, Bn, W, Bl		Sc, Sv, OC (in part)	RWR
1988	Lyng v. Northwest Indian Cemetery Protective Ass'n.	485 US 439	anti	Timber Harvesting	5-3 OC, R, W, Sv, Sc K not participating	Bn, M, Bl		RWR
1989	Robertson v. Methow Valley Citizens Council	490 US 332	anti	National Forest	9-0 Sv, R, Bn, Bl, M, W, OC, Sc, K		Bn	GHWB
1989	Marsh v. Oregon Natural Resources Council	490 US 360	anti	Elk Creek Dam	9-0 Sv, R, Bn, Bl, M, W, OC, Sc, K			GHWB
1989	Penn. v. Union Gas Co.	491 US 1	anti	Coal Discharge Liability	6-3 Bn, M, Bl, Sv, Sc (opinion of the Court for some parts) Bn, M, Bl, Sv (plurality)	Sc, R, OC, K (in part) OC	Sv, W, R, OC, K (in part)	GHWB
1989	Hallstom v. Tillamook County	493 US 20	anti	Waste Management	7-2 OC, R, W, Bl, Sv, Sc, K	M, Bn		GHWB

continued

TABLE 8.2

(continued)

Year	Case Name	Cite	Pro/Anti Env.	Description	Majority	Dissent	Concur	Pres.
1990	California v. Federal Energy Regulatory Commission	495 US 490	anti	Water Rights	9-0 OC, R, Bn, Bl, W, M, Sv, Sc, K			GHWB
1990	Lujan v. National Wildlife Federation	497 US 871	anti	Land Conservation	5-4 Sc, R, W, OC, K	Bl, Bn, M, Sv		GHWB
1991	Wisconsin Public Intervenor v. Mortier	501 US 597	pro	Public Lands	9-0 W, R, M, Bl, Sv, K, So, OC		Sc concurred in the decision	GHWB
1992	Arkansas v. Oklahoma	503 US 91	pro	Clean Water	9-0 Sv, R, Bl, W, K, OC, T, So, Sc			GHWB
1992	U.S. Dept of Energy v. Ohio	503 US 607	anti	Water Pollution	6-3 So, R, OC, Sc, K, T	W, Bl; Sv (in part)		GHWB
1992	Chemical Waste Mgmt. v. Hunt	504 US 334	anti	Hazardous Waste	8-1 W, Bl, Sv, OC, Sc, K, So, T	R		GHWB
1992	Fort Gratiot Sanitary Landfill v. Michigan Dept. of Natural Resources	504 US 353	anti	Solid Waste	7-2 Sv, W, OC, Sc, K, So, T	R, Bl		GHWB
1992	Lujan v. Defenders of Wildlife	504 US 555	anti	Endangered Species	7-2 Sc, R, W, K, So, T (opinion of the Court for some parts) Sc, R, W, T (plurality opinion for some parts)	Bl, OC	K, So Sv (in part and in the decision)	GHWB
1992	Gade v. National Solid Wastes Mgmt. Ass'n.	505 US 88	anti	Hazardous Waste Training	5-4 OC, R, W, Sc, K (opinion of the Court for some parts) OC, R, W, Sc (plurality)	So, Bl, Sv, T	K (in part and in the decision)	GHWB

Year	Case Name	Cite	Pro/Anti Env.	Description	Majority	Dissent	Concur	Pres.
1992	New York v. U.S.	505 US 144	anti	Radioactive Waste	6-3 OC, R, Sc, K, So, T	W, Bl, Sv		GHWB
1992	City of Burlington of Dague	505 US 557	anti	Attorney Fee	6-3 Sc, R, W, K, So, T	Bl, Sv, OC		GHWB
1992	Lucas v. South Carolina Coastal Council	505 US 1003	anti	Land Management	6-3 Sc, R, W, T, OC	Bl, Sv, So	K (in the decision)	GHWB
1994	Oregon Waste Systems v. Dept of Environ. Quality	511 US 93	anti	Solid Waste Management	7-2 T, Sv, K, So, G, Sc, OC	R, Bl		WJC
1994	City of Chicago v. Environ. Defense Fund	511 US 328	pro	Solid Waste	7-2 Sc, R, Bl, K, So, T, G	Sv, OC		WJC
1994	C&A Carbone v. Town of Clarkston	511 US 383	anti	Solid Waste	6-3 K, Sv, Sc, T, G	So, R, Bl	OC (decision only)	WJC
1994	PUD no. 1 v. Washington Dept. of Ecology	511 US 700	pro	Water Quality Standards	7-2 OC, R, Bl, Sv, K, So, G	T, Sc	Sv	WJC
1994	Dolan v. City of Tigard	512 US 374	anti	Private Land Use	5-4 R, OC, Sc, K, T	Sv, Bl, G, So		WJC
1995	Babbitt v. Sweet Home Chapter of Commun. for a Great Oregon	515 US 687	pro	Endangered Species	6-3 Sv, OC, K, So, G, By	Sc, R, T	OC	WJC
1996	Meghrig v. KFC Western	516 US 479	anti	Toxic Waste Cleanup	9-0 OC, R, G, Sv, So, By, T, Sc, K			WJC

continued

TABLE 8.2
(continued)

Year	Name	Cite	Env.	Description	Majority	Dissent	Concur	Pres.
1998	*Steel Co. v. Citizens for a Better Environ.*	523 US 83	anti	Hazardous and Toxic Chemicals	9-0 Sc, R, OC, K, T, By (By in part)		OC, K, By, Sv, So, G (in the decision only) (So and G joined Sv in part) G (in the decision only)	WJC
1998	*Ohio Forestry Ass'n. v. Sierra Club*	523 US 726	anti	Logging Rights	9-0 By, R, OC, Sv, K, Sc, G, T, So			WJC
1998	*U.S. v. Bestfoods*	524 US 51	pro	Industrial Waste Cleanup	9-0 So, R, OC, K, G, By, Sc, T, Sv			WJC
2001	*Whitman v. American Trucking Associations*	531 US ___	anti	Air Pollution Standards	9-0 Sc, R, So, OC, K, G, By, T, Sv		T, Sv, By	GWB

Note: We wish to acknowledge two excellent law review articles that motivated us to put Table 8.2 together. The first is the most recent. It is an article by Richard J. Lazarus entitled "Restoring What's Environmental about Environmental Law in the Supreme Court," *UCLA Law Review*, Vol. 47, no. 3 (February 2000), 703–812; the other article was an earlier article by Richard E. Levy and Robert L. Glicksman, "Judicial Activism and Restraint in the Supreme Court's Environmental Law Decisions," *Vanderbilt Law Review*, Vol. 42 (March 1989), 343–431.

Abbreviations

Bg-Burger, Bk-Black, Bl-Blackmun, Bn-Brennan, Br-Brandeis, Bt-Butler, By-Breyer, Byr-Byrnes, C-Cardoza, D-Douglas, F-Frankfurter, Ft-Fortas, G-Ginsburg, H-Harlan, Hg-Hughes, J-Jackson, K-Kennedy, M-T.Marshall, Mp-Murphy, Mr-McReynolds, OC-O'Conner, P-Powell, R-Rehnquist, Rb-Roberts, Rd-Reed, Sc-Scalia, So-Souter, St-Stone, Sv-Stevens, Su-Sutherland, Sw-Stewart, T-Thomas, VD-Van Devanter, W-White, Wn-Warren

FDR-Franklin Delano Roosevelt; RMN-Richard Milhouse Nixon; JEC-James Earl Carter; RWR-Ronald Wilson Reagan; GHWB-George Herbert Walker Bush; WJC-William Jefferson Clinton; GWB-George W. Bush

We might also add Justice Stephen Breyer to the list of environmentally supportive justices. William Funk has suggested that Breyer's record thus far
would indicate that he is committed to "effective environmental law enforcement."[36] Daniel Farber would also add Justice Ruth Bader Ginsburg, who might
also have some expertise in environmental law based on her years on the D.C.
Circuit Court.[37]

Of those *least supportive* of the environment, Percival listed Antonin
Scalia, supporting the environment only 13.3 percent of the time in 15 cases,
Anthony Kennedy supporting the environment 28.6 percent of the time in 7
cases, Sandra Day O'Connor supporting the environment 29.4 percent of the
time in 34 cases, and Lewis F. Powell, supporting the environment 33.8 percent of the time in 65 cases.[38]

Lewis Powell mellowed in his attitude toward the environment during the
time he sat on the Court. In fact, one might argue that Justice Powell had been an
enemy of the environment before he was selected for the court. In 1971, for example, he represented the U.S. Chamber of Commerce and felt that business and
the economy were under attack. It was his advice to business, given his feeling
that the Court was one of the most influential instruments of political, social
and economic change, that business groups should "launch an aggressive coun-
terattack in the courts, in the media, and on campus, borrowing some of the tactics used by the public interest movement."[39]

Antonin Scalia, however, did *not* change his attitude toward the environment, and remained the most consistent in his opposition to it. According to
Court observer Lettie M. Wenner, Justice Scalia, as leader of the "most conservative wing of the Court, has been very supportive of business's attacks on the
constitutionality of government regulation of property on the grounds that
overregulation amounts to taking property without due process."[40] Moreover,
Scalia's strategy in opposing environmentalism has been to argue against
"standing" for environmental questions.[41] In the *Lujan v. Defenders of
Wildlife* case in 1992, Scalia contended that "Congress has not left the formulation of appropriate federal standards to the courts through application of often vague and indeterminate nuisance concepts and maxims of equity jurispru-
dence, but rather has occupied the field through the establishment of a
comprehensive regulatory program supervised by an expert administrative
agency."[42] Two years earlier, Scalia made it quite clear in *Lujan v. National
Wildlife Federation* that the courts were not places to achieve environmental
reform, but that people should look to other branches of government to satisfy
their need for reform.[43]

Given that many of the justices least sympathetic to the environment are on
the Court today, it is hard to see the current Court becoming "eco-friendly" in the
future.[44] In fact, the Court's involvement with the environment has been less
than notable. As Lazarus stated, "The Court's opinions lack any distinct environmental voice. Missing is any emphasis on the nature, character, and normative
weightiness of environmental protection concerns and their import for judicial
construction of relevant legal rules—how, in other words, the kinds of problems
environmental law seeks to address may warrant special consideration in the
Court's decisions."[45] Lazarus indicated that even when the Court was most supportive of environmental interests,[46] he did not see that the environment played a
central role in the Court's analysis.[47]

The Role of the Chief Justice

For the most part, the nine justices have equal power, but the chief justice is set apart in the performance of judicial duties. The chief justice 1) presides in oral argument as well as over the Judicial Conference, 2) alerts Congress to the views of the Judicial Conference as well as delivers an annual "state of the judiciary" address to Congress, and 3) assigns the opinion of the court if in the majority. None of these duties are as important as the ability of the chief justice to lead by moral persuasion. The Court era is named after the chief justice. We talk of the Warren Court, as well as the Burger Court. These periods of time take on a particular meaning and are identified with the values and outlook that the chief justice may convey.

Leadership of the Court

Does it make a difference who presides and who leads? Has the Court been affected one way or another by the individuals who have led the Court? In this section our focus will be on the last two chief justices—Warren Burger and William Rehnquist—since it has been under these two leaders that most of the environmental cases have been decided.

Warren Burger brought a style to office unlike other chief justices—a style that other justices did not always appreciate. He has been described as being "ambitious for leadership," arrogant, a bully to other Court members, and accused of using questionable tactics to control the vote.[48] There were even those who indicated they "loathed" the chief justice.[49] Warren Burger never really demonstrated a serious commitment to the environment. He revealed in the *Aberdeen and Rockfish Railroad* case that he was still in possession of the same attitude he had had as circuit court judge when he stated:

> Our society and its governmental instrumentalities, having been less than alert to the needs of our environment for generations, have now taken protective steps. These developments, however praiseworthy, should not lead courts to exercise equitable powers loosely or casually whenever a claim of "environmental damage" is asserted. The world must go on and new environmental legislation must be carefully meshed with more traditional patterns of federal regulation. The decisional process for judges is one of balancing and it is often a most difficult task.[50]

Lettie M. Wenner argues that the Court became "increasingly conservative during the early 1980s under the leadership of Chief Justice Warren Burger, and since 1986, when William Rehnquist became chief justice, it became still more probusiness. It was also severely divided in the 1980s, with certain justices vigorously opposed to their colleagues' desire to reduce government regulation."[51]

William Rehnquist's style was quite different. He was more approachable, good-natured, and friendly, and, in Lawrence Baum's words, was in possession of "well-respected intellectual abilities." Baum indicates further that Rehnquist was liked even by those on the Court who disagreed with him.[52] It was Rehnquist who stated, in commenting on the potential influence of the chief justice in presiding over the Court, that he did not preside over subordinates, because, like himself, all of his colleagues were on the Court for life and were "as independent as hogs on ice." The most he could do was try to "persuade or cajole them" into doing what he wanted them to do.[53] Thus the most we might say is that the chief

TABLE 8.3

Comparing the Environmental Records of Chief Justices Burger and Rehnquist

Chief Justice	Years as Chief Justice	# of Environ'l Cases	Pro- Environment	Anti- Environment
			% N	% N
Warren Burger	1969–1986	63	53.8 (34)	46.2 (29)
William H. Rehnquist	1986–present	35	31.4 (11)	68.6 (24)

Note: Derived from Table 8.2.

justice's "authority" to lead is somewhat limited and is going to vary with the individual and with the Court.

Table 8.3 shows that Justice Rehnquist has supported the environment only 31.4 percent of the time, while opposing it 68.6 percent of the time; Burger's voting record, on the other hand, is more supportive of the environment, backing it 53.8 percent of the time, while opposing it 46.2 percent of the time. Rehnquist, interestingly enough, became even more anti-environmental in his voting record once he became chief justice. Looking at the 57 environmental cases during the years Rehnquist served as associate justice (1972–1986), when Justice Burger was chief

CASE STUDY: "THE COURT AND THOSE DAM FISH" *TVA v. HILL* (1978)

What do you do with three-inch, bony perch-like freshwater fish called "snail darters," which number between 10,000 and 15,000 in the Little Tennessee River? Can't roast 'em; can't toast 'em; can't display 'em; can't transport 'em. So what do we do with them? Go to court? Will that preserve 'em? Perhaps—since they are *endangered,* and the Endangered Species Act of 1973 is supposed to protect them. But aren't there 45 other species of darters in the Tennessee River system? Of course, but there are no other *Percina (Imostoma) tanasi!* Is the Little Tennessee River the only place these critters live? Apparently so, although the Tennessee Valley Authority (TVA) tried to relocate these critters to the Hiwassee River area, to allow completion of the multimillion dollar Tellico Dam— that was more than 80 percent completed—that was going to provide electricity for some 20,000 homes, help shoreline development, and provide flood control, recreation, and economic development for an area losing its population. Yet the Court declared that this same area was the snail darter's "critical habitat"—the loss of which would likely reduce the chance of their very survival.

Here we have a problem, dear reader, don't we? Six members of the Court indicated that the Endangered Species Act clearly stated that

continued

survival of species was to be preferred over every other value. Indeed, the majority on the Court accepted the District Court's word on this when it stated: "Whether a dam is 50 percent or 90 percent completed is irrelevant in calculating the social and scientific costs attributable to the disappearance of a unique form of life. Courts are ill-equipped to calculate how many dollars must be invested before the value of a dam exceeds that of the endangered species."[1]

Yet the dissenters, in defending the TVA, felt that it was absurd to think that the Endangered Species Act would bring to a halt a nearly completed project. This decision, they stated, would have damaging results over *any* project regardless of how important it was if it was determined that the project threatened the extinction of an endangered species or its habitat.[2]

Should halting this dam be cause for a victory celebration? It was an immediate triumph for the bony perch in toppling a dam! However, the Court proved it was no real champion of the environment: the majority supported *separation of powers,* commending Congress for writing such a precise act. They said nothing about the environment being preferred over development. The dissenters should also make environmentalists feel even more ill at ease, since they are clear defenders of development—putting *projects* over *fish*—if it helps the economy. Neither perspective bodes well, in the long run, for the environment and for the bony fish of the future!

---

[1] *TVA v. Hill,* 437 U.S. 153, 169 (1978).

[2] *TVA v. Hill,* 437 U.S. 153, 196 (1978).

justice, he supported the environment 50.9 percent of the time, a much higher rate than when Rehnquist was chief justice.

Burger may have been less supportive than the data indicated, since the intensity of support he gave to the environment is questionable. For example, when he wrote the majority opinion in *Tennessee Valley Authority v. Hill* (1978), the snail darter decision,[54] he and the Court voted to protect the snail darter, yet Richard Lazarus argues that in his opinion Burger seemed "somewhat skeptical of the very result that it upholds, suggesting that the statutory language has compelled the Court to endorse such a result, notwithstanding what the Court might believe to be 'common sense and the public weal.'"[55] All in all, the evidence suggests that Rehnquist's voting record has been more anti-environmental, as chief justice, than was Burger's.

The Influence of Congressional Action on Court Decision Making and the Environment

Key legislation passed by Congress has been a critical factor in giving the Court an opportunity to have influence over the environment. Important statutes that have both facilitated and prevented environmental actions have served as sources for numerous court cases (Table 8.4).

TABLE 8.4

Judicial Responses to Major Environmental Legislation, 1970–1992

Legislation	Case	Citation	Description
Federal Water Pollution Control Act of 1946	Train v. City of New York	420 U.S. 35 1975	Federal Environmental Allotment
	EPA v. California ex. rel. State Water Resources Control Board	426 U.S. 200 1976	Federal Exemptions from State Permits
	E.I. duPont de Nemours & Co. v. Train	430 U.S. 112 1977	EPA Jurisdiction
	EPA v. National Crushed Stone Ass'n.	449 U.S. 64 1980	Pollution Discharge
	Middlesex County Sewerage Authority v. National Sea Clammers Ass'n.	453 U.S. 1 1981	Sewage Discharge
	Weinberger v. Romero-Barcelo	456 U.S. 305 1982	Water Pollution Discharge
	Lyng v. Northwest Indian Cemetery Protective Ass'n.	485 U.S. 439 1988	Timber Harvesting
Clean Air Act of 1963	Train v. Natural Resources Defense Council, Inc.	421 U.S. 60 1975	Air Quality Standards
	Hancock v. Train	426 U.S. 167 1976	Air Pollution
	Union Electric Co. v. EPA	427 U.S. 246 1976	Air Quality Standards
	EPA v. Brown	431 U.S. 99 1977	Vehicle Air Pollution
	Adamo Wrecking Co. v. U.S.	434 U.S. 275 1978	Emission Standards
	Chevron USA v. Natural Resources Defense Council	467 U.S. 837 1984	Air Pollution
	Dow Chemical Co. v. U.S.	476 U.S. 227 1986	EPA Investigation
	Pennsylvania v. Delaware Valley Citizens Council for Clean Air	478 U.S. 546 1986	Environmental Activists Compensation
	Pennsylvania v. Delaware Valley Citizens Council for Clean Air	483 U.S. 711 1987	Vehicle Emissions
National Environmental Policy Act of 1969	U.S. v. SCRAP	412 U.S. 669 1973	Recyclables
	Aberdeen & Rockfish Railroad Co. v. SCRAP	422 U.S. 289 1975	Environmental Impact Statement
	Kleppe v. Sierra Club	427 U.S. 390 1976	Environmental Impact Statement

continued

TABLE 8.4

(continued)

Legislation	Case	Citation	Description
	Andrus v. Sierra Club	442 U.S. 347 1979	Environmental Impact Statement
	Strycker's Bay Neighborhood Council v. Karlen	444 U.S. 223 1980	Environmental Impact Statement
	Weinberger v. Catholic Action of Hawaii/Peace Education Project	454 U.S. 139 1981	Environmental Impact Statement
	Metropolitan Edison Co. v. People Against Nuclear Energy	460 U.S. 766 1983	Nuclear Power Plant Operation
	Baltimore Gas & Electric Co. v. Natural Resources Defense Council, Inc.	462 U.S. 87 1983	Environmental Impact Statement
	Lyng v. Northwest Indian Cemetery Protective Ass'n.	485 U.S. 439 1988	Timber Harvesting
	Robertson v. Methow Valley Citizens Council	490 U.S. 332 1989	Environmental Impact Statement
	Marsh v. Oregon Natural Resources Council	490 U.S. 360 1989	Environmental Impact Statement
Occupational Health and Safety Act (OSHA) 1970	*Industrial Union Department v. American Petroleum Institute*	448 U.S. 607 1980	Benzene Exposure
	Gade v. National Solid Wastes Management Ass'n.	505 U.S. 88 1992	Hazardous Waste Training
Endangered Species Act 1973	*Tennessee Valley Authority v. Hill*	437 U.S. 153 1978	Endangered Species— Snail Darter
	Lujan v. Defenders of Wildlife	504 U.S. 555 1992	Endangered Species Regulation
	Babbitt v. Sweet Home Chapter of Communities for a Great Oregon	515 U.S. 687 1995	Endangered Species Interpretation
Resource Conservation and Recovery Act of 1976	*City of Chicago v. Environmental Defense Fund*	511 U.S. 328 1994	Solid Waste
	Meghrig v. KFC Western	516 U.S. 479 1996	Toxic Waste Cleanup
National Forest Management Act of 1976	*Ohio Forestry Ass'n. v. Sierra Club*	523 U.S. 726 1998	Logging Rights
Clean Water Act of 1977	*Chemical Manufacturers Ass'n. v. Natural Resources Defense Council*	470 U.S. 116 1985	Toxic Pollutants

Legislation	Case	Citation	Description
	U.S. v. Riverside Bayview Homes	474 U.S. 121 1985	Water Rights
	International Paper v. Oulette	479 U.S. 481 1987	Water Pollution
	Gwaltney of Smithfield Ltd. v. Chesapeake Bay Foundation	484 U.S. 49 1987	Clean Water
	Arkansas v. Oklahoma	503 U.S. 91 1992	Clean Water
	U.S. Dept. of Energy v. Ohio	503 U.S. 607 1992	Water Pollution
	City of Burlington v. Dague	505 U.S. 557 1992	Attorney Fee
	PUD no. 1 v. Washington Dept. of Ecology	511 U.S. 700 1994	Water Quality Standards
Comprehensive Environmental Response, Compensation, and Liability (CERCL) of 1980	Pennsylvania v. Union Gas Co.	491 U.S. 1 1989	Coal Discharge Liability
	U.S. v. Bestfoods	524 U.S. 51 1998	Industrial Waste Cleanup
Solid Waste Disposal Act of 1980	City of Philadelphia v. New Jersey	437 U.S. 617 1978	Waste Disposal
	City of Burlington v. Dague	505 U.S. 557 1992	Attorney Fee

Source: Derived from Table 8.2.

National Environmental Policy Act

The National Environmental Policy Act (NEPA) of 1969 has been one of the premier pieces of environmental legislation.[56] It declares that "it is the continuing responsibility of the Federal Government ... to improve and coordinate federal plans, functions, programs, and resources" so as to "fulfill the responsibilities of each generation as trustee of the environment for succeeding generations"; to "attain the widest range of beneficial uses of the environment without degradation, risk to health or safety, or other undesirable and unintended consequences."[57] This legislation, as broad as it is, has had important influence on the Court. Robert M. Lynch, who was with the Land and Natural Resources Division of the U.S. Department of Justice, suggested that "by volume alone, the litigation it [NEPA] has spawned attests to the Act's impact on the federal government, and in many respects to state governments as well."[58]

It took the Court several years after passage of NEPA before it began to give it due consideration. This occurred in 1975 in the case of *Aberdeen & Rockfish R. R. v. SCRAP* (1975).[59] While NEPA was initially ignored, the Court recognized that Congress had passed NEPA without providing any body, other than the courts, with the ability to enforce the legislation.[60]

The Supreme Court has treated NEPA in various ways, depending on the particular Court in question. The Court's 1976 decision in *Kleppe v. Sierra Club* tended to narrow NEPA. The Supreme Court indicated in this case that an environmental impact statement (EIS) was not needed until the final stages of an environmental project. Three years later, in the case of *Andrus v. Sierra Club*, the Court continued to narrow NEPA, indicating that the president's budget did not need to comply with any environmental impact statements. In the 1983 case of *Metropolitan Edison Co. v. People Against Nuclear Energy*, 460 U.S. 766, Supreme Court justices indicated that NEPA was not so broad as to take into account psychological trauma caused by the opening of the plant.

In comparing the way lower federal courts and the Supreme Court have treated NEPA, the differences appear to result from how the courts have responded to the need to draw up environmental impact statements (EIS). While the lower courts have attempted to expand the importance of NEPA and its oversight capabilities of governmental activity, the Supreme Court has "dampened lower federal courts' earlier enthusiasm for reviewing the substance of EISs."[61] Daniel Farber went even further to suggest that never, in all of the dozen or so cases that the Supreme Court has handled based on NEPA, has it ever upheld a NEPA claim.[62]

Environmental Statutory Law

Since NEPA, there have been other important environmental statutes passed designed to protect the environment. These include *clean air* (Clean Air Act Amendments of 1990, Pub. L. No. 101-549), *clean water* (The Water Quality Act of 1987, Pub. L. No. 100-4), *ocean dumping* (Marine Protection, Research, and Sanctuaries Act of 1972, Pub. L. No. 92-531), *noise* (Noise Control Act of 1972, Pub. L. No. 92-574), *endangered species* (Endangered Species Act of 1973, Pub. L. No. 93-205 and more recent amendments), *pesticides* (Federal Pesticide Control Act of 1972, Pub. L. No. 92-516 and more recent amendments), *land use* (Coastal Zone Management Act of 1972 Pub. L. No. 92-583 and recent amendments), and *toxic waste* (Toxic Substances Control Act of 1976, Pub. L. No. 94-469).[63]

AIR POLLUTION: AH, FRESH AIR—BUT HOW MUCH THANKS GOES TO THE COURT?

Ah, *fresh air*! We love it . . . we breathe it . . . it's good for us . . . but whom do we thank for it? Do we thank the Supreme Court? Or do we thank others? What has the Court done for air quality? Take the case of *Union Electric Co. v. Environmental Protection Agency* (1976). As a result of the 1970 amendments to the 1963 Clean Air Act, each state was asked to come up with a plan to guarantee that unpolluted air would prevail in their state. Missouri came up with its plan only to have it challenged by Union Electric Company, a St. Louis–based company that claimed that its three coal-fired generating plants could not meet the sulfur dioxide standards without spending more than

$500 million. In this case, the Supreme Court was fully protective of clean air and stated in no uncertain terms that the dangers of "uncontrolled air pollution" were much more important than any expense to the company.[1]

In the 1985 *Dow Chemical Co. v. U.S.* case, a majority of the justices defended the Environmental Protection Agency's (EPA) authority to enforce air quality by allowing it to take aerial photographs of any illegal emissions that might come from Dow Chemical Company. Dissenters, however, took issue, questioning the legality of the procedure.

On other occasions, the Supreme Court has made it difficult to protect clean air. Consider these decisions:

In *Train, Administrator, EPA v. Natural Resources Defense Council* (1975), the EPA allowed the state of Georgia to obtain a change from full compliance with the air quality standards, feeling that the delay they wanted in implementing standards would not interfere with the "timely attainment and subsequent maintenance of national air quality standards."[2]

The *Adamo Wrecking Co. v. U.S.* case, three years later in 1978, found five members of the Court loosely applying the standards for clean air emissions. This allowed the Adamo Wrecking Company to continue to emit asbestos into the air, because the emissions standard was unclear. Justice Stevens dissented, feeling that the emission of asbestos into the air is always a violation of clean air.

In the *Robertson, Chief of the Forest Service v. Methow Valley Citizens Council* (1989) decision, the U.S. Forest Service was asked to disregard its regular three-stage process for issuing special-use permits for building on federal land. In this instance, a 16-lift ski area that would accommodate some 8,200 was allowed to be built without considering what the "worst case analysis" of air quality would be.

So, whom do we thank for protecting our air? Environmental groups, Congress, and some presidents ought to be acknowledged for their role in ensuring clean air for the American public, with less consideration given to the Court.

---

[1]427 U.S. 246 (1976)

[2]421 U. S. 60 (1975)

Clean Air has been a constant as far as the Supreme Court has been concerned. For example, as recently as 2000, the EPA was being sued for insisting on further reductions in the amounts of ozone and soot in the air. The Clean Air Act of 1970 allows the EPA to set standards at a level that allows "an adequate margin of safety" and are "requisite to protect[ing] the public health."[64] If the Court does not approve of this, then other agency grants of authority will also be in question such as "the authority given to the Federal Communications Commission, which must regulate broadcasting consistent with the public interest, convenience, and necessity."[65]

Tightening the clean air standards, many urban dwellers feel, would throw dozens of urban counties out of compliance with the Clean Air Act. Thus, a coalition of industry representatives is suing the EPA and challenging the standards. In 1999, a D.C. appeals court panel invalidated the standards on basis of vagueness, declaring they were so vague that they represented an unconstitutional delegation of legislative authority to the executive branch.

Despite these challenges to the Clean Air Act, it has been a relatively successful piece of legislation. Air quality has improved significantly, often at less expense than first projected. Courts, over the years, have upheld grants of regulatory authority far broader than the Clean Air Act suggested. In a recent 2-to-1 appeals court decision, for example, the Supreme Court ruled that in deciding what constitutes clean air, the EPA cannot take cost into account. This marked the first time that a federal regulatory program had been struck down by a court since 1935, when the Supreme Court responded negatively toward two New Deal programs.[66]

The latest challenge to clean air standards is the not-yet-decided *Whitman v. American Trucking Associations*, #99-1257.[67] This case promises to be an important one for environmentalists and industrialists, because the U.S. Chamber of Commerce and a group of regulated businesses has asked the Supreme Court to read a broad cost-benefit requirement into the agency's rule-making authority.[68]

The *Endangered Species Act* of 1973 is another important but controversial piece of legislation. It was designed to guarantee the habitat of plants and animals that are endangered. It also brought to a halt, or at least delayed, construction and dam projects, as well as logging activity, while preserving endangered species. When the Fish and Wildlife Service determined, for example, that the spotted owl was threatened in the Northwest, the Endangered Species Act was invoked and led to the halting of logging in that region. Congresspersons from Washington and Oregon were instrumental in getting Congress to take jurisdiction from the courts in 1989 and 1990, and the Supreme Court, surprisingly enough, ended up supporting Congress.[69]

Hazardous waste cases have also increased over the years. The Resource Conservation and Recovery Act of 1976, designed to control disposal of solid wastes, was a very important bill in this area. Vice President Al Gore was one of the first persons in Congress to become interested in the need to clean up toxic wastes. Three years after the Resource Conservation and Recovery Act was passed, in 1979, he held the first congressional hearings on this issue. He thereafter participated in assisting in the cleanup of some 443 waste dumps while serving in Congress. In addition, when Congress passed the 1980 Comprehensive Environmental Responses, Compensation, and Liability Act, or Superfund,[70] this also encouraged the Court to become involved in environmental questions. It was an act designed to clean up ignored waste dumps. Case decisions regarding the Superfund have involved many more lower court decisions than Supreme Court cases. The Supreme Court has made few contributions in the area of the Superfund law, only touching the periphery, while leaving major issues like liability of shareholders, officers, and lenders untouched.[71]

As far as the issue of *natural resources* is concerned, there have been a number of important bills that have generated important cases, such as those related to endangered species, energy issues, and public land management cases.[72] These subject categories have remained a focus of the Supreme Court.

Presidential Leadership and the Court

Now that we have examined the Court's relationship with Congress, we turn our attention to the president and the executive branch. It only makes sense, for example, that during the presidency of Richard Nixon, one of the most assertive of our environmental presidents, that we should also have a "growth of public concern for the environment [that] brought a new wave of environmental cases to the Court's doors in the 1970s. Encouraged by decisions expanding citizen access to the courts, both industry and environmental interests increasingly sought judicial review of agency decisions."[73] Yet Nixon brought Warren Burger to the Court as chief justice, again, a justice that, while supporting the environment to a greater extent than Chief Justice Rehnquist has, nevertheless, was not as supportive of the environment as was Richard Nixon.

It is also true that the president who was the most detrimental to the environment, Ronald Reagan, brought some of the justices to the Court who have been most antagonistic to the environment. As mentioned earlier, based on the Percival study of case decisions from 1970 to 1991, there were certain justices who were least supportive of environmental interests. Four of them were Reagan appointees—Justices Scalia, Kennedy, O'Connor, and Chief Justice Rehnquist.[74] We think one could legitimately ask whether there was a "litmus test" to attract anti-environmental justices during the Reagan period as there was for anti-abortion ones. We know, for example, that Reagan, and later George H.W. Bush appointees were certainly more conservative in ideology than most of the other judges. Reagan and Bush appointed lower court federal judges who were more likely than not to vote for reducing the regulatory strength of the Clean Air Act and the Clean Water Act.[75] Moreover, those judges appointed by Reagan and Bush tended to be more willing to reduce budgets and personnel of the Environmental Protection Agency (EPA) than were other presidents' judicial appointees.

Individual presidents have made an impact on environmental law via their appointments to the Court, which follow their own preferences for or against the environment. This has been the case at both the Supreme Court level and, most particularly, at the lower federal court level. Illustrating this, McSpadden calls our attention to the D.C. Circuit Court of Appeals case of *Sweet Home Chapter of Communities for a Great Oregon v. Interior Department*, 1 F. 3d 1 (1993), in which the logging industry charged the Fish and Wildlife Service with misinterpreting the Endangered Species Act. Judge Abner Mikva, a Carter appointee, felt that the Endangered Species Act prevented private property owners from destroying the habitat of endangered species. There was strong dissent from one of the Reagan appointees, Judge David Sentelle, that led to major disagreements on the court. In August 1994 this circuit court turned down the opportunity to rehear the case in order to settle the disagreement. Six Reagan and Bush appointees were united in not wanting to rehear the case. This action tended to polarize the court.[76]

Election 2000: The President and the Supreme Court

What sort of judges will President George W. Bush select if he has the opportunity to do so? Will they be judges more or less sympathetic to the environment than the Reagan-Bush appointees have been? Among the justices now on the Court, George W. Bush admires two of the most conservative, namely,

Antonin Scalia and Clarence Thomas. This is most troubling since neither of these justices could be considered friends of the environment.

Bush, in fact, tried to establish himself in the campaign as an "environmental candidate" for president. He maintained that it was essential that we support clean air and water, and preserve our forests. But much of what Bush suggested would weaken federal regulations in terms of environmental cleanup and would, as a result, protect developers. Moreover, the states, under Bush, will probably have broader authority over how funds would be spent on the environment.

Republican Bush believes more in the marketplace and its ability to solve environmental problems than he does in government solutions. He believes that science and market technologies should set the environmental standards we adhere to; the only role government should have is to encourage these market solutions.[77]

Although considering environmental policy under a Gore presidency is a moot issue, we know that, over the years, he was more involved with and supportive of the environment than was George W. Bush. Gore has been a long-time advocate of cleaning up toxic wastes, protecting clean water, and of warning Americans about the dangers of global warming.[78] In 1979, in fact, he held the first congressional hearings on toxic wastes. More recently he has spoken out about global warming and its dangers in the international arena. As vice president, he chaired a delegation from the United States to the Inter-Parliamentary conference on global warming. Also as vice president he wrote *Earth in the Balance*, published in 1992,[79] promoting the need to protect the environment. It became, for him, a way to educate the public regarding these concerns.

Environmental interest groups were more supportive of Gore than Bush, with Gore picking up endorsements from leading groups including the League of Conservation Voters, the Defenders of Wildlife, the Wilderness Society, and the Sierra Club. Despite all this support, many during the campaign found Gore too timid and cautious, and accused him of failing to stand behind what he believed.[80] This is somewhat surprising given that in his book, *Earth in the Balance*, Gore argued that Americans need to make the "rescue of the environment the central organizing principle for civilization."[81] Consequently, we could have expected his to be a pro-environment presidency with a Supreme Court that would have been more supportive of environmentalism than would be a Bush-appointed Court. This could very well be one of the important results of the controversial presidential election of 2000.

The Public and the Court

De Tocqueville noted in the 1840s that the power of the Supreme Court "is immense, but it is power springing from opinion. They are all-powerful so long as the people consent to obey the law; they can do nothing when they scorn it. Now, of all powers, that of opinion is the hardest to use, for it is impossible to say exactly where its limits come. Often it is as dangerous to lag behind as to outstrip it."[82]

If the people are not supportive of what the Court does, the Court will become ineffective and its decisions will be of little consequence. Thomas R. Marshall pointed out in the 1980s that:

> Most research on public opinion and judicial policy making . . . suggests that judges' decisions tend to reflect public opinion—especially when public opinion itself is clearly expressed, one-sided, and intense.[83]

Marshall does acknowledge that there have been important exceptions to this, as, for example, school prayer.[84] In his research, Marshall found that of the 146 cases he worked on that were decided between 1935 and 1986, "some 62 or 63 percent of the Court's decisions were consistent with the polls when a clear poll majority (or plurality) existed."[85] During Warren Burger's years on the Court, 53 percent of the 76 environmental decisions Marshall looked at went along with the majority of the public.

Riley E. Dunlap's study of the public's attitude toward the environment indicated that "public concern for environmental quality escalated rapidly in the sixties, and by 1970 majorities of the public were expressing pro-environmental opinions ranging from acknowledging the seriousness of pollution to supporting governmental efforts to protect and improve the environment." He argued that "it appears that a majority of the public was sympathetic to the environmentalists' goal of protecting the environment and a sizable minority was explicitly attentive to environmental issues."[86] Dunlap concluded that "[e]nvironmental quality had clearly achieved a position of prominence on the public agenda by 1970."[87]

The public has given mixed signals over the years as to its feeling about the environment. Whenever the *environment* is considered in opinion polls along with other issues, it rarely fares very well.[88] In a June 1992 Associated Press Telephone Poll, for example, the public was asked to name the issue that they considered most important for deciding their presidential vote. In this poll, only 7 percent of the 1,002 polled chose the "environment," while 39 percent selected the "economy," with other issues falling in between these margins.[89] In January 1993, a Voter Research and Surveys Exit Poll, sampling 15,490 individuals, found similar results. The public was asked which issues mattered the most to their eventual vote for president. The environment was selected by only 5 percent of the respondents, while health care was selected by 20 percent of the people, and the "federal budget deficit" was selected by 21 percent of the people.[90] Moreover, in two 1997 Gallup Polls and two 1998 Gallup Polls, the public was asked to identify the most important problem in the country. The environment was identified as the most important problem by only 3 percent of the American public.[91]

When individuals were asked to consider the importance of the environment, without considering other issues, public opinion revealed a very different response to the environment. In a 1992 CNN-Gallup poll, for example, individuals were asked to indicate the importance of the environmental as a subject for presidential debate. Sixty percent of those polled felt that the environment was *very important* to include in a debate between the candidates.[92] The public was also asked to consider how important a candidate's position on the environment would be in casting their vote for president. In a 1996 Gallup Poll, 27 percent felt it was *extremely important* and 48% felt it was *very important*.[93] In a January 2000 Gallup poll, people were asked how important the environment would be to their selection of a candidate for presidency in the 2000 election. Here 23 percent felt it would be *extremely important*, while 45 percent felt it would be *very important*.[94]

It was Riley Dunlap's thesis that the public's added interest in environmentalism during the 1980s and 1990s could be explained by the Reagan and Bush administrations' attitude toward the environment. Neither administration inspired the public's confidence, but instead made the people realize that if the environment was going to be protected it would be up to the public itself and not the elected policymakers.[95] As it has been suggested by Stephen Wasby:

> People react to the Court not only in terms of its procedures but also in terms of its results. They treat it not only as a legal institution deciding specific cases but also as another agency of government, making policy by its decisions just as legislators and executive agencies make policy. As it makes policy, the Court interacts with these other branches of government, and public reaction to the Court's decisions (its policy statements) *forces the Court to become an actor in the political system*: if the Court's actions are to have an effect and if, in the long run, the Court is to survive, the justices must take the Court's environment (i.e., public opinion) into account (emphasis added).[96]

Political Parties and the Court

Has partisanship made any difference in terms of the Courts' decisions? Two of the justices most supportive of the environment—William O. Douglas and Thurgood Marshall—were appointed by Democrats Franklin Roosevelt and Lyndon Johnson. Three of the supportive justices—Harry Blackmun, William J. Brennan, Jr., and John Paul Stevens—were appointed by Republicans Richard Nixon, Dwight Eisenhower, and Gerald Ford. Of those *least* sympathetic to the environment, all were appointed by Republicans. These include Antonin Scalia, Anthony Kennedy, Sandra Day O'Connor, Lewis F. Powell, and William H. Rehnquist (as chief justice). Four of these five justices were appointed by Ronald Reagan, while Powell was appointed by Richard Nixon.

It is not as simple as one party wholly opposing environmentalism and the other party favoring it. For example, "[j]udges appointed by Democratic presidents. . . tend to favor environmental litigants more than Republican appointees do. Republican appointees, however, do not favor business litigants in a similar systematic way. And Reagan-Bush appointees, who now dominate the federal courts, seem to prefer the government perspective regardless of who the opposing party is."[97]

Conclusion

Is the Supreme Court an *eco-friendly* institution? The answer depends on those who sit on the Court. It would appear that the Court has never been an institution to lead on environmental decisions. Further, even when the Court has been staffed with those in support of the environment who work to broaden rules for standing, by making it easier for interested parties to bring environmental questions to the Court, the decisions themselves, with few exceptions, have not reflected a deep-seated commitment to the environment.

Courts and the Direction of Environmentalism

By virtue of their important role in the political system, courts have acted as the enforcement arm of such important statutory measures as NEPA and the Superfund. Federal courts have expanded the opportunities for using litigation to change environmental policy. Where the courts have intervened with regard to environmental policy, decisions have firmed up the advances made in the area of environmentalism. Where courts have come out in opposition to the environment, environmentalism has been slowed in its progress.

Regardless of what period we are talking about, whatever the Court decides to do, it will act on environmental issues without consensus and compromise, because it is the Supreme Court. This will, of course, enhance controversy in the community more so than if the legislature alone should handle the issue. Judicial activism causes positions to be taken that exclude consensus and compromise. Some actors win and some lose whenever the Court makes a decision, further politicizing the issue, which is bound to increase conflict where conflict may not have existed. Moreover, it also encourages other participants in the body politic to take positions.

It Depends on Who Sits on the Court

Daniel A. Farber argues that the Supreme Court up to this time has not played a major role in environmental law. In fact, he argues, most of the important cases decided by the Court have reduced judicial impact.[98] Yet even Farber admits the effectiveness of the justices' decisions will depend on who is on the Court. If Justice Scalia assumes a leading role on the Court in years to come, rather than such justices as Breyer and Souter, who are more supportive of the environment, and conservatives win a majority of the Court, then the Court will continue to fail to play a consequential role in helping to shape environmental law.[99] Writing in the mid-1970s, Werner Grunbaum concluded that:

> future Courts and decisions on environmental quality problems may be influenced by shifts in public opinion. If Americans in the next few years are unwilling to pay for an improvement in the quality of life, efforts at environmental protection may fare poorly in future Court decisions. In any case, the Court has deferred to Congress in several crucial environmental quality cases. Since the Supreme Court, the lower courts, Congress, and the states will in all likelihood continue to share policymaking powers in this area, final priorities will be shaped both by legislative and judicial policymaking.[100]

Grunbaum puts his finger on several of the difficulties the Court has had with environmental policy. He indicates the importance of public support for what the court does, as well as the interrelated nature of the political system. We would only add the inclusion of the executive as well to the mix, to suggest that Congress, the president, and the states will continue to share environmental policy making with the courts in shaping final priorities. Moreover, Thomas M. Hoban and Richard O. Brooks note how interrelated each segment of the country is and each one's impact on environmental decision making:

> [p]luck at any one point in the intricate fabric of our ecosystem and the web of relationships changes shape, disrupting the previous equilibrium so that further changes must be made to offset both intended and unintended effects. This new perception, one in which human beings are merely another component of an immensely complex ecosystem, makes us more fully aware of the magnitude of the environmental problems we face.[101]

The future of Supreme Court effectiveness concerns the Court itself. Despite all we have said about the Supreme Court's involvement in this policy area, it seems to have made less of a contribution to environmentalism than it has to other social issues such as abortion and affirmative action. It has given over leadership in many cases to lower courts and to the Congress. Richard E. Levy and Robert L. Glicksman emphasize this view by suggesting that "the Supreme Court appears to have retreated from this activism by emphasizing judicial restraint in its environmental decisions."[102] They continue, "the Supreme Court has repeatedly underscored its emphasis on institutional restraint with the admonition that environmental policy is to be made by Congress and the administrative agencies, not the courts."[103]

The Court makes a difference in the environmental area when it must decide a conflicting issue. An example of this was the case of *TVA v. Hill* (1978),[104] in which the Court's reading of the Endangered Species Act left it no choice but to block TVA's building of the Tellico dam project to save the snail darters. Here the Court was supportive of the administration and Congress against the TVA.

Ironically, it does appear that the Court's effectiveness has been felt more intensely when it has undercut the environment than when it has supported the environment. This certainly happened with the appointees of Ronald Reagan. As Levy and Glicksman mention, "[s]ince 1976, the Supreme Court has reached prodevelopment results in 32 out of 43 cases, or about 74% of the time."[105] It would appear that the Supreme Court has chosen to follow a policy less protective of the environment than has Congress. Even those cases in which the Court comes out in support of the environmental side, it is "less than wholehearted commitment to institutional results."[106]

Finally, a trend in the Court's role can be seen as it evolved from assisting Congress in its environmental policy to then advocating the importance of separation of powers.[107] Overall, the Court has made economic efficiency more important than Congress has, and it has ignored the desire of Congress for improvements in technology to control pollution.[108]

The Impact of Globalization

One final concern that could weaken the impact of the Supreme Court in environmental decision making concerns the possible global reach of a number of the issues publicized by Vice President Al Gore—namely, issues including global warming, depletion of the ozone layer, and overpopulation. These are the issues

---

Web Sites
The Environmental Court:

U.S. Supreme Court: **www.supremecourtus.gov**

Supreme Court and Court Cases: **oyez.nwu.edu**
    www.courttv.com/legaldocs/supreme
    www.findlaw.com/casecode/supreme2.html
    www.supct.law.cornell.edu: 8080/supct/

Courts and the Law: **www.law.emory.edu/FEDCTS**

that recognize no borders and reach out for international or regional solutions rather than national solutions.[109] Ironically, because these issues do reach global proportions, they demand an international tribunal or forum.

Finally, the Court adds legitimacy to decision making. How the environment will fare in the future will depend, in part, on the Supreme Court and its membership.

Endnotes

[1] Stephen L. Wasby, *The Supreme Court in the Federal Judicial System* (Chicago: Nelson-Hall Publishers, 1994), 2.

[2] Lawrence Baum, *The Supreme Court*, 6th ed. (Washington, DC: Congressional Quarterly Press, 1998), 4.

[3] Stephen L. Wasby, *The Supreme Court in the Federal Judicial System*, 4th ed. (Chicago: Nelson-Hall Publishers, 1993), 2.

[4] S. Sidney Ulmer, "Researching the Supreme Court in a Democratic Pluralist System: Some Thoughts on New Directions," *Law & Policy Quarterly*, vol. 1 (January 1979), 55.

[5] Raymond Tatalovich and Byron W. Daynes, eds., *Moral Controversies in American Politics: Cases in Social Regulatory Policy* (Armonk, NY: M.E. Sharpe, 1998), xxix.

[6] Robert V. Percival, "Environmental Law in the Supreme Court: Highlights from the Marshall Papers," *Environmental Law Reporter*, vol. 23 (October 1993), 10607.

[7] Examples of such critics are Donald Horowitz, *The Courts and Social Policy* (Washington, DC: Brookings, 1977); R. Shep Melnick, *Regulation and the Courts* (Washington, DC: Brookings, 1983); and Lettie McSpadden, "Environmental Policy in the Courts," in Norman J. Vig and Michael E. Kraft, eds., *Environmental Policy: New Directions for the Twenty-First Century* (Washington, DC: CQ Press, 2000), 145.

[8] Robert V. Percival, "Environmental Law in the Supreme Court: Highlights from the Marshall Papers," *Environmental Law Reporter*, vol. 23 (October 1993), 10617.

[9] 427 U.S. 246, 6 ELR 20570 (1976).

[10] Letter from Chief Justice Warren Burger to Justice Thurgood Marshall, May 24, 1976, in Robert V. Percival, "Environmental Law in the Supreme Court: Highlights From the Marshall Papers," *Environmental Law Reporter*, vol. 23 (October 1993), 10617.

[11] 435 U.S. 519 (1978).

[12] *Vermont Yankee Nuclear Power Corp. v. NRDC*, 435 U.S. 543 (1978).

[13] Alexis de Tocqueville, *Democracy in America*, edited by J.P. Mayer, translation by George Lawrence, vol. 1 (Garden City, New York: Doubleday & Co.—Anchor Books, 1969), 270.

[14] Lettie McSpadden, "Environmental Policy in the Courts," in Norman J. Vig and Michael E. Kraft, eds., *Environmental Policy: New Directions for the Twenty-First Century* (Washington, DC: CQ Press, 2000), 145.

[15] Lettie M. Wenner, *The Environmental Decade in Court* (Bloomington: Indiana University Press, 1982), 2–3.

[16] Lettie McSpadden, "Environmental Policy in the Courts," in Norman J. Vig and Michael E. Kraft, *Environmental Policy: New Directions for the Twenty-First Century*, 4th ed. (Washington, DC: CQ Press, 2000), Chapter 7, 145.

[17] Kenneth M. Holland, Chapter 7, "The Role of the Courts in the Making and Administration of Environmental Policy in the United States," in Kenneth M. Holland, F.L. Morton, and Brian Galligan, *Federalism and the Environment* (Westport: Greenwood, 1996), 164.

[18] See Kenneth M. Holland, Chapter 7, "The Role of the Courts in the Making and Administration of Environmental Policy in the United States," in Kenneth M. Holland, F.L. Morton, and Brian Galligan, *Federalism and the Environment* (Westport: Greenwood, 1996), 164, and Lettie McSpadden, Chapter 7, "Environmental Policy in the Courts," in Norman J. Vig and Michael Kraft, *Environmental Policy*, 4th ed. (Washington, DC: CQ Press, 2000), 151.

[19] 420 U.S. 35 (1975).

[20] 426 U.S. 200 (1976).

[21] 430 U.S. 112 (1977).

[22] 421 U.S. 60 (1975).

[23] 426 U.S. 167 (1976).

[24] 469 U.S. 274 (1985).

[25] 504 U.S. 334 (1992).

[26] Al Gore, *Earth in the Balance: Ecology and the Human Spirit* (Boston: Houghton Mifflin, 1992).

[27] Peter Huber, "Al Gore Is No Conservationist," *Washington Post National Weekly Edition*, May 1, 2000, 26.

[28] The statistics came from a listing in *U.S. Law Week* decided from 1970 and 1991 that were analyzed by Percival. See Robert V. Percival, "Environmental Law in the Supreme Court: Highlights from the Marshall Papers," *Environmental Law Reporter*, vol. 23 (October 1993), 10613. The case of *Train v. Natural Resources Defense Council* 421 U.S. 60, 5 E.L.R. 20264 (1975) well illustrates this opinion process.

[29] Werner F. Grunbaum, "Judicial Policymaking: The Supreme Court and Environmental Quality," University Programs Modular Studies (Morristown, NJ: General Learning Press, 1976), 6.

[30] Robert V. Percival, "Environmental Law in the Supreme Court: Highlights from the Marshall Papers," *Environmental Law Reporter*, vol. 23 (October 1993), 10625.

[31] Robert V. Percival, "Environmental Law in the Supreme Court: Highlights from the Marshall Papers," *Environmental Law Reporter*, vol. 23 (October 1993), 10625.

[32] See Richard J. Lazarus, "Restoring What's Environmental about Environmental Law in the Supreme Court," vol. 47, no. 3 (February 2000), 742–743. For the two cases listed by Lazarus see *Avery* at 390 U.S. 474 (1968); for *Hadley* see *Associated Enters*, 410 U.S. 749 (1973).

[33] Werner F. Grunbaum, "Judicial Policymaking: The Supreme Court and Environmental Quality," University Programs Modular Studies (Morristown, NJ: General Learning Press, 1976), 10.

[34] *Dolan v. City of Tigard*, 512 U.S. 411 (1994).

[35] Richard J. Lazarus, "Restoring What's Environmental about Environmental Law in the Supreme Court," vol. 47, no. 3 (February 2000), 766.

[36] William Funk, "Justice Breyer and Environmental Law," *Administrative Law Journal (American University)*, vol. 8 (1995), 735, 741-43. Reference in Daniel A. Farber, "Is the Supreme Court Irrelevant? Reflections on the Judicial Role in Environmental Law," *Minnesota Law Review*, vol. 8 (February 1997), 565.

[37] Daniel A. Farber, "Is the Supreme Court Irrelevant? Reflections on the Judicial Role in Environmental Law," *Minnesota Law Review*, vol. 8 (February 1997), 566.

38 Robert V. Percival, "Environmental Law in the Supreme Court: Highlights from the Marshall Papers," *Environmental Law Reporter*, vol. 23 (October 1993), 10625.

39 From a "confidential memorandum" from Judge Lewis Powell to the Education Committee of the U.S. Chamber of Commerce, in *Attack on American Free Enterprise System* (August 23, 1971) as revealed in Robert V. Percival, "Environmental Law in the Supreme Court: Highlights from the Marshall Papers," *Environmental Law Reporter*, vol. 23 (October 1993), 10607.

40 Lettie M. Wenner, "Environmental Policy in the Courts," in Norman J. Vig and Michael E. Kraft, eds., *Environmental Policy in the 1990s: Toward a New Agenda*, 2nd ed. (Washington, DC: Congressional Quarterly Press, 1994), 159.

41 Daniel A. Farber, "Is the Supreme Court Irrelevant? Reflections on the Judicial Role in Environmental Law," *Minnesota Law Review*, vol. 81 (February 1997), 547.

42 *Lujan v. Defenders of Wildlife*, 504 U.S. 555 (1992).

43 *Lujan v. National Wildlife Federation*, 497 U.S. 871 (1990).

44 See the following two decisions as an illustration of this in *Lujan v. National Wildlife Federation*, 110 S. Ct. 3177 (1990) and *California v. Federal Energy Regulatory Commission*, 110 S. Ct. 2024 (1990). Lettie McSpadden, "Environmental Policy in the Courts," in Norman J. Vig and Michael E. Kraft, *Environmental Policy: New Directions for the Twenty-First Century*, 4th ed. (Washington, DC: CQ Press, 2000), Chapter 7, 149, 154.

45 Richard J. Lazarus, "Restoring What's Environmental about Environmental Law in the Supreme Court," *UCLA Law Review*, vol. 47, no. 3 (February 2000), 737.

46 See the following cases to illustrate the position taken by the Court: *Tennessee Valley Authority v. Hill*, 437 U.S. 153 (1978); *City of Chicago v. Environmental Defense Fund*, 511 U.S. 328 (1994); and *Babbit v. Sweet Home Chapter of Communities for a Great Oregon*, 515 U.S. 687 (1995).

47 Richard J. Lazarus, "Restoring What's Environmental about Environmental Law in the Supreme Court," *UCLA Law Review*, vol. 47, no. 3 (February 2000), 737.

48 Lawrence Baum, *The Supreme Court*, 6th ed. (Washington, DC: CQ Press, 1998), 172.

49 It was Potter Stewart who indicated he felt this way about Burger. See David J. Garrow, *Liberty and Sexuality: The Right to Privacy and the Making of* Roe v. Wade (New York: Macmillan, 1994), 558.

50 *Aberdeen & Rockfish Railroad v. Students Challenging Regulatory Agency Procedures (SCRAP)*, 409 U.S. 1217, 1218 (1972).

51 Lettie M. Wenner, "Environmental Policy in the Courts," in Norman J. Vig and Michael E. Kraft, *Environmental Policy in the 1990s: Toward a New Agenda*, 2nd ed. (Washington, DC: CQ Press, 1994), 158.

52 Lawrence Baum, *The Supreme Court*, 6th ed. (Washington, DC: CQ Press, 1998), 172.

53 William H. Rehnquist, "Chief Justices I Never Knew," *Hastings Constitutional Law Quarterly*, vol. 3 (Summer 1976), 637.

54 437 U.S. 153 (1978).

55 Richard J. Lazarus, "Restoring What's Environmental about Environmental Law in the Supreme Court," *UCLA Law Review*, vol. 47, no. 3 (February 2000), 738.

56 National Environmental Policy Act of 1969, Pub. L. no. 91-190, 83 Stat. 852 (codified as amendment at *42 U.S.C. sec 4321-4370a* (1988).

57 Ray Clark and Larry Canter, eds., *Environmental Policy and NEPA* (Boca Raton: St. Lucie Press, 1997), 17.

58 Robert M. Lynch, "Complying with NEPA: The Tortuous Path to an Adequate Environmental Impact Statement," *Arizona Law Review*, vol. 14 (1972), 717.

59   See Richard I. Goldsmith and William C. Banks, "Environmental Values: Institutional Responsibility and the Supreme Court," *Harvard Environmental Law Review*, vol. 7, number 1 (1983), 4.

60   Kenneth Holland, "The Role of the Courts in the Making and Administration of Environmental Policy in the United States," in Kenneth M. Holland, F.L. Morton, and Brian Galligan, *Federalism and the Environment: Environmental Policymaking in Australia, Canada, and the United States* (Westport, CT.: Greenwood Press, 1996), 168.

61   Lettie McSpadden, "The Courts and Environmental Policy," in James P. Lester, ed., *Environmental Politics and Policy: Theories and Evidence*, 2nd ed. (Durham: Duke University Press, 1995), 247.

62   See Daniel A. Farber, "Disdain for 17-Year-Old Statute Evident in High Court's Rulings," *National Law Journal*, May 4, 1987, 20, in Daniel A. Farber, "Is the Supreme Court Irrelevant? Reflections on the Judicial Role in Environmental Law," *Minnesota Law Review*, vol. 81 (February 1997), 561, n. 66.

63   William E. Kovacic, "The Reagan Judiciary and Environmental Policy: The Impact of Appointments to the Federal Courts of Appeals," *Boston College Environmental Affairs Law Review*, vol. 18 (Summer 1991), 670–671. See footnotes 1–10 in the article as well.

64   Linda Greenhouse, "Court to Hear Clean Air Test of Congressional Authority," *New York Times*, May 23, 2000, A20. Also see Clean Air Amendments of 1970, Pub. L. no. 91-604, 84 Stat. 1676.

65   Linda Greenhouse, "Court to Hear Clean Air Test of Congressional Authority," *New York Times*, May 23, 2000, A20.

66   Linda Greenhouse, "Court to Hear Clean Air Test of Congressional Authority," *New York Times*, May 23, 2000, A20.

67   On appeal the case has taken on the name of *American Trucking Association v. Browner*, #99-1426.

68   Linda Greenhouse, "Supreme Court Roundup: Justices Broaden Their Look at the Clean Air Act," *New York Times*, May 31, 2000, A19.

69   *Robertson v. Seattle Audubon*, 112 S. Ct. 1407 (1991).

70   See Superfund Amendments and Reauthorization Act of 1986, Pub. L. no. 99-499, 100 Stat. 1613.

71   Daniel A. Farber, "Is the Supreme Court Irrelevant? Reflections on the Judicial Role in Environmental law," *Minnesota Law Review*, vol. 81 (February 1997), 553 [Lexis-Nexis].

72   Lettie M. Wenner, "Environmental Policy in the Courts," in Norman J. Vig and Michael E. Kraft, *Environmental Policy in the 1990s* (Washington, DC: CQ Press, 1994), 153.

73   Robert V. Percival, "Environmental Law in the Supreme Court: Highlights from the Marshall Papers," *Environmental Law Reporter*, vol. 23 (October 1993), 10607.

74   The one justice that Percival names who Reagan did not appoint was Lewis F. Powell, 33.8% supportive (in 65 cases). See Robert V. Percival, "Environmental Law in the Supreme Court: Highlights from the Marshall Papers," *Environmental Law Reporter*, vol. 23 (October 1993), 10625.

75   See William E. Kovacic, "The Reagan Judiciary and Environmental Policy: The Impact of Appointments to the Federal Courts of Appeals," *Boston College Environmental Affairs Law Review*, vol. 18 (1991), 669–713.

76   Lettie McSpadden, "Environmental Policy in the Courts," in Norman J. Vig and Michael E. Kraft, *Environmental Policy: New Directions for the Twenty-First Century* (Washington, DC: CQ Press, 2000), 155.

77 See George W. Bush's Web statement at **www.georgewbush.com/issues/domestic/enviro/points.asp** Retrieved May 25, 2000.

78 See Al Gore's Web statement. **www.algore2000.com/agenda/issue_environ.html**. Retrieved May 25, 2000. Also see **www.algore2000...ng_to_protect_our_environment.html**. Retrieved May 25, 2000.

79 Albert Gore, *Earth in the Balance: Ecology and the Human Spirit* (Boston: Houghton Mifflin, 1992).

80 John F. Harris and Ellen Nakashima, "'How Green is Gore?' Despite Previous Bold Talk, the Environment Has Yet to Emerge a Central Campaign Issue," *Washington Post National Weekly Edition*, March 20, 2000, 13.

81 Albert Gore, *Earth in the Balance: Ecology and the Human Spirit* (Boston: Houghton Mifflin, 1992), 269.

82 Alexis de Tocqueville (edited by J.P. Mayer, translation by George Lawrence), *Democracy in America*, vol. 1 (Garden City, New York: Doubleday, Anchor edition, 1969), 150.

83 Thomas R. Marshall, *Public Opinion and the Supreme Court* (Boston: Unwin Hyman, 1989), 71.

84 Robert Weissberg, *Public Opinion and Popular Government* (Englewood Cliffs, NJ: Prentice-Hall, 1976), 121–126.

85 Thomas R. Marshall, *Public Opinion and the Supreme Court* (Boston: Unwin Hyman, 1989), 78.

86 Riley E. Dunlap, "Public Opinion and Environmental Policy," in James P. Lester, ed., *Environmental Politics and Policy: Theories and Evidence*, 2nd ed. (Durham: Duke University Press, 1995), 77.

87 Riley E. Dunlap, "Public Opinion and Environmental Policy," in James P. Lester, ed.,*Environmental Politics and Policy: Theories and Evidence*, 2nd ed. (Durham: Duke University Press, 1995), 74.

88 These polls were all mentioned in a more extensive examination in a chapter by Byron W. Daynes entitled: "The Environment: A Conditional Issue in Presidential Politics," or "It all Depends. . ." that will come out in Keith Bartholomew, ed. *The Presidency and the Environment: The Twentieth Century and Beyond* (Salt Lake City: University of Utah Press, 2002). The book was based on a *Symposium on the Presidency and the Environment*, March 30–April 1, 2000, sponsored by the Wallace Stegner Center for Land, Resources, and the Environment, and the University of Utah College of Law, Salt Lake City, Utah.

89 Associated Press Telephone Poll, June 10–14, 1992. See **http://www.ropercenter.uconn.edu/**.

90 Voter Research and Surveys Exit Poll on behalf of ABC, CBS, and NBC News and CNN. November 3, 1992. Released: January 1993. **http://www.ropercenter.uconn.edu/**.

91 Gallup poll (1997 and 1998). *Gallup Poll Monthly*, No. 396 (September 1998), 34.

92 Gallup telephone poll on behalf of CNN and *USA TODAY*, January 3–6, 1992. Released January 14, 1992. **http://www.ropercenter.uconn.edu/**.

93 Gallup poll on behalf of CNN and *USA TODAY*, July 18–20, 1996. **http://www.ropercenter.uconn.edu/**.

94 Gallup telephone poll on behalf of CNN and *USA TODAY*, January 13–16, 2000. Released January 19, 2000. **http://ropercenter.uconn.edu/**.

95 Riley E. Dunlap, "Public Opinion and Environmental Policy," in James P. Lester, ed., *Environmental Politics and Policy: Theories and Evidence*, 2nd ed. (Durham: Duke University Press, 1995), 94.

[96] Stephen L. Wasby, *The Supreme Court in the Federal Judicial System* (Chicago: Nelson-Hall Publisher, 1994), 3.

[97] Lettie M. Wenner, "Environmental Policy in the Courts," in Norman J. Vig and Michael E. Kraft, eds., *Environmental Policy in the 1990s: Toward a New Agenda,* 2nd ed. (Washington, DC: CQ Press, 1994), 155.

[98] Daniel A. Farber, "Is the Supreme Court Irrelevant? Reflections on the Judicial Role in Environmental Law," *Minnesota Law Review,* vol. 81 (February 1997), 558.

[99] Daniel A. Farber, "Is the Supreme Court Irrelevant? Reflections on the Judicial Role in Environmental Law," *Minnesota Law Review,* vol. 81 (February 1997), 568.

[100] Werner F. Grunbaum, "Judicial Policymaking: The Supreme Court and Environmental Quality," University Programs Modular Studies (Morristown, NJ: General Learning Press, 1976), 32.

[101] Thomas M. Hoban and Richard O. Brooks, *Green Justice: the Environment and the Courts* (Boulder, CO.: Westview, 1987), 6.

[102] Richard E. Levy and Robert L. Glicksman, "Judicial Activism and Restraint in the Supreme Court's Environmental Law Decisions," *Vanderbilt Law Review,* vol. 42 (March 1989), 346.

[103] See Richard E. Levy and Robert L. Glicksman, "Judicial Activism and Restraint in the Supreme Court's Environmental Law Decisions," *Vanderbilt Law Review,* vol. 42 (March 1989), 354, note 37.

Example cases where this philosophy was emphasized include *Vermont Yankee Nuclear Power Corp. v. Natural Resources Defense Council, Inc.,* 435 U.S. 519, 557–558 (1978); *Chevron U.S.A., Inc. v. Natural Resources Defense Council, Inc.,* 467 U.S. 837, 864–865 (1983); *Baltimore Gas & Electric Co. v. Natural Resources Defense Council, Inc.,* 462 U.S. 87, 97 (1983); and *City of Milwaukee v. Illinois,* 451 U.S. 304, 313 (1981).

[104] *TVA v. Hill,* 437 U.S. 153 (1978).

[105] Richard E. Levy and Robert L. Glicksman, "Judicial Activism and Restraint in the Supreme Court's Environmental Law Decisions," *Vanderbuilt Law Review,* vol. 42 (March 1989), 346, note 10.

[106] Ibid., 382.

[107] Ibid., 391.

[108] Ibid., 421.

[109] See Albert Gore, *Earth in the Balance: Ecology and the Human Spirit* (Boston: Houghton Mifflin, 1992) as well as Gore's Web statement: **www.algore2000.com/agenda/issue_environ.html** Retrieved May 25, 2000. Also see: **www.algore 2000...ng_to_protect_our_environment.html.** Retrieved May 25, 2000.

CHAPTER 9

Global Environmental Policy

In the early seventeenth century, English explorer Henry Hudson set off to find the Northwest Passage, which would shorten the sea route between Europe and Asia. Now, almost 400 years later, the Northwest Passage has become a popular tourist site as well as a focal point of an emerging environmental conflict. On the one hand, melting ice resulting from rising Earth temperatures has made travel through the passage much easier; at the same time, however, Canadian officials have raised concerns about personal safety and environmental degradation.[1] Weather conditions in the Canadian arctic have led public officials to allude to the "Titanic" question—namely, the danger posed to tourists in a sinking ship who might not be saved due to the difficulty in getting rescue personnel and equipment to the scene. Moreover, the *Exxon Valdez* disaster—where millions of gallons of oil polluted a pristine Alaskan region in 1989—reminds Canadians of the environmental dangers posed by oil tankers.

As we noted in Chapter 1, voices promoting "pro-environment" governmental policy have been countered by those who argue that the global environment is neither threatened, nor polluted to the degree that some suggest. According to one observer of the global environment, where "catastrophists" focus on environmental degradation, pollution, and resource depletion, "techno-optimists" take the position that the global environment will be just fine as a result of positive human intervention, pragmatism, and technological innovations.[2]

Although our primary focus in this book is on the *political* aspects of environmental affairs, two factors—nature and science—are integral to this discussion in terms of their independent significance, the relationship between the two, and the relationship between nature, science, and political decision making. Our conceptualization of *nature* has changed to an understanding that it is a living ecosystem, whereas it has heretofore been identified as a resource to be used.[3]

Moreover, as James Rosenau argues, "Rooted in the processes of nature and the responses of nature to human intervention, environmental issues are inescapably embedded in a scientific context."[4] The interface of nature, science, and politics is an important dynamic in the study of global environmental policy as each plays an essential role. Amidst the polemics and debates that occur within and between nations about the proper approach to global environmental protection we are reminded that "Politicians cannot exercise control over environmental outcomes without recourse to scientific findings. They may claim that the findings are not clear cut or remain subject to contradictory interpretations, but they are nonetheless dependent on what the practices of science uncover about the laws of nature."[5] Controversies over wetlands protection, global warming, biodiversity, and endangered species are relevant examples of the problems associated with the divergent political and economic interpretations of nature and scientific findings.

For example, where some argue that global warming has become a trend, others hold that the science is inconclusive. Where some argue that we have an obligation to preserve biodiversity because science informs us that plants and animals are diminishing, others question the extent to which the decline in biodiversity is real. In the end, however, it all comes back to the political process. As Paul Wapner contends:

> environmental protection is not the only aim of societies and thus must be balanced with other social goals, such as economic well-being, which, depending on how one thinks about it, can conflict with environmentally sound measures. To reorient human activities on such a scale and order of complexity entails employing a means of governance that can actually influence vast and diverse numbers of people. It requires ways to constrain and direct activities, in a feasible manner, away from environmentally harmful practices and toward more environmentally sound ones. To put it in ordinary language, environmental concern fundamentally involves politics.[6]

A current example of the "problem" of politics and the global environment concerns the continuing controversy surrounding the pesticide DDT. While useful for the agricultural industry, it was devastating to birds including the bald eagle, brown pelicans, and peregrine falcon. Although President John Kennedy had set in motion the effort to begin restriction of the pesticide, which was eventually banned in the United States during the Nixon administration, DDT continued to be used by other countries. In 1998 a United Nations proposal to eliminate 12 highly toxic pollutants including DDT was underway in an effort to achieve a worldwide ban on these deadly environmental hazards. Due to the continuing health threat posed by malaria, public health professionals challenged the UN proposal, which was being negotiated in Geneva.[7] Athough there was general consensus that the threat posed by these environmental hazards required attention, the concerns raised by members of the health community illustrate the potential problems that might arise during international negotiations.

The preceding chapters in this book have addressed environmentalism within the framework of American domestic politics. For example, in the United States alone, there are numerous federal institutions and agencies with jurisdiction over the issue of global warming.[8] While the president has the power to work with the leaders of other countries in the treaty-making process, the United States Senate has the power to ratify the treaty or oppose it. Moreover, in both the House and the Senate, legislators can introduce bills concerning global warming that might reflect the interests of environmental groups or business and industry. The president can then veto or sign the legislation. Whereas the Council on Environmental Quality assumes responsibility for assessing the impact on the environment resulting from actions of the federal government, the Environmental Protection Agency (EPA) has been involved in numerous studies on the effect of global warming on the planet, especially in coastal areas. As the Department of the Interior assesses the impact of global warming on the public lands and waters under its jurisdiction, the Federal Emergency Management Agency (FEMA) has been responsible for establishing a national emergency management system to limit personal and physical losses (although it lacks the capabilities and resources to implement effective programs with subnational governments).[9]

In this chapter, we examine global environmental policy, which shows the linkage between the United States and other nations as well as the impact of transboundary environmental issues. Regarding global warming, in order to make progress toward reasonable goals, national interests may have to give way to future regional and international cooperative efforts. Although political leaders and their delegates at international conferences, as signatories to several international agreements, have made a commitment to work toward reduction of greenhouse gases, they have been divided over objectives and pressured by fellow delegates. As a result, they have argued for voluntary rather than mandatory requirements, among other things.

On the one hand, international treaties are representative of progress; on the other, much more remains to be done regarding the global warming issue. The global *political* environment is comprised of some 200 nation-states, each with their own interests and priorities. Yet the actions of one or a collection of these countries can affect their neighbors as well as the global *natural* environment.

In an effort to address environmental problems on a regional and global scale, nations have been drawn together in regional and international organizations, conferences, and treaties. Moreover, the environment has increasingly become an integral element of the national security debate and is now an essential part of the foreign policy making and diplomatic process. It is to these concerns that we now turn our attention.

Global Environmental Issues

Environmental threats are not limited to one geographic locale but instead have a cross-national impact on either a regional or international level. As rivers travel through one country to another they carry pollutants from their origin point. Coal-fired utility plants in one country impact neighboring countries in the form of acid rain. Wildlife does not recognize human-made political and legal borders. Ocean dumping and climate change have both a regional and global impact.

In his study of international environmental policy, Lynton Caldwell categorized environmental issues in terms of their "criticality."[10] Current issues considered *critical* include endangered species, loss of habitat, expanding human population, loss of forests and overgrazing, pollution of and decrease in freshwater supplies. Issues that are *becoming critical* include loss of topsoil, atmospheric pollution and climate change, energy sources and their alternatives, threats to the biogeochemical processes underlying the biosphere, and the impact of large public works and their maintenance on the availability of resources for the future. For the purpose of illustration, we will focus briefly on one "critical" issue—overpopulation—and another that is "becoming critical"—stratospheric ozone depletion.

AL GORE: THE GLOBAL ENVIRONMENTAL PRESIDENT-TO-BE?

When Al Gore failed to win the presidential contest in November 2000, the people of the United States lost an opportunity to have, perhaps, the first president who would include the global environment as a central feature of the administration's agenda. While most presidents have included the economy, jobs, and national security as the centerpiece of their legislative agendas, the environment has usually been a peripheral issue. Yet during the recent presidential campaign, Al Gore demonstrated in his speeches and debates that he was committed to global environmental protection.

Al Gore began his political career following in the steps of his father, a U.S. senator. Gore served in the U.S. Congress and U.S. Senate prior to his two terms as vice president under Bill Clinton. While in the House and Senate, Gore became an authority on environmental policy and an ardent champion of environmental protection. In choosing Gore as his running mate in 1992, Bill Clinton elevated an environmentalist to the second highest office in the country once they won the White House. As two political researchers have argued, "It is safe to say that Al Gore established the tone of the environmental issue for the 1992 campaign, and for environmentalists there was a feeling of great anticipation that their issue would finally emerge as a priority consideration in the White House."[1]

In 1992, Bill Clinton and Al Gore argued that "environmental protection is fundamental to America's national security" and indicated that they would pursue four major goals if elected: "reduce pollution and solid waste," "preserve America's natural beauty and key resources," "use market forces to encourage environmental protection," and "exert American leadership for a healthier world."[2] The same year, Gore published *Earth in the Balance*, a book that demanded that each one of us assume personal responsibility regarding our actions toward the environment. Moreover, Gore focused on the political system and explained, "my study of the global environment has required a searching reexamination of the ways in which political motives and government policies have helped to create the crisis and now frustrate the solutions we need."[3] In his book, Gore argued that "we must make the rescue of the environment the central organizing principle for civilization"[4] and in the process called for a global environmental "Marshall Plan" to address the increasing world population, development and sharing of appropriate technologies, eco-nomics (environmentally-friendly economics), encouraging global cooperation and international agreements, and enhancing the world's citizenry's level of knowledge about global environmental conditions.[5] According to one reporter who traveled the world to learn more about the global environment, Gore's book "was not the usual politician's hodgepodge of clichés but a thoughtful treatise that showed he understood some of the reforms needed to make the market economy less environmentally harmful."[6]

Although Gore was given responsibility for environmental policy in the Clinton administration, the environment is only one among many important public policy issues. Moreover, for six of eight years, the Clinton-Gore administration was confronted with an aggressively antagonistic Republican-controlled Congress. Further, given the attention of Congress, the media, and the public to Monicagate and the impeachment process, "protecting the environment," according to one political observer, "had been relegated to the back burner."[7]

In the year 2000, Al Gore decided to run for the presidency, making environmental protection central to his campaign. At home, he championed antipollution measures, energy conservation, and opposition to oil drilling in the Alaska Arctic National Wildlife Refuge. Globally, he turned his attention to the threat posed by global warming and stratospheric ozone depletion. The controversial conclusion to the 2000 presidential campaign found Al Gore losing to George W. Bush. Whether Al Gore decides to run for the presidency again in 2004 remains to be seen. If he does it is very likely that his commitment to global environmental protection will once again be an important part of his presidential campaign.

---

[1]Dennis L. Soden and Brent S. Steel, "Evaluating the Environmental Presidency," in Dennis L. Soden, ed. *The Environmental Presidency* (Albany, NY: State University of New York Press, 1999), 336.

[2]Bill Clinton and Al Gore, *Putting People First: How We Can All Change America* (New York: Times Books, 1992), 93–99.

[3]Al Gore, *Earth in the Balance: Ecology and the Human Spirit* (New York: Plume), 11.

[4]Ibid., 269.

[5]Ibid., Chapter 15. The notion of a "Global Green Deal" was suggested in the Earth Day 2000 special edition of *Time* magazine. The global green deal would require government leadership and market incentives. In other words, environmentally friendly business practices could become a profitable enterprise. See Mark Hertsgaard, "A Global Green Deal," *Time* magazine (April–May 2000), 84–85.

[6]Mark Hertsgaard, *Earth Odyssey: Around the World in Search of our Environmental Future* (New York: Broadway Books, 1998), 280.

[7]Jacqueline Vaughn Switzer, *Environmental Politics: Domestic and Global Dimensions*, 3rd ed. (New York: Bedford/St. Martin's, 2001), 62.

Overpopulation

In 1950, when the Korean War broke out, the world's population was about 2.5 billion; 50 years later, in 2000, the world's population almost tripled when the six-billionth person was born. Since population grows exponentially, it takes a shorter amount of time to increase substantially.

For example, in less than three years the world's population would grow by a size equivalent to the population of the United States.[11] While the wealthy countries of the northern hemisphere (in addition to Australia and New Zealand) are aging and have a declining population growth rate, the poor countries of the southern hemisphere are the source of a population explosion, with a substantial proportion of their population comprised of young people. Moreover, the burgeoning populations of the poor countries lack many of the resources needed for survival (e.g., fresh drinking water, adequate health care). It is not surprising that the countries of the south have demanded a more equitable distribution of the world's resources. However, to what extent would the populations of wealthier nations be willing to accede to this demand, with the potential decline in their quality of life? Paul and Anne Ehrlich, who have been writing about overpopulation issues for years, sum up the problem this way:

> A large part of the responsibility for solving the human dilemma rests on the rich countries, and especially the United States. We are the archetype of a gigantic, overpopulated, overconsuming rich nation, one that many ill-informed decision makers in poor nations would like to emulate. Unless we demonstrate by example that we understand the horrible mistakes made on our way to overdevelopment and that we are intent on reversing them, there seems little hope for the persistence of civilization.[12]

An example of the "problem" of politics regarding the U.S. role and overpopulation concerns international family planning practices. International organizations including the United Nations Population Fund (UNPF) have been involved in family planning efforts. Yet during the Reagan-Bush years, U.S. funding efforts for family planning were affected by the domestic political debate over abortion. Funding for the UNPF, for instance, was all but eliminated because Reagan and Bush refused to support any organization involved in family planning practices, even if U.S. funds were used for other activities.[13] Reagan and Bush were also concerned about China's "coercive abortion policy" and did not want to support any agency, in this case the UNPF, that included China in its family planning program.[14] The Reagan-Bush policy was reversed with the election of Bill Clinton, who at home in the United States supported abortion rights for women and in the international arena restored funding to international organizations and the UNPF, which supported family planning in the global arena. However, newly elected president George W. Bush adopted the international abortion policy of the Reagan-Bush years in one of his first official acts as president.

A recent report by researchers at Cornell University informing us that the human population is likely to double over the next century has outlined what impact overpopulation will have on energy resources.[15] For instance, potable water, which has already declined 60 percent over the last 40 years, will be reduced another 50 percent over the next quarter century, and by mid-twenty-first century, global oil resources will be depleted. According to one of the author's of the study, David Pimentel, "It will be much more difficult to survive in a world without voluntary controls on population growth and ever-diminishing supplies of the Earth's resources."[16] Moreover, expanding human population growth impinges on habitat and biodiversity.

CASE STUDY: BIODIVERSITY AND ENDANGERED SPECIES

Although there are obvious natural reasons for the demise of animal and plant species, human activity also plays a large role. A major impact of an ever-increasing human population on the biosphere concerns the degradation of natural habitats. As the number of people increases, there is likely expansion into surrounding ecosystems. Moreover, numbers alone do not tell the whole story. For instance, according to a study by Paul Harrison, there is a direct relationship between human population and the decrease in wildlife habitat.[1]

In his effort to encourage preservation of the "genetic diversity of the biosphere," Lynton Caldwell makes reference to the concept of "genocide." Caldwell argues that the "term is customarily applied to the elimination of genetic types among humans. But humanity has been guilty of genocide against a vast number of life forms. Since prehistoric times, men have systematically—if also inadvertently—eliminated species of plants, animals, and ecosystems numbering uncalculated thousands."[2]

Efforts have been made in the United States as well as other countries to address the problem of species loss. For example, during the administration of Franklin D. Roosevelt, one of the early biodiversity efforts was creation of migratory bird treaties between the United States and Mexico and the United States and Canada, in order to promote wildlife conservation. Four decades later, in 1973, the United States Congress passed and the president signed the Endangered Species Act, which promoted an activist approach to threatened and endangered species in the United States. Moreover, that same year, the Convention on International Trade in Endangered Species of Wild Fauna and Flora (CITES) was concluded. CITES was one among several international agreements in the early 1970s established to preserve the natural environment for future generations.[3]

Despite national and international efforts to preserve wildlife and wildlife habitat, the threat to animal and plant biodiversity continues. In a recent Biodiversity in the Next Millennium survey of biologists, botanists, and others in related fields, 7 out of 10 scientists have raised concerns about a mass extinction explosion unrivaled in any other time in history.[4] Seven out of ten scientists are concerned that by the third decade of the twenty-first century, 20 percent of contemporary species face extinction, while one out of three scientists hypothesize that perhaps 50 percent of all species face this threat. If forests are the primary habitat for a majority of animal and plant species, and a majority of the world's forest habitat has been lost, international cooperation is needed to address this urgent threat.[5] Deforestation in Brazil is a clear example of this dilemma. In describing the problems resulting from the relationship between economics, politics, and the environment, G. Tyler Miller explains:

continued

Brazil is divided geographically into a largely impoverished tropical north and a temperate south, where most industry and wealth are concentrated. The Amazon basin, which covers about one-third of the country's territory, remains largely unsettled. This is changing as landless poor migrate there, hoping to grow enough food to survive, and as its tropical forests are cut down for grazing livestock, timber, and mining or are flooded to create large reservoirs for hydroelectric dams."[6]

During the summer of 2000, the Convention on Biological Diversity (a product of the 1992 Earth Summit in Rio) convened in Kenya to address contemporary and future threats resulting from the impact of the human population on biological diversity, and the continuing escalation of species loss. The impending demise of thousands of animal and plant species will require extraordinary political will among government leaders and citizens alike to reverse the trend in the loss of biological diversity.

[1]See "Facing the Future: People and the Planet: Extinction of Species" at **http://www.facing thefuture.org/environment/enviro-4.htm**. Retrieved August 8, 2000.

[2]Lynton Keith Caldwell, *International Environmental Policy: From the Twentieth to the Twenty-First Century* (Durham: Duke University Press, 1996), 318.

[3]See Edith Brown Weiss, "Intergenerational Equity: Toward an International Legal Framework," in Nazli Choucri, ed. *Global Accord: Environmental Challenges and International Responses* (Cambridge, MA: The MIT Press, 1993), 339.

[4]See Ed Ayres, "Worldwatch Report: Fastest Mass Extinction in Earth History" at **http://www. enn.com/enn-features-archive/1998/09/091698/fea0916.asp**. Retrieved August 8, 2000.

[5]See "Governments Sound Biodiversity Alarm in Nairobi" at **http://www.enn.com/2000/ NATU...22/biodiversity.conference.enn/index.html**. Retrieved August 8, 2000.

[6]G. Tyler Miller, Jr., *Living in the Environment,* 7th ed. (Belmont, CA: Wadsworth Publishing Company, 1992), 225.

Stratospheric Ozone Depletion

Climatic change is one of the third-tier issues that are considered puzzling, complex, and controversial and that, in turn, leads to dissension between experts, public officials, and citizens. The motivation to address the depletion of stratospheric ozone—one type of climatic change—occurred when the wealthy countries of the world achieved consensus that it was a serious global environmental problem. Representatives of world governments, business leaders, and organized interests worked together to forge an agreement to begin to phase out the chemicals that threaten stratospheric ozone. In the effort to deal with the problem, political divisions emerged as rich and poor countries exhibited divergent interests. Moreover, economic problems arose resulting, in part, from the increased costs associated with developing viable alternatives to the chemicals causing the problem.

Concentration of ozone in the stratosphere is important for the biosphere in many ways, including protecting people from ultraviolet radiation, which can lead to skin cancer if not filtered prior to reaching ground level. The focus of attention has been on chlorofluorocarbons (CFCs), which were developed in the 1930s and eventually became an important component for aerosol cans, refrigerants (e.g., air conditioners), cleaning agents, and insulation. During the congressional debate concerning the Supersonic Transport in 1969, initial concerns were raised about the impact of human activities on the stratosphere, which led to research activity to learn more about threats to the atmosphere.[17] In 1974 two researchers proposed a hypothesis that suggested that once in the stratosphere, solar radiation breaks down CFCs, releasing chlorine that, in turn, breaks down ozone—a process that could continue for years.[18]

A decade later, subsequent to studies by the United Nations Environment Program, the United States and the European Community began the process of coordinating efforts to address the global threat posed by CFCs. This resulted in the 1985 Vienna Convention for the Protection of the Ozone Layer. (It is interesting to note that the same year the agreement was signed, scientists discovered a massive "hole" over Antarctica, indicating that a large proportion of ozone had been depleted. An event with similar historic proportions repeated itself in 1987.)[19] This convention provided the foundation upon which the 1987 Montreal Protocol was signed by the United States as well as by 23 other countries.[20] By 1996, some 150 countries became parties to the agreement.

Signatories to the protocol agreed to a 50 percent phaseout of CFCs by the year 1999. However, in order to facilitate and expedite this process, in 1989, 81 countries became signatories to the Helsinki Declaration on the Protection of the Ozone Layer, which mandated total elimination of CFCs by the end of the century. The actions by Dupont (U.S.) and Imperial Chemical Industries (ICI) (U.K.) also played an important role in the establishment of the agreement. Whether doing so for the right reason or due to business or economic calculations, as one analyst of the diplomatic effort has argued, "While initially opposed to any restrictions on markets, both companies changed their positions over time. Dupont actually sought—and ICI soon after accepted and supported—the international regulation of CFCs."[21]

Two problems associated with the stratospheric ozone depletion issue involve international politics and business and consumer affairs. First, although the Montreal Protocol exemplifies a successful international effort to address a common global problem, political differences divide the rich and poor countries over the implementation process. Representatives from the poor countries—some of which were early signatories to the protocol—wanted to ensure that there was equity in the agreement toward all of the signatories, as well as financial support from the wealthy countries so that poorer ones could fulfill their obligations. Second, in the process of phasing out CFCs, there is a need to find suitable replacements. While some industries were uneasy about the potentially high costs associated with eliminating CFCs and developing substitutes, business and consumers have raised concerns about the effectiveness of new alternatives.[22]

International and Regional Organizations

In discussing global governance and the formation of international regimes, Oran Young finds it useful to organize the notion of international *environmental* regimes into three categories: the international commons, shared natural resources, and transboundary externalities.[23] The *international commons* is comprised of elements of the biosphere in which members of the world community have shared interests including global warming, biodiversity, stratospheric ozone depletion, and inner as well as outer space, among others. Animals, bodies of water, underground fossil and mineral resources, for instance, constitute *shared natural resources* where these elements cross over national borders of at least two countries. When one country engages in behavior that has an adverse impact on its neighbor(s), *transboundary externalities* occur. For example, when an industrial site in one nation is polluting a river that travels through other countries, it has committed a transboundary water pollution violation. These categories are helpful in understanding the role of international and regional organizations that are directly or indirectly involved in environmental affairs.

The United Nations/United Nations Environment Program

The United Nations is a mixed blessing. It has been instrumental in bringing together representatives from countries around the world into an international forum to debate and discuss rather than engage in conflict. Yet it has not lived up to the expectations that it could provide global governance. One significant attempt to engage the United Nations in playing a crucial role in global environmental affairs has been establishment of the United Nations Environment Program (UNEP).

UNEP, which will celebrate its 30th anniversary in 2002, was created in 1972 subsequent to the United Nations Conference on the Human Environment. Despite its lack of sufficient resources, UNEP has been relatively effective in the formation and coordination of international environmental conventions, negotiations, and research.[24] For example, in 1977 an international scientific forum in Washington, D.C., was organized by UNEP to study threats to the ozone layer. It produced a "World Action Plan" and future research agenda.[25] In 1988 UNEP gave the Intergovernmental Panel on Climate Change (IPCC) the task of evaluating global climate change, in order to provide data about the circumstances involving the human impact on the climate.[26] More recently, in 1995, the Global Biodiversity Assessment, a scientific analysis of the relationship between human beings and biodiversity, was promoted by UNEP.[27]

The European Union

In an effort to more fully integrate the nations of the European Community (EC) that resulted from the 1957 Treaty of Rome, the Treaty on European Union (Maastricht Treaty) of 1992 established the current European Union (EU). The EU is comprised of five key institutions—namely, the European Council and Council of Ministers, the European Commission, the European Parliament, the European Court of Justice, and the European Environment Agency.

Forty years ago, the political elite of the EC were primarily concerned with economic growth and national security and gave little, if any, attention to environmental matters. Beginning in 1973, however, a series of Environmental Action Programs (EAPs) was created by the EC to harmonize environmental policy on a cross-national basis. As one of many policy areas under the jurisdiction of the newer EU, the environment gradually became an integral aspect of decision making in the EU.[28] After all, the densely populated European continent is threatened by pollution, a high rate of natural resource consumption, and increasing waste production.[29] In 1995 the European Environment Agency reported that although much progress had been made, much more work needed to be done by the EU in order to more fully integrate the member states into a comprehensive environmental policy.[30]

Two important considerations about environmental policy in Europe include public opinion and the policy-making process of the EU. Although the EU is comprised of 15 member states each with its own history, culture, political systems, and stages of development, public opinion across the continent has increasingly reflected concern about environmental quality. When asked which institution they preferred to be responsible for making decisions about the environment, two-thirds of the people making up the EU preferred the EU—a regional organization rather than national governments.[31] Support for the EU was rather consistent across the 15 member states. Moreover, public opinion supports the EU institutional framework now in place to improve the environment.

Environmental policy making in the EU has been characterized by legislative directives that are binding on member states. At the same time, 15 different members have varying political motivation, financial resources, and administrative capacity to respond to EU mandates. Consequently, while the EU has made progress in its effort to improve environmental conditions in Europe, implementing legislation across the diversity of member states remains a critical EU problem for the future.

The World Trade Organization and "Green" Nongovernmental Organizations

Since 1947, international trade policy had been governed by the General Agreement on Tariffs and Trade (GATT). This institutional structure changed in 1994 when it was replaced by the World Trade Organization (WTO) at the Uruguay Round of trade relations.[32] For the purpose of our discussion, the WTO had the potential for great environmental impact, but only "modest provisions" and a "weak reference to sustainable development" were included in its charter when the organization was established.[33] In other words, the environmental laws of a country might become subservient to economic decisions of the WTO which raised fears among environmentalists.

For example, four years ago the United States, which acts under the Clean Air Act of 1990, was required by the WTO to revise its air pollution standards because the WTO viewed them as a "restraint of trade" in favor of domestic sources at the expense of foreign producers.[34]

A week before a new round of WTO trade negotiations in Autumn 1999, President Clinton delivered a speech explaining his position on a host of trade related issues. As far as the environment was concerned, Clinton stated that in the negotiations the United States would act in full accordance with environmental protection as a top priority.[35] Moreover, the president issued an executive order mandating that when trade agreements have an environmental impact, a review process would be implemented.[36]

The November 1999 WTO trade round in Seattle witnessed protest demonstrations by trade unions, civil rights groups, and environmentalists—all concerned about implications of the trade agreements that would result from the negotiations. For environmentalists, apprehension centered on the secrecy of the decision-making process, the power of the WTO, and the role played by corporate lawyers in the organization. As the United States was heading into the twenty-first century, environmentalists saw environmental protection threatened if WTO regulations could nullify national laws of the United States as well as of other countries. The WTO meeting became a top story for the news media as tensions increased and clashes occurred on the streets of Seattle between protesters and the police. In response to recent trade meetings, demonstrations occured in New York City, Washington, D.C., and Quebec among other cities.

Environmental groups have been active within many countries around the world. At the same time, "green" nongovernmental organizations (GNGOs) have also exerted political pressure on world governments in order to influence their environmental policies. Transnational environmental activist groups (TEAGs) have not only been active in national politics but also have been active in "global civil society."[37]

TEAGs or GNGOs include Greenpeace International, Friends of the Earth, the World Wildlife Fund, and Earth Island Institute, among many others. Although Lamont Hempel suggests that GNGOs can influence the activities of internationally based environmental organizations, John McCormick argues that despite large memberships among some of these groups, they tend to have more success exerting political power at the national rather than the international level.[38]

International Conferences and Agreements

During the post–World War II period, delegates from numerous countries have met to discuss and then find solutions to environmental problems. The nature of ecological issues has changed in recent years, as new threats have emerged while old issues remain a source of contention. Early regional and international agreements tended to focus on wildlife and marine conservation (Table 9.1). By the early 1960s, national security and the environment became an issue as the United States, Soviet Union, and United Kingdom signed the 1963 Limited Nuclear Test Ban Treaty. From the 1970s until the current time, biodiversity and endangered species have emerged as important issues as well as global climate change (global warming and depletion of stratospheric ozone). Between 1972 and 1997, three major international conferences brought together world leaders to address environmental issues.

Attempts to secure international cooperation regarding the environment occurred in several conferences, most importantly, in Stockholm, Sweden, in 1972; 20 years later in Rio de Janeiro, Brazil, in 1992; and again in Kyoto, Japan, in 1997. Although differences in opinion were quite evident among the participants, the conferences were a tangible representation of the effort to address global environmental problems.

In 1972, the United Nations sponsored the Conference on the Human Environment in Stockholm. This conference, the first to bring together delegates from rich and poor countries (although the Soviet Union and East European countries refused to attend), resulted from a proposal by Sweden in the 1960s. (The foundation for a global conference was established by the earlier Biosphere Conference in Paris in 1968.)[39] The Stockholm conference resulted in "common principles" that established a framework within which international cooperation could be fostered, with the goal of improving the health of the global environment. A Declaration on the Human Environment contained the common principles and more than 100 action plans.[40]

TABLE 9.1

Regional and International Environmental Agreements (selected)

	Conventions, Protocols, and Treaties
1930s–1940s	Convention for the Protection of Migratory Birds and Game Animals, 1936
	Convention on Nature Protection and Wildlife Preservation in the Western Hemisphere, 1940
	International Whaling Convention, 1946
1950s–1960s	International Convention for the Prevention of Pollution of the Sea by Oil, 1954
	Convention on Fishing and Conservation of the Living Resources of the High Seas, 1958
	Limited Nuclear Test Ban Treaty, 1963
1970s–1980s	Convention on International Trade in Endangered Species of Wild Fauna and Flora (CITES), 1973
	Conservation of Polar Bears Treaty, 1976
	Montreal Protocol on Substances that Deplete the Ozone Layer, 1987
1990s	Climate Change Convention, 1992[1]
	Convention on Biological Diversity, 1992[2]
	Kyoto Protocol, 1997

[1]Only after the convention was revised to reflect voluntary rather than mandatory emission reductions did President Bush sign it.

[2]President Bush opposed the convention. President Clinton signed it but the U.S. Senate refused to ratify it.

Source: Adapted from Peter M. Haas with Jan Sundgren, "Evolving International Environmental Law: Changing Practices National Sovereignty," in Nazli Choucri, ed. *Global Accord* (Cambridge, MA: MIT Press, 1993), 420–429; Lamont C. Hempel, *Environmental Governance* (Washington, DC: Island Press, 1996), 170–172; Carolyn Long, Michael Cabral, Brooks Vandivort, "The Chief Environmental Diplomat: An Evolving Arena of Foreign Policy," in Dennis L. Soden, *The Environmental Presidency* (Albany, NY: State University of New York Press, 1999), 194–219.

Two decades later, what became known as the Earth Summit in Rio brought together thousands of delegates to discuss environmental conditions near the close of the twentieth century. Expectations about this United Nations Conference on Environment and Development were perhaps too high. Given the gathering of numerous political leaders, journalists, and representatives of NGOs, among others, one observer characterized the conference in this way:

> Faced with an agenda of more than one hundred environmental policy issues, more than a thousand pages of negotiating texts, and the unprecedented security requirements of the assembled presidents, prime ministers, and other VIPs, the organizers of the summit understandably wanted to be remembered more for what they overcame politically than for what they achieved in policy terms.[41]

Nonetheless, the conference provided a forum in which a common theme—"sustainable development"—was accepted and several agreements were concluded: namely, the Climate Change Convention and the Biodiversity Convention. As a guiding principle of the summit, sustainable development meant the "meeting of today's true needs and opportunities without jeopardizing the integrity of the planetary life-support base—the environment—and diminishing its ability to provide for needs, opportunities, and quality of life in the future."[42]

Earlier in this chapter we discussed the issue of genetic diversity and the problems associated with the production of greenhouse gases and the phenomenon of global warming. According to Article 2 of the Climate Change (Earth Summit) Convention, the overall objective of the signatories was the "stabilization of greenhouse gas concentrations in the atmosphere at a level that would prevent dangerous anthropogenic interference with the climate system."[43] As we pointed out in Chapter 6, however, President George H.W. Bush successfully encouraged fellow delegates at the Earth Summit to accept a weaker version of the original proposal concerning timetables and the reduction of emissions of greenhouse gases.[44] The Biodiversity Convention was also an important consideration at the Earth Summit because it signaled an effort to preserve the planet's fauna and flora. According to the convention:

> Despite mounting efforts over the past 20 years, the loss of the world's biological diversity, mainly from habitat destruction, over-harvesting, pollution and the inappropriate introduction of foreign plants and animals, has continued. . . . Urgent and decisive action is needed to conserve and maintain genes, species and ecosystems, with a view to the sustainable management and use of biological resources.[45]

Once again, however, the Bush administration became an obstacle to achieving unanimity among the delegates by refusing to sign the convention—the only participant to do so.

Agenda 21 was another outcome of the Earth summit. While focusing on a "global partnership for sustainable development," it also stressed the need for financial assistance from the rich to the poor countries to soften the burden in meeting the sustainable development objective.[46] Agenda 21 was a complex effort including four major sections—namely, socioeconomic concerns, conservation and natural resource management, the role of participants, and the implementation process.[47] Each section was further divided into numerous categories including demographics, poverty, deforestation, biological diversity, oceans and coastal zone preservation, women, workers, unions, business, finances, science, education, and decision making.

Whether and to what extent international cooperation would be obtained in support of these agreements, financial assistance to poor countries was seen as a necessity in order to make the international environmental process work. Rich and poor countries eventually agreed to employ the Global Environment Facility. This financial mechanism established in 1990 assisted poor countries in taking action to address "third-tier" environmental issues.[48]

AIR POLLUTION: GLOBAL WARMING AND THE GREENHOUSE EFFECT

Global warming is an alteration in the natural climatic processes in which, due to a buildup of carbon dioxide and other greenhouse gases, sunlight (solar radiation) that ordinarily reflects off the earth is trapped and absorbed on the earth, in the oceans, and in the clouds and other gases in the atmosphere.[1] The buildup of carbon dioxide and other greenhouse gases is due to the increased burning of fossil fuels, among other human activities. The result is a warming effect with attendant negative consequences that might include the melting of the polar caps and the rise in sea level; more severe hurricanes, storms, and drought; coastal flooding;[2] changes in agricultural patterns; desertification; and alteration in animal, plant, and insect populations, among others.[3] Moreover, another victim could be international tourism as coastal areas flood, ski resorts lack sufficient snow, and hiking and camping areas become too hot.[4] Nonetheless, some argue that there might be winners as well as losers in this area, as changes in the distribution of favorable and unfavorable growing patterns affect food production, and new economies and political relations change in response to global warming.[5]

The issue of climate change resulting from an alteration in the components of the atmosphere was raised in 1861 in an article in the *Journal of Science* by J. Tyndale, and again in 1896 when Svante Arrhenius, a Swedish chemist, noted that an increase in carbon dioxide in the atmosphere due to industrialization would have a warming effect on the future global climate.[6] Although scientists had accepted the notion that there had been a buildup in carbon dioxide in the atmosphere due to industrialization, the general consensus was that it would dissipate naturally. In 1938, the impact of human production of carbon dioxide was demonstrated by G. Callendar.[7] Twenty years later, on the basis of their research on the buildup of carbon dioxide in the atmosphere, scientists at Scripps Institution of Oceanography argued that "mankind is now engaged in a great experiment."[8] Three decades later, in 1988, Stephen Schneider of the National Center for Atmospheric Research suggested that global warming "could well cause climate change over the next two generations as large or larger than civilization has experienced."[9]

Automobiles are but one example of the human impact on the biosphere. Increasing amounts of carbon dioxide and other greenhouse gases in the atmosphere result, in part, from automobiles, which burn fossil fuels. At the current time, tens of millions of automobiles are produced with half a billion in operation globally.[10] Although the rich countries of the north are able to implement air pollution standards for these vehicles, opposition comes from the petroleum and automobile industry as well as auto workers who feel that their jobs are at risk. The poor countries of the south might be willing but lack the financial resources to implement substantive changes. Added to the accumulation of carbon dioxide in the atmosphere is the increasing use of nonrenewable resources including coal and natural gas, which also contribute greenhouse gases into the atmosphere.

One of the difficulties in addressing the global warming problem is securing international cooperation. Although several agreements are in effect, compromise has been needed, given the self-interest of each

continued

national government in agreeing to new obligations and responsibilities. Setting goals and time frames has divided wealthy countries. Concerns about industrial development on the part of the poor countries and their lack of finances is another problem. Furthermore, organized interests within countries provide yet another constraint on the decision-making process and international agreements.

In order to make progress toward reasonable goals regarding global warming, national interests may have to give way to future regional and global cooperative efforts. Political leaders and their delegates at international conferences have made commitments to work toward the reduction of greenhouse gases as signatories to several international agreements (Earth Summit 1992, Kyoto 1997), but they have been divided over objectives, pressured by fellow delegates, and argued for such things as voluntary rather than mandatory requirements. Although international agreements reflect progress, much more remains to be done regarding the global warming issue.

[1]Robert E. Morrison, *Global Climate Change* (Washington, DC: Congressional Research Service, Library of Congress, October 6, 1989), 2–3.

[2]The threat of coastal flooding is becoming a more severe concern for world governments because an increasing proportion of human populations live in coastal areas.

[3]See, for example, **http://www.state.gov**.

[4]See "Big Threat to Tourism in Global Warming," *International Herald Tribune* (August 30, 1999), 1.

[5]See, for instance, Eugene B. Skolnikoff, "Technology and the World Tomorrow," *Current History* 88 (January 1989), 7.

[6]See Gordon J. MacDonald, "Scientific Basis for the Greenhouse Effect," *Journal of Policy Analysis and Management* 7 (1988), 427; Michael Weisskopf, "The Evidence on the Greenhouse Effect," *The Washington Post National Weekly Edition* (August 29–September 4, 1988), 8. See also Lester Lave, "The Greenhouse Effect: What Government Actions Are Needed," *Journal of Policy Analysis and Management* 7 (1988) and Irving Mintzer, "Living in a Warmer World: Challenges for Policy Analysis and Management," *Journal of Policy Analysis and Management* 7 (1988).

[7]See MacDonald, "Scientific Basis for the Greenhouse Effect," 427.

[8]Ibid, 9.

[9]Quoted in Richard Wolkomir, "The Greenhouse Revolution: Climates are Changing—And So Will Coastlines as Sea Levels Rise," *Oceans* (April 1988), 19.

[10]See "Facing the Future: People and the Planet: The Atmosphere," at **http://www.facing thefuture.org/environment/enviro-5.htm**. Retrieved August 8, 2000.

Five years after the Earth Summit in Rio, delegates from industrialized countries met in Kyoto, Japan, to discuss climate change and the emission of greenhouse gases. The major problem that challenged participants concerned the level of reduction in greenhouse gases. While the goal was to reduce emissions to 1990 levels, the participants were given from 11 to 15 years to do so.[49] Due to variation in previous emission outputs, different targets in the amount of emission reductions were established as an incentive to encourage governments to sign the agreement. For example, where the United States was obligated to reduce its emissions by 7 percent, Japan had a 6 percent objective. However, in early 2001 President George W. Bush withdrew the U.S. commitment to the Kyoto Protocol.

National Security and the Environment

National security interests are likely to come into conflict with other interests, including environmental protection on a regional or international level. Several years ago, for instance, the environment was characterized as the "national-security issue of the early twenty-first century" because it had the following characteristics:

> The political and strategic impact of surging populations, spreading disease, deforestation and soil erosion, water depletion, air pollution, and possibly rising sea levels in critical, overcrowded regions like the Nile Delta and Bangladesh developments that will prompt mass migrations and, in turn, incite group conflicts will be the core foreign-policy challenge from which most others will ultimately emanate, arousing the public and uniting assorted interests left over from the Cold War.[50]

The linkage between national security and protecting the environment includes waging war, the nuclear arms race, and continuing access to vital natural resources located in ecologically sensitive areas, among others. Although Daniel Deudney argues against the notion that war waging and the preparation for war are major contributors toward environmental degradation, he acknowledges that environmental destruction is directly related to national defense because of the use of resources that could be employed for other sectors of society; the environmental destruction resulting from military explosives; and pollution as a direct result of national security measures.[51] For example, it is estimated that during U.S. military involvement in Vietnam, 80 percent of forestland and 50 percent of coastal habitat were destroyed due to the use of Agent Orange, an herbicide defoliant.[52] During the Persian Gulf War in 1990, the coastline of the gulf was polluted by oil spills, marine life suffered, and oil wells burned, emitting debris into the atmosphere.[53]

The Soviet-American nuclear arms race during the post–World War II period resulted in several treaties meant to reduce international tensions. The Antarctic Treaty of 1959, Limited Nuclear Test Ban Treaty of 1963, Outer Space Treaty of 1967, and Seabed Treaty of 1971 were established to prevent the placement and testing of weapons of mass destruction in strategic locations on land, under the sea, and in outer space. For example, in responding to the importance of the Limited Nuclear Test Ban treaty, Theodore Sorenson argued that President Kennedy made the United States a party to the treaty with the Soviet Union and United Kingdom because he was genuinely concerned about national security as well as the environmental and public health threat resulting from nuclear weapons explosions.[54] In the autumn of 1999, while reflecting on the history of the nuclear arms race, a member of the Russian Academy of Sciences and former advisor to then Russian President Boris Yeltsin stated that the Cold War arms race "has created environmental problems with which future generations will have to contend."[55] At about the same time, both President Clinton and the Russian government supported the Comprehensive Nuclear Test Ban Treaty, which was opposed by the Republican-controlled U.S. Senate. Moreover, preparation for nuclear war has had additional consequences. For example, the U.S. National Academy of Sciences recently reiterated what environmentalists were concerned about in the 1980s—namely, that preparation for nuclear war and nuclear testing has created "nuclear sacrifice zones"—public lands that are uninhabitable and will remain contaminated for years to come.[56]

Finally, former Secretary of State Madeleine Albright made it quite clear that the environment is now a central element in American foreign policy. Albright focused on threats to the global environment, their negative impact on the quality of life for Americans, and what should be done:[57]

- collaborative efforts are needed among countries to protect the environment
- political and economic instability are in many cases the result of conflicts over the environment
- the environment is threatened by human activities, which requires cooperative measures by the United States and other countries

For example, in the mid-1990s, as a result of sanctions imposed on Taiwan by the United States, Taiwan reversed its policy from being a participant in the rhino-horn and tiger-bone trade (prohibited under the Convention on International Trade in Endangered Species) to a working partner with the United States, in an effort to terminate this wildlife threat.[58]

Environmental Opinion: Citizens and Business Leaders

In Chapter 3, we discussed public opinion about the environment among American citizens. In this section, we provide a portrait of the political orientation of citizens in a few selected countries as well as the views of selected leaders concerning corporate responsibility.

Similar to their counterparts in the United States, citizens in other countries are confronted with numerous public policy problems. To what extent is the environment a salient issue for them? What is public concern about the role of business and environmental pollution? How might members of business groups conceive of the role of corporations regarding environmental protection?

In a 1993 global survey that asked citizens to list their country's "most important problem," responses included typical concerns about the economy and national security. Table 9.2 shows the environmental opinions of citizens in five countries of the industrialized world and in five poor countries. Almost 4 out of 10 citizens in Ireland and the Netherlands, followed by almost 3 in 10 in Mexico, view the environment as a most important problem. In contrast are the countries of Brazil and Nigeria, where the environment is much less prominent as a concern among citizens. The table shows wide variation in opinion about the environment as a most important problem. However, as we can see, citizens' concerns transcend the particular country's level of development, i.e., we find citizens in both industrialized and poor countries ranking the environment as either the most important or least important problem compared to other issues.

A recent poll of business groups in the United Kingdom, Germany, and France shows that the environment has become a more salient issue for the global busi-

TABLE 9.2

Citizens' Views of the Environment (selected countries)

	Environment as Most Important Problem	Difference from the Mean*
Ireland	39%	+22
Netherlands	39	+22
Mexico	29	+12
India	21	+4
Denmark	13	−4
United States	11	−6
Germany	9	−8
Russia	9	−8
Brazil	2	−15
Nigeria	1	−16

Source: Adapted from Riley E. Dunlap, George H. Gallup, Jr., and Alec M. Gallup, "Of Global Concern: Results of the Health of the Planet Survey," in Dennis L. Soden and Brent S. Steel, eds. *Handbook of Global Environmental Policy and Administration* (New York: Marcel Dekker, Inc., 1999), 11.

* Mean = 17

ness community.[59] Findings from the poll indicate that corporate responsibility must now take into consideration the impact of business practices on the environment.[60] Table 9.3 focuses on several environmental issue areas and their priority among members of the survey's business groups. Among the eight major environmental issues under consideration, air and water quality were considered most important followed by waste and recycling. Although the third-tier (and more complex) issues of climate change and biodiversity ranked third (18 points behind air and water quality), almost 4 out of 10 members of the business community ranked them as important.

What is clear is that the environment is an important issue for citizens in industrialized and poor countries, as well as an important consideration in terms of corporate responsibility. As we move forward into the twenty-first century it is very likely that the environment will remain a significant global issue for citizens and for political and economic elites.

In this chapter we have discussed several important issues that have implications for the global environment. In the following guest essay, Jaya Tiwari

TABLE 9.3

Business Sector Opinion about Environmental Issues

	Most Important Issue	Percentage Difference		
		(1–2)	(2–3)	(1–3)
1. Air and Water Quality	57%	+10		
2. Waste and Recycling	47		+8	
3. Climate Change and Biodiversity	39			+18

Source: Adapted from "Big Business Puts Environment in Its Big Picture, June 27, 2000, at **http://www.enn.com/news/ennstories/2000/06/06272000/envirosurvey_14227.asp?p=2**. Retrieved June 28, 2000.

discusses the role played by the two most populous countries in the world—India and the People's Republic of China—with their increasing demand for energy and the potential impact on the environment.

GUEST ESSAY:

Population, Energy, and Environment in India and China: A Difficult Balance

Jaya Tiwari
Graduate Programs in International Studies
Old Dominion University

According to a recent estimate published by the United Nations Population Information Network (UNPIN), the world population is currently increasing at a rate of 77 million per year.[1] Within the next five decades, by 2050, it is expected to grow to more than 9 billion. UNPIN estimates that most of the new population growth will be concentrated in the developing countries of Asia, Africa, and Latin America.[2] Rapidly growing populations and a continued march toward economic development in these countries will, most certainly, lead to increased energy demand for both domestic and industrial uses. In light of growing populations and economies, the International Energy Agency (IEA) has estimated the world energy demand will increase 65 percent by 2020, with two-thirds of this increase projected to take place in developing countries.

Current per-capita energy use in developing economies like India and China is less than one-tenth of that used in the United States (Table A). This situation, however, is slowly changing. IEA studies have shown that a country's energy demand rises in line with increasing gross domestic product (an indicator of economic growth or development).[3] As many countries in the developing world move toward further economic growth, their energy demand can be expected to rise. According to future energy trends projected by the IEA, developing countries like India and China, with their huge populations and rapidly growing economies, will experience a considerable increase in their energy consumption and production—sometimes at even higher growth rates than the industrialized world. For example, the IEA estimates that in the next decade the average annual demand for electricity (which is only a portion of a country's total energy needs) in the developed countries will increase by 1.9 percent while the increase in the demand in the developing world during the same period of time will be at least four times higher—5.4 percent in China and 5 percent in India.[4]

India and China, two of the most populated countries in the world, expect their energy needs to multiply tenfold in just a couple of decades. How to meet this growing demand for energy without causing irreversible damage to their natural environments—land, air, water, global temperature—will be one of their biggest challenges. Both China and India are major consumers and producers of energy and their energy decisions have global consequences. For example, in 1997 China became the world's second largest energy consumer following the United States. It is also the third largest energy producer, trailing the United States and Russia, and it is expected to surpass Russia in the near future. Currently China is the second largest emitter of carbon dioxide (CO_2) after the United States. During 1997, China's energy-related CO_2 emissions totaled

TABLE A

Energy Overview of China, India, and the United States

	Population (1999)	GDP (1999)	Real GDP Growth Rate	Total Energy Consumption (1998)	Per-Capita Energy Consumption (1998)	Energy-Related Carbon Emissions (1998)	Per-Capita Carbon Emissions	Energy Consumption by Sector			
								Industrial	Transportation	Residential	Commercial
China	1.2 billion	$1.03 trillion	6.9% (1999)	33.9 quadrillion Btu	28.25 million Btu	300 million metric tons	2.5 metric tons (1997)	62% (1996)	5% (1996)	28% (1996)	5% (1995)
India	1 billion	$406.1 billion	6.0% (1999) 6.4% (2000)	12.5 quadrillion Btu	12.9 million Btu	252.6 million metric tons	0.3 metric tons (1998)	68.0% (1997)	15.7% (1997)	12.6% (1997)	3.6% (1997)
United States	275 million	$9000 billion	4.5% (2000)	96.1 quadrillion Btu (1999)	350.7 million Btu	1494.6 million metric tons	5.5 metric tons	38.3% (1997)	26.4% (1997)	19.5% (1997)	15.7% (1997)

Source: United States Energy Information Administration at **http//:www.eia.doc.gov/emeu/cabs.htm.**

more than three billion tons, some 13 percent of the global total.[5] Because China still relies on coal for nearly three-quarters of its energy, it is predicted to exceed the U.S. share of carbon emissions by 2020.

Similar to their Chinese counterparts, Indian policymakers and other officials have also been struggling to meet the energy demands of more than a billion people and a rapidly growing economy. India is the world's sixth largest energy consumer and, despite low per-capita energy consumption, India was responsible for some 5 percent of total global CO_2 emissions in 1997.[6] Indians, like the Chinese, are heavily dependent on coal as the major source of their energy supply. Due to India's heavy reliance on coal, its share of total CO_2 emissions is expected to increase, as the country hikes its energy consumption and production. Large-scale emission of CO_2 gases by India and China is bound to have global environmental consequences since, unlike local and regional pollutants that mainly affect the environment close to their source, greenhouse gases, regardless of their place of origin, are diffused throughout the planetary atmosphere.[7]

Energy Needs and Environmental Protection: An Assessment of India and China

Population growth, energy use, and the environment are closely linked. While consumption of energy is vital to the survival and improvement of human life, the process of production and consumption of energy by human populations requires them to make certain changes in their environment. Some of these changes are minor and temporary—for example, a person chopping some branches from a single tree for the purpose of heating a home would give rise to a temporary and minor effect on the local environment. Such changes are quickly and naturally corrected. In the above example, new tree branches would grow to take the place of those removed. However, in the case of large populations, meeting energy needs in the above manner could engender large-scale deforestation, with associated environmental consequences that could be severe and long lasting. Unfortunately, India and China, each with over a billion inhabitants, as well as other developing countries, are facing such a situation when it comes to meeting the energy demands of their populations and industries.

Both India and China have experienced rapid population growth and increasing industrialization in the past few decades. In the case of India, during the past two decades the population has grown at an annual rate of 2 percent, passing the one-billionth person mark in May 2000.[8] India's economy and energy supply also grew considerably during the latter half of this period. The average growth rate for India's gross domestic product (GDP) between 1992 and 1997 was 6.9 percent.[9] The average annual growth rate of India's total energy supply jumped to 6.2 percent during the period 1990 to 1995, compared to 5.9 percent between 1971 and 1995.[10] The steady increase in Indian per-capita income has resulted in a high demand for electricity, driven considerably by domestic uses. India's total electricity demand over the next decade is expected to increase by 5 percent per year as compared to the global average increase rate of 3 percent during the same time.[11]

As in the case of most developing countries, India's tremendous population growth, coupled with a rapidly developing economy, has resulted in large-scale industrialization and urbanization, which have not necessarily been very well planned. Due to uneven economic growth patterns centered in certain parts of India, a large number of rural poor continue to migrate to selected metropolitan areas, creating an unbearable strain on the infrastructure and environment. For example, three Indian metropolitan regions, Delhi, Mumbai, and Chennai, are now among the world's 10 most polluted cities.[12] Major sources of pollutants in these cities are vehicular emissions, untreated industrial smoke, and untreated water effluents.

Close to 80 percent of the road vehicles in India use diesel fuel, a highly carbon-intensive source of energy that is one of the biggest contributors to air pollution in India.[13] Smoke and carbon emitted from road vehicles currently account for a staggering 70 percent of national air pollution.[14] The situation is worsened by industrial pollution. A large portion of Indian industry is still fueled by poor quality coal that releases massive amounts of carbon and sulfur into the atmosphere. Total pollution from industries, over the past two decades, has quadrupled while pollution from road vehicles has increased eight times during the same period.[15] Increasing air pollution in major Indian cities is blamed for thousands of deaths every year. According to India's Central Pollution Control Board, in 1995 there were 3,650 deaths and over 154,000 serious illnesses due to air pollution, twice the number that occurred during 1991–1992.[16]

Successive Indian governments have taken a number of steps to combat pollution. In 1976, India became the first country to include an addition to its constitution (the 42nd Amendment) for allowing the state to intervene and protect public health, forests, and wildlife. Under the Environmental Protection Act of 1986, the Ministry of Environment and Forests (MEF) was assigned overall responsibility for administering and enforcing environmental legislation and policies whose main focus has been to reduce industrial pollution. The government has also begun to take steps to enforce emission standards on automobiles.

Similar to India, China is also facing the difficult challenge of balancing its growing energy needs while maintaining environmental balance. A large population and rapid economic growth in China have certainly affected the environment in an adverse way. According to 1999 estimates, China's population is 1.24 billion.[17] During the past decade, the Chinese economy has registered an average growth rate of more than 9 percent, and it is expected to continue at 5.5 percent per annum for the next two decades. As in India, the industrial and urban centers in China continue to attract large numbers of people, overwhelming the infrastructure and environment in these areas. According to a report released in 1998 by the World Health Organization (WHO), out of the 10 most polluted cities in the world, 7 are in China. Respiratory diseases, contracted mostly due to air and water pollution, are now a leading cause of death in China.[18] Interestingly, because of the communist social structure where the transport system is mostly government-owned, private vehicle ownership is small. Thus China's road transport–related pollution is relatively low. Currently, passenger vehicle ownership is 3 per 1,000 people, a very modest number even when compared to a developing country.[19] Bicycles and animal carts are still the primary means of transportation.

Large-scale deforestation due to energy, housing, and industrial needs along with soil erosion has been responsible for an estimated loss of one-fifth of agricultural land since 1949.[20] In fact, in the summer of 1999, uncontrolled soil erosion was believed to be the major cause of a devastating flood that killed 3,600 people and left millions homeless.[21] As the Chinese premier acknowledged, this and other tragedies might be an indication that China, in its drive for economic development, had for too long ignored nature and the environment and that there should be "coordinated development of the economy and ecological environment."[22]

China is the world's largest coal producer and coal accounts for about 60 percent of the country's total energy supply.[23] Chinese coal is relatively high in ash and has high-to-medium sulfur content.[24] The overwhelming use of high-ash, high-sulfur coal as a fuel in China has led to abundant air pollution and acid rain and has caused enormous environmental damage. While acid rain is a particular problem in the southeastern and south-central parts of China, it is estimated to affect more than 30 percent of China's total land area, destroying forests and ecosystems.[25] Parts of China's neighboring countries, including South Korea and Japan, are also affected by acid rain originating in China. Chinese industries emit a total of 21 million tons of sulfur dioxide into the atmosphere each year.[26] Adding to that are some 14 million tons of smoke-filled dust and another 13 million tons of powder-like particulates which, through wind, rain, or snowfall, are carried and dumped over a large portion of the country and its neighboring states.[27]

In order to control increasing levels of pollution, the Chinese government has taken a number of steps. For example, in the capital city of Beijing, the government has ordered city vehicles to convert to liquefied petroleum gas and natural gas to reduce the level of air pollution.[28] Chinese Prime Minister, Jiang Zemin, has appealed for a more environmentally friendly economic development and his government has been considering some drastic changes for managing industrial pollution. These changes include gradually replacing coal combustion with clean energy resources such as "renewable" energy forms and natural gas; banning the discharge of air pollutants above a certain level in the atmosphere; and imposing heavy fines on industries and people violating environmental laws.[29]

Energy Supply in India and China: Current Sources and Future Trends

Each type of energy generation produces a certain amount of waste potentially harmful to humans and the environment. Coal and oil produce the largest amount of waste, while nuclear power produces the least (Table B). As far as the relative efficiency of these energy sources is concerned, the fossil fuels rank (from lowest to highest efficiency) as follows: coal, oil, and natural gas. Nuclear energy is the most efficient of the energy sources listed in the table. While nuclear energy is highly efficient and its compressed waste is considerably smaller than the waste produced by other sources, due to its highly radioactive nature, the waste requires long-term storage and is difficult to clean up if released into the environment.

TABLE B

Energy Sources: Waste Production and Energy Efficiency

	Non-Nuclear Sources of Energy			Nuclear Energy
	Coal	Oil	Natural Gas	Nuclear Energy
Annual Solid Waste Production, 1000 MW Plant	500,000 MT	300,000 MT	200,000 MT	20 M^3
Energy Efficiency	Low	Medium	High	Highest

Note: MT= Metric Tons

MW = Megawatts

M^3 = Cubic Meters

Source: Adapted from Richard Rhodes and Denis Beller, "The Need for Nuclear Power," *Foreign Affairs* 79 (January–February, 2000), 39.

Coal

In India and China, coal is the principal fuel for both power generation and industrial production. In addition to being an inefficient source of energy compared to other sources, coal is the most carbon intensive of all conventional fossil fuels. During the combustion process, coal releases high amounts of carbon monoxide (CO), nitrogen oxides (NO_X), carbon dioxide (CO_2), and sulfur oxides (SO_X), all of which are gases known for polluting the environment.[30]

Despite being a major source of environmental pollution, coal currently accounts for about three-quarters of total electricity generation in China and for about 70 percent in India.[31] Electricity demand in both countries is expected to increase rapidly, and the share of coal in power generation will remain considerable. China, the world's largest coal producer, has an estimated reserve of some 114.5 billion tons, which is 11 percent of the known global reserve.[32] In 1997, China dug 1.37 billion tons of coal, making up about 60 percent of the country's total energy supply.[33] It is estimated that the currently known Chinese coal reserve is sufficient to sustain the current rate of production for 82 years and new reserves may be identified.[34] During a recent one-year period (1998–1999), India's coal production totaled 290.04 million tons and consisted of 67 percent of the country's total commercial requirements.[35] India imports about 20 percent of its coal, while its own current coal reserves are estimated to be sufficient for sustaining the current rate of production for the next 30 years.[36]

As detailed in the previous section, due to the high use of coal to meet energy needs, both India and China are confronted by major pollution challenges. Efforts are under way in both countries to reduce their dependence on coal and also to move toward cleaner burning coal.

Oil and Natural Gas

From an environmental point of view, liquefied natural gas (LNG), which consists mainly of methane gas (CH_4), is the cleanest source of energy among fossil fuels. Efficient combustion of natural gas produces mainly carbon dioxide (CO_2) and water (H_2O), with variable quantities of nitrogen oxide (NO_X) generated during the combustion process, when the air is raised to high temperatures.[37] Crude oil, on the other hand, consists of a complex range of hydrocarbons, a number of which are known carcinogens. In addition to carbon and hydrogen, it contains variable quantities of nitrogen and sulfur. Combustion of oil results in emission of carbon monoxide, CO_2, and H_2O (depending on the efficiency of the combustion process), a range of hydrocarbons, and significant quantities of nitrogen and sulfur oxides.[38]

After coal, oil and natural gas are the most important contributors to the energy supplies of China and India. In 1996 and 1997, 22.9 percent of India's total primary energy supply consisted of oil and gas, with crude oil accounting for 19.1 percent.[39] India does not have abundant oil and gas resources, yet the country's demand for these fuel sources is growing at a rate of 5 percent per year.[40] India imported 38 million tons of crude oil and 25.5 million tons of oil products in 1997, some 60 percent of its oil.[41] Given the increasing demand from the industrial and transport sectors, it is likely to import large quantities of petroleum in the coming decades.

Among the components of India's total energy needs, LNG demand is the fastest growing. It is expected to meet 15 to 18 percent of the total energy demand in the next century.[42] In its quest to move toward cleaner sources of energy, the Indian government has been considering replacement of a number of its coal-fired power generators with plants fired by natural gas. Consequently, India plans to import more than 10 million tons of LNG in the next decade.[43]

As in India, a significant portion of the Chinese energy supply comes from oil and LNG. China is Asia's largest oil producer and ranks sixth in the world.[44] Despite China's large domestic production, since 1993 the country's increasing energy needs have forced it to import petroleum. Chinese oil reserves are large and currently estimated to be around 28.8 billion tons. Still, due to the rising demand, it is estimated that it will import half of its oil by 2010.[45] China has considerable reserves of natural gas, estimated around 1.16 trillion cubic meters. However, due to lack of infrastructure, the production and consumption of natural gas are low.[46] Natural gas's current share—only 2 percent of the total energy supply—is projected to quadruple by 2020.[47]

Nuclear Power

Although the most efficient of the energy sources, nuclear energy has problems of its own such as operational safety and waste disposal. Currently, nuclear power constitutes a small percentage of India's and China's total energy supply; however, it is viewed as an important source of future energy. Both India and China have extensive nuclear infrastructures and ambitious plans for increasing their nuclear energy production by 2020. Nuclear energy's share in China's total energy use has been steadily increasing since 1995 and, by 2020, China's use of nuclear power is expected to increase fourfold.[48] Official estimates call for 20 Gigawatts (GW) of nuclear power capacity by 2010, and 40 to 50 GW by 2020.[49] There are four new nuclear plants under construction. With its newly purchased reactors from the United States, and offers from French, Japanese, and British companies for construction of new plants, China's nuclear energy sector is poised to flourish in the coming decades.

India initiated its civilian nuclear program in 1969 with the commissioning of the Tarapur power plant. The country currently has 10 operating power plants, which contribute about 2 percent of the energy supply. There are four more plants, each with 202 Megawatt (MW) capacity, under construction.[50] India plans to increase its nuclear power capacity to 20 GW by 2020 with the help of two new reactors recently purchased from Russia.[51]

Hydroelectric Power

Both China and India are rich in hydro resources, which have been put forward as an alternative source of energy in both countries. While it is a relatively clean source of energy as compared to coal or oil, it is still problematic. Because of its role in displacing people and destroying local ecosystems, environmentalists have criticized hydroelectric projects.

Hydroelectric power currently makes up less than 2 percent of the Chinese primary energy supply.[52] In 1996, China's total hydropower capacity stood at 56 GW, which is expected to reach about 200 GW by 2020.[53] The most significant portion of the increased hydropower supply would come from China's most ambitious hydro-project, the Three Gorges. Upon its completion in 2010, this 185 meter high, 1.6 kilometers-wide dam will be the world's largest. With its 26 generators, each capable of producing 700 MW of electricity, the Three Gorges will have a capacity of 18.2 GW.[54] The project, however, has faced strong criticism from political activists and environmental lobbying groups for its impact on the environment and people. Many fear it will be damaging to the regional ecosystem and environmental balance. It has been argued that very little attention is being given to potential accretion of toxic waste and other pollutants from industrial sites that will be flooded after construction of the dam. The project required that the third-longest river in the world, the Yangtze, be diverted from it natural course in 1997. Completion of the project would require displacement of some 1.26 million people.[55]

India, which has abundant potential in the area of hydropower, has thus far developed 15 percent of its total hydro resources, with plans under way to develop an additional 7 percent. Plans have already been approved to build 12 large-scale hydro projects, which will add 3.7 GW of power generation capacity.[56] In the near future, an additional increase of 5.81 GW of hydropower from new state sector projects and some 350 MW from private sector projects are expected as well. However, like the Three Gorges project, large hydropower projects in India, including the Narmada River Dam Project, are facing massive protests because of their environmental and human consequences.

Renewable Energy

Currently, India has the largest programs in the world for renewable energy. According to current planning, by year 2012, close to 10 percent of total power generation capacity in the country is likely to come from renewable sources.[57] The government is considering a comprehensive policy to accelerate development of renewable energy sources as a substitute for fossil fuel. In 1998, India was the world's fourth largest wind-power producer, with a capacity of 1,024 MW, and the third largest in photovoltaics with 47 MW.[58] At the same time, biomass, a high-waste, low-energy density source is one of the major means for cooking and heating energy in poor rural households.

The Shangdu wind farm in Inner Mongolia and geothermal energy sources in Tibet are significant examples of renewable energy in China. However, as in India, the majority of rural households in China rely on biomass for their energy supply. China is the world's largest consumer of biomass energy, having some 800 million people and half a million rural enterprises depending on biomass.

A Difficult Balance: India China, and the Environment

Energy production and consumption are the most significant contributors to the buildup of greenhouse gases in the atmosphere.[59] Currently, energy uses in developed countries, namely the United States, Russia, and Western Europe, account for some 85 percent of total greenhouse gas emissions.[60] However, energy-related emissions in the developing world, including India and China, are rapidly increasing. As a country's energy demand grows, its choice of energy sources becomes important for environmental balance, not only for the country itself but also for its neighbors.

The environmental impact of energy decisions by leaders of countries as large as India and China (both in terms of geography and population) has already proven to affect more than those leaders' own countries. This is especially the case with acid rain, which results in one country's emissions of pollutants being transported through air currents to neighboring nations. China's close geographic neighbors such as Japan and South Korea have firsthand experience with the results of poor quality coal burning in China. Carbon emitted from the tremendous amount of coal burned to meet Chinese energy needs has been drifting over the Japanese and Korean shores and created acid rain damaging the ecosystems in these countries.

Because China already accounts for more than a tenth of world CO_2 emissions, and India for more than 5 percent, the way in which they choose to meet their energy needs will be critical for the future regional and global environment. Problems of transboundary pollutants such as acid rain and greenhouse gases can only be combatted through cooperative means. For example, efforts of the developed countries to reduce CO_2 emissions would make little difference if they failed to bring India and China into a reduction framework, since over the next two decades India's and China's combined CO_2 emissions will surpass total emissions from all the developed countries. Neither India nor China ratified the Kyoto Protocol and thus were not legally obligated to reduce their CO_2 emissions. Also, given that both countries joined the race for economic development later than most European countries and are the two most populated countries, it is not surprising that they resist pressure for reduced CO_2 emissions.

The international community is slowly turning its attention to the serious pollution problems in India and China. During President Clinton's visit to India in March 2000, a number of bilateral agreements were discussed and signed to help India develop cleaner sources of energy and reduce the current pollution level. On a regional level, China, South Korea, and Japan have agreed to launch a five-year project to control transboundary air pollutants and acid rain. While these are steps in the right direction, given the rapid growth in the energy needs of India and China, more comprehensive regional and international cooperation will be needed.

Guest Essay Endnotes

1   *World Almanac 2000* (New Jersey: World Almanac Book, 1999), 878–879.

2   Ibid.

3   International Energy Agency, *World Energy Outlook 1999* (Paris, France: OECD/IEA, 1999), 35.

4   Ibid.

5   Ibid. 101.

6   International Energy Agency, *World Energy Outlook 1998* (Paris, France: OECD/IEA, 1998), 323.

7   Ibid., 39.

8   According to the 1999 estimates provided by the Indian Government, the Indian population is currently estimated to be growing at an annual rate of 1.68 percent.

9   *World Energy Outlook 1999*, 130.

10 Ibid., 132.

11 Ibid.

12 Reshma Prakash, "Democracy not enough to combat population and poverty in India," *Earth Times*, Dec. 23, 1999, **http://www.earthtimes.org/dec/population democracynotenoughdec23_99.htm**.

13 *World Energy Outlook 1998*, 333.

14 United States Energy Information Administration (EIA), "India Environmental Issues," EIA, November 1999, **http//:www.eia.doc.gov/emeu/cabs/indiaenv.htm**.

15 Ibid.

16 "Air Pollution Touches Alarming Levels in City," the *Times of India*, March 25, 2000.

17 Due to a successful population control policy, China was able to bring its population growth rate below 1 percent in 1999. Chinese policymakers are confident that they will be able to meet the country's goal of keeping population within 1.3 billion by the year 2000. Xinhua News Agency, "China Confident of Meeting Population Control Goal," June 24, 1999.

18 United States Energy Information Administration (EIA), "China: Environmental Issues," EIA, November 1999, **http//:www.eia.doc.gov/emeu/cabs/chinaenv.htm**.

19 *World Energy Outlook 1999*, 285.

20 United States Energy Information Administration (EIA), "China: Environmental Issues," EIA, November 1999, **http//:www.eia.doc.gov/emeu/cabs/chinaenv.htm**.

21 "Toxic China," *Time International*, March 1, 1999, vol. 153, no. 8, 16.

22 Ibid.

23 *World Energy Outlook 1999*, 95.

24 Ibid.

25 United States Energy Information Administration (EIA), "China: Environmental Issues," EIA, November 1999, **http//:www.eia.doc.gov/emeu/cabs/chinaenv.htm**.

26 Ibid.

27 Ibid.

28 Ibid.

29 Ibid.

30 Michael B. McElory, "Industrial Growth, Air Pollution, and Environmental Damage: Complex Challenge for China," in Michael B. McElory, Chris P. Nielsen, and Peter Lydon, eds. *Energizing China: Reconciling Environmental Protection and Economic Growth* (Cambridge: Harvard University Press, 1998), 246.

31 *World Energy Outlook 1999*, 38.

32 Ibid., 95.

[33] Ibid.

[34] Ibid.

[35] Ministry of Information and Broadcasting, *India 2000: A Reference Annual* (Government of India Press, Patiala House, New Delhi: 2000), 192–193.

[36] Shebonti ray Dadwal, "India's Energy Security Policy: A Case for Nuclear Power," *Strategic Analysis*, vol. 28, no. 8 (November 1999), **http://www.idsa-india.org/an-nov9-4.html**.

[37] Michael B. McElory, "Industrial Growth, Air Pollution, and Environmental Damage: Complex Challenge for China," in Michael B. McElory, Chris P. Nielsen, and Peter Lydon, eds. *Energizing China: Reconciling Environmental Protection and Economic Growth* (Cambridge: Harvard University Press, 1998), 246.

[38] Ibid.

[39] *World Energy Outlook 1999*, 132.

[40] Juli A. MacDonald and S. Enders Wimbush, "India's Energy Security," *Strategic Analysis*, vol. 28, no. 5 (August 1999), **http://www.idsa-india.org/an-aug9-9.html**.

[41] *World Energy Outlook 1999*, 133.

[42] Juli A. MacDonald and S. Enders Wimbush, "India's Energy Security," *Strategic Analysis*, vol. 28, no. 5 (August 1999), **http://www.idsa-india.org/an-aug9-9.html**.

[43] Ibid.

[44] Ibid.

[45] Ibid., 97.

[46] Ibid., 99.

[47] Swaran Singh, "China's Energy Policy for 21st Century," *Strategic Analysis*, vol. 27, no. 12 (March 1999), **http://www.idsa-india.org/an-mar9-5.html**.

[48] United States Energy Information Administration (EIA), "China: Environmental Issues," EIA, November 1999, **http//:www.eia.doc.gov/emeu/cabs/chinaenv.htm**.

[49] *World Energy Outlook 1998*, 289.

[50] Ibid., 337.

[51] *India 2000: A Reference Annual*, 155.

[52] *World Energy Outlook 1998*, 288.

[53] Ibid.

[54] Ibid.

[55] Ibid.

[56] Shebonti ray Dadwal, "India's Energy Security Policy: A Case for Nuclear Power," **http://www.idsa-india.org/an-nov9-4.html**.

[57] *India 2000: A Reference Annual*, 511.

[58] *World Energy Outlook 1999*, 136

[59] Ibid., 36.

[60] Ibid.

Conclusion

More than two decades ago in his May 1977 *Environmental Message to the Congress*, President Jimmy Carter directed the Council on Environmental Quality and the Department of State, along with several other federal agencies, to assess the state of the environment. In his message, the president observed that "Environmental problems do not stop at national boundaries. In the past decade, we and other nations have come to recognize the urgency of international efforts to protect our common environment."[61] The subsequent study evaluated a variety of global environmental problems and potential consequences. The urgency of these problems was emphasized, as was the need to formulate goals and implement strategies to resolve them before they worsened. The major finding of the 1980 report suggested that:

> If present trends continue, the world in 2000 will be more crowded, more polluted, less stable ecologically, and more vulnerable to disruption than the world we live in now. Serious stresses involving population, resources, and environment are clearly visible ahead. Despite greater material output, the world's people will be poorer in many ways than they are today.[62]

As we have seen, regional and international cooperation has resulted in numerous agreements for the purpose of improving the quality of the environment. Moreover, GNGOs have been active in promoting environmentalism on a global scale. At the same time, while some international organizations have been effective in promoting environmentalism (e.g., UNEP) others have been the center of controversy and criticism for putting material interests above environmental concerns (e.g., WTO).

Whether and to what extent environmentalism will have the same impact as "the Renaissance, the Reformation, and the Industrial Age," as one observer argues,[63] remains to be seen. Nonetheless, the human impact on the environment has received increasing attention by governments both rich and poor as well as by citizens around the world.

For example, on the one hand, in 1987 political leaders were able to come together to forge an agreement to address the problem of stratospheric ozone depletion. On the other hand, global warming and the greenhouse effect continue to be a contentious yet crucial issue. Recently a group of scientists reported in the *Proceedings of the National Academy of Sciences* that the impact of carbon dioxide is not as great as originally assumed and that other greenhouse gases are apparently responsible for global warming.[64] Political leaders and members of the scientific community argue over what type of action to take with regard to greenhouse gas emissions, and the debate over climatic change continues. In late August 2000, scientists working with the United Nations' Intergovernmental Panel on Climate Change confirmed that for the first time in human history, "an ice-free patch of ocean . . . has opened at the top of the world . . . and is more evidence that global warming may be real."[65] Where Antarctica was the center of attention regarding the "hole in the ozone" issue, the Arctic has now assumed an important place in the environmental debate over global warming.

In his recent book *Earth Odyssey*, Mark Hertsgaard relates his experiences traveling around the world during the 1990s to almost 20 different countries to learn more about the health of the global environment and the future of the human species. He concludes his journey of several years with the following admonition:

> The outlook is uncertain, the hour late, the earth a place of both beauty and despair. The fight for what's right is never ending, but the rewards are immense. Humans may or may not still be able to halt the drift toward ecological disaster, but we will find out only if we rouse ourselves and take common and determined action.[66]

Web Sites
Global Environmental Policy:

United Nations Environment Programme: **www.unep.org**

United Nations Commission on Sustainable Development: **www.un.org/esa/sustdev/csd.htm**

Convention on International Trade in Endangered Species: **www.cites.org**

Convention on Biological Diversity: **www.biodiv.org**

World Wildlife Fund: **www.worldwildlife.org**

Organization for Economic Cooperation and Development: **www.oecd.org/env**

United Nations Population Fund: **www.unfpa.org**

U.S. State Department: **www.state.gov**

European Environment Agency: **www.eea.eu.int**

International Whaling Commission: **www.iwc.org**

World Meteorological Organization: **www.wmo.org**

Greenpeace International: **www.greenpeace.org**

World Trade Organization: **www.wto.org**

Intergovernmental Panel on Climate Change: **www.ipcc.ch**

International Chamber of Commerce: **www.iccwbo.org**

Endnotes

[1] See James Brooke, "Arctic Shortcut for Shipping Raises New Fears in Canada," *New York Times,* July 29, 2000, A1, A6.

[2] Vaclav Smil, "Our Changing Environment," *Current History* 88 (January 1989), 12.

[3] See David John Frank, "Science, Nature, and the Globalization of the Environment, 1870–1990," *Social Forces* 76 (December 1997).

[4] James N. Rosenau, "Environmental Challenges in a Global Context," in Sheldon Kamieniecki, *Environmental Politics in the International Arena: Movements, Parties, Organizations, and Policy* (Albany: State University of New York Press, 1993), 257.

[5] Ibid., 258.

[6] Paul Wapner, *Environmental Activism and World Civic Politics* (Albany: State University of New York Press, 1996), 1.

[7] See "Malaria Peril Derails Efforts to Ban DDT," *International Herald Tribune,* August 30, 1999, 2.

[8] See Lynne T. Edgerton, *The Rising Tide: Global Warming and World Sea Levels* (Washington, DC: Island Press, 1991), Chapter 4.

[9] See Jonathan P. West and Glen Sussman, "Implementation of Environmental Policy: The Chief Executive," in Dennis L. Soden, ed. *The Environmental Presidency* (Albany: State University of New York Press, 1999), 102–104.

10 Lynton Keith Caldwell, *International Environmental Policy: From the Twentieth to the Twenty-First Century* (Durham: Duke University Press, 1996), 5–10.

11 See G. Tyler Miller, Jr., *Living in the Environment*, 7th ed. (Belmont, CA: Wadsworth Publishing Company, 1992), 6.

12 Paul R. and Anne H. Ehrlich, "The Most Overpopulated Nation," in Lindsey Grant, ed. *Elephants in the Volkswagen: Facing the Tough Questions About Our Overpopulated Country* (New York: W.H. Freeman and Company, 1992), 130.

13 "International Population Assistance: U.S. Support for Family Planning Practices and Reproductive Health," *Congressional Digest* 76 (April 1997), 99.

14 "Cold War's Demise Shapes $26.3 Billion Spending Bill," *Congressional Quarterly Weekly Report* (October 10, 1992), 3178.

15 See Margot Higgins, "You Wouldn't Want to Live Here, Report Says," September 24, 1999 at **http://www.enn.com/news/enn-stories/1999/09/092499/creport_5856.asp**. Retrieved August 8, 2000.

16 Ibid.

17 See David E. Gushee, *Stratospheric Ozone Depletion: Regulatory Issues* (Washington, DC: Congressional Research Service, Library of Congress, October 17, 1989), 3.

18 See Tyler, *Living in the Environment*, 296–301.

19 See William Booth, "Severe Ozone Depletion Likely Again This Year," *Washington Post*, October 6, 1989, A18; Susan J. Buck, *The Global Commons: An Introduction* (Washington, DC: Island Press, 1998), 123.

20 For a full discussion of ozone diplomacy see Richard Elliot Benedick, *Ozone Diplomacy: New Directions in Safeguarding the Planet*, enlarged edition (Cambridge, MA: Harvard University Press, 1998).

21 Joanne M. Kauffman, "Domestic and International Linkages in Global Environmental Politics: A Case-Study of the Montreal Protocol," in Miranda A. Schreurs and Elizabeth C. Economy, eds. *The Internationalization of Environmental Protection* (Cambridge: Cambridge University Press, 1997), 75.

22 See Malcolm W. Browne, "In Protecting the Atmosphere, Choices are Costly and Complex," *New York Times*, March 7, 1989, C1, C13.

23 See Oran R. Young, "Rights, Rules, and Resources in World Affairs," in Oran R. Young, ed. *Global Governance: Drawing Insights from the Environmental Experience* (Cambridge, MA: The MIT Press, 1997), 7–9.

24 James Connelly and Graham Smith, *Politics and the Environment: From Theory to Practice* (New York: Routledge, 1999), 198.

25 See Young, *Global Governance*, 98.

26 See David G. Victor, Abram Chayes, Eugene B. Skolnikoff, "Pragmatic Approaches to Regime Building for Complex International Problems," in Nazli Choucri, ed. *Global Accord: Environmental Challenges and International Responses* (Cambridge, MA: The MIT Press, 1993), 463.

27 See United Nations Environment Program, "UNEP Achievements," August 16, 2000 at **http://www.unep.org/Documents/Default.asp?DocumentID=43&ArticleID=250**. Retrieved August 16, 2000.

28 Kurt Tudyka, "Regulation Problems of a General European Environmental Policy," in Markus Jachtenfuchs and Michael Strubel, eds. *Environmental Policy in Europe* (Baden-Baden: Nomos Verlagsgesellschaft, 1992), 234.

29 United Nations Environment Program, *Global Environment Outlook* (New York: Oxford University Press, 1997), 75.

30 European Environment Agency, *Environment in the European Union 1996: Report for the Review of the Fifth Environmental Action Program* (Luxembourg: Office for Official Publications of the European Communities, 1995), 1.

31 See Glen Sussman, "The European Union and Environmental Policy," in Dennis L. Soden and Brent Steel, eds., *Global Environmental Policy and Administration* (New York: Marcel Dekker Publishers, 1999), 485–486.

32 See Caldwell, *International Environmental Policy*, 133.

33 See Konrad von Moltke, "The Structure of Regimes for Trade and the Environment," in Oran R. Young, ed. *Global Governance: Drawing Insights from the Environmental Experience* (Cambridge, MA: The MIT Press, 1997), 259.

34 See Gary Bryner, *From Promises to Performance: Achieving Global Environmental Goals* (New York: W.W. Norton & Company, 1997), 227.

35 See "The Clinton Administration Agenda for the Seattle WTO," Office of the Press Secretary, The White House, November 24, 1999.

36 Ibid.

37 See Paul Wapner, "Politics Beyond the State: Environmental Activism and World Civic Politics," *World Politics* 47 (April 1995).

38 See Lamond Hempel, *Environmental Governance: The Global Challenge* (Washington, DC: Island Press, 1996), 137, and John McCormick, "International Nongovernmental Organizations: Prospects for a Global Environmental Movement," in Sheldon Kamieniecki, *Environmental Politics in the International Arena: Movements, Organizations, and Parties* (Albany: State University of New York Press, 1993), 141.

39 See Peter M. Haas, *Saving the Mediterranean: The Politics of International Environmental Cooperation* (New York: Columbia University Press, 1990), 8; Kirkpatrick Sale, *The Green Revolution: The American Environmental Movement, 1962–1992* (New York: Hill and Wang, 1993), 40.

40 See Ibid.; Bryner, *From Promises to Performance*, 15.

41 Hempel, 30.

42 Caldwell, *International Environmental Policy* 243.

43 Stanley P. Johnson, *The Earth Summit: The United Nations Conference on Environment and Development (UNCED)* (Boston: Graham & Trotman/Martinus Nijhoff, 1993), 62.

44 For more information about the actions taken by the United States and other signatories to the convention see, for instance, Bill Clinton and Al Gore, *The Climate Change Action Plan* (Washington, DC: Executive Office of the President, 1993) and International Energy Agency and Organization for Economic Co-Operation and Development, *Climate Change Policy Initiatives: 1994 Update, Volume 1, OECD Countries* (Paris, France: IEA/OECD, 1994).

45 Johnson, *The Earth Summit*, 288.

46 Ibid., 129.

47 Ibid., 126–127.

48 See David Fairman, "The Global Environmental Facility," in Robert O. Keohane and Marc A. Levy, eds. *Institutions for Environmental Aid* (Cambridge, MA: The MIT Press, 1996), 66–69.

49 See Kline, *First Along the River*, 135–136.

50 Robert Kaplan, "The Coming Anarchy," *The Atlantic Monthly* (February 1974) at **http://www.facingthefuture.org/environment/enviro-1.htm**. Retrieved August 8, 2000.

51 See David Deudney, "The Case Against Linking Environmental Degradation and National Security," in Ken Conca and Geoffrey D. Dabelko, eds. *Green Planet Blues: Environmental Politics from Stockholm to Kyoto* (Boulder, CO: Westview Press, 1998), 306.

[52] See E. W. Pfeiffer, "The Ecology of War: Degreening Vietnam," *Natural History* 99 (November 1990), 37–40.

[53] See Charles H. Southwick, *Global Ecology in Human Perspective* (New York and Oxford: Oxford University Press, 1996), 318.

[54] See Theodore C. Sorenson, *Kennedy* (New York: Harper & Row, 1965), 621.

[55] See "Russian Scientist Mulls Legacy of Nuclear Race," *The Japan Times,* August 31, 1999, 10.

[56] See Matthew L. Wald, "Nuclear Sites May Be Toxic in Perpetuity, Report Finds," *New York Times,* August 8, 2000, A16.

[57] See "Environmental Diplomacy: The Environment and U.S. Foreign Policy," The United States State Department at **http://www.state.gov/www/global/oes/earth. html**. Retrieved June 10, 1999.

[58] Ibid.

[59] The business groups included institutional investors, financial and business media, regulators, and nongovernmental organizations.

[60] See "Big Business Puts Environment in Its Big Picture," June 27, 2000, at **http://www.enn.com/news/enn-stories/2000/06/06272000/envirosurvey_14227.asp?p=2**. Retrieved June 28, 2000.

[61] See *The Global 2000 Report to the President: Entering the Twenty-First Century* (New York, Penguin Books, 1982), preface.

[62] Ibid., 1.

[63] See Smil, "Our Changing Environment," 48.

[64] See Andrew C. Revkin, "Study Proposes New Strategy to Stem Global Warming," *New York Times,* August 19, 2000, A13.

[65] John Noble Wilford, "Ages Old Icecap at North Pole Is Now Liquid, Scientists Find," *New York Times,* August 19, 2000, A1, A13.

[66] Mark Hertsgaard, *Earth Odyssey: Around the World in Search of Our Environmental Future* (New York: Broadway Books, 1998), 335.

10

Conclusion: American Politics and the Environment

Environmental policy is one of the oldest social issues. Because it has been with us for so many years, it is no surprise that many United States citizens see themselves as "environmentalists." Jedediah Purdy estimates that "[m]ore than two-thirds of Americans call themselves environmentalists."[1] Other researchers have estimated that the percentage is even higher.[2] Purdy maintains that those considering themselves environmentalists are of varying types in society, including "every serious presidential candidate, a growing list of corporate executives, some of the country's most extreme radicals, and ordinary people from just about every region, class, and ethnic group."[3] Yet it is still *unclear* what these people mean when they call themselves "environmentalists."

One reason why it is difficult to agree on the meaning of environmentalism can be attributed, in part, to the divisions within the issue area itself. Environmentalism can be divided into at least three diverse persuasions: 1) romantic environmentalists, 2) managerial environmentalists, and 3) environmental justice advocates.[4] The first two date from the days of John Muir and Teddy Roosevelt, the most visible creators and articulators of these two types, and represent approaches that have long distinguished the environmental movement. Their followers are commonly referred to as *preservationists* and *conservationists.* Environmental justice is the most recent approach to the environment. Advocates are particularly concerned with the potential dangers to the environment and to those who might live in urban areas of poverty who have to confront air pollution, the dangers of chemical waste, excess garbage, and other health hazards.

Within each of these three approaches to environmental policy exist distinct objectives, unmistakable priorities, and specific methods of achieving their intentions. The three often conflict with each other. As an example, *preservationists* are inspired by their love of beautiful landscapes, as motivated by the ideas of John Muir and the Sierra Club, and wish to set aside wilderness areas, without any concern for economic needs or public access. *Conservationists,* on the other hand, look to the goals and aspirations of Teddy Roosevelt in attempting to balance ecology with considerations of the economy, in response to human needs. Those advocating *environmental justice* focus not only on the environment, but also on equality and human rights, suggesting that regardless of who we are or where we live we all have a right to a liveable environment.[5] Advocates of these three approaches to the environment may each well demand that their distinct approach be given priority in the public forum.

Policymakers have been more likely to adopt conservationist principles. For instance, among modern presidents, Franklin Roosevelt turned the nation's attention to conservation in the United States by aggressively supporting such issues as land management and conservation of national resources. Bill Clinton, however, emphasized environmental justice by advocating that citizens have the right to a clean and safe environment regardless of where they live and spend their time.

The environmental movement lacks philosophical unity in several respects. This is because environmentalism is an issue area of such great complexity and diversity. It is the most elaborate and segmented of our social issues, and it reaches and touches more aspects of society than any other social issue. Environmentalism extends to every part of our federal system—local, state, and national government—and also can influence the international community. It may even reach each of these jurisdictions all at the same time. Acid rain, for example, may be a problem for a northern city at the same time as it is considered a regional problem by those states in the path of the rain, and it may, as well, be looked on as an international problem, as it reaches across the border into Canada.

The environment's complexity, diversity, and global reach can also make it difficult for both the public and the policymaker to easily understand the issues involved. As we made clear elsewhere in this book, understanding the environment in the 1930s, then defined in conservation terms as the need for protecting national forests, public land, air, and water, was much easier than it is today when the sort of issues mentioned by Al Gore in his book, *Earth in the Balance*, dominate the agenda. These issues include global warming, overpopulation, genetic diversity, and ozone depletion, among others.

Scientific and technological aspects of environmental legislation also distance congresspersons and judges from environmental issues given that they have neither the time nor the incentive to develop an expertise in the subject area. Yet congresspersons need to remember that this sort of expertise probably does exist in the executive branch in such agencies as the Environmental Protection Agency and other agencies staffed by the president. Also they should keep in mind that if members of Congress expect to have substantive input on environmental legislation, they need to precisely write the legislation, to reduce the possibility for discretionary interpretation by other decision makers who also want control.

Observations About American Politics and the Environment

Throughout this book we have examined how the American political system has responded to the environment and which political decision makers have been most important in shaping environmental policy. We now present several observations in a series of propositions.

PROPOSITION #1A: *Activist presidents supporting the environment have been and will continue to be major actors in shaping environmental policy.*

Even though many policymakers are activists for the environment, presidents have been and will continue to be most influential in shaping environmental policy, if they are sympathetic to environmental needs and also exert aggressive leadership. If the environment becomes an integral part of a president's social agenda, the chief executive can make a major difference in how the government responds to the environment. Theodore Roosevelt, as our first activist environmental president, used his powers and authority, in addition to the authority granted him by the Antiquities Act of 1906, to protect more land than any other president, preserving it in the form of national parks and monuments, as well as securing forest lands.[6] He and Gifford Pinchot, who would later head the U.S. Forest Service, set down a conservationist strategy that later presidents would follow, including Franklin Roosevelt, Richard Nixon, George H.W. Bush, and Bill Clinton.

Franklin Roosevelt also became enamored with forestry and was able to use this interest in responding to the Great Depression through his newly created Civilian Conservation Corps (CCC) where he found work opportunities for the unemployed millions as they were asked to plant trees, correct soil erosion, and protect wildlife refuges in national parks and forests.

Richard Nixon also showed how important presidential leadership could be when he became a leading force for the environment by proposing establishment of the Environmental Protection Agency, as well as encouraging passage of major environmental legislation that became key to the movement during his administration. His leadership helped to pass legislation affecting clean water and air, as well as the protection of open spaces and the addition of new national parks.

George H.W. Bush, early in his presidency, declared that he also wanted to be a president in the tradition of Teddy Roosevelt, following conservationist principles. His primary contribution to advancement of environmentalism was his support of the Clean Air Act Amendments. But he was unsuccessful in winning the support of environmentalists in the later years of his presidency because of his increasing association with Reagan administration anti-environmental policies along with pressure from fellow Republicans, business, and industry.

Bill Clinton, as well, was initially seen as a major supporter of the environment. But because of partisan conflicts with Congress, Clinton ended up with a mixed record on the environment. Where he made his primary contribution in his first term was in bringing a number of individuals with proven environmental experience to his administration. These included Vice President Al Gore and Secretary of the Interior Bruce Babbitt, among others supportive of the environment.

During his second term, Clinton was quite active in using the Antiquities Act to set aside land in the form of national monuments. During the last year of his presidency, he used the act to establish or expand 10 new national monuments, with 8 other sites under consideration.[7] As a result, Bill Clinton has become the president who has preserved more land in the 48 contiguous states as national monuments than any other president.[8]

Through the actions of these presidents, one can see how important sympathetic presidential leadership is to the advances of the environmental movement.

PROPOSITION #1B: *Activist presidents opposing the environment have been and will continue to be detrimental to the advances of the environmental movement.*

Presidents maintain a unique role in the political system because they are the most visible of all policymakers and are at the very center of the political system. With those presidents who have actively opposed the environmental movement, environmental advancement has been decidedly slow, demonstrating their influence over environmental policy. Indeed, damage to the movement during their years in office has been evident.

Among the limited number of presidents who might be placed in this anti-environmental category, none fits better than Ronald Reagan. His attitude toward the environment proved detrimental, as did those persons he appointed to key positions in his administration. Ann Burford (EPA head) and James Watt (Secretary of the Interior), as two representatives of the administration's attitude against the environment, splendidly carried out the wishes of the president in their effort to diminish environmental programs. Reagan did his best to undercut prior bipartisan support for the environment on matters such as clean air, safe drinking water, and the Superfund. Environmental budgets devoted to water conservation, for example, were significantly reduced in 1985.

The Reagan years were unprecedented for unsympathetic leadership toward the environment. One positive aspect of Reagan's anti-environmentalism might be noted—namely, due to the attitude of his administration, environmental interest group membership did grow stronger, made up of both environmentalists and those disillusioned with the administration. Environmentalists hoped these groups could offer some core resistance to administrative policies.

Reagan's efforts were damaging to the environment but because his anti-environmental position proved to counter public opinion, he failed, beyond his two terms, to chart an anti-environmental direction for presidents who would follow. However, President George W. Bush failed to include substantive conservation measures as part of his environmental agenda. Moreover, he divided rather than united the public with his advocacy of oil drilling in the Alaska Arctic National Wildlife Refuge. A majority of Americans are opposed to drilling for oil in environmentally sensitive areas in Alaska.

PROPOSITION #2: *A pro-environment Congress is pivotal to the success of the environmental movement.*

A Congress that is against the goals of environmentalism or, at the very least, ignores them, regardless of which party is in control, can prove damaging to the environmental movement. Supportive statutory law is essential to the growth of environmentalism. Without such landmark legislation as the National Environmental Policy Act (1969), the Clean Air Act (1963) and its amendments in 1990, the Safe Drinking Water Act, the Surface Mining Act, the Toxic Substances Control Act, the Endangered Species Act (1973), and the Comprehensive Environmental Responses, Compensation, and Liability Act ("Superfund Act") (1980), to mention only a few, the environmental movement would have enjoyed little progress and would have lost its direction.

Strong environmental legislation not only becomes the means for Congress to shape environmental policy, but also it serves as a source for other institutions like the Court and the president to become involved with the environmental movement. In addition, supportive legislation is able, among other things, to counterbalance anti-environmental efforts by other institutions that might be supporting development and business, as occurred during the Reagan years. Congresspersons in favor of the environment saw legislation of consequence pass during these years despite having a president who was by all measures anti-environmental.

Passage of landmark environmental legislation is difficult for Congress due to the dispersed and decentralized power and fragmented authority and leadership in Congress. Legislation is always going to reflect the institution. In Congress there are multiple committees and subcommittees with authority over some aspects of the environment. Michael Kraft, in fact, made clear that some 11 different committees in the House and Senate have authority and jurisdiction over environmental affairs.[9] Estimates are even higher by other students of politics, with some suggesting that as many as two-thirds of the standing committees in the House and Senate have some input on environmental legislation. The latter estimate surely takes account of all of the environmental areas covered by committees and subcommittees, including natural resources, forestry and land management, air and water, fisheries and wildlife, energy and public works.

In addition to legislation, a Congress in support of the environment can also expand the powers of such administrative agencies as the EPA. This extension of power is another tool Congress uses to shape policy during the implementation stage, since it is such agencies as the EPA that will implement the legislation Congress passes.

PROPOSITION #3: Unlike the Supreme Court's response to other social issues, it has resisted assuming a leadership role with regard to the environment.

The Supreme Court has been more assertive and dominating over other social issues, such as abortion, than it has over the environment. The environment is more complex than other social issues and lends itself more to technological expertise than it does to judicial decision making. For this and other reasons, then, the Court has *not* been a primary actor in this issue area.

The Court originally got into the environmental area reluctantly, with justices having concerns about their initial involvement. The elaborate nature of the environment, its complexity and diversity, has proven a problem for the justices. As a result, leadership has shifted to Congress, the president, and the administrative branch.

This is not to say, of course, that the Court has stayed out of environmental concerns altogether. It was more willing to become involved with the environment in the 1930s and 1940s, when the environment was thought to be limited to air, water, hazardous wastes, land management, and public health. As environmental issues coming to the courts began to include the broader issues of the 1990s, the Court has been even more reluctant to broach these issues.

As to whether the Court has been eco-friendly in its decisions, one may say that it has depended on who sits on the bench. Justices such as William O. Douglas, Thurgood Marshall, Harry Blackmun, William J. Brennan, Jr., John Paul Stevens, and Stephen G. Breyer have been quite supportive of the environment. Other justices have been opposed to environmental concerns, including Antonin Scalia, Sandra Day O'Connor, Anthony M. Kennedy, and Lewis F. Powell, Jr.

In addition, the Supreme Court has never had a chief justice who has been fully supportive of the environment. Chief Justice Warren E. Burger and Chief Justice William H. Rehnquist have served on the court when it has been the most involved with environmental cases. Burger, the more supportive of the two justices, upheld environmental concerns 50 percent of the time, whereas Justice Rehnquist has supported the environment less than 40 percent of the time. It can only be presumed that had the chief justice been a champion of the environment, the Court might well have been a more viable part of the growth of environmentalism.

Nor did things change when environmentally supportive presidents were elected to office, since those who have been appointed to the Court have not always shared the president's own feelings about the environment. Richard Nixon's positive attitude toward the environment, for example, was not reflected in three of his four judicial appointments. Those he appointed included Justices Rehnquist, Burger, Powell, and Blackmun. Justice Blackmun was the only justice who actively supported the environment in the cases that came before the Court.

By virtue of the fact that the Court is a part of the political system and has always maintained an important role, we cannot discount it entirely when talking about the environment. The effectiveness of this institution with regard to the environment, however, will depend on who sits on the Court at any one time.

PROPOSITION #4: *Environmental policy is, by and large, originated at the federal level, and implemented at the state and local level.*

In those state and local areas where there are conflicts over environmental values, that portion of the citizenry, to be sure, would probably prefer that environmental policy were controlled by state and local government because any alternative is seen as an intrusion by a central authority. Nevertheless, it is at the federal level where environmental policy is initiated and where the environment is largely managed. In some of the more important legislation like the National Environmental Policy Act (NEPA), it is specified that Congress, the president, and the federal courts would have a deciding role, while little mention is given to local areas. What is left largely for the state and local jurisdiction is the policy's implementation.

It only makes sense that, given the resources that must be involved in any environmental program, the federal level would be the source of policy initiation. Recognizing the need to solicit state and local support, however, federal decision makers use both the methods of coercive regulation as well as nonregulatory means such as collaboration and grant money, to persuade state and local governments to support these programs.

It is always uncertain, of course, whether states will fully support federal policy. States have varied a great deal in their commitment to the environment. Some states have made an effort to support legislation that would improve the environment, whereas other states have opposed any federal effort to improve the environment. Those states most supportive of the environment as measured by the portion of their budget devoted to the environment have included Wyoming,

Alaska, Wisconsin, Idaho, Montana, Nevada, South Dakota, Maine, California, and Vermont. Those states that have devoted fewer funds to environmental improvement in terms of their budgets include North Carolina, Massachusetts, New Jersey, Ohio, and Arizona. As far as regions of the country are concerned, it is the South that has been the most resistant to supporting environmental legislation.[10]

PROPOSITION #5: *Public support for the environment is crucial to the environment's success in the political system.*

The public has been generally committed to protecting the environment over the years, but support has varied over time and with the individual issue in question. In 1965, for example, Opinion Research Corporation found that only 28 percent of the American public saw air pollution as a serious problem, yet five years later, in 1970, some 69 percent of them saw air pollution as a severe problem.[11]

It is also unclear how strong the public's commitment is when the environment is compared with such issues as economic and political concerns. When pitted with other issues, the environment has done less well than when the public is asked to consider the importance of the environment alone, without considering other issues. When the public is asked which issue is considered most important for deciding who is to be president, the environment rarely scores more than 5 to 7 percent; but when people are asked to indicate the importance of the environment as an issue, without considering other issues, a sizable percentage of respondents feel it is important.[12]

Public support for the environment, then, appears to be an uncertain subject on surveys not only because of the way the question is asked but also based on the particular circumstances at hand. Riley Dunlap pointed out that, at times, public eagerness for environmental support could be explained by the nature and attitude of the administration in power at the time. It was during the Bush administration, for example, that the public strongly felt that the government ought to be doing more to protect the environment.[13]

Public support of institutional involvement with the environment is particularly important for any conservation or preservation actions to be implemented. As Thomas Marshall indicated, most decisions do reflect public sentiment,[14] but if the public is uninformed, one can see how policymakers will be affected. Public "education" largely takes place through radio, television, newspapers, and the Internet, all of which are involved in distributing information to the public. Samuel Hays's conclusion is that environmental concerns become mainstream, "only when environmental information becomes more central in the mainstream media."[15] This can be a problem, though, because the media tends to give emphasis to sensational news stories, a category under which environmental issues normally do not fall.

PROPOSITION #6: *Active environmental groups are essential to making environmental policy more visible and understandable to the public and policymakers.*

In addition to the media, the public learns about the environment also through information distributed by environmental groups. While today there are many groups in support of environmental protection, the groups differ in their tactics, goals, and strategies. On the political left are such groups as the Friends of the Earth and the Sierra Club (an interest group founded by preservationist John Muir). Other important interest groups in the political system include Greenpeace, Defenders of Wildlife, the National Wildlife Federation, and the National Audubon Society, among many others.

Each of these groups is independent of one another, often reflecting the diversity of the environmental movement itself. Earlier groups like the Sierra Club, the National Audubon Society, the Wilderness Society, and the National Wildlife Federation, established when environmentalism was more focused on public lands and wildlife, share more in common with one another than they share with the more recent groups such as Environmental Defense Fund, Friends of the Earth, and Natural Resources Defense Council—groups that tend more to mirror the new environmental interests. Some groups have been able to adjust their focus over the years to respond to new causes. Such a group is the National Wildlife Federation, which has expanded its focus and takes on air and water pollution, biodiversity, global warming, and ozone depletion. If these groups could come to some kind of consensus, they would be more effective contributors to the environmental movement.

Groups also differ in their narrowness and breadth of interest, in their resources, and in their political clout. There are the single-issue interest groups like the National Audubon Society, People for the Ethical Treatment of Animals (PETA), and the "Save the _____ (fill in the animal)" groups with very narrow bases, which can focus all of their membership and resources on a very confining area. The broader-based groups like Friends of the Earth and the League of Conservation Voters are more diversified in their efforts and need more resources to be as effective. Some of the larger groups, like the National Wildlife Federation, can rally their larger membership in support of a cause, while smaller groups like PETA employ unusual, even shocking, tactics to get their message to the people.[16]

PROPOSITION #7: The Democratic party tends to be more supportive of the environment than the Republican party is.

Over time, there have been partisan differences between the parties over environmental policy in Congress. This became particularly intense during the Republican-dominated 104th Congress, in which such committees as the Senate Environment and Public Works Committee found conflict over environmental issues particularly rancorous.[17] Democrats, on the whole, tend to be more supportive of the environment at the federal as well as the state and local level than are Republicans, as demonstrated by their party platforms over the years. During the decade prior to 1944, the Democrats' focus on the Depression and war momentarily diverted their attention from environmental issues. However, ever since 1944, Democrats have included a statement on the environment in their party platforms.

Republicans, on the other hand, have not been so predictable, but have varied depending on the nominee for office. When Richard Nixon ran in 1968, there was a platform statement on the environment, but four years earlier, in 1964, with Barry Goldwater's candidacy, there was no such statement.

In examining the Congress from the 1970s through the 1990s, it would appear that the Democrats have increased their support for the environment at the same time as Republicans have weakened their support for it. The gap between the parties appears greatest in the West, and less significant in the South.[18] Congressional leaders in each party reflect an even more extreme position on the environment than do the rank-and-file party members, thereby pushing the parties further and further apart. Having said this, of course, each party has members on both sides of the issue.

Among the Democrats, for example, Senator Robert Byrd (D-WVA) is much less supportive of environmental legislation than is someone like Senator Tom Harkin (D-IA). In the Republican party also we find very different attitudes in response to the environment. In the House, for example, Sherwood Boehlert (R-NY) has been very supportive of the environmental movement, while his colleague from California, Richard W. Pombo (R-CA), has been critical of environmental protections.[19]

Several differences distinguish the two parties. For example, Democrats tend to seek governmental means for reaching their environmental objectives, whereas Republicans frequently look for market-based ways to resolve them. Thus, many Republicans tend to be less supportive of governmentally sponsored environmental programs like the Endangered Species Act, which in 1997 conservative Republicans attempted to undercut, over its flood-control projects. One Republican, Congressman Sherwood Boehlert (R-NY), risked irritating his fellow conservatives by demanding that the Endangered Species Act apply to flood-control projects as it does to other projects—and he introduced legislation that would do that very thing.[20]

Partisan differences are not as clear on the Supreme Court as they are in the Congress, but they do exist. Republican appointees tend to be more opposed to the environment than are Democratic appointees. For example, William O. Douglas and Thurgood Marshall, both Democrats, were the most supportive of the environment of any justices in the past or present. Those justices least supportive of the environment were all appointed by Republicans, including Justices Scalia, Kennedy, O'Connor, Powell, and Rehnquist. Four of these were appointed by Reagan, while Powell was appointed by Nixon. Some of the justices, although appointed by Republicans—Stevens, Blackmun, and Brennan—became more liberal while on the Court and changed their views on the environment, becoming much more pro-environment.

PROPOSITION #8: *Responses to future environmental concerns need to take account of the entire ecosystem and not be confined to political or geographic boundaries or outdated strategies.*

Some students of the environment urge us to begin to think of environmentalism in a greater context—in an ecosystem context, if you will. They point out that we can no longer focus our attention on only the most obvious environmental problems in a segmented way;[21] in other words, we can no longer focus just on the "belching smokestacks and orange rivers that fouled the landscape," but that it is now necessary to also consider the "fertilizer runoff from thousands of farms and millions of yards; emissions from gas stations, bakeries, and dry cleaners; and smog produced by tens of millions of motor vehicles."[22] Our piecemeal approaches relying on fragmented law are not adequate for our needs today.[23] While such a comprehensive consideration of the environment has the advantage of forcing policymakers to think of alternate responses to environmental problems in all of their interconnective facets, it does not help simplify our understanding of environmentalism in the twenty-first century.

But what we must understand is that the relative simplicity of earlier years is gone. The critical issues for the new century that were identified by Lynton Caldwell a number of years ago, namely, endangered species, overpopulation, depletion of forests, overgrazing, water pollution, loss of top soil, climate change, energy reduction, and threats to biogeochemical processes,[24] demand those sort of broad responses today and will need those responses in the future. Moreover, many other important environmental threats today are not geographically specific and recognize no borders, such as air and water pollution, acid rain, wildlife depletion, and ocean dumping, among many others. The unanswered environmental challenges of today suggest that environmental concerns for the twenty-first century will exceed our current remedies. Nor do the future projections offer much relief. According to the *Global 2000 Report* to the president, the world "faces enormous, urgent, and complex problems in the decades immediately ahead. Prompt and vigorous changes in public policy around the world are needed to avoid or minimize these problems before they become unmanageable."[25]

Because these environmental problems have become intense and widespread, there seems to be greater need for global remedies; we may need to rely more and more on the international sector. The problem with that comes in the institutions we have set up to handle international concerns. Today, world environmental problems are given to the United Nations, a body lacking resources to respond to the problem areas. The UN, in other words, is strapped for funds, and the United States has not been very sympathetic and supportive of the UN's efforts in this arena. It is problematic whether institutions like the European Union or the World Trade Organization will prove more or less effective than the UN in offering responses to our environmental challenges, since the WTO, for one, is allowed to override national environmental laws.

It is our prediction that unless effective global resolutions are found and supported to respond to some of the more basic needs of our environment, the next 20 years will find conditions to be even worse in terms of overpopulation, pollution, and ecological instability. We need to begin thinking in interconnected ways, in terms of entire ecosystems, and in ways that will facilitate ecosystem solutions. With an ecosystem approach we will at least be able to harness new creativity and implement cooperative remedies supported by collaborative efforts by many nations. That might allow for the survival of our fragile biosphere.

Endnotes

[1] Jedediah Purdy, "Shades of Green," *The American Prospect*, January 3, 2000, 6.
[2] Marian R. Chertow and Daniel C. Esty suggest that the polls seem to indicate about 80 percent of Americans think of themselves as environmentalists. See Marian R. Chertow and Daniel C. Esty, "Environmental Policy: The Next Generation," *Issues in Science and Technology Online*, Fall 1997 @ **http//bob.nap.edu/issues/14.1/esty.htm**. Retrieved September 13, 2000.
[3] Jedediah Purdy, "Shades of Green," 6.

4   Ibid.

5   Ibid.

6   Douglas Jehl, "West Takes a Stand Against Clinton Plan," *New York Times* on the Web, September 14, 2000 @ **http://www.nytimes.com/2000/09/14/national/ MONU.html**. Retrieved September 14, 2000.

7   Robert Keiter, Director of the Wallace Stegner Center for Land, Resources, and the Environment, suggested this at a conference on "Learning from the Monument: What Does the Grand Staircase–Escalante Mean for Land Protection in the West?" at the University of Utah Law School, Salt Lake City, Utah, September 15, 2000.

8   Douglas Jehl, "West Takes a Stand Against Clinton Plan," *New York Times* on the Web, September 14, 2000 @ **http://www.nytimes.com/2000/09/14/national/ MONU.html**. Retrieved September 14, 2000.

9   Michael E. Kraft, *Environmental Policy and Politics: Toward the Twenty-First Century* (New York: HarperCollins College Publishers, 1996), 62–63.

10 See, for instance, Glen Sussman, "The Environment as a Public Policy Issue: Assessing Virginia from a Regional Perspective," in Quentin Kidd, ed. *Government and Politics in Virginia: The Old Dominion in the 21st Century* (Needham Heights, MA: Simon and Schuster Custom Publishing, 1999).

11 See Riley E. Dunlap, "Trends in Public Opinion Toward Environmental Issues: 1965–1990," in Riley E. Dunlap and Angela G. Mertig, eds., *American Environmentalism: The U.S. Environmental Movement, 1970–1990* (New York: Taylor & Francis, 1992), 93.

12 See Chapter 8 for an elaboration on poll response.

13 Riley E. Dunlap, "Public Opinion and Environmental Policy," in James P. Lester, ed., *Environmental Politics and Policy: Theories and Evidence*, 2nd ed. (Durham: Duke University Press, 1995), 94.

14 Thomas R. Marshall, *Public Opinion and the Supreme Court* (Boston: Unwin Hyman, 1989), 78.

15 Samuel P. Hays, *Explorations in Environmental History* (Pittsburgh: University of Pittsburgh Press, 1998), 384.

16 An example of a controversial advertisement used by the People for the Ethical Treatment of Animals recently was their "Got Beer?" advertisement, which was directed to college students. The ad cautioned students about drinking of milk, suggesting that it might be responsible for breast cancer and prostate cancer. It also indicated that it might be safer for students to drink beer than to continue to drink milk. The ad had a very short run due to the controversy it stirred up. See "Opinion: PETA's Controversial Ad Campaign Was Irresponsible," *NewsNet@BYU*, March 20, 2000. **http://newsnet.byu.edu/print_story.cfm?number=8527&year= current**.

17 Allan Freedman, "Prospects in Senate Brighten for Rewrite of Species Law," *Congressional Quarterly Weekly Report*, vol. 55 (20), 1997, 1125.

18 See Chapter 4.

19 See Allan Freedman, "Tensions Mount within House GOP," *Congresional Quarterly Weekly Report*, vol. 55 (20), 1997, 1126.

20 Ibid.

21 Both Robert Keiter, Director of the Wallace Stegner Center for Land, Resources, and the Environment, and David Williams, a Wallace Stegner Fellow of the Center, suggested this at a conference on "Learning from the Monument: What Does the Grand Staircase–Escalante Mean for Land Protection in the West," at the University of Utah Law School, Salt Lake City, Utah, September 15, 2000.

22 Marian R. Chertow and Daniel C. Esty suggest that the polls they have seen indi-
    cate that about 80 percent of Americans think of themselves as environmental-
    ists. See Marian R. Chertow and Daniel C. Esty, "Environmental Policy: The Next
    Generation," *Issues in Science and Technology Online*, Fall 1997 @ **http//bob.
    nap.edu/issues/14.1/esty.htm**. Retrieved September 13, 2000.
23 Ibid.
24 Lynton Keith Caldwell, *International Environmental Policy: From the Twenti-
    eth to the Twenty-First Century* (Durham: Duke University Press, 1996), 5–10.
25 See *The Global 2000 Report to the President: Entering the Twenty-First Century*
    (New York: Penguin Books, 1982), 5.

INDEX